LANSDOWNE ROAD

- **THE STADIUM**
- **THE MATCHES**
- **THE GREATEST DAYS**

Gerard Siggins & Malachy Clerkin

THE O'BRIEN PRESS
DUBLIN

Gerard Siggins was born in Dublin in 1962 and has lived
almost all his life in the shadow of the old East Stand at Lansdowne
Road. His earliest memory of the ground is at age seven, when he
was flattened by Ken Kennedy when the Ulster hooker crashed into
the touchline seats. He has written on sport in the *Sunday Tribune*
since 1985, where he was sports editor from 1989-94 and is now
assistant editor. This is his fourth book.

Malachy Clerkin is the chief sportswriter of the *Sunday Tribune*
where he has worked since winning a sportswriting competition
organised and overseen by his co-author Gerard Siggins in 1999.
He has been assured by his co-author that there was more than one
entrant, but has yet to see documentary proof that this was the case.
He has covered every conceivable sporting event for the *Tribune*,
from Olympic Games to World Cups in soccer and rugby.
This is his first book.

Dedication

To Paul Howard, who couldn't be orsed

Acknowledgements

GERARD SIGGINS wishes to thank everyone who helped him in putting together his chapters. Especial thanks to Deryck and the late Billy Vincent for the magnificent rugby collection. Thanks also to Malachy Logan, Gavin Cummiskey and Irene Stevenson of *The Irish Times*, Frank Greally of the *Irish Runner*, Gerard Whelan of the RDS Library, Ned Van Esbeck, Frederic Humbert of www.rugby-pioneers.com, Brian Siggins, Peter Dunne, Bohemians FC and Old Wesley RFC for their help and kindness. I am grateful to the staffs of the National and Gilbert Libraries for their guidance and patience, and to my colleagues at the *Sunday Tribune* for their help and advice.

Thanks to Michael O'Brien for believing in the project and cajoling us along, and to Helen Carr for seeing us home with fantastic skill and fortitude. I also thank the many people who chipped in with stories and leads over the years, and apologise for not having room to list you all. Special thanks to the many who have stood and sat alongside me as we roared Ireland on over the last forty years at Lansdowne Road. May we get the chance to roar on many more victories in the new stadium. And thanks to all my family and friends who have indulged my passion for sport and its history, especially my dad who first lifted me over the turnstiles. He wouldn't do it now. And to Martha, Jack, Lucy and Billy, who make every day as joyful as all the tries and goals ever scored.

MALACHY CLERKIN wishes to say thanks to everyone who answered a phone, chased up a photo and found a phone number. A special word of gratitude to the indefatigable Jim O'Brien of Boston for turning what might have been just a passing reference into a fully-formed chapter.

To the staff of the Pearse Street Library in Dublin not only for their archives, but for their glorious workspace too. To P.J. Cunningham at the *Sunday Tribune* for making it a job, but never work. To Rachel Collins, Eimear Lowe, Pat Nugent and Emma Somers for pep talks and patience. To the family for all that and more. And to Olivia Doyle for the best time of my life.

CONTENTS

10. WILLIE-JOHN McBRIDE
BALLYMENA and IRELAND
Second-row forward: **63 caps (1962–1975)**

D. Givens *(Luton)*

Cigarette cards and stickers featuring Irish sportsmen.

At eight o'clock on the Sunday morning of New Year's Eve 2006, John Kelly arrived at Lansdowne Road for a final day's work. His book of numbered stickers in his hand, he headed off around the stadium. He passed the bins under the North Terrace that were half-filled with water, rounded the radio station people who were stitching up their promotional banner near where the East Stand met the South Terrace and carried on his careful, precise way along the front few rows of Lower West Stand. All in all, his circuit of the stadium took just over an hour to complete. His job? Checking each seat to make sure its number hadn't been washed off by the Saturday night rain.

This was Lansdowne Road on its last legs. We spent the day there to see out the last game the old place would host before the diggers moved in. With a nice tip of the hat to history, the final match replicated the first ever rugby fixture – Leinster versus Ulster. But to be there to witness it was to know that 'replicated' was the wrong word entirely. The place was different, the rugby itself was different, the world was unimaginably different.

Just about the only similarities, in fact, were the team names. Within hours of the DART ferrying the last of the crowds into the Dublin night after Leinster's 20-12 victory, Setanta Sports footage of Brian O'Driscoll's stunning pass to himself in the second half was up on YouTube and had begun its journey to well over three-quarters of a million hits. No part of that sentence would have made sense to Henry Wallace Dunlop back in 1872.

And despite all the changes, nobody was in any doubt that still more change was needed and needed badly. Just after 11 am, we went right up to the top of the Upper East Stand and sat for a while to take the place in. There was no getting away from it – what you could see from up there was a stadium that nobody in their right mind could have imagined had they started with a blank sheet of paper.

Down to the left was the South Terrace where the schoolboys stood for the internationals. Its back wall started off high, but began to slope away around its midpoint, as if slumping its shoulders in apology to those in the houses on Lansdowne Road behind for obstructing their view.

A 1977 leaflet for the Lansdowne Road Development Fund

Pushed over to the side of the terrace nearest the West Stand was the security centre – a solid, square concrete box with a ladder up to it. Then on around to another box, this time one with a wide window through which on big match days you could see an RTÉ panel fulminating amongst themselves in studio light. By the time you reached the end of the terrace, these constructions had encroached right into the standing space so that it finished at a point, as if pinched by a giant thumb and forefinger.

We looked across and saw the West Stand, separated from the North Terrace by a lone floodlight pole and the Wanderers pavilion that had stood there since 1912, as if a twee old cottage in the middle of an international sports stadium was the most natural thing in the world. On then to the Lower West Stand, pockmarked with plastic seating of all different colours and shades, the legacy of wear and tear and one dark night of riots in 1995. And the Upper West Stand looking for all the world like the old Hogan Stand in Croke Park – all brown wooden benches covered by the same dun roof that had peeked out over it for fifty-one years.

The upper stand had the press box in the centre, built in a time before Wi-Fi, before ISDN, before the uniform use of three-point plugs even. (Presumably also before the size of the average press buttock grew beyond that of, say, an Olympic gymnast – but we digress). Underneath was the lower stand where the dignitaries sat and below that again the tunnel from which players would emerge for games.

The venerable RTÉ floor manager Tadhg de Brún has the best story about that tunnel. When the newly-elected President Mary Robinson arrived for her first official engagement at a Five Nations match in

1991, she and her husband took tea in the holding area while the players filed onto the pitch and lined up ready to meet her. But between that tunnel and the pitch there was a big, iron, sliding door and as the band prepared to play the presidential salute, that door stayed shut. 'Have they forgotten about me?' the new president wondered aloud as she stood there ready to take the pitch.

Suddenly, an almighty racket arose as someone on the outside of the iron door started kicking at it noisily and repeatedly. The official on the inside of the door, clearly unaware that he was the one holding the whole show up, heaved it across in a rage and upbraided the chap who was doing the kicking. 'Would you stop that please – what's the matter with you?' he asked. And the official on the outside, oblivious to just how close an tUachtarán standing, gave him his answer. 'Would you leave the door open, the fuckin' president has to come out!' De Brún reports that ne'er a flinch came from anyone in the presidential party, least of all the lady herself.

But back to New Year's Eve 2006; we looked on down to the end of the West Stand and the Havelock Square end. They came to call it 'Currow Corner', after the small Kerry parish that gave the world Mick Doyle, Moss Keane and Mick Galwey, all of whom scored tries for Ireland on that patch of grass. Just behind the corner flag was the Lansdowne Pavilion, formerly a place for players to change before and after matches, latterly a press conference room where Ireland soccer managers went to squirm and occasionally wish the DART rumbling overhead had room for one more.

The back wall of the North Terrace was similar to its southern equivalent, starting off high and proud but gradually draining away as it met the corner with the East Stand. Opened in 1984, the East Stand was by far the most modern-looking section of the stadium. It had seats rather than benches throughout and the PA system didn't crackle as much over there as it did in the West Stand. Down below, catering vans powered with the low hum of out-the-back generators sold burgers and pizza slices

Above and opposite: Tickets from Lansdowne Road matches: Ireland v England, 1949 and Ireland XV v Barbarians, 2000

PRESS

PRESS

FOOTBALL ASSOCIATION OF IRELAND

OPEL GM

REPUBLIC OF
IRELAND VS ALBANIA
WORLD CUP GROUP 3
WEST STAND UPPER
Lansdowne Road, Dublin, Tuesday 26th May 1992
Kick-Off at 5.00 pm

0000000094

PLEASE RETAIN THIS PORTION

ISSUED TO

BLOCK	ROW	SEAT
	06	094

for a fiver and tea and coffee for €2.50. The East Stand might have been an improvement on the rest of the place, but the notion of a purpose-built concession stand in the ground was laughable.

And yet, here's the thing. Lansdowne Road was full that day, full to bursting. Fathers brought kids and fathers brought fathers, whole battalions of families and friends turned out to be part of what the marketing people called 'The Last Stand'. As a slogan, they'd argue it did its job – a footfall of forty-eight thousand adds up to some serious unit-shifting after all – but inside the ground it felt like it had struck the wrong note. This was no defiant action. Nobody was chaining themselves to turnstiles and declaring theirs the dead body over which the diggers would need to roll. There was a general, shrugging acceptance that the old place had to go. The sooner the better, most of us reckoned.

But people loved it like they loved a pair of torn and faded old jeans. They loved the peculiar microclimate that would cause a visiting kicker to see his first penalty carried one way on the wind and his second go quite the other. They loved that the stands loomed over the pitch to such an extent that the players' voices carried into the upper tiers on quiet nights. They loved the idea of the Lansdowne Roar and asking aloud in groups of drinkers after a game where it had gone to at all, at all. It was a kip of a place, but it was *our* kip of a place.

That's why those forty-eight thousand people were there on a freezing final day. To grab one last thread of a garment that had been part of us since shortly after the Famine. No, of course nobody with a blank sheet of paper would ever have built a stadium like it, but building stadiums all in one go is a wholly modern enterprise. People didn't build the great stadiums of the past, history did. Stage by stage and decade by decade, brick by brick and quirk by quirk.

Lansdowne Road was crumbling long before it was felled, but the memories and the stories and the days it gave the nation were great indeed and were always going to be sturdy enough to last long after the rain washed the last of John Kelly's stickers away.

But just to make sure the stories live on, we've tried to fit 134 years of the place between two covers. Some of the days are as familiar to your average rugby or soccer fan as the weekend just gone, some won't register in the slightest. From the initial efforts of Henry Wallace Dunlop to create a sports complex by the Dodder in the late nineteenth century to the first All Blacks in 1905, from early soccer internationals to athletics meetings in the forties and fifties and American football in the eighties. Days like the one where England turned up to play rugby at the height of the troubles, keeping the real world at bay while we watched some sport. And nights when sport took a back seat, most obviously when soccer fans tore the place to bits in 1995.

Some stories sag with tragedy, others make you giggle and indeed goggle at the Ireland of the day. The thing with a stadium that becomes the focal point of a country a few times each year is that what goes on within its walls must reflect something of the state of the nation beyond them. And so we've set each day in its context and framed the hours between the touchlines as they affected the times.

The old Lansdowne Road is gone and in its place an impressive venue of shimmering glass adorns the skyline on Dublin's southside, visible and identifiable to all from Pearse Street to Ringsend, from Ballsbridge to Sandymount. The past wasn't a better place, just a different one and in time the new stadium will tell its own stories and host its own great days. For now, however, you'll have to make do with these. Enjoy.

Gerard Siggins and Malachy Clerkin,
March 2010

Opposite and below: Ticket from Ireland v Albania, 1992 and Ireland v San Marino, 2006, both in Lansdowne Road

LANSDOWNE ROAD: TIMELINE OF ITS DEVELOPMENT

May 1872	Irish Champion Athletic Club founded
Dec 1872	Dunlop buys sixty-nine-year lease on 8.25 acres from Pembroke Estates for £60
May 1873	Ground opened for first athletics meeting of ICAC
1880	Wanderers rugby club move in
1881	ICAC dissolved
1904	Dunlop sells lease to IRFU treasurer Harry Sheppard
Dec 1906	Harry Sheppard dies. IRFU pays £200 to his mother for the lease
1907	The IRFU sign a new lease for fifty years, paying £50 a year ground rent
1907	Pitch realigned north-south from previous east-west orientation. Covered West Stand built
1908	Uncovered North-West Stand built, with dressing rooms in building behind
1912	Lansdowne and Wanderers pavilions completed.
1919	Land reclaimed from River Dodder enabled two back pitches to be installed
1925	IRFU memorial erected to players who died in Great War
1927	East stand with terrace beneath opened, where previously there was a big grassy hill with a pavilion for reporters
1930	Lansdowne Lawn Tennis Club moved out
1954	West Stand rebuilt as a two-tier stand, capacity now fifty thousand
1974	IRFU purchase freehold to ground from Pembroke Estates
1977	Lower West Stand rebuilt and refurbished
1978	Old 'red stand' and pavilion at north-west end demolished and North Terrace extended. New Lansdowne FC pavilion built in corner of back pitch
1982	East Stand rebuilt with a capacity of 13,400, at a cost of £5 million
1995	Floodlights installed
Dec 2006	Ground closed
May 2007	Old stadium demolished
Aug 2010	Reopens as the Aviva Stadium

CHAPTER 1

**The 1870s
Dunlop's
dream**

With many stories in Ireland, nothing is quite as it seems. The beginnings of the home of Irish rugby are actually rooted in athletics and the vision of a leading race walker, Henry Wallace Doveton Dunlop. His sports administration skills were to see him inaugurate the Irish championships in athletics, tennis and archery, as well as provide Irish rugby with a permanent home. When Dunlop opened the ground in 1873, rugby was something of an afterthought, a minority activity to keep the ground in use and the members fit in the winter months.

Track and field had taken root in Dublin after Trinity College codified the sport in 1859, and within a decade there were dozens of athletics clubs throughout the country, usually springing out of cricket clubs. H.W.D. Dunlop founded The Royal Irish Athletic Club in June 1872; shortly afterwards it was renamed 'The Irish Champion Athletic Club'.

Henry Dunlop came to Ireland via a circuitous route; he was born in February 1844 in India, where his father William was Superintendent of the Bombay Harbour Police. William died when Henry was four and the boy was sent back to England. He later joined his older sister and mother in Germany, where Mrs Mary Anna Dunlop worked for some years as a governess. The family moved to southern France where Henry was educated at Montauban College before coming to Dublin aged seventeen to study at the Engineering School in Trinity College. Having taken a BAI degree he was appointed as junior clerk to Judge Hargreave.

Dunlop was something of an all-rounder; in 1930 his obituary noted that he was a musician, dancer, athlete, sculptor and painter. He developed quite a reputation in his later years as a model maker, and was a noted naturalist and bird-watcher. He was twice married, the second time at the age of sixty-eight, fathering a future member of Lansdowne FC, Eric, who lived to see the old stadium demolished in 2006.

Henry Dunlop, an 'outstanding pedestrian', was a good enough race walker to win the Spencer Challenge Cup and, in 1869, the Provost's Cup at the College Races. Wearing a Stewart tartan belt, he won the seven mile race in 1 hour, 3 minutes, 11 seconds. He was one of the students who argued for a cinder 'running path' to be set out around College Park in 1872, a motion only defeated by twenty-seven votes to twenty-six with

In May 1873 The Irish Times printed a list of those who had made donations towards the foundation of the ICAC

the opposition of the cricket and rugby clubs. His entrepreneurial and administrative skills were also shown when he proposed and saw through the redirection of the standard running track to the now internationally accepted anti-clockwise.

Having been frustrated by the Trinity authorities, Dunlop hit upon the idea of forming a governing body for the sport. In May 1872 he met with the Civil Service Athletic Club, as well as the Dublin University Harriers. Feelers were put out to the other universities, who agreed to act as provincial convenors, and circulars sent around the country. By the following summer 270 members had signed up, 'all of these are men of some standing,' said The Irish Times, 'and many are well-known'. The newspaper also noted that the club was open to all gentlemen amateurs, which was 'a unique feature' at the time.

The Irish Sportsman of 18 January 1873 reported that 'After a due period of incubation a new Athletic Club has burst into existence with the lofty title of the Irish Champion Athletic Club (ICAC). The founding has all the appearance of vigorous life about it and the patronage under which it makes its appearance gives it every reasonable chance of a long and prosperous career.' The eighteen patrons included Lord O'Hagan, Lord Harte and Sir Arthur Guinness. The Honorary Secretaries were named as H.W.D. Dunlop and R.W. Morgan, the latter's address of 39 Grafton Street being that of Lawrence's sports outfitters and publishers where several sporting bodies held their meetings.

The club took its definition of amateurism from English rowing to create a 'gentlemen' class of athletes:

'Any person who has never competed in an open competition or for public money, or for admission money, or with professionals, for a prize, public money and admission money or at any period of his life taught or assisted in the pursuit of athletic exercises as a means of livelihood; or is a mechanic, artisan or labourer.'

The ICAC next came to public attention at the annual prize-giving of the Royal Dublin Society's school of art in February 1873. The Lord Lieutenant, Earl Spencer, announced that 'a society in Dublin, which has been lately got up', had commissioned RDS students to produce statues as prizes for its athletic meetings. The winning plaster models, 'A Flying Mercury' and 'Jason', were to be two of a series of ten cast in bronze, fourteen inches high, and mounted on ebony pedestals with an engraved shield for the winner's name.

Celebrated soldier Garnet Wolseley, who presented the prizes at the inaugural event. His portrait was painted by Paul Albert Besnard

Athletics, like some other sports in the Victorian era, became codified at Trinity College Dublin; it was here that the first recorded athletics meeting took place in 1857; the College Park ground was an important sporting and social centre for Dubliners for the next half century.

Dunlop secured the permission of the Provost, Humphrey Lloyd, to use College Park for the first ICAC meeting on Saturday 5 July 1873, but foul weather forced a postponement to the Monday. That day turned out cool and windy and the attendance, about eight thousand, was much less than at that year's College Races. The *Irish Times*' eccentric, unbylined, reporter took great interest in the weather, fearing that there would be a rise in demand for 'cough mixtures and pectoral candy', and the fashions on parade, bemoaning 'that ladies' outfitters have become infected with Miss Anthony's women's rights notions.'

The events themselves suffered from the withdrawal of many entries, caused by the postponement. Competitors were in the main from the Dublin clubs: the Champion, Dublin Amateur, Civil Service and Trinity, but among the visitors who featured were the Davin brothers from Suir Rowing Club in Co. Tipperary, and others from Foyle College (Derry), North of Ireland (Belfast), Queen's College (Cork), and Cambridge University.

Tom Davin won the high jump, jumping his own height after his opponents had failed at a foot lower. The height of 5 feet 10-and-a-quarter inches was hailed by Bells' Life as a world record. The chief attraction was the Seven Mile Walking Race, the event at which Dunlop had excelled, but the founder did not compete, having retired from race walking never having been beaten. W.H. Hart took an early lead and held it till the tape, but his chief rival H.E.W Barrington 'over-exerted himself when the race was early and had to be assisted to the tent'.

Tom's brother Maurice Davin, who was placed second in four weight-throwing events, was a leading athlete of the era and a founder member of the GAA in 1884.

The ICAC showed its ambitions by sending two members to Lillie Bridge in Fulham to compete in the UK championships. P.W. Todd finished second in the half mile and Tom Davin second in the high jump. The handful of Irish spectators named in the press as having attended included two young Dubliners called 'W. and O. Wilde', which may be the first time young Oscar was mentioned in the national press, and was certainly his first mention on the sports pages. Given his antipathy to sport – shown by his celebrated aphorism that 'football is all very well as a game for rough girls; but it is hardly suitable for delicate boys' – it was perhaps his last, too.

Meanwhile, the board of the university had taken exception to the participation of non-students at the May ICAC meeting, and to the fact that Provost Lloyd had given permission for the event without consulting the board. Dunlop was told he would not be allowed to hold any subsequent events in Trinity and was thus forced to look elsewhere. The Champion club set its sights on land 'of which the centre will be a cricket ground and the remainder used for the laying down of a proper cinder running path, now recognised as essential for really good athletic performances.'

In 1921 Dunlop wrote a short memoir of the foundation of ICAC and Lansdowne. In December 1872, and having looked at sites in Serpentine Avenue and Sydney Parade, Dunlop explained, *'after careful consideration, I chose the present Lansdowne Road one. In*

A poster for the ICAC meeting in College Park

conjunction with the late Edward Dillon (my trainer), I took a sixty-nine year lease from the Pembroke Estate, paying a ground rent of £60 per annum, of part only of the premises stretching from the railway to about 60 yards from the Dodder.'

The eight and a half acres lay by a bend in the river. An unassuming plot, it was bounded by the railway line, Haig's Avenue, and the Dodder and Swan rivers.

The surrounding area has long been among the sought–after properties in Dublin. In 1170 the lands around what are now the villages of Donnybrook, Sandymount and Irishtown were granted by King Henry II to Strongbow, Earl of Pembroke, who had led the Norman Invasion of Ireland the year before. These lands changed hands often over the centuries, at one time being owned by Anne Boleyn, ill–fated wife of Henry VIII.

In 1707 Queen Anne appointed Thomas Herbert, the 27th Earl of Pembroke as Lord Lieutenant, her representative in Ireland. He started to develop the dangerous marshy lands to the south of the city, which had long been a haunt of highwaymen and vagabonds.

The 1905-06 Trinity hockey team that won the Irish Senior Cup under the captaincy of D.L.C. Dunlop. He was the son of Henry Dunlop, who is the man wearing the top hat on the right of the group

The first industrial development in the area was the Dodder Bank Distillery, founded in 1759 by Robert Haig, a descendent of the famous Scots distiller. The plant occupied a vast area to the east of the river, and was a notorious concern, which the authorities feared to visit. One report stated that Haig's was 'infamous for its nightly distilling and rumours that some unpopular revenue officials disappeared within.' The proprietor fought the Revenue 'both physically and legally by every means that his ingenuity could devise', but the distillery closed in the 1830s. It gave its name to Haig's Avenue, which was the name of Lansdowne Road to the east of the railway until 1855. The road to the west of the line was called Watery Lane, little better than a ditch with water constantly seeping from its mud banks and passable only via a line of stepping stones laid along it.

By the 1830s, the pollution, overcrowding and widespread poverty in

A map of the district in 1867, with the location of the stadium marked. Havelock Square lies to the north and the river to the east. The map also shows the streams that ran over the ground. The Swan River still runs underground along the north boundary, while the other mill streams are now also underground.

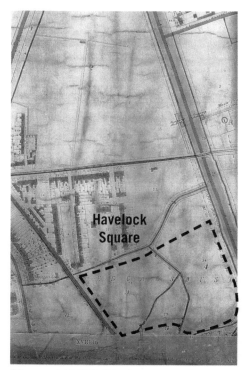

Havelock
Square

the city made it unpleasant to live in for the professional and merchant classes, and there was a flight to the prosperous villages to the south, which led to the expansion of Rathmines, Rathgar, Donnybrook, Ballsbridge and Sandymount. The arrival of the railways (the six-mile line between Dublin and Kingstown – now Dún Laoghaire – opened in 1834) accelerated this process.

Lansdowne Road was named in tribute to the third Marquess of Lansdowne, who lived from 1786-1863. He was a noted Whig politician at Westminster who supported the repeal of the Penal laws and the abolition of slavery, and twice refused the office of prime minister. The houses on the western end of the road were built around 1855 and were aimed at the wealthier professional classes. The houses were not as fabulous as those built in the Georgian period, but conformed to the Pembroke Estates' policy of only allowing development that would keep out the 'lower classes'. The houses along the other perimeters at Shelbourne Road (formerly Artichoke Road) had started to be erected in 1832, and Bath Avenue in 1840.

The railway station opened in 1870. The high-class residents of the area had lobbied for a station, but the railway company asked that the Pembroke Estates contribute half of the cost of construction. If the station made a profit the company would repay Pembroke. There was an attempt to call it 'Pembroke Estate Station', but 'Lansdowne Road' was settled upon. In the event the station was a success and the cost repaid.

Having a railway station beside the ground was a huge attraction for Dunlop, and his decision has been a boon for spectators ever since. But despite its advantages, turning this site into a sports ground was not achieved overnight, as the founder explained half a century later:

'I will not say much about my difficulties and struggle in connection with the ground and its enclosing and preparation, (of which I could say much) further than to record the following facts: I laid down a cinder running path

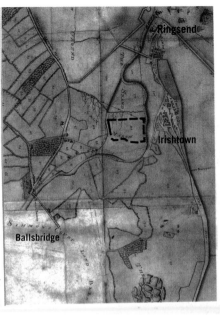

of a quarter-mile, laid down the present Lansdowne Tennis Club ground with my own theodolite, started a Lansdowne archery club, a Lansdowne cricket club, and last, but not least, the Lansdowne Rugby Football Club – colours red, black and yellow. On the tennis club grounds the first tennis championship was held long before Fitzwilliam meetings.'

This collection of amenities was an enormous boon to the city, as the annual *John Lawrence's Handbook of Cricket* explained: 'The absence of any ground open to all gentlemen athletes has been a great bar to training and progress in athletics.

'A very fine piece of ground in close proximity to the aristocratic neighbourhood of the Lansdowne Road station on the Kingstown line, has been taken on lease from the Earl of Pembroke. It is in contemplation to form a permanent running path, with all the necessary accompaniments, while a first-class cricket crease, with archery and croquet grounds, will be added as adjuncts.'

By May, enough work had been done – the 578 yard cinder running track was laid down – to open the facility to the city's athletes. 'A large covered grandstand to accommodate some four hundred people and reserved seats on a graduated foundation have been erected', beamed *The Irish Times*, 'and the fine band of the 17th Lancers will perform'.

'A carefully handicapped series of athletic contests will, for the first time in Ireland, be run on a cinder running path, which has never before been used.'

On Saturday 23 May 1873, the Irish Champion Athletic Club grounds were opened by the Viceroy, the Earl Spencer, and his wife Lady Georgina Hamilton. The presence of the cream of Castle society did not help draw the crowds, however, and the newspapers complained that the grandstand was never more than half full and the standing room was sparsely populated. There were complaints about the facilities: the cinder track was in poor condition and was much narrower on the far side, while the scoreboard was 'of a century long gone by'. *The Irish Times* also urged the club to ban 'saddle horses', as 'one day the committee of management may be taking its trial for manslaughter if a restive steed, frightened at the passing trains on the Dublin, Wicklow and Wexford line, managed to kill some of the spectators.'

A map from the 1760s shows the meanderings of the River Dodder. The location of the Lansdowne Road stadium is marked

Two days later the Dublin Amateur Athletic Club hired the facilities for its sports. An unexpected guest was Sir Garnet Wolseley, who helped present the prizes. Wolseley was an enormous celebrity of the day, a Dubliner who fought in battles from Crimea to Burma, and China to Canada. He had just returned from waging war with the Ashantees in the Gold Coast, for which he received a testimonial to his 'courage, energy and perseverance' from parliament, and the sum of £25,000. He is best remembered as the target for the Gilbert and Sullivan lampoon 'The Very Model of the Modern Major General'.

The ground was next open for business on 6 June, when the Irish Civil Service Club held its sports day. Again the Lord Lieutenant and Lady Hamilton came along to present the prizes, which included a biscuit box, fish slice and revolving butter cooler, modest indeed compared to the stakes in modern sport. This was a more successful event than the first two meets, with 'a crowded and fashionable assemblage of ladies and gentlemen'.

By the end of its first season, the complex was taking shape. *Lawrence's Annual* itemised the facilities installed: 'ground enclosed, first running path in Ireland laid, cricket ground, hurdle course, archery ground, four hundred seat grand stand erected, sloping seats for six hundred more, archery and croquet hut, Gate lodge, Dressing room under the railway arch.'

It was a stunning arrival on the Dublin sporting scene. But Dunlop was clearly not content with athletics meetings, and had far greater ambitions.

The motto of the ICAC was adopted that winter, too, taking a line from the poet Horace: '*nunc cuiris homini contigit adire Corinthum*'. It translates as 'It is not every man's lot to go to Corinth', a reference to the Greek city that was a byword for luxury and refinement. This is taken to mean that not every man will get to see great cities, a modest statement for an arena that would grow into one of the world's finest.

CHAPTER 2

1875-1884
The
Champion
rises,
and falls

THE rapid progress of the first twelve months was carried on by Dunlop and his efficient steward, Mr B. Byrne. A carriage drive and stand was erected, and the grandstand 'thoroughly painted and tarred and thus safe from deterioration'. An area for archery was established under the railway embankment, 'roofed with felt and thus made into a habitable dressing room', but there was still much to keep the ICAC busy: 'A railing around the pitch is still much required,' said *Lawrence's Handbook*.

Besides the physical development of the project, it seems Dunlop had greater mountains to climb. The club minutes make clear that he regarded the Irish Champion Athletic Club as 'a National Club,' and 'not the product of mere rivalry'.

Dunlop was clearly not content with being merely master of a club in Ballsbridge, but aimed to form a federation of existing clubs, thereby imposing some sort of discipline on the chaotic world of Irish sport. Perhaps he saw Lansdowne as akin to the Jockey Club or Marylebone Cricket Club (MCC), an elite club with a leading role in administering the sport. As it was, in 1873 there were no governing bodies for rugby, athletics, cricket or tennis in Ireland, while the association football body had just been formed in Belfast.

J.T. Hurford, editor of *Lawrence's Handbook*, explained in a note: 'the progress, and unexpected commercial and athletic success of the Irish Champion Athletic Club give it a fair claim, as an essentially national association, to the premier place in our records.'

While Lansdowne Road would soon evolve into primarily a rugby stadium, its main function in the 1870s was as a venue for athletics. It was a glorious era for track and field in Ireland, with many world bests being recorded by such as the Davin brothers from Carrick-on-Suir, John Purcell from Dublin and Dan Shanahan from Limerick. The athletics club was where a budding sports administrator called Michael Cusack cut his teeth: he would go on to help form and shape the country's leading sports body over the next 125 years, the Gaelic Athletic Association.

The 1875 championships took place on 'a very disheartening day, wild and tempestuous', according to *Bell's Life*. There were fine double victories for Maurice Davin (shot putt and hammer), and Alfred Courtney (mile

and half-mile), but the newest star of Irish athletics was unveiled as George Kenny, a student at Clongowes Wood College.

Kenny's appearance at the event was much anticipated, as the boy 'was reported to have done some wonderful performances in private', according to Pat Davin in his reminiscences many years later. Fourteen stone and six feet tall, Kenny, from Galway, won the long jump that day with a leap of twenty-one feet six inches (6.55m), beating the world record holder John Lane of ICAC, who had jumped 7.05m at the College Races the year before.

Douglas Ogilby, IRFU founder who lived a colourful life when he left Ireland for Australia

Kenny entered TCD later in 1875, and won everything he entered for at the College Races. He entered for some events at the ICAC meeting of 1876 but, still suffering from a rugby injury incurred over the winter, he was forced to retire after a single attempt at the long jump. He never competed again, and died of typhus later that year, aged just twenty-one.

According to Davin, 'No finer type of athlete than George Kenny ever stood in the athletic arena. Had he lived his name would undoubtedly occupy a prominent place amongst the list of athletic champions.'

George Kenny's other claim to a footnote in Irish sports history is that on one glorious afternoon in 1876 he blazed his way to 266 for Trinity's second XI against Rathmines School's Past & Present selection. Until 2009 it was the highest cricket score recorded by an Irishman.

On 7 August 1875, as part of the centenary celebrations of the birth of Daniel O'Connell, a 'monster athletics meeting' was staged at Lansdowne Road, but was 'rendered a complete failure because of adverse weather'. Less than one hundred attended, and rain cleared for just one hour of the day. Kenny won three races while Michael Cusack was second in the shot putt.

The ICAC chairman, Thomas Casey, reported to the AGM in December that the ground was developing well: 'the grandstand has been painted; the running pitch exceeded the committee's expectations; the arch under the railway has been roofed with felt; two splendid croquet pitches have been laid down; a tent and shower bath have been purchased, with the water supply secured from Vartry.' The club reported total income at £500, with a surplus of £228, reducing the capital debt to £299. The other major decisions of the AGM were to adopt blue and gold as the colours of the club, and 'the ancient arms of Ireland above three gold crowns' as the crest.

The championship meeting of 1876 was well-attended, despite there being a counter attraction of a military review in the Phoenix Park to mark Queen Victoria's birthday. Tom Davin took the prizes for long jump and high jump, while his brother Maurice took the hammer with a new world record of 128 feet (39 metres) but lost out in the shot putt to Dr John Daly of Borrisokane, who set an Irish record. Daly won the tug of war from Matthew Stritch, the event being added to the programme as part of the build up to the international against England ten days later. Bicycling took its place in the championships for the first time, with the enormous front wheels (58 inches diameter) ensuring that, as Pat Davin recalled, 'It debarred any but a very tall man from competing in races'.

The Irish Times had hailed the efforts of the ICAC to stimulate sport, and saw in their activities a great boon to public health. It highlighted the performances of the Davins, Kenny and Lane as prime examples of 'the systematic development of Irish muscle by means of athletics. We know by calculations made by the late Dr Edward Forbes of Edinburgh, and others, that Irish labourers are capable of greater physical efforts than members of their class in either of the sister countries, or in France, Belgium or Germany.'

The newspaper went on to complain, however, that Irishmen were not prominent in the world of English athletics:

'It must be confessed that English gentlemen, as a rule, carry the palm from their Irish fellows in most of the departments of sport which require exceptional muscular development.'

Perhaps stung by this slight, the Champion club challenged the leading English clubs to assemble a side to contest what would be the first international athletics meeting. Strangely, the public imagination wasn't captured by this novel concept and the attendance on 5 June 1876, Whit Monday, was less than expected. *The Irish Times* fancifully blamed the Trinity races:

'Probably the approach of the great annual Olympiad of the University when sixty to eighty thousand people flock together in the gloss of summer fashion and youthful beauty, has caused many people to avail themselves of other opportunities of pleasure-seeking yesterday, particularly along the sea-coast, and to put-off indulgence in respect of foot-races until the great Isthmian display next week'.

Besides the gloriously over-the-top sentiments, there is no evidence that the College Races ever attracted more than twenty-thousand spectators, even at its peak.

The 'Celt v Saxon' contest, as some newspapers styled the event, did not see a true representative side of Englishmen – or Irishmen – but a side got up by the elite clubs of Oxford and Cambridge universities, London AC and the Amateur AC. The AAA was not founded until 1880. The Irish side conformed to the norms of the era, where sport was the preserve of those who could afford the time to play it.

A printed programme was produced, but the press complained it was meagre in its information, being simply a list of events and participants. The reporters pondered, too, on whether England were as strong as they could be, suggesting that there were 'men of straw' among the visitors, but that was rather rudely disproved.

The contest was slated to begin 'at one o'clock punctually', but it was

2.20 pm before 'the first hammer was seen curling its tail through the air'. The delay is mysterious, as both English competitors, including the Hon. Arthur Pelham, failed to appear. John Daly threw 98 feet 11 inches, but Maurice Davin hurled the hammer well past to a reported mark of 131 feet 6 inches. There is some doubt about that figure as it is not recorded as a world record, which it was by more than four feet. Were it so, Davin would have been the first to pass 40 metres as it equates to 40.08m.

One world record that was recognised was that for the 880 yards by the great middle-distance runner Walter Slade, who was paired with Harry Hill against a sole Irishman, H. Moore. The English champion passed the half way mark in fifty-seven seconds and beat Moore by ten yards as Hill dropped out. His 1-59.5 was three-tenths faster than the absent Pelham's world record. Astonishingly, Slade lowered the mark by 0.7 seconds at the Civil Service sports the following day at Lansdowne Road, and a further 0.6 seconds in Belfast four days later.

Charles Lockton, Australian-born athlete who conquered the Davins

Hill may have been injured, as he failed to start in the one mile race, Slade romping home by twelve yards from CH Ford in four minutes 35.6 seconds.

In the sprints Ireland's James Douglas Ogilby won the 100 yards from Albert Powles, with the result reversed in the 220. Montague Shearman of England, later an athletics historian, finished last in both races. The visitors objected to the length of the track which was re-measured and found to be accurate.

Ogilby had an even better run the following day in the Civil Service AC sports: with twenty yards to go he was still behind a Tasmanian-born star, C.L. Lockton. 'Hopelessly beaten', wrote Pat Davin many years later, but Ogilby caught up with his opponents and finished nearly a yard ahead of Lockton, with Shearman well behind.

The Ulsterman is regarded as one of the finest nineteenth-century

Maurice Davin, first president of the GAA and star athlete of the 1870s

sprinters, a specialist over the shortest distance, which was unusual at the time. A fair man, he was strongly built, weighing 12st and standing 5'9". He had a short running stride, but won most of his races in the last few yards when he had something in reserve.

In addition to his flair on the athletics field, Ogilby led a colourful life; he hailed from Donemana in Co. Tyrone. Educated at Trinity, he rebelled against his wealthy family by falling in love with a factory seamstress, Mary Jane Jamieson. After his family vetoed the relationship, he disappeared for seven years, working in the British Museum and the US. He returned in 1884 to reclaim Mary Jane, with whom he eloped to Australia. He worked at the Australian Museum from 1885 to 1890, when he was sacked for his 'extreme and undiscriminating affinity for alcohol'. He later became a famous ichthyologist, writing many volumes about the 154 new species of fish he identified.

Ireland's other three victories were won by men called Davin. Pat – who celebrated his nineteenth birthday the day before – and Tom shared first place in the high jump with leaps of 5 feet 8 inches. Charles Lockton, running for England, opted out to save himself for the hurdles, which he won by four yards. Lockton also prevailed over the Davin brothers in the long jump.

Maurice Davin had a titanic battle with Thomas Stone for the shot putt pendant. Davin threw forty feet with his second throw, fourteen inches ahead of Stone, and rested on his laurels. Stone, according to his teammate Shearman, was 'a fine specimen of manhood, weighing fourteen stone and being over six feet, but beautifully proportioned, and no mean performer at a sprint.' The Englishman, and Ireland's J.C. Daly, continued to try to match Davin and when Stone threw 40 feet Davin re-entered the fray. The giant Tipperary man tossed the shot 40 feet 2 inches for a narrow victory.

Under the headline 'Well Done Carrick!', the *Tipperary Free Press* reported on what it styled 'Ireland v Carrick' (presumably it meant to print 'England v Carrick'):

'*Their names in any programme mean a triumph for any Tipperary men; as men they are 'all there', and we congratulate them on their marked victory (which, as they have always done), they have achieved without brag or ostentation. The triumph was duly celebrated in Carrick on Tuesday evening amid the rattle of music and blaze of bonfire.*'

The final event was the tug-of-war, 'this new description of athletics'. The press believed that as Dr John C. Daly had more experience of the event he was bound to pull his opponent over, but perhaps they were not well briefed about the enormous William Winthrop. The Englishman was 18 stones, Daly a mere 14 stone 8 pounds. Winthrop was also 'better acquainted with the science of the game' and bested Daly by two pulls to one.

In all, England won nine events (220, 440, & 880 yards, mile, four miles, 120 hurdles, long jump, three mile walk and tug-of-war) to Ireland's four. The new concept of international team sport failed to rouse the venue that later gave the world the Lansdowne Roar: 'There was rather an absence of spirit and verve about the amusements and the spectators'.

Medals were presented by the Lord Mayor of Dublin, Sir George Bolster Owens, and a banquet was held for the teams in the Shelbourne Hotel.

The London-based *Globe* newspaper remarked that

'*Ireland can at any rate compete on pretty equal terms with the best men in England…*

'*All the races for which long preparation and careful training are required – such as walking and long-distance running – were, as might have been expected, won by the Englishmen. For the short-distance running and the non-training competitions, such as jumping and throwing the weight and hammer, Ireland had the best of it.*'

'*It is a wide gap which separates us from our neighbours across the Channel, and such a friendly contest as that of Monday does an immense deal towards bridging over the disagreeable gulf*'.

● ● ●

The increased number of big events meant the ICAC annual general meeting in December 1876 was able to report income was up to £987, excluding donations.

Athletics was still the bedrock sport, and few would have guessed that its time was running out rapidly. Internal divisions were reported in ICAC in 1877, and the championships, held in mid-May, were not well supported, despite extensive improvements to the track. 'The attendance was twice as large as it generally is and about half as large as it ought to be', said the *Freeman's Journal*. The entry was weak, with just two men, Maurice Davin and Patrick Hickey of Queen's College Cork, competing in the throwing events.

There were a couple of spats at the 1878 championships involving Pat Davin, who went home with three titles. The Tipperary man was reckoned by observers to have won the 100 yards by half a yard, but the judges called it a dead heat. A rerun was called, but Davin declined the opportunity and James Stewart of ICAC had an easy win. Later in the day Davin was coming out of the long jump pit after a trial jump when he collided with the leading cyclist in the track race. Davin was 'quite shaken' and the cyclist lost his chance to win.

In 1879 a new star was seen for the first time in Tom Malone of Milltown Malbay who won the 100 yards in 10¼ seconds and the 440 yards in 51.2. Malone went on to win the AAA long jump title in 1882 before emigrating to Australia where he became a professional athlete. The championships also saw the last major appearance of Maurice Davin, who won the hammer and shot, his ninth and tenth titles.

The Irish Sportsman was certainly impressed with the state of the stadium:

> *'The ICAC grounds are rapidly becoming a resort of beauty and fashion as well as strength and fleetness. The gentleman who brings here his wife, his daughters, or his sisters, may rest assured that nothing to offend the eye or to shock the ear, even of the most fastidious, can come within their reach, and we rejoice to see the ICAC ground so rapidly becoming, not only the leading resort of form and physique, but also of beauty, fashion and innocence.'*

Despite Pat Davin winning five titles at the 1880 championships, the Irish Champion club was in trouble, and an executive committee was formed to see it out of the crisis. A thirty-three-year-old Co. Clare-born teacher called Michael Cusack took a prominent role. Cusack had been a leading figure of the Dublin Amateur Athletic Club (DAAC), and when he left that body in 1878 he was immediately co-opted onto the Champion club committee. He was a fanatical believer in sport, enshrining it in the curriculum of Cusack's Academy and being an eager participant in athletics, rowing, cricket and rugby before being the main mover in the birth of the Gaelic Athletic Association in 1884; he is immortalised by that body in the name of one of its Croke Park grandstands. Cusack was a committed Home Ruler too, which conflicted with the predominantly unionist and elitist outlook of the three main clubs, ICAC, Civil Service and Trinity.

An eccentric-looking gentleman, he cut a fine figure on the streets of Dublin, wearing home-spun clothes, a soft felt hat and hob-nailed boots, and carrying a blackthorn stick. He was of medium height, with powerful arms and legs and, when not in training, a large belly. His voice was loud and booming, and his opinions often got him into trouble. James Joyce immortalised him as The Citizen in *Ulysses*, describing him as 'a broadshouldered, deepchested, stronglimbed, frankeyed, redhaired, freelyfreckled, shaggybearded, widemouthed, largenosed, longheaded, deepvoiced, barekneed, brawnyhanded, hairylegged, ruddyfaced, sinewyarmed hero'.

Back in 1877 Dunlop had struggled to turn the club into a company to help finance the expansion and development at Lansdowne Road. There was considerable internal opposition to the scheme which went on for months, but Dunlop pushed it through that December. The dissenters persisted however and in July 1878 Dunlop took High Court action against the club 'to have accounts taken in order to indemnify himself in respect of claims for which he made himself responsible on account of the club'. Cusack, who is judged to have had a foot in both camps, was called in to intercede.

The debts were enormous however – more than £4,000 – and at a

The eccentrically-dressed Michael Cusack, who helped wind up the Champion club

meeting in December 1880 twelve leading officials of the club, including Dunlop and Cusack, unanimously decided to dissolve the Irish Champion Athletic Club and to use its property, including trophies, in part-discharge of its liabilities. The tenancy was handed over to Lansdowne FC, which was by then a thriving club.

Dunlop, also secretary of the rugby club, soldiered on at the stadium, and new funds were found to continue development when Lord Pembroke and Lord Longford offered financial assistance.

'It was excellently drained and levelled and became one of the best grounds in Ireland', wrote Dunlop in the 1920s, 'better in fact than the present one, which, owing to the shelter of the grand stand, does not dry properly during wet seasons.'

Dunlop recalled that one winter he paddled a canoe over the pitch in about eighteen inches of water, while a few sheep stood stranded in a little island in the middle. 'To prevent a recurrence of this, three hundred cartloads of soil were transferred from a trench alongside the neighbouring railway line and this raised the playing area two feet and no further "ark" incidents have been recorded.'

With the demise of the Champion club, athletics' days were numbered at the stadium, even though the old ICAC championships were taken up by the Dublin Amateur Athletic Club and run under Amateur Athletics Association (AAA) rules.

In 1881 Cusack, then aged thirty-four, made a comeback and won the 16lb shot at the Irish championships with a mark better than the current British champion. The event was rain-affected and standards were otherwise poor: 'The worst championship meeting we have ever seen', complained the *Freeman's Journal*. The event was most notable for a meeting held in the Lansdowne pavilion afterwards, at which the Amateur Athletics Association of Ireland was founded. The association had more egalitarian ideals than ICAC, but it never got off the ground. It would be another four years before the Irish Amateur Athletics Association was founded.

The 1882 championships were again hosted by DAAC, but 'no more than a dozen pounds' were taken on the gate and the following year was similarly ill-starred. 'This seemingly unfortunate ground ... invariably fails to draw a good gate', wrote one pressman.

The last Irish championship to be held at Lansdowne Road was on 5 July 1884. *The Irish Sportsman* was highly critical, but the report of Michael Cusack was coruscating. He criticised the organisers aloud on the day and an ugly scene developed in which he said his wife was insulted and attempts were made to eject him. He was reporting for *United Ireland*, a Home Rule weekly, where he later railed against the standard of judging and the prominence of the foot races at the expense of what he saw as the 'more Irish' throwing and jumping events. He also criticised the arrogance of the bookmakers and the dangers they clearly held for sport. His passionate words of disgust were a fine epitaph for what he saw as the death throes of the premier Irish athletics meeting.

CHAPTER 3

1876 Rugby takes root by the river

Wanderers comes to join Lansdowne at the new headquarters

THE first rugby club in Ireland was that at Trinity, where the game was played from 1848 by former pupils of Cheltenham and Rugby schools, and the first club was founded in 1854.

There is no evidence that Dunlop was a rugby player – he certainly did not make the first team in Trinity when he was there – but he clearly had a strong interest in the game. Following the foundation of the ICAC, and its acquisition of a base in the southern suburb, Dunlop started a rugby side, comprised almost entirely of current and former Trinity students.

Dunlop himself described the first fixture – against Wanderers, who had formed the year before – as 'a fiasco', but the seeds were sown. At the time there were just two other sides in the city – Wanderers and Trinity – but within a decade there would be more than thirty.

Lawrence's Handbook of 1873-74 described the facilities: 'Lansdowne Road FC is the name of the football section of the ICAC scheme. The Eastern side of the Champion ground, Lansdowne Road Station is specially laid out for the game, and affords a plot about 125 yards long by an average of 60 wide.'

The last match of that season on the ICAC ground was Wanderers v Lansdowne Road, which brought out most of the best players in Dublin on one side or the other. Mr Cronyn scored the only try for Wanderers.'

By 1874 Lansdowne were finally able to overcome their local opposition, with Frederic Kidd scoring a try. Kidd was an early captain of the club and a top local sportsman. He still holds the Irish record for the esoteric – but then common at athletics meetings – event of 'throwing the cricket ball', with a throw of 114 yards, 1 foot 7 inches.

Kidd was the heaviest man on the Ireland team that played England at the Oval in London in 1877, weighing in at 13 stone 8lbs (on modern Irish teams only the scrum-half would weigh less). He was later a successful doctor and Master of the Coombe Hospital in Dublin.

By 1876 the rugby ground had become 'the centre of the ICAC enclosure', but one difficulty the nascent club had was that as so many of the members were students, they would not play against the college. Indeed, Dunlop bemoaned that they were known as 'Second Trinity'. For the 1876-77 season he took an unusual step: 'I reduced our firsts to a

Left: the 1875 Ireland team that played England at Kennington Oval
Below: R.M. Peter, early rugby pioneer and editor of the first Irish rugby annual

paper one, selected the best men (who were not Trinity men) and formed them into the Lansdowne second team ... from this team arose the present Lansdowne football club.'

Lansdowne at first wore the blue and yellow colours of ICAC, but in 1876-77 Dunlop picked the black, red and gold colours of I Zingari to become those of Lansdowne. I Zingari was founded in 1845 as a travelling team of English gentlemen cricketers; its name means 'The Gypsies' and motto defines the colours: 'out of darkness, through fire, into light'.

In 1879 Dunlop resigned as secretary, but remained on as President until he stepped down in 1904.

By 1880, when R.M. Peter produced his first, and only *Irish Football Annual,* there were seventy-eight clubs in Ireland, of which Lansdowne 'holds the foremost position amongst the clubs in Dublin'. They had fifty members, almost double the previous season, each paying £1 subscription. It was a booming club by then, with fifty-six fixtures for the two sides, and 'great pecuniary advantages' for its members, according to *Lawrence's Handbook*, as members were entitled to 'free admission to all sports held at the athletic ground from 1 October to 31 March, (including) all interprovincial and international matches.'

Lansdowne's undivided use of the ground during the winter months was to come to an end, however, at the end of its first decade. Wanderers, who were founded in 1871, played on a ground at Clyde Road, Ballsbridge, but in December 1879 they were asked to move as the

landowner wanted the land for tillage. The club did a deal with Dunlop and 'played the second half of the season side by side with the Lansdowne FC in complete harmony.' The first game as co-tenants was against each other, with Wanderers winning by a goal and three tries to a goal.

In 1882 competition started in the province, with the first running of the Leinster Senior Cup, a development that ensured the previously chaotic practice of men playing for several clubs died out. The cup was dominated by Trinity up to World War I, while Wanderers were clearly the next best club, but Lansdowne won the cup for the first time in 1891 with a famous win over the students.

Dunlop remained actively involved with Lansdowne, even after he stepped down as President. His son Eric recalled visiting the changing rooms in the 1920s when his father would offer Player's Drumhead cigarettes to the players.

'He designed netting gloves and toe caps for players such as Eugene Davy', he explained. 'His wife made them and though it was considered a bit "sissy", the players would try them out rather than offend him.'

Dunlop died suddenly on 16 April 1930 at his home at Sidney Avenue, Blackrock. He was in his eighty-seventh year. Dunlop had joined the legal service as a teenager and retired in 1921 aged seventy-seven after fifty-eight years, but there is no doubt his greatest work took place on a piece of land occupying eight-and-a-quarter acres of Ballsbridge.

Top: The Wanderers club moved from Clyde Road to Lansdowne Road. This team group is from 1888
Above: Rugby was growing in popularity, as this advertisement from *Lawrence's Annual* shows

nternational rugby took its first steps in 1871, when Scotland beat England in front of four thousand spectators at Raeburn Place in Edinburgh. Just seven weeks earlier the English clubs had founded the Rugby Football Union (RFU) and Trinity College Dublin joined up soon after.

The student club was founded in 1854, laying claim to being the oldest club in continuous existence anywhere in the world. Charles Barrington, club captain, recalled how he and secretary R.M. Wall had written down the first modern laws of the game in their student rooms in 1868:

'Wall sat gravely at his little table. A small dark wiry hardy chap with a short black beard and kindly dark eyes. He wrote and I dictated. Gradually and gradually as one could remember them the unwritten laws governing the immortal Rugby game were put on paper.'

The formation of the RFU was noted in Dublin, and attempts were put in train to set up a similar body. Again the Trinity captain was to the fore, and George Hall Stack's rooms saw several meetings of the clubs. In December 1874, the Irish Football Union (IFU) was founded at the premises of sports equipment seller John Lawrence at 38-39 Grafton Street (now occupied by the Monsoon Accessorize clothes store, and a Burger King restaurant). Things did not run smoothly for the new body, as the northern clubs were irked at not being involved and formed their own Northern Football Union (NFU) in January 1875.

The relations between the two unions were civil, however, and each provided ten men to the first Ireland team, which played England at the Kennington Oval the following month. That the game was twenty-a-side was at the insistence of the Irish, who clearly felt that their best hope of overcoming the more experienced English side was by crowding the field. Ireland's players, it was reported by *Sport*, were 'immaculately innocent of training'. Wearing stout woollen sweaters, the Irish side went down by two goals and a try to nil. (Until 1875 internationals were decided by the number of goals – conversions and dropped goals – but from that year the number of tries was used as a 'tiebreak' if teams were level on goals. A formal point scoring system was not introduced until the late 1880s, when a try scored one point, a conversion two and a drop goal three.)

Ireland was captained by Donegal man Stack, who had hosted the

1878 The first rugby inter- national

Ireland v England, 11 March 1878

nascent IFU, and that day took the first step in the long history of Irish rugby when he kicked-off the game. Stack was fated not to play a large role thereafter, however, as he died nineteen months later in November 1876. At that time, Stack was a twenty-six-year-old barrister with rooms in Trinity. He had recently undergone a painful and unsuccessful operation and was staying at the Royal Albert Hotel in Dominick Street, close to the courts. On Sunday lunchtime he sent a waiter on an errand to Hamilton's Chemist for a bottle of hydrate of chloral, a popular sedative. Stack suffered from painful indigestion – for which he took opium – and may have needed help in sleeping.

The following morning he was found unconscious in bed, with the bottle empty beside him. He died before a doctor could be summoned. 'Chloral', as the substance was known, was widely used in Victorian times, but overdosing was fatal; the celebrated Irish scientist, John Tyndall, died in such a manner. Stack's inquest found that his death was caused by misadventure.

England were the first visitors to Dublin, but not to Dunlop's stadium, which would have to wait a little longer. The RFU offered 19 December 1875 for the fixture, which the Irish Football Union originally wanted to play in Trinity College. That ground was considered unsuitable, as was the Nine Acres in the Phoenix Park. Dunlop offered the Champion ground, but that was rejected out of hand, despite the founder making repeated efforts to persuade the committee. Lansdowne Road, it was

Handbill for the first international at Lansdowne, with the late change on the Irish team noted

reported, was 'quite inadequate for an international rugby match'. Eventually the Leinster Cricket Club arena in Rathmines was hired – at a cost of £10 – with goalposts, ropes and a flagpole provided by Trinity. The IFU must have been concerned that this novelty might inspire public misbehaviour, with Honorary Secretary H.D. Walsh warning spectators that 'Stewards and representatives of the Press alone are allowed within the ropes'.

England again were too strong – by a goal and a try to nil – and the press blamed the result partly on the 'wretched thin cotton vests' Ireland wore. These were coloured white (as were England's) and the only distinguishing part of the kit was the blue knickerbockers and green velvet cap. Ireland also wore a gold badge and lace. The shamrock crest was the property of the Trinity club, but when Trinity switched to the college coat of arms in 1880 the Irish union requested they be allowed take over the emblem.

The gate takings were just £22 and nine shillings – which at one shilling admission meant fewer than 450 paid in, although women were admitted free. The IFU managed to negotiate the rent down from £10 to £7 ten shillings.

Dunlop must have been feverishly keen to host these popular fixtures. His persistence with the IFU paid off, and the first interprovincial in Dublin was staged in Lansdowne on 16 December 1876. Dunlop offered the options of the ground for £5 rent, or to share the expenses and receipts; the IFU opted for the latter. There was torrential rain in the morning which reduced the crowd, and Leinster beat Ulster by a goal and a try to two tries.

After the game, representatives of the provinces met in the Arcade Hotel in Suffolk Street – now the Ulster Bank – to pick the team to play at the Oval the following February. That was the first of Ireland's fifteen-a-side internationals, and another defeat to nil resulted. Ireland played the inaugural fixture against Scotland in Belfast two weeks later, which the visitors won by six goals and two tries to nil. There were two Leinster men on the side, of whom the acerbic reporter Jacques McCarthy said they 'might have been much better at home in bed.'

It was more than a year before the next international – Ireland's fifth

– came around, and this time the IFU offered it to the Irish Champion club, commencing a run of 244 games as the sole venue in the capital, which only ended in 2006 when the old ground was closed for demolition.

The press was confident that the attendance would be good for the visit of England on 13 December 1875. 'The ground is in capital order, and a reserved portion has been set aside where ladies can obtain a most commanding view of the contest'. Stewards were enlisted from the captains and secretaries of the city's clubs, plus past members of the Irish team. The slightly haphazard organisation can seen in the newspaper notice that read 'both teams are requested to be at the ground at 2 o'clock, and the public may count on the kick off at 3 o'clock.'

The Irish Times editorial hailed the new organisation, saying it 'may take credit for having done much to foster and encourage the manly game throughout the country'.

Ireland made nine changes from the previous game, picking six new caps, but the selection did not go down well in some quarters. It was the first Irish team that was open to Munster players, and three Limerick men were called up. However the honorary secretary of the Cork club wrote a letter to the editor of *The Irish Times*, complaining that his men had been totally ignored.

Robert Walkington and James Macdonald were the only survivors of the Oval game in 1875, with Walkington the only man to play in all four games to date. He was an important figure in those early days, playing ten games up to 1882, in which year he was also president of the IRFU.

In a late change, Kingstown schoolboy George Fagan – who had just turned eighteen – was called in a few minutes before kick off to replace Gus Whitestone of Trinity at half back. Fagan was 'well worthy of his place', but it proved to be his only cap, and he died in Calcutta seven years later. His younger brother, Arthur, played for England against Ireland in 1887.

Concerns about the arrangements proved well-founded:

'The rush at the gates was somewhat unexpected, and much pushing and shoving was indulged in. The entrance to the turnstile was too wide, creating a block and preventing the machine from turning.'

The teams were photographed before the game, the England team haphazardly arranged under a tree inside the grounds. A strong, bitter north-westerly wind blew over the ground, which was rather exposed. It was reported that two thousand people turned up, and a rope was needed to keep them back from the pitch: 'the public kept fairly within the touch line and the utmost good order prevailed, which the players of either team received commensurate amounts of applause according to their desserts,' wrote *The Irish Times*.

Shortly after 3pm England won the toss and asked Ireland to kick off into the wind towards the river end. Walkington started the game, his kick resulting in a scrum, from which a Kelly break saw the ball dribbled close to the English line. Enthoven rescued the situation for the visitors and started another attack.

Matier made a relieving kick for Ireland but England came back again and again. A penalty for 'hand-ball play' led to a Hunt break. He passed to Bell who ran it close to the Irish line, where England forward Herbert Gardner touched down for the first of the 864 international tries at the stadium. Pearson kicked the goal 'in splendid style'. Herbert Prescott Gardner, aged twenty-one, was playing his only game for England. He later emigrated to Australia where he was a local representative in Queensland in 1915 and is believed to have died there in 1938.

Walkington kicked off again from half way, when as the pressman put it 'Hornby returned the Gilbert' – an early plug for the ball's manufacturer – but Walkington 'replied with interest' and a promising situation was set up close to the England 25 yard line, eventually ruined when 'the wind proved Kidd's worst enemy'.

An England attack ended with Bell failing to ground the ball and Walkington touched down to save a try. There was much comment on the quality of play in the game, and the end-to-end attacking made it entertaining for the spectators.

The press was full of praise for the Englishmen: 'The style of play of our visitors was generally remarked, while the running and dropping was

Above:
England's A.N. 'Monkey' Hornby, who was also a top cricketer

greatly admired.' The unselfishness of the England players was also noted; 'No matter how close to the goal line they would prefer to pass back, and doing it so quick, one after another, they may be said to fairly bother the opposing team.' The reporter railed against the attitude of the Irishman: 'In Ireland men like to play the gallery game, and "Moriarty" thinks it a grand thing if the *Irish Times* next morning announces he "secured a try".'

Ireland's forwards continued to match their opponents – Kelly, Macdonald and Schutte were singled out for praise – but a great run by Jackson saw England twenty yards from the Irish line. 'The careless play of Matier now let Verelst gain a try, but the try at goal was a failure'.

England crossed again when a Hornby run ended with a scoring pass to Penny. This time Pearson goaled, 'notwithstanding the great angle to the posts'.

Albert 'Monkey' Hornby was a major figure in English sport: one of only two men to captain his country at both rugby and cricket, he also played football for Blackburn Rovers. Hornby was immortalised by the English poet Francis Thompson in one of the most celebrated of all sporting poems, 'At Lord's'.

> For the field is full of shades as I near a shadowy coast,
> And a ghostly batsman plays to the bowling of a ghost,
> And I look through my tears on a soundless-clapping host
> As the run stealers flicker to and fro, to and fro:
> O my Hornby and my Barlow long ago!

Ireland upped their game in the second half, when they 'several times seemed like wiping off the score against them'. England were playing into a stiff wind but 'closely penned their opponents'; with ten minutes to go Ireland were camped on the England line. The ball was fed back to Fagan but 'he was so quickly pounced on he could not drop a goal'.

But the Englishmen by slow degrees relieved the siege. Hornby and Enthoven made some excellent runs before a final relieving kick by Pearson spun into touch and 'no side' was called. The match was an England win 'by two goals to nil, with one try to spare'.

Much of the criticism went the way of three-quarter R.N. Matier, who 'did not come up to expectations, perhaps because of nervousness' –

several times he 'muffed' the ball, and once he interfered with Walkington, and later with Kidd, while his picking up was rarely clean.

There was praise for the half-backs, notably Kidd, while Walkington 'was equal to the occasion', although the trenchant *Irish Times* reporter, Jacques McCarthy, criticised Ireland for playing one full back when the English had two. Ireland had lined out in a 1–2–2–10 formation, England 2–2–2–9.

The teams adjourned to the Shelbourne Hotel, where the IFU hosted the post-match dinner at 7 pm. The toasts, 'which were given and responded to with much enthusiasm', were made to the Queen, the English XV, the Irish XV, the Rugby Union, the Irish Union and 'The Ladies'.

While the match was a success, it was clear Ireland's rugby had a fair way to go before it would start winning games. It was not a glorious introduction to international rugby – Ireland lost their first ten games without scoring a point, while prior to the first victory over England in 1888, the record in all games read: won 1, drew 1, lost 23. In only six of those games did they even score.

IRELAND: R.B. Walkington (NIFC, captain), R.N. Matier (NIFC), F.W. Kidd (Lansdowne), G.L. Fagan (Kingstown School), T.G. Gordon (NIFC), E.W.D. Croker (Limerick), W.D. Moore (Queen's, Belfast), F. Schute (Wanderers), H.W. Murray (DUFC), W. Finlay (NIFC), J.A. Macdonald (Methodist College & Windsor), H.G. Edwards (DUFC), H.C. Kelly (NIFC), R.W. Hughes (Queen's, Belfast), W. Griffiths (Limerick)

England: H.W. Pearson (Blackheath), W.J. Penny (King's College), A.M. Hornby (Preston), H.J. Enthoven (Richmond), A.H. Jackson (Blackheath), J.L. Bell (Durham), G.F. Vernon (Blackheath), H.S. Gardner (Richmond), F. Dawson (Cooper's Hill), T. Blatherwick (Manchester), C.L. Verelst (Liverpool), A. Budd (Blackheath), E.B. Turner (St George's), M.W. Marshall (Blackheath, captain)

Referee: E. Swainston (Manchester), Umpires: H.L. Robinson (Leinster), R. Bell jnr (Ulster)

CHAPTER 5

1875-1925
A sporting Zoological Gardens

Tomahawks and triple plays, Cossacks and Caledonians

The sporting complex at Lansdowne Road was an expensive concern to run, and Dunlop was always on the lookout for an event that would fill the seats and standing areas. That pattern continued over the years, with sporting and entertainment entrepreneurs from John Lawrence to Billy Morton to Oliver Barry hiring the grounds for their promotions.

That renting out of the stadium began on Day Two: the morning after the gala opening ICAC meeting in 1874, the Lansdowne Road complex was open once again, this time for a paying customer, the Irish Civil Service Athletics Club, hosting its annual sports day. There were more people at this event, and more still at the Dublin Amateur Athletics Club meeting two weeks later, when the word had clearly spread about this sporting nirvana by the Dodder.

Dunlop had originally seen the grounds as a centre for athletics, cycling, cricket, tennis, croquet and rugby, but there were many other sports, including such obscure ones as pigeon-shooting, skating and lacrosse, played there over the first decade.

A whole new set of sports were introduced in 1884 when the Dublin Caledonian Society, a grouping of Scots immigrants, organised the first Caledonian Games. The event was the brainchild of A. Morrison Miller, a friend of Michael Cusack who later joined him in setting up *The Celtic Times* in 1887. This was a weekly newspaper of Celtic sport and culture which lasted less than twelve months but set up an annual hurling versus shinty international that lasted another thirty years. Cusack saw Ireland as part of a wider Celtic race, and was particularly close to the Scots.

The games were 'an unqualified success, financially as well as athletically'. A huge crowd – up to twenty thousand – paid in that Whit Monday, despite an overcast day. There were many side attractions, with pipe bands and dancing competitions especially popular. The *Irish Times* reporter wrote sarcastically that 'the hearts were stimulated of a highly select, though not a numerous constituency… who revel in the skirl of the pipes'.

The tartan costumes drew much attention, while the Highland events of caber-tossing, putting the stone and sword dancing were a delight to the Dublin crowd. There was an extensive programme of bicycle races and athletics events, with Cusack judging the weight throwing and jumping competitions.

The athletics correspondents of the Dublin newspapers agreed that it was the best meeting held at Lansdowne for many years, although there was disappointment that Pat Davin, although entered for several events, failed to make an appearance.

The highlight of the day was the Hop, Step and Jump, at which John Purcell of Metropolitan Harriers set what was hailed by Cusack as a 'best-on-record' mark of 46 feet seven and a half inches (14.21 metres).

The triple jump was a sport of distant and murky origins. It had been part of the ancient games at Olympia and, as the *geal-ruith*, of the Irish Tailteann games, a multi-sport festival held in Co. Meath from 1829 BC till the arrival of the Normans in 1169 AD.

Cusack had asked the Caledonian committee to include the event, promising them that it would see a world record at what he called 'a shamrock of successive one-legged leaps': the Irish style at the time was more Hop, Hop and Jump. Sure enough, Purcell's first attempt saw him soaring eight inches past the established mark, set by Trinity medical student John Daly at 45'4" the year before. Cusack then prevailed on

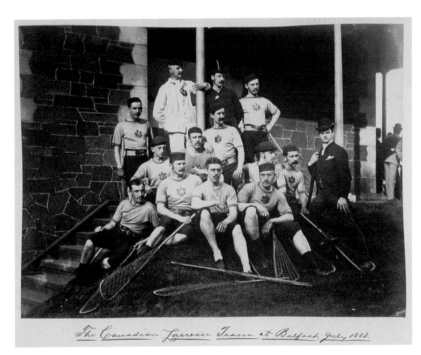

The Canadian lacrosse team before their first game in Ireland, at the North of Ireland club, Belfast

Purcell to have another go, whereupon he added another seven and a half inches.

Sadly, Cusack was mistaken in believing this was a world record. Daniel Looney of Cork had set 46'11" (14.30 metres) in 1879, although Purcell was to break the record twice in the following years as it switched between him and Limerick man Dan Shanahan. Purcell was a top-class athlete, twice winning the British AAA long jump championship in the mid 1880s, and breaking that event's world record at Monasterevin in 1886.

A large number of Scots athletes travelled over, while the local society's more active members also competed. There was a 100 yard race confined to the Caledonian Society's committee which drew much laughter due to the rotund shape of several members. Most events were open to all amateur athletes; only caber tossing, putting the ball, throwing the hammer, pipe music and some dancing events were confined to the Scots. The 'Irish bagpipes', better known as uileann pipes, were also given an outing. John McLeod won £3 for being best dressed Highlander.

One sport where there was no need to consult the record books was bicycling: the mile race on the track was won in an almost pedestrian 3 minutes 4.2 seconds.

The following year the event moved to The Royal Dublin Society showgrounds where it was held in 1885 and 1886, before falling off the calendar.

● ● ●

Big John and the Kahnawake line up on their European tour

The most exotic overseas visitors arrived in May 1876, when two lacrosse teams travelled across the Atlantic for a tour of Britain and Ireland. The sport originated among American and Canadian Indians tribes, where it was seen as a form of martial training–cum–religious ritual. One writer in an 1832 edition of the *Dublin Penny Journal* claimed that hurling and lacrosse were identical:

'it is not so fantastical to suppose, if, as is claimed, St Brendan, the navigator who was a native of Kerry, and died in 577, visited America, and that his followers

introduced hurling there, which developed into lacrosse.'

The Iroquois side had played in England first, winning the endorsement of Queen Victoria who said lacrosse was 'very pretty to watch'. They attracted great attention when they arrived in Ireland, first playing the Canadian selection at the North of Ireland club at Ormeau in Belfast. Two days later they arrived in Dublin where there was much interest in what the newspapers called 'the savages'. The press delighted in listing the names of Blue Spotted, Hickory Woodsplit, Pick the Feather, Hole in the Sky, Flying Name, Deer House, The Loon, Crossing the River, Outside the Multitude, Scattered Branches, Spruce Branches, Great Arm and Wild Wind. The Indians enchanted the crowds with their painted faces and feathered headbands.

Only one of the side, Blue Spotted, spoke English and was thus appointed captain for the tour. He wore scarlet knickerbockers and a feathered headdress, carried a tomahawk and smoked a white clay pipe. However, according to *The Irish Times* 'he spoiled his appearance by wearing a grey shooting jacket'.

The day's entertainment included a tug of war between police and army, a sprint between the Irish and Canadian champions, and a snow-shoe hurdle race.

Before play started in the main event, the teams were introduced to the Lord Lieutenant, whereupon all the players sat on the grass in a circle while Blue Spotted addressed them while brandishing his tomahawk. After an early version of 'the haka', the game began, which Canada won by 3-2.

As a result of the publicity, lacrosse clubs sprang up all over Ireland, and an international match was staged at Lansdowne the following year when Scotland won 3-0 against a team that included Irish Rugby Union secretary R.M. Peter.

Peter (who was also a founder of the Irish Amateur Swimming

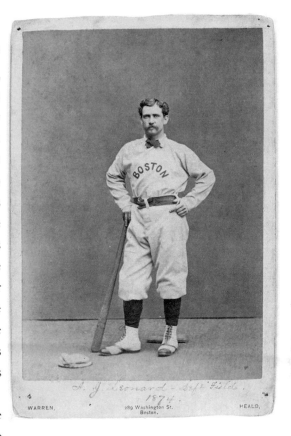

Cavan-born baseball star Andy Leonard

THE AMERICAN BASE-BALL PLAYERS IN ENGLAND—MATCH BETWEEN THE RED STOCKINGS AND THE ATHLETICS, PRINCE'S GROUND, BROMPTON.—[See Page 750.]

HARPER'S WEEKLY.

The 1874 teams in action in London

Association) was a leading light of the Champion Lacrosse club which played at Lansdowne Road but – despite a visit by another Native American side led by Big John Scattered Leaves in 1883 – the sport died out soon afterwards.

In the early 1930s it was revived by a group of young women who had been educated in England and an international was staged at Lansdowne Road in 1935. There were very few opportunities for women to play sport there over the 130 year history of the old ground, with the best-known being the visit of legendary Olympic athlete Fanny Blankers-Koen in 1948. The Irish women's rugby team, for example, has yet to play at 'headquarters'.

The lacrosse women were able to secure the ground, however, and it was again made available for the visit of England in 1949, when the visitors won 15-1 against an Ireland team captained by Clarissa Crawford of Pioneers. An American side beat Leinster 5-4 in 1951 in the last lacrosse game to be staged at Lansdowne Road.

● ● ●

Back in August 1874 cricket was still arguably the most widely played game in the land. Dunlop had ambitions to challenge the supremacy of the Trinity club in its staging of lucrative annual matches against touring sides and English counties, and teamed up with publisher and sports goods seller John Lawrence to invite over the London Imperial Clowns for games against Eleven Gentlemen of Ireland. It was a raucous Victorian version of Twenty20 cricket, with the Clowns being actual circus performers, augmented by some useful professionals. The Gentlemen of Ireland was a strong selection, with several of the best players of the day, including celebrated scholar and wit J.P. Mahaffy, who taught Oscar Wilde; and Leland Hone, who later played test matches for England. The play was interspersed with musical interludes while the Clowns entertained the audience with acrobatic fielding.

The Irish Times man was unimpressed:

'Many lovers of cricket objected to their game being burlesqued, and consequently absented themselves from a match where they expected nothing but buffoonery.' Not quite so generous was the man from *Saunders Newsletter*.

'We may content ourselves now by hoping we ne'er may look upon its like again. Buffoonery, through the medium of cricket, may amuse the village Yokels, or create a laugh in the circus, but we doubt much whether Irish gentlemen will again be found arrayed against such competitors in such costume.'

Sadly for Lawrence, there was little spectator interest in such frivolity either, and the weather was no help: the attendance was described as 'wretched'. He lost £100 on his promotion, which was not repeated. Ironically, Dunlop's rivals at the Leinster club put up a purse to attract the greatest cricketer of the age, W.G. Grace, who brought a huge crowd to Rathmines for a proper match a few weeks later.

Before that game there was another fixture to tantalise the sporting public: the visit of the 'American Base Ball Teams'. The tour of the Americans was an attempt to popularise the game which had just developed the professional shape it retains today. English-born Harry Wright, player-manager of the Boston Red Stockings (in time, the Stockings moved to become the Atlanta Braves; the modern Boston Red Sox are a different club), was keen to spread the game to his native land. Wright sent Albert Spalding, later to be a major sporting figure, across the Atlantic to drum up interest. Spalding returned with a programme of games in England, Scotland, France and Ireland.

Spalding had linked up with Charles Alcock, hailed as 'The Father of Modern Sport' in a twenty-first century biography. Alcock was secretary of the Football Association when he first suggested the FA Cup, and as Secretary of Surrey County Cricket Club organised the first test match in England. His administrative skills are acknowledged, but his marketing talents fell short and the baseball tour proved a financial disaster. He insisted the Americans played a cricket match as part of each day's entertainment, and Wright taught his team-mates the sport on the ship across the Atlantic.

In Dublin, a group of local players were prevailed upon to provide opposition in a series of 'odds' cricket matches between eleven men of Ireland and eighteen Americans. The cricket was to start on each of the three days at 11am, followed at four o'clock by a baseball match between Boston and the Philadelphia Athletics. Admission was one shilling, or 2/6 for a three-day pass (1/6 for ladies). As it turned out only one cricket match was played – Ireland had a more important game the same week – and a weakened side was put out, which was bowled out for thirty-two by the Americans. The tourists, incidentally, won every cricket match on their travels around England and Ireland.

Boston and Philadelphia were the two leading sides in the National Association of Professional Base Ball Players, the first professional league in the United States. Only seven who played in that league have been elected to baseball's Hall of Fame, and five of them played in Dublin: Wright, his brother George, Spalding, Cap Anson and Jim O'Rourke.

Cap Anson was a legendary right-fielder, probably baseball's first superstar. His name is sullied for his playing a large part in the game being segregated along racial lines: he several times refused to play with or against black players. George Wright too, was one of the most celebrated players of his day, the star of the first all-professional team the Cincinnati Red Stockings. O'Rourke was the best pitcher of his generation while Ross Barnes is acknowledged as the champion bat of the era.

A cigarette card of Cap Anson, controversial star of the Philadelphia Athletics

The final day's entertainment was billed to include a baseball match between eighteen Irishmen and nine Americans, but the organisers could not prevail upon sufficient local sportsmen. In the end, just seven Irishmen turned out while, *The Irish Times* reported, 'it is very questionable whether the home party comprehended the merest outline of the game...' The reporter enjoyed it, however, and expressed the hope that 'in a little time it will have taken root in Ireland'. The man from the *Freeman's Journal* claimed the game thus: 'Base Ball is a scientific adaption of the Irish game of rounders'. The attendance was disappointing, as it was on the tour as a whole, and the clubs lost $2,500 between them.

It was not the only visit of baseball players to Lansdowne: in March 1889 two thousand spectators thronged Ballsbridge for the visit of Chicago and an All America selection, and in October 1917 a fund-raising game was arranged between teams representing America and Canada with proceeds going to the Dublin Castle Red Cross Hospital.

● ● ●

Dunlop made strong efforts to establish a permanent cricket club at the ground. Lansdowne CC lasted several years, but never reached the front rank in Dublin circles.

The stars of the early sides were the Exham brothers from Cork, who later found sporting fame in England. Arthur Exham took an impressive seventy-

ADRIAN C. ANSON.
ALLEN & GINTER'S
Cigarettes.
RICHMOND, VIRGINIA.

five wickets in the 1876 season, while Percy made one of only two centuries scored for Lansdowne, against Leinster at Rathmines. Percy was an excellent all-round sportsman who played football for Derby County and cricket for Derbyshire. Other notable members were internationals Horace Hamilton from Carlow and Freddie Lambkin from Cork.

Lansdowne were not immediately granted fixtures by the leading local sides – Leinster, Phoenix and the University – but eventually worked their way up the pecking order. By 1879 they were heavily praised in *Lawrence's Annual* for becoming competitive and having a good crease and abundant room. The pitches played better too, with more scores over a hundred, including one of 225 made against the leading Phoenix club.

However within a couple of years it was struggling, having lost 'its oldest and best members'. By 1881 the club was only able to play five games, compared to twenty-seven the year before, and all of them 'away' games. The committee complained it was 'unable to get use of the ground as in the past', and that the wickets were in a very bad state.

In 1884 Jack Hynes scored the only century recorded at the ground. Hynes also played for Trinity and Phoenix and won twenty-seven caps for Ireland over a career that stretched from 1883-1896. He was the most significant player of his day, labeled 'the champion bat of Ireland' by Wisden after scoring 113 for the MCC.

The club fell away in the 1890s, but the ground continued to be used for cricket, with Sandymount CC establishing a home there before it folded around 1907, while schools and junior clubs also hired it out for games. The sport generally went into steep decline after the First World War and there was little played at Lansdowne Road. *The Irish Times* staff XI played its junior league games on the back pitch throughout the twenties, but the last cricket match was played there in 1930.

● ● ●

The 2 July 1885 meeting of the Irish Rifle Association was a low-key affair, with less than three hundred spectators, but it caused quite a scandal thanks to a minor unscheduled event featuring a visiting American.

There was a US team competing in the championships, but an unattached compatriot, Captain Adam Bogardus, announced on the second day that he wished to perform a rare feat of target shooting. Bogardus, described in the press as 'The Champion Wing Shot of America' said he would 'kill fifty pigeons at a distance on the wing of twenty-one yards, load his own gun throughout and gather up the dead pigeons, all within a quarter of an hour.'

The captain, who earned his title on the Union side of the US Civil War, had a bit of form in this line of sport. He was a noted exponent of trap shooting in America, and once killed five hundred pigeons in under nine hours for a $1000 bet. The sport was under siege however, as humane societies had sprang up all over the country and succeeded in making the shooting of live birds for sport illegal in many states. Bogardus later invented a bloodless compromise, with glass balls stuffed with feathers springing out of the traps for the gunmen.

His performance at the IRA meeting at Lansdowne Road was roundly condemned in the Irish press. In a piece headlined 'Wholesale Pigeon Slaughter', the *Irish Times* reporter decried what he called 'a merciless and unsportsmanlike slaughter of pigeons':

'How can it be considered sport to fire a few yards distance at birds which have been confined in a box, and are half paralysed – many of them as they emerge from the trap? What pleasure can be derived from seeing the quivering, panting, bleeding pigeons roll about the field in their death agony, or drag behind them a broken leg or wing? The exhibition is positively in a sense disgusting, but yesterday it was doubly so.'

Bogardus had a man stand at the basket, throwing two birds in the air at a time. Often the birds hadn't even opened their wings before they were blasted by his double barrel fowling-piece, ripped apart by an ounce and a half of shot. He missed twenty-four birds, but as some of them flew back again he was able to gain his fifty kills in eight minutes twenty-nine seconds. He then leisurely strolled around, joking with the onlookers as he collected the dead. The lot were bagged within twelve minutes 14.2 seconds, so his wager was secured.

The *Times* reported that Bogardus had chosen a poor place to shoot, with the wind blowing the smoke back into his face, while he once shot a bird about four feet from his assistant's head. Some non-paying spectators were warned not to sit on the railings surrounding the ground and were only convinced of the need to do so when Bogardus rattled the fence with his pellets.

The bloodlust extended to some local members of the Irish Rifle Association, who started a contest to shoot three birds each, with the £5 prize won by Mr Humphrey of the County Dublin Gun Club. More than a hundred birds were shot that day, and most reporters were unsympathetic. The cynical correspondent of *Lawrence's Annual* carried a report entitled:

'PIGEON SHOOTING'

'This pastime we should be sorry to advocate but we think that by its great success financially, when tried this year on the ground it gave rather severe testimony to the fact that the sensibilities of the public as expressed in the press must be, like beauty, only skin deep.'

There was a less bloody use of livestock the following winter, when Dunlop promoted a sheepdog trial, the first time such an event was held in Ireland. It was a cold January day, but the attendance was good.

● ● ●

Some of the other efforts to introduce new sports proved abortive. In March 1876, at what can only be described as a particularly untimely point in the calendar, the formation of the Lansdowne Skating Club was announced. There were ambitious plans to lay down wooden floors of 600 square yards in the corner closest to the railway station, with room to extend it to 2,000 square yards if it was successful. Half the area would be roofed over, with canvas over the rest, if necessary. A newspaper report said it had attracted many subscribers but nothing came of the proposal. An early attempt to form a quoits club was also abandoned.

Hurling was popular in Dublin at the time, too, and an attempt was

Captain Bogardus, who left a bloody trail around Lansdowne Road

made to form a club in 1877, seven years before the foundation of the Gaelic Athletic Association. A notice in *The Irish Times* announced 'It is proposed to hold a meeting to organise a hurley club under the patronage of the Irish Champion Athletic Club at Lansdowne Road, and to form a committee. All gentlemen please attend.' No further notices appeared and the club seems to have died at birth. The Trinity College club was formed a year later with future unionist leader Edward Carson an early member.

The initial layout of Lansdowne included two croquet lawns, and with two more being temporarily laid on the cricket square, the club hosted the second Irish Croquet Championship in August 1875. The attendance was dismal – barely two dozen – and there were just fourteen competitors. One of the entrants was a Mr Cusack, who may have been Michael, while a General Stannus beat the defending champion, Thomas Casey, in the men's final. Casey was a leading sportsman of the day, one of three brothers capped at cricket. Mrs G. Vance won the women's prize. At the next annual general meeting of ICAC, H.W.D. Dunlop testified to the success of the club, but it swiftly died out. The game was revived in the 1900s, when Mr S.A.W. Waters tried to make Lansdowne Road the home of the new All Ireland Croquet Club. The funds offered were insufficient to

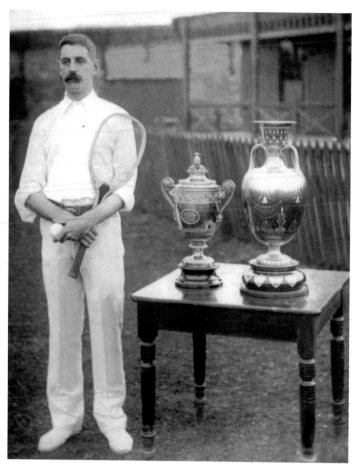

Lansdowne tennis club star Joshua Pim, who won two men's singles titles at Wimbledon

entice the landlords, the IRFU, and the club instead moved to Kenilworth Square.

Another sport that was in vogue in the early days of the ICAC was race walking, at which Dunlop himself was a leading exponent. There developed a taste for longer and longer races, with one epic fifty-mile match organised in October 1876. Willis C. Williams, 'the doughty champion of the club' challenged C. A. Ford, 'an oarsman of repute', and gave him a five mile start.

The race commenced at 7am on Saturday morning, but Williams's challenge proved mere bluster. He completed the first twenty miles in three and a half hours, by which stage he hadn't even lapped Ford once. With a five mile handicap he had no chance, so retired. Ford kept going, stopping just once to adjust his boot, and covered the distance in nine hours four minutes and 52.5 seconds. He was in 'surprisingly good form at the close', according to reports. Ford won a cup for his efforts, but the spectacle of a nine hour race didn't appeal to the public, which 'did not muster strongly'.

Long distance races were regular occurrences at the Irish Champion Bicycling Club, which was founded in 1875. The club came to an agreement with Dunlop for the use of the track and a depot at Lansdowne Road. It held its first meeting on 24 June and the mile race was won by Mr D. H. Pring in three minutes 19.5 seconds.

The club's first championship meetings were held in tandem with those of the athletic club, on Easter Monday 1877. The ICAC had previously included cycling events in its programme but this was the first attempt to run a separate club. It continued to use the track at Lansdowne into the 1880s, but when that fell into disrepair it moved to the RDS.

●●●

Tennis was another sport that was adopted early by the ICAC. Dunlop wrote in his memoir 'On the tennis club grounds the first tennis championship was held long before Fitzwilliam meetings'.

The sport had evolved from various racket games in the 1870s and the first lawn tennis club was founded in England in 1874. A Major Wingfield developed and patented a game he called '*sphairistike*' (Greek for 'skill at playing at ball') and sold sets containing racquets, balls, a net and his rules. Thousands of the sets were sold and at least one found its way to Lansdowne Road where a club, the All Ireland Lawn Tennis Club, was founded in 1875, membership one shilling, with two courts laid down.

The Fitzwilliam club was founded two years later – the same year the first All England championships were played at Wimbledon – and its championship quickly became the premier event in the country. The All Ireland Club was renamed as Lansdowne LTC in 1880, and the first Lansdowne man to play in the Fitzwilliam event was H.K. McKay, who won five games through to the semi-final in 1884. On his way he beat Willoughby Hamilton who, six years later, became the first Irishman to win Wimbledon.

Two Lansdowne men spearheaded the glory years of Irish tennis, the 1890s. The greatest Irish tennis player of all was a Lansdowne member, Joshua Pim, who won two men's singles titles at Wimbledon and lost two more finals. Born in 1869 on Meath Road, Bray, Pim learned his game from Thomas Burke, coach at Lansdowne. In 1890 he teamed up with Frank Stoker, cousin of Bram, the celebrated author of *Dracula*, to form a successful doubles partnership. Stoker was also a rugby player with Wanderers and won five caps for Ireland. Between 1890 and 1895 the pairing won five Irish and two Wimbledon titles.

Pim fought a four year series of epic Wimbledon finals against the English champion Wilfred Baddeley, who won the 1891 and 1892 titles. Pim lost the first set of the 1893 final, but rallied to win 6-1, 6-3, 6-2. The next year he won in straight sets, 10-8, 6-2, 8-6.

Sir William Orpen, the celebrated portrait painter, recalled in his memoirs watching the pair in action at Lansdowne:

'I used get up early in the mornings and go and watch Josh Pim, the amateur *champion of the world, being trained by Burke at Lansdowne Road. People were real amateurs in those days, and Pim used to play with Burke at eight o'clock in the morning before his day's work began. That was the only time he could afford for tennis. Pim and Stoker, what a pair! Our little chests swelled out with pride when we mentioned them. Oh it's true, young Ireland took its lawn tennis very seriously in those far-off days.'*

Lansdowne was naturally the strongest club of the era, and won the first Irish Senior Cup in 1892. One of the team, Manliffe Goodbody, became the only Irishman to play in the US Open final two years later.

The grass tennis courts were just inside the wall on the Lansdowne Road end of the ground, and were covered with planks of wood when the big rugby matches were staged. After more than half a century, however, the expansion of the rugby stadium squeezed out the tennis club, and when a tenancy agreement expired, Lansdowne LTC moved across the river to a new site on the grounds of the Irish Hockey Union (IHU) on Londonbridge Road.

A farewell tournament was staged in 1930, at which competed rugby star Mark Sugden. The club lifted its carefully-tended grass courts from the area that soon became the South Terrace, and installed nine new ones (and four hard courts) at its new ground. The club still occupies the site, although the IHU moved out in the 1970s.

The use of Lansdowne Road for spectacular events continued throughout its lifetime. While recent years saw full-houses for the likes of Michael Jackson, U2, the Eagles and Frank Sinatra, the tastes in entertainment of earlier generations of Dubliners was quite different. In August 1925 a company of two hundred Cossacks arrived to give an exhibition of their equestrian skills. The Russians had given a display in Paris which was so successful they won a booking at Olympia in London. After that became a hit they embarked on a world tour with Lansdowne Road as the first port of call.

They were filmed by a newsreel company and their film shows them leaping on and off moving horses and lying across the backs of their steeds. Various lunatic feats were achieved and the crowd seemed duly impressed. One of the Russians broke his leg in a fall, and was reported as being very distressed at having to remain in Dublin while his colleagues moved on to Belfast and abroad.

It was Horse Show Week in Dublin, and as the Cossacks' shows took place in the evening they were assured of big crowds. Two thousand people turned out for the opening night of their week-long run, including the justice minister Kevin O'Higgins and three fellow members of the cabinet. There were no floodlights on the ground, but a lighting rig was built in the centre of the field to illuminate proceedings. Part of the entertainment saw the lights switched off for a massed march with traditional Russian songs, which was a great success with the attendance.

As the week went on the numbers grew and ten thousand attended on the Friday, paying the enormous ticket prices of 10 shillings or 7/6. The show was such a success that they stayed for a further six days of two performances a day, with prices reduced by a half, and rugby club members admitted for three shillings.

Even with substantial discounts for rugby players, one can't imagine a similar event drawing crowds to the new stadium.

CHAPTER 6

1887
Long time coming

The first win at Lansdowne, 5 February 1887

By the late 1880s rugby was unrivalled as the premier sport at Lansdowne Road, and the ground's status as the premier venue for the sport firmly established. But as defeat after defeat mounted up, the realities of international rugby were becoming obvious to the men who played for Ireland.

The IRFU, which came into being in November 1878 after the Dublin and Belfast-based unions amalgamated, then brought the clubs from the southern province into the fold and Lansdowne Road played host to the first Ulster v Munster game in January 1879. The Connacht branch was formed in 1885 and a full four-team championship started in the 1920s.

Ireland had played England six times (and the Scots once) and had still not scored a try prior to the English visit in January 1880. It was the first international at Lansdowne since the inaugural one two years before.

On a pleasant day, and in front of three thousand spectators, England duly recorded their seventh successive win. But what made that day special was the try scored by John Loftus Cuppaidge, the first by a man in an Irish jersey.

Cuppaidge, from Warrenpoint, Co. Down, was a heavy, hardworking forward who played for Trinity, Wanderers and the Dublin Hospitals XV.

The match was 'a very hard-fought one', but according to the Rev. F. Marshall's early history of the sport, *Football – The Rugby Union Game*, the English selectors were unable to get together their best team. A violent storm in the Irish Sea had laid low several of the English party, and it became clear at training the day before the game that replacements would be needed. The captain, Fred Stokes, asked some students who were watching the run out in College Park if they knew of any Englishmen and one recalled an Ernest Woodhead. A fine sprinter, Woodhead was doing post-graduate study in Trinity, but was not a good enough rugby player to make the Trinity second team. So the 3rd XV three-quarter was called up to represent his country at Lansdowne Road.

Ireland played with the wind in the first half, and from a 25 yard drop out, the forwards footrushed the ball to the England 25. An attack was built by Forrest who took the ball into touch close to the line. From a long throw Kelly seized the ball and 'bounded' it out to Cuppaidge who went over and grounded under the posts to deafening cheers.

Robert Walkington – who having missed only one of Ireland's games since 1874 was by far the most experienced – was reported to have 'trembled like a leaf, from head to toe' over the conversion, which he missed. Two tries, one converted, gave England the win.

After writing his name in the history books, Cuppaidge did not fade into obscurity, although his fame was earned far from Ballsbridge. He graduated from TCD with a degree in surgery in the summer of 1880, a few months after the last of his three caps. He moved to Australia where he worked for many years in rural Queensland. In 1884 he was based in Roma, a mining town three hundred miles west of Brisbane, when he became involved in a high profile murder. Cuppaidge wrote a prescription for hydrate of chloral for a man called Robert Birkett. His wife, Ruth Robinson, added an ounce of laudanum to the chloral and fed it to her husband, who soon expired. Cuppaidge refused to sign the death certificate and called in the police.

By 1896 Cuppaidge was vice Surgeon-General of Queensland, but later he moved to England, where he was partner in a medical practice in Devon. In 1901 he dissolved the practice and returned to Australia. He resumed as a medic in the mining industry in Queensland, living in the gold town of Gympie, one hundred miles north of Brisbane. Dr J. L. Cuppaidge, scorer of Ireland's first try, died in November 1934, aged seventy-seven.

Ireland was still struggling to keep up with the English and the Scots when the final piece of the Four Nations jigsaw popped into place. In January 1882 Wales came to Lansdowne Road, and announced their arrival with a thumping victory by two goals and two tries to nil.

England returned to Dublin in 1882 when each side scored two tries, but neither was 'goaled' so a scoreless draw was declared. Ireland's second attempted conversion was taken by Robert McLean, but one umpire called it 'good' and the other 'wide'.

And the defeats kept mounting up until February 1887, when desperate measures were called for. A fractious IRFU selection meeting saw nine men called up for debuts, including John Macaulay, a forward from Garryowen. Macaulay had a seemingly insurmountable problem however,

as he had used up his annual leave and his employer was reluctant to allow more time off. His ingenious solution was to claim the extra holidays he would get were he to get married – so he brought forward his wedding day to ensure his honeymoon was spent winning the first of his two caps. His self-sacrifice was duly rewarded in 1894-95 when he was made President of the IRFU.

Another future holder of that office, Richard Warren, was picked as captain, and was the only one of the six backs who had played before. In 1897 he began a thirty-six year spell as honorary secretary of the International Board.

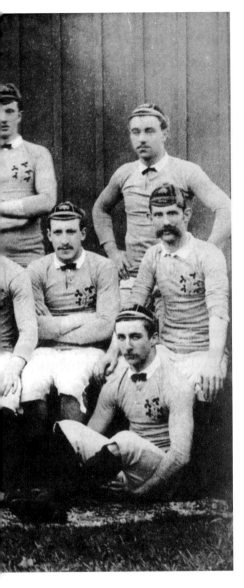

Schoolboy tickets were on sale for the game – but had to be presented by two o'clock. The kick was timed for 'after the arrival of the three o'clock train'. By that hour about four thousand had crammed into the stadium, the biggest crowd ever seen there according to the press.

Ireland's forwards quickly asserted their supremacy, and things turned for the worse for England when three-quarter Arthur Fagan of Guy's Hospital broke down shortly after the start. Fagan, who had started with a sprained ankle, was the brother of George, who made his only appearance for Ireland nine years earlier in the first international at Lansdowne.

Reports told glowingly of the 'wonderful dash of the Irish team', and the game was played at high pace. Victor Le Fanu, nephew of the writer Sheridan Le Fanu, was 'vigorous' in the loose. Ireland were on top for much of the first half, although England narrowly missed a try just before half time when the ball ran out of the in-goal area.

Into the second half, Ireland's pack continued to dominate their hapless opponents, English writers blamed defeat on their 'mediocre forwards, who allowed themselves to be hustled all over the field by their opponents, and never gave their players behind a ghost of a chance.' Chance after chance was created: a McLaughlin drop kick screwed off the posts, and a minute later David Rambaut saw his drop kick shave the upright.

Opposite:
The Ireland team that beat England in 1887: BACK ROW: W.L. Stokes (president), J.S. Dick, C.B. Tillie, T.R. Lyle, H.J. Neill, V.C. Le Fanu, R. Stevenson, MIDDLE: D.F. Rambaut, D.B. Walkington, J. Chambers, R.G. Warren (captain), E.J. Walsh, J.H. McLaughlin, J. Johnstone; FRONT: John Macauley, R.S. Montgomery.

Then, with twelve minutes to go Rambaut picked up the ball up from the feet of the English forwards, burst through the pack, ran around the two full backs and laid off to Trinity three-quarter Charlie Tillie, who ran in under the posts. The crowd's reaction was described thus:

'The enthusiasm which greeted this performance has probably never been approached on an Irish football ground, and it burst it afresh when … Rambaut spun the ball over the bar'.

There were more cheers when, with two minutes to go, Robert Montgomery picked up a loose ball and 'flashed through the defence'. Rambaut, bluntly called 'a fat little fellow' by *Sport*, converted the goal and a glorious victory was finally achieved.

Jacques McCarthy hailed the team's preparation:

'We beat England all ends up, fore and aft, but there are secrets about this match which must remain for the instruction of a future generation. Everything was arranged ready, cut and dry even to the very ball which was played with. There was not a weak point in the team.'

The *Irish Sportsman's* reporter, 'Green and Gold' was even more excited as he addressed the heroes:

'Gentlemen of the Irish fifteen, thus far by means of play that was grand, you have marched on despite impediment. England, the erstwhile successful boar, whose ravenous appetite had swallowed up our teams, gave our poor country a taste that rudely cropped its ripened hopes of fair prosperity, is now even chockfull of bile.

'St Patrick, who after all was a gentleman, has caught St George between wind and water and the latter eminent personage is now weeping by the waters of Babylon with a leg on either side of his tail.. You have licked the Saxon, and you have done it nobly …'

Not to be outdone, 'Jakes' McCarthy produced a parody on 'Two Lovely Black Eyes' – a famous music hall song by Charles Coborn which was itself a parody – to celebrate the win:

Two goals off two tries,
Oh, what a surprise;
Were ever Englishmen leathered like this?
Two goals off two tries.

It was a momentous month for Irish sport: two weeks later Ireland's association footballers recorded their first international win too, beating

Wales 4-1 in Belfast, and on the 17 February the nascent GAA banned policemen from playing its games, a rule that survived in part into the twenty-first century.

ENGLAND: S. Roberts (Swinton); E. Lockwood (Dewsbury), W.N. Bolton (Blackheath), A. Fagan (United Hospitals), M.T. Scott (Cambridge University), A. Rotherham (Richmond), capt., W.G. Clibborn (Richmond), G.L. Jeffery (Blackheath), C.J.B. Marriott (Blackheath), J.H. Dewhirst (Cambridge University), R. Seddon (Broughton Rangers), A.T. Kemble (Liverpool), A. Teggin (Broughton Rangers), J.L. Hickson (Bradford), F. Pease (Durham)

IRELAND: D.B. Walkington (NIFC & Dublin University); C.R. Tillie (Dublin University), D.F. Rambaut (Dublin University), R. Montgomery (Queen's College, Belfast); R.G. Warren (Lansdowne, captain), J. McLaughlin (Derry); T.R. Lyle (Dublin University), J. Chambers (Dublin University), V.C. Le Fanu (Lansdowne & Cambridge University), H.J. Neill (NIFC), E. J. Walsh (Lansdowne), J. Dick (Queen's College, Cork), J. Johnstone (Albion), R. Stevenson (Lisburn), J. Macauley (Limerick)

Referee: Phillips (Wales)

CHAPTER 7

1888
'Not very black'

Dublin welcomes The New Zealand Native team, 1888

WHILE nowadays Lansdowne Road reverberates regularly to the twanged accents of the Aussie, Kiwi and Springbok, in 1888 it was a very different world. Overseas sporting visitors were rare and certainly none were as exotic to the Victorians as the New Zealand Maori team. That was the year that the New Zealand Native Football Team played Ireland as part of their ground-breaking epic 107 match, twelve-month tour of Britain, Australia and New Zealand. Besides those 107 games, they also played eight Australian Rules and two soccer matches.

It was quite an extraordinary journey for the twenty-six men from the Land of the Long White Cloud. The side were originally labelled 'the New Zealand Maoris', but although many members of the NZ aboriginal race were keen rugby players, it was difficult to raise a full squad and so a smattering of whites ('*Pakeha*') were selected too and the title 'New Zealand Native Football Representatives' agreed upon. The tour was organised by an entrepreneur called Thomas Eyton who – in the absence of any New Zealand union – saw an opportunity to cash in on British curiosity at the time for the 'colourful' citizens of its empire. He put up the enormous sum of £2,000 to guarantee the tour and filled the roles of tour manager, promoter, press agent, *chef-de-mission* and entrepreneur.

The first modern tour in any sport is acknowledged to be that by a team of Australian aboriginals who played forty-seven cricket matches in England in the summer of 1868. The native Australians delighted crowds with their displays of boomerang throwing and athletic feats, but their cricket skills were rudimentary and they are best remembered because one of their number, King Cole, died of pneumonia on tour.

New Zealand rugby was one of the few examples (in any activity or any land) where the colonials and their descendants embraced the indigenous inhabitants. Maoris were common on NZ provincial sides by 1879, something that was not the case in rugby or cricket in South Africa and Australia for many, many years. When the first team to represent New Zealand was selected in 1884, Jack Taiaroa and Joseph Warbrick were in the team on merit.

The Maori side gathered in a training camp in May 1888 and after a few warm-up games they were sent on their way with the derision of the New Zealand rugby public as a team that couldn't beat the strongest club sides. On their return – when they closed the tour by winning seven out of eight games on home soil – they were hailed as 'a fine exhibition of what several months of combination and practice can do'.

The journey to England took six weeks by steamer, and the Maoris' efforts to keep fit by shovelling coal and doing exercises up on deck were hampered by the complaints of some passengers. Eyton's hunger to make the trip a success meant the itinerary was constantly expanding and the players were flogged relentlessly. Two-thirds of the games took place in the north of England, with only one game in Scotland, three in Ireland and five in Wales. The tourists won two-thirds of the games, despite playing on average every 2.3 days. They once played three days in a row and four times on consecutive days. Unsurprisingly there were repercussions – for much of the tour no more than twenty of the squad of twenty-six were fit and at one point only eleven men were up to playing.

On the 19 November 1888, the IRFU annual general meeting detailed the arrangements for the upcoming fixture and agreed that caps should

The New Zealand Native team party

J. A. WEBSTER.   G. H. WYNYARD.

(From a Photograph by H. A. Chapman, 235, High Street, Swansea.)

NEW ZEALAND NATIVE FOOTBALL TEAM, 1888-1889.

P. KEOGH. T. EYTON A. WARBRICK. G. A. WILLIAMS. T. R. ELLISON. W. KARAURIA. J. R. SCOTT H. J. WYNYARD.
(Treasurer).   (Manager).
W. ANDERSON. F. WARBRICK. J. A. WARBRICK (Capt.). E. McCAUSLAND. H. LEE. D. STEWART.
D. GAGE.   W. ELLIOT.   W. T. WYNYARD.   R. G. TAIAROA.

The Two Umpires.

not be awarded but expenses would be paid to men coming from the provinces. It was the twenty-ninth international played by Ireland and the first to veer from the unrelenting diet of England, Scotland or Wales.

Following a game in Leeds, the Native Team arrived in Dublin at 9pm on Friday 30 November, having played thirteen matches in four weeks. They stayed at Jury's Hotel on Dame Street, next to the current site of the Central Bank. The following morning Mr Scott, manager of the Maoris, called to the centre city offices of the *Sport* newspaper to meet its famous correspondent Jacques McCarthy, 'but as I was in a state of semi-suffocation from bronchitis,' the reporter confessed later, 'I told him that I was out.'

There was quite a controversy raging about the Irish team, as two half backs declined to play for Ireland, preferring to play for Trinity against the Maoris the following Monday. There were no university men on the Irish team, although nine were capped the previous season and eight in the championship games of 1888–89.

The attendance of about three thousand was described as 'moderate' when the game kicked off 'after the arrival of the 2.30 train from Westland Row'. Although it was on this tour that the tradition of performing the Haka was instituted, there was no reference to the visitors doing so at Lansdowne Road. *The Irish Times* reported:

'A very stalwart, formidable looking lot, too, they were, and every man of them seemed as fit as the proverbial fiddle. No time was put to waste in arranging preliminaries and Warren having won the toss Ellison started the leather at 2.45pm against the stiff breeze blowing from the railway end.'

Tom Ellison, who died in 1904 at the age of thirty-six, 'was the first true genius of New Zealand rugby' according to historian Terry McLean,

Above and opposite: the tour attracted much press attention in Britain and Ireland

and penned *The Art of Rugby Football*, which 'had a profound impact on the game'. He was also the first Maori lawyer to be admitted to the New Zealand bar. His great grandson Rhys Ellison, an All Black trialist, got to walk in his illustrious ancestor's footsteps more than a century later. Ellison, a powerful centre who played more than 150 provincial games in New Zealand and thirty games for the Maoris, played with Shannon in the late 1990s and was on the side that won the All Ireland League final at Lansdowne Road in 1998.

Tom Ellison developed the wing forward role of harrying the scrum half to stave off possession at the base of the scrum. He also captained the first official New Zealand team in 1893 and proposed the official kit of black shirt with a silver fern, although the fact that he also suggested white shorts hints that he wasn't quite up with modern marketing techniques.

Ireland were resplendent in their light green shirts with olive green sashes, white pants and dark stockings. Their opponents were, for the era, an imposing group. Their average weight was 12st 7lb and two men weighed in over fourteen and a half stone. The Irish press calculated that they had a five stone advantage over the Irish and that was most pronounced in the pack.

The Maori were so comfortable with their forward superiority that they used only eight men in the pack against the current norm of nine. In the Ireland game they lined up with one full back, three three-quarters, three half-backs and eight forwards. Ireland by contrast had one full back, one centre, two quarter-backs, two half-backs, and nine forwards. The tourists' influence on tactical developments was not limited to reducing the scrum to eight; they introduced specialist scrummaging positions, instead of the previous practice of the forwards packing down according to who first arrived on the spot. The media were also perplexed by

A sudden outburst of Joy. on getting the 1st Goal of the Jour.

some of the visitors' tactics, notably the trick whereby 'their line-out thrower threw the ball to hit an opponent's forehead and bounce into Maori hands'.

It was all too much for the hapless local referee, Mr Chambers, who was widely panned. *Sport* complained that he 'seemed to extend the courtesy to the visitors', as he seemed to 'allow palpably illegitimate scores against their own side'. McCarthy reported that the referee's failings 'leaned to the natives' side' and was 'What the Yankees would call "all darned fine"'. The Maori management agreed they had never received such 'judicial consideration' before. That said, there was a remarkable display of sportsmanship when the Maoris stopped playing when they received line-out ball from a crooked throw.

Above and opposite: the cartoonists of the time were not sensitive to racially insulting their visitors

There were also complaints that the Maori were 'quite rough' although this may have been in response to an early tackle by Frank Stoker which necessitated five minutes of treatment for the Maoris' star Warbrick. Reports of over-physical play followed the tour, although it seems that the Maori were given as much as they got. The game was extremely dangerous at the time, and a study revealed that no less than seventy-one rugby players died in Yorkshire alone in just three seasons in the early 1890s.

Ireland took an early lead, but were rocked by a second half Maori rally. 'The partisans of the home team now considered the match as good as won', wrote *The Irish Times,* 'but a bitter awakening was in store for them and between this and the finish disaster followed disaster with almost bewildering rapidity.'

Ellison scored the visitors' third try and two more were run in before a late Irish rally. Despite intense Irish pressure, the tourists defence held: 'For a long time now the ball was kept close to the Maoris' goal, and any cripple would have scored where these athletes failed,' reported *Sport*. When the Irish debutant three-quarter Michael Bulger was sent clear he ran into the unfortunate referee with the line at his mercy. The visitors ended up with four goals and one try to Ireland's one goal and one try, equating to a 13-4 win.

The Irish press were unhappy:

'These Maoris are not a good team as far as footballing erudition goes; and consequently, it is somewhat of a disgrace to be beaten by them. But they are the makings of the best lot that ever was seen, being of tremendous strength and weight, good wind, splendid heart, thorough determination and quick intelligence.'

Quarter-back Paddy Keogh 'from Enniscorthy, they say', was the Maoris' best back. In tribute to the land of his birth he wore an emerald sash and had a green Irish committee badge attached to his waist.

The race of the visitors was remarked upon in all the reports, and there seemed to be much bemusement that the team was 'not very black'. Even the full-blooded Maori members of the team 'could only be said to be badly sunburned'. The standards of the time cannot be judged by those of the twenty-first century, but it is still likely that the visitors would have been offended by the cartoons carried in *Sport* in the week of the game.

The teams met up at the international dinner in the Central Hotel that night. There are no reports of incidents, but alcohol was a poor friend to the Maoris on several occasions on the tour. Some players 'innocently made the most of the many good things that Lord Sheffield's genuine hospitality provided' before the match against Middlesex. Two who were missing when the team photograph was to be taken were

SPORT WELCOMES THE PAKEHA MAORI AND HIS FOURTEEN CHIEFS TO DUBLIN.

All Black Patrick Keogh, who wore his Irish origins with pride

found asleep in some bushes. After the dinner in Belfast later in the week, one of the tourists got into an alcohol-fuelled row and was left to sleep it off overnight in a police cell. The tourists were not immune to other temptations, and one young student earned the nickname 'Don Juan', being presented with a diamond ring by a smitten English barmaid. Another player is believed to have died of syphilis contracted during the tour.

At College Park on the Monday, before 'a large audience of spectators, including Prince Edward of Saxe-Weimar', the tourists played out a draw with Trinity College. The press averred that it was a much better game than the international and that the 'Maoris played much more brilliantly'. Under dull and threatening skies – and with two Maoris playing barefoot – the teams scored a goal and a try apiece.

On the Wednesday afternoon at Ormeau, before a 'very small number', the New Zealanders won 2-0. The Dublin press drew a veil over the game, but complained that 'There was nothing but gutter rooting at the Maori and NIFC match on Wednesday.'

Interestingly, the visit had the effect of making the locals assess their approach to the game. Two weeks after the game Wanderers 'tried the Maori experiment' of playing four three-quarters.

But with the 'broken-time' schism around the corner, there was much concern at the Maori's commercial arrangements. 'Pendarius' in *The Irish Sportsman* newspaper railed against the sham amateurism already raising its head:

'I cannot regard the Maoris as amateur exponents of football. I do not know how they arrange their monetary affairs, but I have heard that they cannot afford to play under a certain sum fixed upon by agreement. So far as I can make out, not even the usual 'share of the gate money' arrangement will satisfy these New Zealanders. They must have their price planked down, or else _____ _____.'

One can only imagine what venom those carefully spaced blanks concealed!

Pendarius also alleged that the Native Team were told that 'there were doubts that their market price would be forthcoming in Ireland and they tried to break the fixture for a game in Yorkshire, more lucrative'.

It seems unfair to blame the team for the desire of Eyton and Scott to ensure the tour's financial success. The New Zealand newspaper, *The Lyttelton Times*, asserted:

'The list of fixtures was far too long, which was solely due to the desire of the [promoters] to make money over the trip without due regard to the wishes of the team. When next a band of footballers leave these shores to do battle on English soil, it should be seen that the engagements are of good number and quality. There should be no risk of having men disabled in small matches which are no credit to win and are only played with the expectation of putting a few pound in the pocket of the promoter'.

It seems certain that the Maori side would have done better in the internationals had they not had to flog themselves all over the islands. They lost, creditably, to Wales by 5-0 and seemed to have been robbed at Twickenham. With the RFU secretary Rowland Hill refereeing, England were given two tries when a Maori seemed to touch down first and when the Native XV surrounded an English player who had lost his 'knickerbockers', a sneaky Saxon slipped away to score. Several of the tourists left the field in disgust and were only persuaded back on after several minutes.

While the famous All Black sides of 1905 and 1924 live on in legend, it can be argued that the 1888 side faced far sterner opposition, playing most of their games against Yorkshire and Lancashire clubs that had turned to rugby league by the time of the later tours.

IRELAND: T. Edwards; D.C. Woods, A. Walpole, M.J. Bulger; J. Stevenson, R.G. Warren; H.W. Andrews, E.G. Forrest, J.H. O'Connor, J. Moffat, J.N. Lytle, J. Waites, R. Stevenson, J.S. Jameson, F.O. Stoker.

MAORIS: W. Warbrick, D.R. Gage, E.E.M. McCausland, F. Warbrick, P. Keogh, W.T. Wynyard, C. Madigan, W. Elliott, G.A. Williams, W. Taiaroa, T.R. Ellison, W. Anderson, J.A. Warbrick, Maynard, Goldsmith

Referee: J. Chambers

CHAPTER 8

1894 &
1899
The First
Triple
Crowns

Irish teams
taste glory

THE win over England in 1887 did not open the floodgates for the Irish rugby team. Defeat after defeat mounted up, and by the start of the 1894 championship, Ireland's overall record read: Played 43, Won 5, Drew 3, Lost 35.

Ireland hadn't won more than a single game in any one season, and had only won one in total over the previous four campaigns. On the field, it was almost two years since they had even scored a point.

So it was with little optimism that Ireland headed into the new international season. It was a reasonably experienced team, however, and under a new captain, Edmund Forrest of Wanderers, who had taken over from the North of Ireland (NIFC) centre Sam Lee. It was the first time a selection committee had picked the team – rather than the full union committee – and that first Big Six comprised J.R. Blood and R. Warren (Leinster), R. Garrett and R. Stevenson (Ulster), and J. Hook and H. McOstrich (Munster). Only Warren and Stevenson had played for Ireland. The committee made the momentous decision to follow the Welsh model and have a four man three-quarter line. It also called up three new caps in the forwards: Tom Crean (Wanderers), George Walmsley (Bective Rangers) and Jim Lytle (NIFC).

Tom Crean, although no relation to the polar explorer, was himself a legendary figure, born in Morrison's Hotel at the bottom of Dawson Street in Dublin city centre. Crean attended Belvedere College and Clongowes Wood, and was notable as the only Roman Catholic on the 1894 Irish team. He played nine times for Ireland and, on tour with the 1896 British and Irish Touring Side (the term 'Lions' had yet to coined) to South Africa, he decided to settle in Johannesburg. His sister Alice married Tom's English teammate on the tour, Alexander Todd. Their son, Richard Todd, went on to be a leading Hollywood film star. An opponent on that tour, P.S.T. Jones, described Crean as 'as fine a forward as I have ever seen, and besides doing the scrum work was a veritable terror to the opposing backs. The opposing wing was his particular fancy, and he had a nasty habit of sailing into him near the corner flag when the wing saw visions of an easy score.'

Crean went on to have a glittering military career, winning the Victoria Cross in the Second Boer War and seeing action in the First World War.

He was appointed Medical Officer at Ascot racecourse, where he once performed a life-saving operation on a fallen jockey. Crean dashed out on to the course in his shirtsleeves and took a hammer and chisel to the jockey's skull, the action saving his life. Crean found it hard to adjust to civilian life and was declared bankrupt in 1922. He died from diabetes the following year, aged forty-nine.

Ireland were not fancied to beat England at Blackheath – bookmakers quoted them as 5/1 outsiders – and were trailing 5–3 with time running out. A couple of English backs drew the wrath of the media for kicking the ball over the grandstand to waste time, but after some loose English play under their own posts, the ball went out to Irish captain Forrest.

'*He steadied himself with great coolness, and with a good drop he sent the ball sailing in the direction of his opponents' goal.*

'*During the few seconds that elapsed before the ball had landed safely over the crossbar the suspense was painful but that Ireland had once more got in front was quickly communicated to the spectators by an exhibition of "cart wheels" and somersaults which several of the Irish team found it necessary to indulge in to give vent to their unbounded delight ...*'

The Irish Times, 4 March 1894

Dropped goals were worth four points at the time, so a 7–5 victory set Ireland on the way.

The second game was at Lansdowne Road, with Scotland the visitors.

John O'Conor of Bective Rangers, at 13-and-a-half stone he was the biggest man in the Irish pack

THE DOINGS O' LARRY O'HOOLIGAN.

BRAVO, IRELAND.

At Cardiff, on Saturday last, Larry O'Hooligan presented the Triple Crown to the captain of the Irish Rugby team, on the successful termination of their season's International engagements. Larry made some appropriate marks of a complimentary character, but owing to the press of spectators our reporters were unable to take them down. However, they caught his concluding words, which were, "Bravo, Ireland," and "We'll do it again."

The triple crown wins were greeted with delight; this from Belfast sports newspaper 'Ireland's Saturday Night'

Walmsley had broken his leg and missed the game – he never played for Ireland again – and the selection committee also brought in P.J. Grant at full-back for William Sparrow. Grant had started the season on the Bective 2nd XV, and is believed to have been the man James Joyce had in mind when he wrote the line in the Nighttown passage of *Ulysses*:

'I'll tell my brother the Bective rugger fullback on you, you heartless flirt.'

The phrase was spoken by Martha, a prostitute in Monto, the celebrated red-light district of Dublin.

After the win over England the Scots game was highly-anticipated, and the sale of advance tickets was 'the greatest ever seen'. It was the first time Scotland played in Dublin, all their previous visits being staged in Belfast. The papers noted that the pitch at Lansdowne Road had been widened to 'the standard dimensions', and that the number of entrances had been increased to seven. Extra trains were put on for the day, while trams going down Bath Avenue would stop at Havelock Square to facilitate spectators.

Estimates of the crowd put it at over ten thousand; these spectators witnessed a dour forward struggle littered with mistakes. There was a long stoppage while Bective three-quarter H.G. Wells was strapped up after a suspected broken collar bone. ('H.G. Wells' would not have registered unduly with supporters of the era; his namesake did not publish his first novel, *The Time Machine*, until 1895.)

In the last half hour the Irish pack pulverised the Scots, but the scores did not come. Then, with three minutes remaining, Bective scrum-half Ben Tuke collected the ball on his own 25 and brought the house down as he ran as far as the Scots' 25, where he passed to Lucius Gwynn. The Trinity man drew Wotherspoon and McGregor before slipping the ball to Sam Lee, who was tackled on the line by Gadge and Campbell. But Lee had got the ball away to Wells, who sidestepped Cameron before crossing for a stunning try. Lytle converted to give Ireland a 5-0 lead which they held.

Bective forward John O'Conor, the biggest man in the pack at 13½ stone, explained some years later that the team was 'tall and speedy':

'In those days, handling was not developed to the same extent that came later. The game was left almost entirely to the forwards and the scrums were grim affairs, with all the forwards giving full weight to the shove. There were no specialised positions such as hooker or wing forward, and every forward was expected to be an accomplished hooker. First up, first down was the rule. The backs were used mainly in defence.'

Wells' injury ruled him out of the final match of the season, breaking up Ireland's first four man three-quarter line of Gardiner, Lee, Gwynn and Wells. Just eighteen men were capped that season: the run of success was obviously a factor, but the presence of a smaller committee must have allowed for the greater consistency in selection. Thirteen of the eighteen were from three Dublin clubs – Trinity, Bective and Wanderers – with the other five from Ulster.

Belfast was the venue for the final game of the season, with Wales visiting Ormeau, home of the North of Ireland club. The River Lagan had overflowed the day before and the pitch was in shocking condition, and Ireland again opted to play a tight game utilising their experienced pack.

Around six thousand spectators attended, boosted by eight hundred travellers from Dublin who had arrived by train.

Local forward John Lytle was six feet tall and fifteen stone, and 'unquestionably the strongest man in the Irish pack'. So, when the Welsh forwards were penalised for offside 10 yards inside their own half, Forrest took Lytle aside and asked him did he think a kick at goal was possible.

The ground was saturated and a hailstorm was sweeping the ground when Lytle started his long run in the clinging mud and, with a mighty kick, sent the ball over.

It proved to be the only score of the game, and Ireland had claimed its first international

Trinity and Monkstown forward Charles Rooke

trophy, albeit a mythical one.

On the Monday after the game *The Irish Times* began its report:

'*After long years of seemingly hopeless struggle, Ireland has achieved the triple crown honours of Rugby football*'.

This is believed to be the first recorded reference to the Triple Crown, coming five years earlier than one previously hailed as the original, in the *South Wales Daily News*.

Ireland was well led that season by Edmund Forrest, later described by Jacques McCarthy as 'a clever player with tremendous speed ... a deadly tackler and hard worker, in the scrum and out of it.' Forrest first came to

L. M. Magee (Bective Rangers) playing for Ireland. "Overtaken".

prominence with an excellent display in the Leinster v Munster interprovincial in January 1888. He was first capped against the Maoris that year, and in December 1889 played on the Ireland Schools team that beat England Schools at Lansdowne Road.

Two days after that 1894 win over England, Forrest collected his medical degree from Trinity, with *The Irish Times* reporting that 'He intends studying for the army'.

Forrest played once more for Ireland in 1895, and twice in 1897, but his career in the Royal Army Medical Corps was under way and he was soon serving the Empire around the globe. He was promoted to captain in 1899 and posted to India. He was taken ill there and invalided home, but his condition worsened on the voyage and he was taken off ship at Aden. He lingered in the Yemeni port for several weeks before he died on 20 February 1902, aged thirty-one.

The Triple Crown win heralded an unprecedented period of success, although that wasn't immediately obvious the following season when all three games were lost, with a side including nine of the 1894 heroes.

Louis Magee, running with the ball in this postcard, was one of the greatest players of the era

In 1896 a win away to England was followed by two games at Lansdowne: a 0-0 draw to Scotland and a win over Wales, giving a second championship, but no crown. The 1897 and 1898 seasons were not completed due to an amateurism dispute involving the Welsh RFU and a house built for its star player Arthur Gould.

So, by 1899, all that glorious first Triple Crown team had retired or been discarded one by one, while two of them − Gwynn and Lee − had graduated to the selection panel. The team that lined up for the first game of the season − against England at Lansdowne on 4 February − included six debutants, including a Campbell College schoolboy. It wasn't an entirely raw selection, as soon some fine players had come in to the side. The powerful Ryan brothers from Rockwell, Mick and Jack, had been regulars for two seasons, but the most experienced was half-back Louis Magee of Bective Rangers.

Aloysius Mary 'Louis' Magee learned his rugby at Clongowes Wood – and was good enough in 1895, at the age of twenty, to be picked for his first cap after just one season of senior rugby. A Lion in South Africa a year later – alongside his brother Jim, who never played for Ireland – he played all four of the tests in the series, which was won 3-1.

He was one of the greatest players of the era, and his half-back partnership with Glynn Allen was hailed as the best in the game. In 1923 the journalist 'EJFH' recalled Magee and his style:

'One remembers his manner of running – the short, quick steps and the small feet that pattered so lightly and could side-step so neatly; his curly dark head so wise in the game that it brought him straight to where the ball was coming; his strange attraction to, or for, mud, and the knack he had of getting on to his nose, so that he was at all times the dirtiest as well as the cleanest of players. This his apparent ubiquity, giving the idea that he was doing about twice as much work as anybody else on the ground; his wondrous football-speed and that uncanny gift of overtaking sprinters. One thinks of his unerring tackle, which could strike a man off his feet and flatten him in one simultaneous movement, or (more often) bear him almost gently to earth, closely, clingingly enwrapped, ball and all; of his hands so neat at the giving and taking of passes, his huge punts, his drops at goal. Verily

you are in for a long evening when you begin on Louis Magee.'

It was typically cold, wet and dreary day in Dublin when the English came to town. There was some muttering that the England side had some 'stiffish veterans', and it was apparent that their pack was a lot heavier than Ireland's.

Twelve thousand people packed the stands and standing areas, and the *Irish Times* correspondent was moved to pay tribute to the stadium, now owned by IRFU treasurer Harry Sheppard, 'Without our Lansdowne Road, Dublin would be a weary waste so far as functions social and national are concerned'.

The Irish forwards asserted their strength and superiority early, but Ireland found it hard to get points on the scoreboard. At one stage in the first half Magee and McIlwaine were in the clear running at the English three-quarters when Magee's pass hit the referee.

It was still scoreless at half-time, but Ireland started the second like a hurricane and

Ireland.—P. O'Brien-Butler, Monkstown, back; F. Purser, Dublin University, S. Lee, North of Ireland, L. H. Gwynn, Monkstown, and L. Bulger, Lansdowne, three-quarter-backs; C. Allen, Derry, and L. M. Magee, Bective, half-backs; J. Ryan, Tipperary, M. Ryan, Tipperary, H. Lindsay, Wanderers,   J. H. Franks, Dublin University, James Little, North of Ireland, J. M'Ilwaine, North of Ireland, G. Byron, North of Ireland, and J. J. Davis, Monkstown, forwards.

THE IRISH TEAM: THE WINNERS

created several chances. England held on desperately before a penalty goal near the touchline was landed by Magee – quite an achievement with a sodden and heavy ball.

From a scrum on the Irish 25 Magee kept the ball in the pack before a 'wild rush' by the forwards brought the ball fully sixty yards on. The England full back, Byrne, weakly kicked to touch. Allen pretended to take the line-out throw long, which fooled the English and he 'simply bounced the ball on the field of play and walked in for a try'. Magee again kicked the conversion just in from touch. Magee had another penalty on the final whistle, but narrowly missed.

Magee, who was captaining Ireland for the first time, 'gave a grand display, and his head work was delightful to witness'. Ireland's forward power was overwhelming, and Magee and Allen controlled the game. His work around the scrums was described as 'beautiful to watch' and far too elusive for his opposite number Rotherham. It meant Ireland had won four games in a row against the English.

Seventy-five years later *Irish Times* rugby correspondent Edmund Van Esbeck interviewed one of the debutants that day, George Harman, who was then just three months short of his hundredth birthday. 'We deserved to beat England that day,' he recalled. 'Our captain Louis Magee was a magnificent half back, the back line was solid and we had some magnificent forwards, especially the Ryans and Sealy.'

Harman was injured playing for Trinity the following weekend and missed the visit to Edinburgh. A spate of injuries and influenza meant Ireland fielded only two of the seven backs that beat England – centre Allison and Magee. There were three changes in the pack too, including the return of Jim Lytle, the only man surviving from the 1894 team, and thus the only one to feature in two triple crown campaigns.

Ireland scored three tries in a 9–3 win, with the scores coming from James Sealy and two of the debutants: Edward Campbell (Monkstown) and Carl Reid (NIFC). It was Ireland's first win on Scottish soil.

Lytle was dropped for the final game of the season in Cardiff, where a championship record crowd of forty thousand turned out. Such was the crush that the railings around the pitch collapsed and spectators lined the touchlines and the in-goal area. 'Wales had a thousand full-backs, some of who came up even to the 25', wrote an Irish correspondent, as half-time was extended by ten minutes to enable the officials to usher the mob back, assisted by Magee. Wales were reduced to fourteen men when their captain, Billy Bancroft, was thrown into the crowd by the Ryan brothers. Bancroft fractured several ribs as he fell awkwardly.

Ireland won through a try by Gerry 'Blucher' Doran of Lansdowne, the only score of the game. Mick Ryan, writing many years later in the *Rockwell College Annual*, recalled a dramatic late episode:

'Lloyd whisked the ball out to Nicholls. Straight through the opposition he went, swerved and transferred to Skrimshire, who seemed to have a perfectly clear field. He had lightning speed and there appeared to be nothing to prevent him scoring between the posts. Suddenly Magee flashed up and dived for his heels. Amidst

frantic cheers from the Irish supporters, Skrimshire came down and lost the ball…'

Harman, who was recalled after missing the Scottish game, said in 1975 of the Cardiff game that 'my abiding memory is that we got very drunk'.

If Ireland thought that three championships in six seasons was just the start of a period of glory they were sorely mistaken. It wasn't until 1935 that what was by then the Five Nations was next won, while two world wars and almost half a century would intervene before the next Triple Crown.

1894 IRELAND v SCOTLAND, Lansdowne Road

IRELAND: P.J. Grant (Bective Rangers), H.G. Wells (Bective Rangers), S. Lee (NIFC), W. Gardiner (NIFC), L.H. Gwynn (Dublin University), W.S. Brown (Dublin University), B. Tuke (Bective Rangers), J.N. Lytle (NIFC), E.G. Forrest (Wanderers) capt., H. Lindsay (Dublin University), T.J. Crean (Wanderers), A.T.W. Bond (Derry), J.H. O'Conor (Bective Rangers), C.V. Rooke (Dublin University), J.H. Lytle (NIFC)

SCOTLAND: A.W.C. Cameron, G.T. Campbell, G. MacGregor, W. Wotherspoon, H.T.S. Gedge, J.W. Simpson, W.P. Donaldson, H.T.O. Leggatt, J.D. Boswell (capt.), A.H. Anderson, A. Dalgleish, W.R. Gibson, W.B. Cownie, G.T. Nielson, R. MacMillan

Referee: H.L. Ashmore (England)

1899 IRELAND v ENGLAND, Lansdowne Road

IRELAND: J. Fulton (NIFC), I.G. Davidson (NIFC), J.B. Allison (Campbell College, Belfast), G. Harman (Dublin U), W.H. Brown (Dublin U), L. Magee (Bective Rangers, capt.), G.G. Allen (Derry), M. Ryan (Rockwell College), J. Ryan (Rockwell College), W.G. Byron (NIFC), J McIlwaine (NIFC), T. McGown (NIFC), T. Ahern (Queens College Cork), J. Sealy (Dublin U), H. McCoull (Belfast Albion)

ENGLAND: J.F. Byrne, E.F. Fookes, P.W. Stout, J.T. Taylor, S. Anderson, E.W. Taylor, A. Rotherham (capt.), F. Jacob, C. Thomas, A. Darby, J.H. Blacklock, H.W. Dudgeon, J.H. Shooter, F. Jacob, J. Davidson

Referee: D.G. Finlay (Scotland)

CHAPTER 9

1900 Soccer takes a bow

The first football international, 17 March 1900

ASSOCIATION FOOTBALL was a latecomer to the world of Irish sport. The game first took root in Belfast, soon spreading to Derry and Monaghan before Dublin Association became the first club formed in the capital in 1883, followed soon after by Trinity College. The Dublin press corps was not impressed with this new game, decrying its play as 'butting the ball like a pack of young goats'.

By the time soccer arrived in Dublin, a decade after H.W.D. Dunlop set up his multi-sport club, there was little room for it at Lansdowne Road. And as the club's rules excluded anyone who was 'a mechanic, artisan or labourer', many of those who played the game would have been unable to do so in Lansdowne. A Dublin journalist wrote at the time that football had 'no pretensions to be considered the pet game of the highly respectable, but it rejoices in the fact that it is the chosen sport of the democracy, and is mainly of a plebeian nature.' The game had taken a huge step forward in Britain when parliament had instituted the Saturday half-day, allowing working men time to watch and play sport.

Ironically, two of the leading clubs in Irish soccer were founded in the neighbouring village of Ringsend, a working class community that has seen more than forty of its sons capped by Ireland at the round ball game. Shamrock Rovers were founded there in 1901, while six years earlier a group of men walked from the fishing village to Finglas, some seven miles away to the north-west of the city, to register Shelbourne as a club with the Leinster Football Association.

Shelbourne's first home was a piece of waste ground beside Havelock Square, next to the Lansdowne stadium, rented at a cost of £6 a year. The club even shared a common root with its exalted neighbours, with both names coming from the original landowners' Somerset origins: the Marquess of Lansdowne's sons were the Earls of Shelburne.

Four years after the Irish Football Association (IFA) was founded in Belfast in 1880, an Ireland team joined England, Scotland and Wales in the Home International championship. They struggled for many years in the face of the dominance of the English and Scots, who never finished outside the top two until Ireland finished second in 1904.

With two other established 'football' games – rugby and Gaelic football

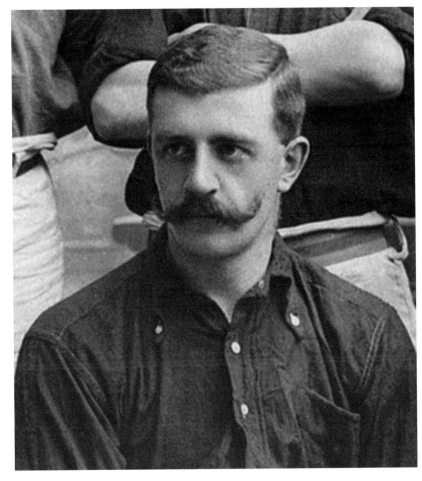

Ireland captain George Sheehan, the only southern-based player

— soccer had to fight its corner. In 1891 the rugby writer, Jacques McCarthy, defined the sports thus: 'Football in Ireland may be said to consist of three parts Rugbeian, Associationist and Gaelic. The rule of play in these organisations has been defined as follows: In Rugby, you kick the ball; in Association, you kick the man if you cannot kick the ball; and in Gaelic you kick the ball if you cannot kick the man.'

Association football in Ireland continued to be run from Belfast, where the teams and administrators were more powerful than their Dublin counterparts. From 1884 to 1914 forty-four of fifty home matches in the British International Championship were played in Belfast, including all twenty-seven in the nineteenth century. This caused resentment in the other cities, which all came to a head after a disastrous 13-2 defeat to England at Roker Park, Sunderland in 1899.

The Leinster Nomads delegate to the IFA, Tom Kirkwood Hackett, knew where the blame lay: 'This has come upon us because of the

hidebound prejudice of the men who select the teams preventing anyone outside the close circle of Belfast being chosen to represent his country. Northern prejudice is the bane of Irish football.'

The Dublin newspaper the *Freeman's Journal* reported that the Leinster delegates formed an alliance with those of Derry to defend their interests against the Belfast powerbase and 'very satisfactory results have accrued', with a sharing of plum fixtures.

The game had grown enormously in the capital, with 259 clubs registered to the Leinster FA by 1901. In February 1906 there were thirty-one football pitches in the Phoenix Park, twenty-nine of which were allocated to association and two to Gaelic. This was raised by a Nationalist MP in the House of Commons as evidence of a bias against Irish games, but it was shown that the allocation reflected demand.

Kirkwood Hackett's racket paid off, and the IFA announced that the 1900 game against England would be played in Dublin. It may also have had one eye on the rugby fixture lists, as 17 March was also set as the date for the Ireland v Wales international at the Balmoral Showgrounds in Belfast. The Welsh came seeking the triple crown, and duly won the game 3–0.

The Dublin public was excited at this rare treat. One, calling himself 'Soccer', wrote to *The Irish Times* to exhort the public to 'go see the cream of English footballers'. 'So buck up Dublin, and don't forget Lansdowne Road.'

Irish centre-half Archie Goodall, who was later a music hall star

With just one Dublin-based player, Dr George Sheehan of Bohemians, there was some muttering that the side might still have been selected by the Belfast IFA clique: 'The selecting five have not followed out the business view of the matter taken on by the association,' wrote the *Freeman's Journal*, 'because had they done so, a couple more places would have been given to Leinster men.'

There had been a long-standing policy not to select 'Anglos', or players based in England, but that had been done away with the year before. Two such players were selected for the 1900 game, Portsmouth goalkeeper Matt Reilly and Archie Goodall of Derby County.

'Ginger' Reilly had never played the game as a boy: growing up in Dublin his sport was Gaelic football. He took up soccer after he joined the British army and by 1895, aged twenty-two, he was keeping for the Royal Artillery, The Army, and Hampshire. In 1899 he left the military life behind to become Portsmouth's first professional signing. He played 206 games for the club before joining Notts County and later returned home to play with Shelbourne. He ended his career with two Ireland caps.

Archie Goodall was born in Belfast to a Scottish soldier father, while his brother John was born in London. The rules of the time insisted men play for the lands of their birth so, although raised in Kilmarnock, Archie had to play for Ireland and Johnny for England.

A goalscoring half-back, he was a rough character who several times crossed swords with the football authorities. In 1894 he refused to play the extra time period of the United Counties League Cup final against West Bromwich because he said his contract ended after ninety minutes. He almost missed the 1898 FA Cup final for Derby County because he was outside the ground touting his ticket allocation.

Bizarrely, his post-playing career included spells as full-time coach at the exclusive schools at Clongowes Wood and St Vincent's College in Castleknock, before he hit the music hall stage with his 'sensational performance called "Walking the Hoop".' An advertisement of the time screamed:

'here is an undescribable sensation that has startled two continents. Goodall (the former greatest footballer of the past decade) will defy the laws of nature and walk the interior of a hoop fifty feet in circumference, five inches wide, three inches thick and weighs two hundred pounds.'

The professional members of the England team arrived at the North Wall ferry terminal on the Thursday night, after a rough crossing. The two gentleman amateurs, Gilbert Smith and Bill Oakley, missed the train

Above: An international cap won by Matt Reilly from Donnybrook, which now resides in the Portsmouth city museum

and would arrive on the Friday.

The team were billeted in the Gresham Hotel on O'Connell Street (Ireland were in the Central on Exchequer Street) and were taken on a tour of the city next morning. They visited the Guinness brewery, the Phoenix Park, Dublin Castle and Trinity College before heading out to Lansdowne for 'a spin'. That evening they met up with the Irish team at the Rotunda for a 'smoking concert' in aid of Bohemians football club, which had to be moved to a larger hall such was the public interest.

Saturday dawned bright and sunny, but intensely cold; it was a much-anticipated day in the life of the city. There had been a dry spell leading up to the game, giving rise to concerns that the pitch was too hard, but a downpour on Thursday night allayed those fears.

The IFA were probably a bit surprised, maybe even offended, that the 'patron' of the game, Lord Lieutenant, the Earl of Cadogan, opted not to attend and instead went to the races in Baldoyle. There was a more fraternal attitude on the part of sporting bodies, as all rugby and hockey matches were called off to allow players attend Lansdowne Road.

The morning newspapers set the scene, but damped down any idea of an Irish win:

'although the result of today's game is almost a foregone conclusion, and that

The gentlemen of Bohemians were dominant in Dublin football

Ireland's unenviable title as "wooden-spoonists" is practically assured,
interest in the match is nevertheless intense in Irish football circles'.

On the Wednesday before the game it had been decided to
put back the kick off from 3.30 to 4pm, 'to allow spectators to
see the Lord Mayor's Procession' arranged for St Patrick's Day.
The city centre parade was a troublesome affair, with no less
than eighteen police baton charges needed to quell the dissent.
The trouble was sparked when a Boer flag was unfurled near
Fleet Street and 'warmly cheered' by the populace. The second
Boer War had broken out the previous October and there was
much support for the South Africans among Irish nationalists.
In reply, a trio of students unfurled Union Jacks from the top
floor of Trinity College. The unrest did not augur well for the
visit of Queen Victoria just over two weeks later.

Admission to Lansdowne Road was one shilling, with tickets on sale in
Cook's of Grafton Street. Reserved seats cost an extra shilling or 2/6d,
while sixpence was charged for those wishing to 'promenade'. Trains
carried spectators from all corners of the country and by 4pm there were
well over ten thousand people in the ground, perhaps as many as twelve
thousand.

There was some murmuring as the teams ran on, as the Irish side was
clad in shirts of St Patrick's blue, with a shamrock on the breast. *The
Freeman's Journal* was livid:

Charlie Sagar of
Burnley who
scored England's
second goal

'Why this colour was chosen puzzled a great many, and the choice was strongly
commented on. Ireland has a very distinctive national colour and there seems no
necessity to go out of the way to seek in heraldry for a different one.' It was only
in 1931, when it governed football in just the six north-eastern counties,
that the IFA changed the shirt colour to green.

After the teams stood for photographs and anthems played by the Royal
Irish Constabulary band, the Irish captain, George Sheehan, won the toss
and asked the Englishmen to play into a bright sun.

Dr George Faber Sheehan was a founder member of the Bohemian
club, formed in a Phoenix Park gate lodge ten years before. They were a
strictly amateur club, who gloried in three principles: 'Never say die',
'Keep the ball on the floor', and 'The best defence is attack'.

Football in those days was very different to the modern, scientific approach. Bohemians were reported to have been shocked by the approach of Distillery when they played them in 1895. The Belfast side 'played the ball with machine-like regularity, the ball passing sharply from man to man, each man being in proper place to receive the pass.' The Dublin side were adherents to the 'fast rushes' style of massed charges upfield, which only fell out of vogue in the following decade.

George was one of three brothers who formed the backbone to an almost instantly successful side. 'Bohs' won the Leinster Senior Cup six years in a row from 1893 to 1898, with George scoring in each of the last four finals. Emphasising the elite nature of the club, nine members of one of those cup winning teams went on to be doctors or surgeons.

OGDEN'S CIGARETTES.

E. NEEDHAM.

Ernest Needham
(Sheffield United)

Sheehan was first capped in 1899, when Ireland was hammered 9-1 by Scotland at Parkhead. He was appointed captain for the game in Wales, where Ireland suffered a 2-0 defeat. His third and final cap was at Lansdowne Road in 1900, as he was ordered to join up with the Royal Army Medical Corps in South Africa on 22 March, the day before Bohs played Cliftonville in the IFA cup final. 'It is hard lines on Bohemians', sympathised the *Freeman's Journal*. Perhaps a football-supporting superior officer relented and delayed his departure, as in the end Sheehan turned out for Bohs, scoring in a 2-1 defeat. He eventually made a career in the army, rising to the rank of colonel.

His opposite number at the toss was Gilbert Oswald Smith, considered by football historians as 'the first great centre forward'. Smith was renowned for exceptional balance and timing and his skill in close controlling the ball. He stood 5'11", tall for the day, and was slightly built, although described by opponents as 'as hard as a whip cord'. He suffered from asthma and was a reluctant header of the ball, lobbying for it to be banned from the game. His defining skill was his ability to hold up the ball before slipping it to a teammate. He played for the great amateur club Corinthian Casuals, and scored eleven goals in twenty games for England, including four against Ireland in that 13-2 win in 1899. He also found time to play first-class cricket for Surrey.

None of the English players played for the modern glamour clubs, but a glance at the 1899-1900 league table shows that they were representative of the powerhouses of the Victorian game. Aston Villa finished that season as champions, two points ahead of Sheffield United. Only Liverpool of the twenty-first century 'big four' was in the top division, finishing tenth, ahead of clubs such as Bury, Notts County and Glossop.

After sixteen wins and two draws in previous games between the sides, the England team was expecting an easy run-around. Their selectors had seen the game as an opportunity to experiment, and five men were handed their first caps, including four of the five forwards.

Ireland fielded only one debutant, Ginger Reilly, but another was originally selected. Andy Gara, a free-scoring centre forward from Roscommon who played with Preston North End, was injured the week before, delaying his debut for two seasons. When he was eventually capped he marked his debut with a hat-trick against Wales.

Ireland started briskly, and in the first minute Roberts in the England goal was forced to fist away a free-kick. Sheehan had a chance saved shortly afterwards but in the twelfth minute, half-back Harry Johnston drove a ball goalwards which ricocheted off Mick Cochrane and flew past Reilly into the net. 'A softy', moaned *The Irish Times*.

Ireland retaliated swiftly, with a Sheehan run meeting the boot of James Pyper. Sadly, 'Pyper's shot was nearer the North Star than the goal'.

Just four minutes after the first goal, England extended their lead through Charlie Sagar from a tight angle, though the goal owed everything to the man described as 'the best centre-forward in the world'.

'There was a buzz as G. O. Smith made fast tracks into Irish ground, keeping his eye all the time on his left wing, but he smartly popped the ball in the opposite direction and a few quick passes gave possession to Sagar, who sent past Reilly amid a silence which betokened rather surprise than a lack of appreciation.'

Top: Bill Oakley (Corinthians)
Above: Gilbert Smith, 'the first great centre-forward'

Ireland never gave up, and assumed a dominance for much of the rest of the game. 'It was not as nice to watch, but was just as effective,' wrote the *Freeman*. A weakness in front of goal cost Ireland dearly, as chance after chance was squandered. James Pyper, who like his full-back brother Jack, became a Presbyterian minister, was blamed for much of the profligacy.

The English press corps — of which fifty travelled to Dublin — were much taken with Sheehan, whose 'fleetness' was remarked upon. The London media expressed relief that England had won, as Ireland were 'desperately unlucky'.

'Never did an English team receive such a gruelling as that which played at Lansdowne Road on Saturday', wrote the *Evening Herald*.

It was the only all-Ireland football international to be played at Lansdowne Road. By the time the Belfast administration was feeling generous again, Bohemians had developed 'The Pisser Dignam's field', a former vegetable plot in Phibsborough, into Dalymount Park and was able to provide a suitable venue. Besides one Army Cup Final in the 1920s, and the first home game by the Irish Free State in 1927, soccer was not played at Lansdowne Road again until the late 1960s.

IRELAND: Matt Reilly (Portsmouth); Jack Pyper (Cliftonville), Mick Cochrane (Distillery); John McShane (Cliftonville), Archie Goodall (Derby County), Hughie Maginnis (Linfield); George Sheehan (Bohemians), James Campbell (Cliftonville), James Pyper (Cliftonville), Alfred Kearns (Distillery), Joe McAllen (Linfield)
ENGLAND: John Robinson (Southampton); Bill Oakley (Corinthians), James Crabtree (Aston Villa); Harry Johnston (Sheffield United), John Holt (Reading), Ernest Needham (Sheffield United); Archie Turner (Southampton), Dan Cunliffe (Portsmouth), Gilbert Smith (Corinthians), Charlie Sagar (Burnley), Fred Priest (Sheffield United)
Referee: Mr Marshall (Third Lanark, Scotland)

CHAPTER 10

**1905
Originals
of the
species**

The Donegal
man who
followed the
test from a
hospital bed

The Maori visit of 1888-89 established the link between Irish rugby and those who played the game in New Zealand. The 1905-06 visit of the team now hailed as The Originals was an arguably more significant tour however, announcing a new power in the game and a new way of playing it. It also allowed the veteran captain of the All Blacks make his first, and last, return to the land of his birth.

Dave Gallaher was born in Ramelton, Co. Donegal on 30 October 1873. It is possible that he might have struck up a friendship with some other great Irish sportsmen from that village. Lucius Gwynn, who played on the 1894 Triple Crown team, was born five months before Gallaher, while Arthur Gwynn, who won one cap in 1895, was born eight months after him. But whether they ever met in Ramelton is not recorded, and Gallaher, at the age of five, emigrated with his family to the other side of the world on the Lady Jocelyn steamship. By the time Gallaher returned with the 1905 All Blacks, the Gwynns were dead, both dying before they saw their thirtieth birthdays.

The large Gallagher family – eight sons and two daughters – settled in Katikati, near Tauranga in the Bay of Plenty. The family travelled with a plan to open a woollen business, but their patron died suddenly and James was forced to take to farming while Mrs Gallagher taught at the local school. They had left an infant called James Patrick, who later died aged six, behind in Ireland. It is likely he was a sickly child and his parents believed he would not survive the voyage.

Mrs Gallagher died while the children were young and they later moved to Auckland where young Dave began playing rugby with the Parnell club, before transferring to the famous Ponsonby. He first played for Auckland in 1896 and was a regular for his province before NZ played their first test in 1903. He was selected as a hooker on the side that toured Australia, although he finished the tour – in which the All Blacks won all twenty games – as a wing-forward. It was in this position, in which he had only played occasionally for Auckland, that he was to reach greatness.

The family name was originally Gallagher, but Dave was irked at how it was frequently misspelled or mispronounced. On his return from fighting in the Boer War in 1903 he dropped the second 'G'.

David Gallaher

He was selected to play in the first ever test between New Zealand and the touring British & Irish side at Athletic Park in Wellington in August 1904, which the home side won 9-3.

But it was as captain of The Originals that Gallaher is immortalised. The centenary history of New Zealand rugby maintains that this was their greatest ever tour, and the statistics certainly bear that out: played 35, won 34, lost 1, points for 976, points against 59.

Those numbers do not fully convey the enormity of the impact the tour had on the game on both sides of the world. It was a controversial tour, mainly due to Gallaher himself and his newly-developed position of 'The Rover' – a wing-forward acting occasionally as scrum-half. He received much criticism, with frequent complaints that he was off-side or obstructing play, and even that he spun the ball into the set scrum. Almost twenty years later, in a book on rugby players who died in the Great War, the English writer E.H.D. Sewell maintained 'This is not the place for a discussion upon the wing-forward position. We do not like the position, and it will never be part of the game in the four Home Unions'.

Gallaher, who weighed thirteen stone and stood six foot tall – big for a forward at the time – was known as a disciplinarian and his firm, well-developed views on tactics led him into dispute with the tour management.

Dave Gallaher, Donegal-born captain of the Kiwi tourists

His appointment as captain was not universally popular and a tough training regime on the ship to Britain did not help. There was a feeling among the team that the players should select the captain, not the NZRFU, and Gallaher offered his resignation, as did his vice-captain, Billy Stead. A vote was taken on board to support the union's appointments, which was passed by 18-11, a weak showing that demonstrated how divided the party was. But once the tour began the Ulsterman asserted his superiority and results were his evidence. The only defeat on the tour came at Cardiff, by 3-0 when, in one of the most controversial incidents in the history of the game, a Bob Deans 'try' was disallowed.

Gallaher never got to play rugby in the land of his birth. He was injured in the game against Scotland, and his recovery was not complete by the time of the visit to Dublin one week later.

The Scottish leg of the tour was an unhappy one. The home crowd did not appreciate the new style of play and greeted the 12-7 win for the 'All Blacks' (this tour was where the nickname was first coined) in virtual silence. The Scots union did not officially welcome the visitors, did not award caps, and although it treated its own team to dinner after the game, did not invite the New Zealanders. The frosty atmosphere was worsened when the Kiwis declined the theatre tickets the SRU had booked for the night before the international. Happily for the tourists however, the game was a great success at the gate. The tour organisers had demanded a guarantee for each fixture, but the Scots refused to agree. They offered the net gate receipts instead, which yielded the sum of £1,700 – more than four times what they would have under the guarantee.

After playing West of Scotland, the New Zealanders got the ferry to Belfast, and the morning train to Dublin, where they were warmly received on the Thursday evening when both teams met at the Empire Palace Theatre for a performance of *The Geisha*.

The New Zealanders' triumphant march around Britain had not gone unnoticed – they had won all twenty-one games – and there was such interest in Dublin that the IRFU made the game all-ticket. It was the first international anywhere to require such an arrangement. Henry Dunlop sold the lease on the ground to IRFU treasurer Harry Sheppard in 1904. Sheppard died young in December 1906 and his mother transferred ownership to the rugby union for £200.

A concerned member of the public wrote a letter to *The Irish Times* the day before the match, expressing his dissatisfaction with facilities for spectators:

A postcard of the time carried the tour's results and fixtures

Results of tour of New Zealand Rugby Team in Great Britain.

	for	agst
Devon County	55	4
Cornwall	41	0
Bristol	41	0
Northampton	32	0
Leicester	28	0
Middlesex	34	0
Durham	16	3
Hartlepool	63	0
Northumberld	31	0
Gloucester City	44	0
Somerset	23	0
Devon & Albion	21	3
Midland Counties		
Surrey		
Blackheath		
Oxford University		
Cambridge		
Richmond		
Bedford		
Scotland		
West Scotland		
Ireland		
Munster		
England		
Cheltenham		
Cheshire		
Yorkshire		
Wales		
Glamorgan		
Newport		
Cardiff		
Swansea		
TOTALS		

Published by Chas. H. Lewis & Co., Wellington, N.Z.

The New Zealand touring party

'May I draw attention to the very inadequate accommodation there is being provided for the general public to view this match on Saturday. I believe there are something like 5,000 shilling tickets sold (not to speak of schoolboys), and so far as I can see this enormous crowd is to be accommodated on one side of the ground and behind the railway goal posts. Surely the responsible parties should see to the immediate erection of tiers for standing upon. At one time they engaged empty barrels, which were a boon to the schoolboys. They are going to make a pot of money over the match, and it's not too much to ask them to give us a plank to stand upon.'

The New Zealanders relaxed the day before the game, and came across a 'speak-your-weight' machine. It was with some consternation they discovered that several members of the party had put on several pounds, and Bill Cunningham almost two stone.

As the build-up to the game continued, other sports realised they were on a hiding, and all senior friendlies in rugby, hockey and football were called off for the day of the game.

After some morning drizzle, the gates opened at one o'clock, and by 2pm – an hour before kick off – a reported ten thousand spectators were present. The Chief Secretary of Ireland and a party of bigwigs were escorted to a special viewing platform erected on the Wanderers' touchline.

The Originals were the first New Zealand international team to perform the *haka*, the traditional Maori dance, which they did before some fixtures. The *Irish Times* report is vague on whether this was done in Dublin: 'Allen, after the customary invocation, selected the railway goal, and Cunningham kicked off for New Zealand'.

After two minutes Billy Wallace kicked the ball over the grandstand and into a neighbouring back yard. It proved impossible to recover the ball and it was replaced, but five minutes later the new ball burst. The two sides chatted while a third ball was found.

It became quickly apparent that Ireland believed its best chance was keeping the ball amongst the forwards. A couple of the fabled Irish foot rushes gave the crowd plenty to cheer on, but after a relieving kick was dropped by the centre J.C. Parke he was quickly set upon by half a dozen black shirts, before the saving boot of Harry Thrift came to the rescue.

Parke was an extraordinary sportsman, arguably Ireland's finest all-rounder. Born in Clones, Co. Monaghan, he was also a leading tennis player of the era, winning an Olympic doubles gold medal, two Wimbledon mixed doubles titles and a Davis Cup for Britain as well as eight Irish titles. He was also a scratch international golfer, accomplished senior cricketer, top ranked sprinter and (as a child) a chess prodigy. As a rugby player he was a centre for Monkstown and Trinity, and won twenty caps between 1903 and 1909, two of them as captain.

The New Zealanders had enthralled the crowds on tour with their

passing movements, and the game at Lansdowne Road was no different:

'*From one to the other the leather was transferred in bewildering fashion above the heads of the Irish lot, but Maclear, with an experience of their methods, gleaned in several cross-Channel engagements, went straight for Deans, and as the New Zealand centre handled, he was instantly bowled over by the Munster stalwart.*'

(The Irish Times)

Charlie Seeling and 'Massa' Johnstone, two of the New Zealanders

Basil Maclear was an Englishman, but his appearance in the white had been vetoed by RFU secretary Rowland Hill on the grounds that he was 'not good enough'. Maclear, stationed in Fermoy, Co. Cork, threw his lot in with Ireland and it proved a huge coup. As luck with have it, his first cap was against England, at the Mardyke in Cork. Ireland ran out 17-3 victors, with the 'not good enough' centre scoring a try. Maclear went on to play eleven times for Ireland and crossed for four tries. He died at the Battle of Ypres in 1915.

As the game at Lansdowne Road proceeded at ferocious pace, Ireland surprised many with the pressure they put the All Blacks under. Ireland failed to convert territory into scores however, the best chance being from a Tedford penalty attempt that was only just missed.

After thirty-two minutes the game was scoreless, the longest blank period the Kiwis had suffered on the tour to date. However, *The Irish Times* report of the first try is a telling example of how Gallaher's men were bringing a new dimension to the sport:

'*Roberts, receiving from his forwards, got those behind him in motion, the leather travelling out towards the right wing. Though each of the Irish backs seemed to grass his man, yet at the finish there remained a trio of the visitors unopposed, and of these Deans was the one to race round for a try.*'

Among the other far-reaching innovations of Gallaher's team that are still practised today was the use of the hooker to throw the ball into the line-out; the use of codewords to signal pre-ordained moves; splitting the line-out and throwing the ball into the gap; and the use of dummy runs.

Ireland half-back Tom Robinson, who had been tackling fiercely, was forced to retire for a time, but resumed at the start of the second half when the New Zealanders had a distinct advantage with the wind.

Three minutes into the second half the Irish full back, Cork man Maurice Landers, became bottled up and ran into touch, and with the Irish temporarily disorganised, the New Zealanders seized their opportunity.

'Their wonderful system of passing was again brought into vogue, and after almost all the backs had handled, Deans registered his second score by grounding the ball close under the posts.'

(The Irish Times)

New Zealand continued in the ascendant in the second half, and a third try came after sixty-eight minutes. The Kiwis swarmed all over the Ireland try-line, but were repeatedly repulsed before McDonald broke through, rode a final tackle, and grounded.

There was apprehension that the tour pattern of superior stamina producing plenty of late tries would be repeated, but excellent tackling by Parke, Maclear and George Hamlet kept the tourists at bay. The great pace at which the game was played at left the Irish forwards floundering, but no more scores resulted.

The Irish could feel no shame in losing to such a fantastic team – simply marvellous' said one report – but the fifteen-point margin 'didn't exaggerate their superiority over Ireland'. Ireland had matched the New Zealanders in strength and stamina, but lost out to their superior skills. Ireland's lack of cutting edge proved costly.

The Irish Times editorial writer enthused: 'A more perfect team has never before been seen in this country', while its rugby reporter insisted: 'Many famous football battles have been fought in the same arena, but never was witnessed such a struggle as this'.

Dave Gallaher is reputed to have followed the progress of the game

Below & overleaf:
The cartoonists had a field day with the exotic visitors

from his hospital bed with frequent telegrams and telephone calls from the ground, with the assistance of a Dr Savage. He was still unfit when the All Blacks travelled to play Munster in Limerick.

The tour management had asked to postpone the game as they wanted a full week to prepare for the England game the following weekend, but

the IRFU insisted they travel south. A huge crowd gathered at the station to greet the exotic visitors, although just three thousand actually turned up at the Markets Field to watch the game.

'Everywhere we went people followed us, but there was hardly anyone at the game itself,' wrote New Zealand manager G.H. Dixon in his diaries. 'It's clear that despite the low admittance price, many of the locals just couldn't afford it.'

Basil Maclear captained Munster to a 33-0 defeat. It was his fourth appearance against the tourists – he also played for Blackheath and Bedford – and not one of the sides he played with scored a point.

Gallaher retired at the conclusion of this tour and co-authored the game's seminal coaching tract *The Complete Rugby Footballer* with Billy Stead, a volume they are reputed to have written in seven days during the tour. The book still reads with an extraordinary freshness and lays down the commandments for how All Black rugby was to be played. The following passage on the 1905-06 tour, which still resounds in many ways, gives a flavour of the man and his philosophy:

'We have noticed shocking neglect in the choice and cultivation of the men of the front rank. The prevailing idea in Britain seems to be that anything is good enough for a forward, and that you put in that department all those men who are not thoroughly capable for any other task. Our principle is that every forward should be a potential back and in the team that Britain there was not a man in the pack who could not have fulfilled the duties of a back if the emergency had demanded.'

Gallaher married the sister of a team-mate and worked as foreman in a freezing works, while serving as an All Black selector from 1907 to 1914. Having served in the Boer War in 1901, rising to the rank of sergeant major, he wanted to enlist at the outbreak of the First World War, but his family ties held him back. However, on hearing of the death of his brother in action he joined up the same day and was transported to Europe.

There he was to die, suffering mortal wounds at the bloody battle of Passchendaele in Belgium.

On the freezing morning of 4 October 1917 Gallaher was leading his men through a muddy river to where they would relieve another battalion for the second stage of an attack. Just as they 'stepped over' the top of the slope the men came under fire from a German gun placement on the Gravenstafel Ridge and Gallaher was shot through the head. He was evacuated from the battlefield to an Australian field hospital, little more than a tunnel attached to the trenches. There he died, aged forty-four, and was later buried in the Nine Elms cemetery, Poperinghe.

A fellow member of 'the Originals', Ernest Booth, wrote of Gallaher:

'Dave was a man of sterling worth …. girded by great self-determination and self-control he was a valuable friend and could be, I think, a remorseless foe. To us All Blacks his words would often be 'Give nothing away: take no chances'.'

In New Zealand Gallaher is still recalled as one of their greatest ever players – since 1922, the Auckland club championship has been played for the Gallaher Shield – while in his birthplace he was acknowledged by Letterkenny RFC, who renamed their ground Gallaher Park on the centenary of The Originals visit. Captain Tana Umaga, and other members of the 2005 All Blacks touring Britain and Ireland at the time, attended the ceremony.

IRELAND: M.F. Landers (Cork Constitution); H. Thrift (Dublin University), B. Maclear (Cork County), J.C. Parke (Dublin University), C. Robb (Queen's College Belfast); E.D. Caddell, T.H. Robinson (Dublin University); C.E. Allen (Derry, capt.), A. Tedford (Malone), Joseph Wallace (Wanderers), H.J. Knox (Lansdowne), G. Hamlet (Old Wesley), G.H. Wilson (Malone), J.J. Coffey (Lansdowne), H.S. Sagars (Dublin University)

NEW ZEALAND: W. Wallace; C.W. Smith, R. Deans, H.J. Mynott; W.J. Stead (capt.), J. Hunter; J. Roberts; G. Gillett; A. McDonald, S. Seeling, T. Glasgow, W. Cunningham, J. O'Sullivan, G. Tyler, S. Casey

Referee: C. Finlay (Scotland)

CHAPTER 11

1914 Irish rugby's fallen volunteers

Despite the pleadings of those who love the purity of sport, it has never been able to divorce itself from politics and intrigue. From the 'bread and circuses' attitude of Roman emperors, sport has always been a useful tool in the hands of powerful men. In Ireland, the GAA first took heed of this, and its close links to the national liberation movement ensured politics was written into its rule book – and took many years to be written out.

By 1914 Ireland was at a crossroads: the Great War had broken out, putting the Third Home Rule Bill on hold. Moderate nationalist leader John Redmond urged his supporters to enlist in the forces, believing this would put his party in a strong position after the war. More militant nationalists opposed this, and continued preparations for an uprising. Unionist opinion, north and south, was supportive of the war and many men signed up. The rugby community at the time in Dublin was dominated by middle-class Protestants, and was willing to play its part. Other rugby men took the opposite course.

Today, on international days and nights, the streets around Lansdowne Road echo with nothing more lethal than the cries of those hawking souvenirs and chocolate. But just under a century ago there were rifles barking and bullets whizzing close to the stadium. One of the bullets tore into the flesh of a man called Frank Browning, ending the life of a revered sportsman.

Browning was best known as a cricketer, playing thirty-nine times for Ireland from 1888 to 1909, but in 1914 he was president of the IRFU, a fine honour bestowed at the end of his active career as a half-back with Wanderers. At the outbreak of the war, Browning played a major role in the formation of the Irish Rugby Football Union Volunteers Corps, which met and drilled at Lansdowne Road. Such battalions, known as 'Pals', were popular across Britain, allowing groups of men with something in common to join up and fight alongside each other. Pals regiments were drawn from sports clubs, work places and colleges.

Once Britain declared war on Germany on 4 August 1914, Browning wrote to the Dublin rugby clubs urging them to encourage their members to enlist. Once he saw the enthusiastic response he decided to form an IRFU Volunteers Corps, with its HQ at Lansdowne Road. The corps was both a focus for recruitment and an active 'home guard' grouping for those unable to serve as front-line troops.

An old Monkstown player, Lt-Col Geoffrey Downing, was in command of the 7th Battalion of the Royal Dublin Fusiliers, and agreed to open a company for the rugby pals.

The Irish Times of 25 August 1914 reported that the 'opening muster' of the volunteer corps at Lansdowne Road was 'most satisfactory in every respect', with more than a hundred attending. Enrolments were taken at the ground every day from 4.30pm to 6pm, with an hour's drilling for volunteers every evening. Within a week the numbers were up to two hundred and fifty men, mainly, but not exclusively, drawn from the professional classes of the city.

On 11 September the RFU at Twickenham cancelled all international fixtures and urged clubs to do the same. The union also announced 'Nearly every football player is physically fit and between the ages of nineteen and thirty-five, and all should, therefore, enlist. If, owing to special circumstances, some cannot enlist for service at the front they can, and should, join some military organisation for home defence.'

A week later, under the headline 'The New Army', *The Irish Times* reported on the volunteer corps' departure for training on The Curragh. The group of 110 men gathered on Trinity's parade ground, which lay behind the houses on Westland Row. Browning addressed the men and acknowledged the remarks of Major Tate who wished them 'God speed and a speedy return after engaging in a struggle in a just and righteous cause'. The men marched through the university, along Dame Street and the south quays to the station at Kingsbridge, all the way cheered by crowds waving Union Jacks and singing 'It's A Long Way to Tipperary'.

With the first detachment off training,

Frank Browning, founder of the 'Pals' and victim of the Easter Rising

"This is not the time to play Games" (Lord Roberts)

RUGBY·UNION·FOOTBALLERS
are
DOING·THEIR·DUTY
over 90% have enlisted

"Every player who represented England in Rugby international matches
last year has joined the colours."—Extract from The Times, November 30, 1914.

BRITISH ATHLETES!
Will you follow this
GLORIOUS EXAMPLE ?

recruitment continued, and four hundred more gathered to fill their places. In mid October the Volunteer Corps played D Company in a rugby match at Lansdowne Road. There was a huge crowd – many wearing khaki – at the game, which ended in a 8-8 draw. Colonel Downing of the Royal Dublin Fusiliers presented Browning with a gold watch in recognition of his efforts in starting the corps. It was a rare afternoon of action at the ground, as much of the complex was given over to growing vegetables for the next four years. Rugby continued only at schools level.

The enthusiasm of the first recruiting fervour started to pall, however, once the first casualty lists started to be published. In May 1915, their training over, The 'Pals' were sent to Basingstoke in southern England to await deployment. In July they sailed to the eastern Mediterranean to join the allied assault on the Gallipoli peninsula, in a bid to keep open the sliver of waterway called the Dardanelles strait.

Many of the IRFU contingent were chosen for the initial assault on Suvla on 7 August, and as they approached the bay some were heard to mutter how like Dublin Bay the landscape appeared. Walter Paul, former captain of Clontarf's schoolboy side, was killed in the landing, which was

Above: Sportsmen were targeted by recruitment campaigns
Right: The 'Pals' mustered in Lansdowne Road, with Browning and Downing at the front

initially successful, but incompetent leadership ensured it later turned into a bloodbath. The next day the 7th Dublins captured – at heavy cost – a promontory called Chocolate Hill.

'Under concentrated shell and rifle fire they took up formations almost as though they were on the Curragh. They had confidence in their leaders and they themselves retained coolness and courage, full of a determination to live well or die hard. They passed through infernos of shell-fire unshaken and even the thick rifle-fire from the Turks did not stop them as they charged the first ridge – Chocolate Hill'.

(The Pals at Suvla Bay, 1916)

Their grounding in rugby seems to have stood to the Pals, as an officer in another company wrote in a letter home: 'D Company came into our ditch with a dash for all the world like a wild forward rush at Lansdowne Road'.

Twenty-two men of D Company died in taking Chocolate Hill, but worse was to come. On Sunday 15 August an assault on the Turkish position high on the ridge called the Pimple was successful. During the night the Turks retook their post, which they used to lob grenades into the Irish trenches. Orders were given to charge the Turkish position, and No.14 platoon of D Company sallied forth. All bar four men were killed in the futile assault, including one of the original Pals, Lieutenant Edward Weatherill of Lansdowne. Other rugby pals to die in that foray included Thomas Elliott (Trinity), George Kearney (hockey international) and Charles MacDonald (IRFU). In the clamour of the battle many others were slain, their bodies never found. The Pals who went missing that day included John Boyd (Clontarf), William Boyd (Bective Rangers), Hugo Pollock (Wanderers) and Arthur Crookshank (St Columba's College rugby captain). In all that morning eleven officers and fifty-four men were killed or wounded, and thirteen were missing: D Company was reduced from 239 men to 108.

The Pals set off on their journey to the Curragh

As the months passed, the 'Roll of Honour' list in the newspapers got

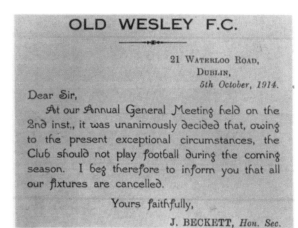

OLD WESLEY F.C.

21 WATERLOO ROAD,
DUBLIN,
5th October, 1914.

Dear Sir,

At our Annual General Meeting held on the 2nd inst., it was unanimously decided that, owing to the present exceptional circumstances, the Club should not play football during the coming season. I beg therefore to inform you that all our fixtures are cancelled.

Yours faithfully,

J. BECKETT, *Hon. Sec.*

Above: The war ended normal sport for more than four years

Below: Wanderers erected a memorial plaque on the club pavilion in Lansdowne Road

longer and longer as the Pals were shipped to the Western Front: Michael D'Alton (Lansdowne) invalided home; William Mathews (Wanderers), killed; Richard Swan (Lansdowne) died of typhoid fever; Edward Millar (Monkstown), killed. The latter's brother, Harry, played four times for Ireland and was company commander of the IRFU volunteer corps in Dublin.

Back home, there was a fund-raising drive to help the wounded. In October Browning organised a gymkhana and sports day at Lansdowne Road. The athletic events were mostly run by schoolboys and girls, with the hundred yards won by Denis Cussen of Blackrock College. Cussen went on to be one of the greatest Irish right wingers, scoring two famous tries when Ireland beat England 19-16 in Lansdowne Road in 1926. Cussen also reached the second round of the 100 metres at the 1928 Olympics.

The volunteer corps continued to aid recruitment, but its main activity now was drilling those men who were too old or unfit for service. By November 1915 there were 170 men among its ranks who continued to drill at Lansdowne Road, now wearing a khaki uniform. They also sported a red armband with the initials 'GR' short for *'Georgius Rex'*, the Latin for 'King George'. With the wit for which Dubliners are renowned, the GRs became known as the 'Gorgeous Wrecks'.

With fighting on the Western Front a bloody stalemate, it became clear the war could last years, and nationalist opinion grew impatient. The old republican slogan 'England's difficulty is Ireland's opportunity' was dusted down and the Irish Volunteers prepared for rebellion.

On Easter Monday 1916, the Gorgeous Wrecks were on manoeuvres in Ticknock in the foothills of the Dublin Mountains when the Rising

broke out in O'Connell Street. Hearing of the insurrection on the way back to their barracks at Beggars Bush, the unarmed group split up at Ballsbridge. One party marched down Shelbourne Road where they came under sniper fire from the railway bridge over Bath Avenue, while Browning's group marched through the intersection of Lansdowne Road and Pembroke Road, along Northumberland Road.

In a house on the corner where Haddington Road intersects, a pair of rebels, Michael Malone and Jim Grace, were holed up with two fifteen-year-old boys, Michael Rowe and Paddy Byrne. As the uniformed column marched towards them, the two men opened fire and thirteen men fell, five fatally. A woman living in a neighbouring house watched the veterans from her window:

The 'Gorgeous Wrecks' drilling in College Park

'*A sharp report rings out, and the man in the foremost rank falls forward, apparently dead, a ghastly stream of blood flowing from his head? Bullet follows bullet with lightning rapidity.*'

One of those lethal slivers of lead caused fatal damage to forty-seven-year-old Frank Browning. He was carried to the barracks and later to Baggot Street hospital, but died there two days later. He left a wife and young son.

The news that an unarmed group had been fired upon was greeted with fury in Dublin and helped ensure the Rising was highly unpopular

at the time. Padraig Pearse issued an order that night that no unarmed persons were to be fired upon, whether wearing uniform or not. The two fifteen-year-olds escaped that night under cover of darkness, as did Grace later in the week, but Malone was killed in a last-ditch battle for the house and his name is remembered in the area in the name of Malone Gardens.

Browning's headstone in Dean's Grange was erected by the IRFU and carried this dedication: 'He will live in the memory of all as an honourable comrade and true and distinguished sportsman, who by his untiring efforts and splendid patriotism obtained from his corps over three hundred recruits for His Majesty's Forces during the Great European War.'

While many Dublin rugby men were unionists, many of those who fought against British rule also played the game. Eamon de Valera, future Taoiseach and President of the Republic, was a keen follower, having played the game at Blackrock College. He had little time for gaelic football, stating that 'the game of rugby is best suited to the Irish temperament', but he was rarely able to attend internationals in the years after independence due to the power of the GAA and its strong links with his party. A UCD player called Kevin Barry was hanged for his part in the killing of a soldier guarding a bread van, and his iconic photograph shows him wearing a Belvedere College rugby shirt.

Belvedere rugby player Kevin Barry was hanged for his part in an assassination during the War of Independence

Lansdowne Road was occasionally utilised during the war years – in September 1917 a military tournament was staged to raise funds for Dublin Fusiliers held as prisoners of war in Germany. Reporters drew comparison between the pre-war tournaments held at the RDS – with the red uniforms and gaily-coloured banners – and the austere wartime displays at which khaki was the dominant colour.

It was a grim time for rugby, with eight former internationals dying in the war. The oldest of them, at thirty-two – and the most capped, with eleven – was the career soldier, Captain Basil Maclear, who was killed at Ypres in May 1915.

Later that year Ernest Deane (Monkstown, 1 cap) and Robert Burgess (Trinity, 1 cap) were killed in France; Vincent McNamara (UCC, 3 caps) lost his life at Gallipoli.

The youngest rugby international to die was twenty-one-year-old Jasper Brett from Kingstown. A nippy winger, Brett's rise to a cap was meteoric. In January 1912 he was on the Monkstown 3rd XV, but by the end of the following year he was playing for Leinster. He went to Paris as travelling substitute for the international on New Year's Day 1914, but was not required. He had a starring role in the interprovincial in Cork in late January which Leinster won 5–3 – 'Whenever Brett got the semblance of a chance he made plenty of ground', reported *The Irish Times*.

Leinster beat Ulster 11–0 the following weekend and Brett won his place on the 'Possibles' team for the final trial, although he failed to force his way into the side. He was again picked as travelling reserve for the game against Wales at Balmoral on 14 March 1914. Brett was called in at a very late stage when star winger J.P. Quinn, who had scored a try in each of the previous games that season, cried off with an attack of rheumatism.

In what was described as 'the roughest game ever seen in Ireland', Wales won 11–3, and Brett was commended for playing 'in a very plucky style', but he was no replacement for the dashing Trinity wing.

Six months later Brett, still a teenager and an apprentice solicitor, signed on with D Company at Lansdowne Road. He took part in the landings

Rugby aficionado Eamon de Valera greets the Scottish captain in 1960

The IRFU memorial was erected in 1925 and is retained in the new stadium

at Suvla Bay, where many of his friends died, and was commissioned as an officer in October 1915. He was evacuated with enteritis, and later fought in Serbia, Bulgaria and Greece, but by August 1916 was admitted to the Latchmere Hospital in Richmond, Surrey, an establishment that treated officers suffering from 'shell-shock'.

In January he was discharged from the army as 'medically unfit', and his father William went to London to bring him home. The pair met in a café where Jasper was jeered by passers-by, a common occurrence for young men who were not 'at the front'. The mental hospital told his father that Jasper was 'cured', but William was shocked by his son's condition. The doctors insisted he be taken home.

Jasper's mental state worsened on his return to Crosthwaite Park, Kingstown, but he was reported to be in good health on Sunday 4 February when he left home for a walk at 8.45pm.

A couple of hours later he lay down on the railway track inside the Khyber Pass tunnel, just past Dalkey station. The driver of the 22.10pm train from Amiens Street, which had rattled past Lansdowne Road and the Monkstown RFC grounds on its journey, felt a jolt and telephoned back to Dalkey from the next station. Inside the tunnel a search party found the decapitated body of Brett.

At Crosthwaite Park a letter was found which asked all to think of him as he once was, and concluded with an informal will and the words 'God's will be done'.

Three more Irish internationals were to die in that horrific year of 1917: Albert Stewart (NIFC) had scored a try on his debut against Wales in 1913, the first of his three caps. A major in the Royal Irish Rifles, he was killed in action in Ypres. Alfred Taylor (Queen's University, Belfast) died in the same battle, blown up by a shell while dressing the wounds of a fellow officer. He won three caps in the centre in 1909 and was recalled for the game in Paris in 1912, when he scored the try that beat France.

The eighth rugby cap to die was William Edwards, who was killed in action in Jerusalem on 29 December 1917. Edwards (Malone) made his debut as wing forward in that 1912 win in Paris, but played only once more for Ireland. Edwards had joined up with the rugby pals in August 1914 and served in France, Flanders and Egypt before being sent to Palestine. A strong man, Edwards was also a water polo international and Irish swimming champion. He was the first man to swim across Belfast Lough.

Below: Jasper Brett, rugby international who took his own life after experiencing Gallipoli and Flanders

Those men were not the only Irish rugby men to die in combat in the twentieth century – a further seven perished in the Second World War. Irish rugby players had a long and feared reputation as warriors – three of the four rugby internationals to win the British army's highest honour, the Victoria Cross, were Irishmen, and all three were members of Wanderers. Robert Johnston and Tom Crean won their VCs for actions in the Second Boer War, while Frederick Harvey won his in France in 1917.

Left: D. Company v the rest of the IRFU Volunteer Corps, Lansdowne Road, 17 October 1914. Frank Browning is in the blazer in the front row; Jasper Brett is sitting on the ground at right

CHAPTER 12

1924-1935
Between
the wars

Still no
beating the
visitors from
New Zealand

Through Ireland's long history of test rugby against New Zealand, a solitary victory has yet to be achieved. In a century of rivalry, one game was drawn and twenty ended in victory for the All Blacks.

Between the wars there were two epic encounters that could have produced a win for Ireland, games that still stir emotions in Irish rugby followers.

They were extraordinary times, an exciting period for those who had escaped the slaughter of the war and Spanish flu that followed it. Perhaps the carefree attitude produced characters such as Ernie Crawford, Jammie Clinch and Mark Sugden, men whose deeds and attitude to the game seem almost alien in the fully professional era.

Crawford was a Belfast man who played with Lansdowne when he moved to Dublin. A top soccer player too, he was reserve for the Ireland team that played in the 1924 Olympic Games, and played for Cliftonville and Bohemians, where he is still venerated. In one famous incident after a Bohs v Shamrock Rovers derby match, he took off his shirt and offered to fight Bob Fullam of Rovers. Bohs fans still air a chant in memory of the incident,

Ernie Crawford, he's our friend,
He's our friend, he's our friend
Ernie Crawford, he's our friend
He hates Rovers

As a rugby player he was an outstanding full-back, and certainly impressed the England captain Wavell Wakefield, who wrote about him thus:

'Although Crawford was the most cheery companion off the field, he has always seemed sinister to me during a game, a kind of brooding intelligence directing the play, crouching and waiting like a spider for the unfortunate man who has to try and pass him.'

Crawford won thirty caps from 1920-27, captaining Ireland to a fantastic 19-15 win over England at Lansdowne, when the speedy Denis Cussen was twice sent over by dummies thrown by Sugden, and centres Frank Hewitt and George Stephenson each scored a try. That team went to Swansea on the brink of a Grand Slam in 1926 but lost 11-8. His final

Un incident du match : en pleine action, le ballon a été envoyé hors de touche, près du but irlandais.

Left: Lansdowne Road was still under-developed in 1920, as this action from the France game shows **Below:** England captain W.W. Wakefield, who described Ernie Crawford as 'sinister'

year as captain again saw Ireland win three out of four, losing only at Twickenham.

He was quite a character, with several tales told of his occasionally sharp practices, such as tapping the ball and scoring a try while the defending side waited for a penalty kick to be taken, and duping attackers by shouting 'pass' as they neared the line. He is credited with inventing that peculiarly rugby phrase 'alickadoo', which came about on a train trip to London. Failing to prise a teammate away from a book to join the poker school, he scoffed at the biography of a middle-eastern figure thus: 'You and your bloody Ali Khadu!'

Crawford played one of the greatest games of his career against the All Blacks on All Souls Day 1924.

The New Zealanders arrived with a fearsome reputation, and a deserved one. History would know this team as the Invincibles, Cliff Porter's legends that won all thirty-two games on its epic tour around Britain, Ireland, France and Canada from September 1924 to March 1925. They had, in George Nepia, one of the greatest ever players of the game but one who, on this day, had to bow to Crawford. The *Irish Independent* was sure who was superior:

'New Zealand had to fight desperately hard to overcome a great Irish team in which George Stephenson's tackling disrupted the tourist machine and Ernie Crawford emerged with a great respect, further enhanced as he played a better game

The popular craze of collecting cigarette cards made household names of Irish rugby players

at full back than his famous opposite number George Nepia.'

Nepia is hailed as 'New Zealand rugby's first superstar', a fierce tackler, brave fielder and powerful kicker of the ball. A member of the Maori race, he was just nineteen on the tour, and made his international debut at Lansdowne Road.

The All Blacks arrived in Dublin on the crest of a triumphal wave that surged through the north of England, packing crowds in at football grounds such as Roker Park, Villa Park and Old Trafford. They had a full week off in the run-up to the international, and enjoyed their time training in Sydney Parade and Palmerston, playing golf in the afternoon and relaxing at the Salthill and Hibernian hotels.

The IRFU had organised extra car parking spaces at Milady's Field at the Havelock Square end – O'Connell Gardens was yet to be built – and a remarkable twenty-five thousand people turned up on a day of sheeting rain.

The Irish tackled like demons from the off, refusing to let the All Blacks settle and it soon developed into a kicking game. One New Zealand attack was only halted when Crawford made a diving tackle at the ankles of Parker.

The game was played in driving rain and sleet, 'grim and relentless stuff in the mud and slush'. Ireland had some good chances in the first half, with Crawford narrowly missing a place kick and Gardiner tackled just short of the line after being sent through by his captain George Stephenson. It was scoreless at half-time, but when Stephenson's brother Henry was caught in possession early in the second period, the New Zealanders swiftly capitalised and Karl 'Snowy' Svenson ran in to score in the corner. Immediately afterwards John McDowell was penalised under the posts for not playing the ball, 'although it seemed to many as if he had not much chance of doing so with several opponents on top of him …' White kicked the goal, but by now it was apparent that the wind gods had been kind to Ireland, having joined the teams in changing ends at half-time.

Despite Hewitt playing on one leg – and off the field for much of the half – Ireland kept the pressure on and created several scoring chances to no avail. The final scoreline of 6-0 was the narrowest defeat in tests on the tour.

By the time New Zealand returned in 1935, Nepia had departed for English rugby league and there were no survivors on either team. It was a very different stadium they returned to as well, as the new East Stand had been opened in 1927. A novel structure, it incorporated terracing on the ground level, with a covered grandstand on stilts rising above. The Irish army was enlisted to jump up and down in the grandstand to test its strength. The stand stood up to the test, but unfortunately the roof was not completed in time for the visit of Scotland.

That game, in February 1927, was described in the *Sporting Life* as 'the most amazing rugby match of all time'. The soubriquet was not awarded for the quality of play – Ireland won 6-0 thanks to two first half tries by T.O. Pike and Jim Ganly – but due to the horrendous conditions in which the game was played.

'The Irish arrived on the field with jerseys of brilliant green and snowy shorts while the Scots were similarly attired in cheerful blue. Within a few minutes however, all thirty had acquired a rich coating of nice brown mud.

'Conditions for the players and for those unhappy wretches on the uncovered stand were appalling. The former at least had something to do, and were sure of a hot bath immediately after the game, but the latter had no such consolation. For ninety perishing minutes they sat in a pitiless downpour of rain. And what rain it was!'

There were up to forty thousand spectators in the ground, and all were soaked to the skin by the relentless torrent. Reporters' notebooks were returned to a sodden pulp in their brand new press box in the middle of the new stand, while the first use of numbered jerseys by Ireland was of no benefit as the numbers disappeared under the mud within minutes.

G. NEPIA

Above: George Nepia, one of the legends of rugby, made his All Black debut as a teenager in Lansdowne Road in 1924

Below: Increased prosperity and transport links made travelling to games an attraction

The Scots had refused to wear numbers, with one official announcing 'This is a rugby match, not a cattle sale!'

The conditions were so bad that players were tackling members of their own team, and by the end were truly horrendous, according to the *Sunday Independent*:

'*So bitter was the high wind and heavy rain that in the second half George Stephenson, the famous Irish centre, after refusing once was induced to leave the field in a semi-conscious condition due to exposure. He went off staggering and reeling like a man unconscious of his actions or surroundings*'

Some players were numbed cold, the referee's hand was 'still and lifeless' for two hours afterwards. The tough soldier prop 'Horsey' Browne collapsed after the whistle and was out cold for more than thirty minutes. Browne was forced to retire due to illness in 1929 and died two years later, aged twenty-eight.

One of those who froze that day, and one of the greatest players of the 1920s was Mark Sugden, whose play at scrum-half is best remembered as the inventor of the dummy. Several of his contemporaries recalled with awe his skill: Eugene Davy said 'You almost thought the ball was in flight, that it had left his fingertips'. Centre Morgan Crowe explained it: 'The dummy was so perfect you would think you had the ball in your hands yourself'.

Sugden himself explained the move in an interview with Ulick O'Connor toward the end of his life: 'I used to maintain the dummy was hypnotic. You did it with your eyes. First you gave the chap you are selling it to a lot of time to see it coming. You didn't look at him but at your own player who was to receive the ball. You should look into his eyes appealingly as if to say – for instance, if it was Denis Cussen – "here you are Denis, you take it". If you convinced him he was getting it he would affect the fellow who was going to tackle you.' One teammate was, reputedly, so taken in by the beautifully executed dummy that he dived over the line without the ball.

Sugden started as a centre, winning a place on the Leinster

LONDON MIDLAND AND SCOTTISH RAILWAY

RUGBY

INTERNATIONAL MATCH

ENGLAND
versus
IRELAND

Friday Night, February 10

DAY EXCURSION TICKETS
TO

KINGSTOWN
AND
DUBLIN

XV, but was playing out-half at Trinity when former international Harry Thrift told him 'Sugden, you're the worst fly-half I've seen. Why don't you take up snooker.' So he tried scrum-half and became the best in the world.

For the last five years of his international career Sugden never played a club game, as he was teaching at Glenalmond School in Scotland, far from any senior clubs. He used arrive at Lansdowne Road on a Friday in January and the next day play the first game of his season in the international. 'I was fresh as a daisy while all the others were suffering from bad ankles,' he explained. His eccentric attitude to preparation extended to giving up smoking a week before an international, 'but I always smoked one at lunch on the day of the match.'

The Scots match was fated in the inter-war period – the 1933 game was postponed after a howling blizzard covered the pitch with a blanket of snow and several Irish players failed to get to Dublin because of the conditions. The Scots did make it to the city, but not until they had endured a miserable night and day in the Irish Sea being tossed by a savage easterly gale in the *Lairdsburn*. They left Glasgow on Thursday night, and expected to dock at 7am on Friday, but actually arrived at 11pm in no state for international rugby.

Above: Brochure to mark the 1924-25 All Blacks tour

Below: The Ireland team that had a brilliant 19-15 win over England in 1926; BACK: M. Bradley, J. Farrell, A. Buchanan, J. McVicker, W.J. Llewellyn (referee), C.T. Payne, M. Sugden, S. Cagney; MIDDLE: T. Hewitt, G.V. Stephenson, E. Crawford (captain), C. Hallaran , F.S. Hewitt; FRONT: E. Davy, J. Clinch, D. Cussen.

TINORI CURES CORNS Without Pain SOLD EVERYWHERE. E. MAC SWEENY, Ph. Chemist.

SUNDAY INDEPENDENT CITY SPECIAL Drink Victor's Café au Lait COFFEE & MILK

VOL. 22. NO. 9. DUBLIN, SUNDAY, FEBRUARY 27, 1927. PRICE TWOPENCE.

IRELAND PLOUGHS HER WAY TO VICTORY

Members of the Scottish team being introduced to his Excellency the Governor-General before the commencement of yesterday's match.

The Irish team going on to the field in yesterday's downpour, to the accompaniment of rousing cheers from every part of the enclosure. The battery of camera men had a shocking day for their part of the work.

To alter an old adage, these gentlemen at Lansdowne liked yesterday thought any perch good enough in a storm. How the fragile-looking tree held them was a marvel to the spectators placed in lower altitudes.

FIGHT WITH STORM | U.S. AIRMEN DEAD | NOT ENCOURAGING. | **PLAYERS COLLAPSE** | THE ELECTION DATE. | THIRD SMASH | LABOUR'S ERROR

Sailing Ship's Drift of 500 Miles | Dreadful Collision Near Buenos Aires | Terrible Experiences at Lansdowne Road | Hull Station's Run of Ill-Luck | Lord Birkenhead on Extremist Element

● ● ●

In June 1935 The *Irish Times* expressed its surprise that Mike Gilbert had been selected as the sole full back in the All Blacks' touring party, due to visit Lansdowne in December. 'George Nepia is playing as well as ever, and is almost certain to gain a place in the Maori team to visit Australia'. In New Zealand Nepia's omission was less of an issue, and although he played on the 'Probables' on the last of six trial games, Gilbert's selection was welcomed.

The Ireland game was twenty-third on the fixture list, and they arrived in Dublin with twenty wins, one defeat to Swansea, and a hard-fought 3-3 draw with Ulster. Having escaped Ravenhill, the party arrived in Dublin on Monday and again had a leisurely week: they visited the Guinness brewery, played golf in Royal Dublin and attended a performance of *The Gondoliers*. The three Catholic members of the team, Hadley, Mahoney and McKenzie, visited CUS where they were given a warm reception. They also visited Leinster House where they were welcomed by the President of the Executive Council (a post later to be called 'Taoiseach') Eamon de Valera. A report appeared in the New Zealand newspapers that 'Dev' had played in a final trial in 1903 at full back, which was untrue. De Valera was a keen supporter of rugby, and frequently attended games at Lansdowne until it became politically imprudent. In March 1902 he was given a present by two students he had been tutoring for their solicitors' apprenticeship exams. Florrie Green and Patrick Donegan gave him a ticket for the covered stand at the Ireland v Wales game at Lansdowne, priced four shillings.

After their scare in Belfast, the All Blacks took no chances for the international, fielding their strongest available team. Despite a wet morning, there were thirty thousand spectators – including the Dutch soccer team who were to play Ireland the following day in Dalymount Park – when the sun came out in time for the kick off. There was minor drama on the day of the game when it was discovered the Scottish referee had missed the boat and IRFU secretary R.W. Jeffares – an experienced referee – stepped in. There were no complaints about him, the New Zealand press saying he did 'a splendid job'.

The match started disastrously for Ireland, who were 8-0 down within eight minutes. First Caughey made a brilliant break and from the opening Mitchell scored in the corner, then after a mis-kick by the Irish full back, Dermot Morris, Charles Oliver went over for a gift try.

The Irish pack soon asserted their superiority, but found it hard to get the points on the board. Eventually Aidan Bailey scored a penalty goal, but Brushy Hart replied with a try for the tourists.

Light drizzle made the ball slippery, but Ireland's first try against the All Blacks – at the third attempt – finally came after George Morgan slipped away from the scrum and passed to captain Jack Siggins who was tackled close to the line. Prop George Beamish picked up the loose ball and crossed for a try. The conversion was missed – and a penalty hit the crossbar – and New Zealand led 11-6 at the break.

The rain grew heavier and poured down throughout the second half. The powerful Irish pack set off at a frantic pace, with number eight Siggins crossing the line before being called back for an earlier infringement, an unpopular

decision by Mr Jeffares. The Ireland captain kicked a penalty in front of the points to narrow the gap to two points but two late penalties from Mike Gilbert gave the tourists a 17-6 win.

1924

Ireland: E. Crawford (Lansdowne); H. Stephenson (United Services), J. Gardiner (NIFC), G. Stephenson (Queens University, capt), T. Hewitt (Queens University); F. Hewitt (Instonians), J. Mcdowell (Instonians); A. Spain (UCD), R. Collopy (Bective Rangers), T. Brand (NIFC), J. McVicker (Collegians), T. McClelland (NIFC), J. Clinch (Dublin University), W. Collis (Wanderers and Harlequins), R. Crichton (Dublin University).

New Zealand: G. Nepia, S. Svenson, F. Lucas, A. Cooke, A. Hart; M. Nicholls, W. Dalley; W. Irvine, O. Donald, M. Brownlie, R. Masters, J. Richardson (capt.), L. Cupples, A. White, J. Parker.

Referee: A. Freethy (Wales)

1935

Ireland: D. Morris (Bective Rangers); C.V. Boyle(Dublin University), l.G. Malcolmson (NIFC), A. Bailey(UCD), J.J. Oconnor (UCC); V. Hewitt (Instonians), G. Morgan (Clontarf); T. Dunn (NIFC), C. Graves (Wanderers), C. Beamish (NIFC and RAF), S. Deering (Bective Rangers), W. McRoss (Instonians), J. Siggins (Collegians, capt.), C. Wallis (Wanderers), S. Walker (Instonians).

New Zealand: M. Gilbert; G. Hart, C. Oliver, T. Caughey, B. Mitchell; J. Griffiths, B. Sadler, A. Lambourn, W. Hadley, D. Dalton, R. King, S. Reid, H. Mclean, J. Manchester (capt.), A. Mahoney.

Referee: R.W. Jeffares (Ireland)

Today, Lansdowne Road's worldwide fame rests on its status as the home of Irish international sport, for both rugby and football. The resurgence in Irish soccer in the last twenty years was in part due to the intimidating atmosphere engendered by the 'Lansdowne Roar', a phenomenon that many hope will carry into the new era. When Dalymount Park started to show its age in the early 1970s, the FAI started hiring the IRFU's stadium, but there was one little-remembered earlier visit to Dublin 4.

It was in the early days of the new state, and a plum fixture for the new governing body for football in the twenty-six counties, the Football Association of the Irish Free State (FAIFS). The body had been founded when the Leinster FA pulled out of the IFA in 1921 due to the long-standing grievance about pro-Belfast bias. At first both the FAIFS and IFA claimed jurisdiction over the whole island (a Belfast club won the 1923 FAIFS Cup) but when the FAIFS joined FIFA in 1923 it was as the governing body for the new state. A fractious relationship continued for many years; players could play for both the Irish Free State team and (Northern) Ireland, and many did until 1950 when FIFA called a halt.

The newly-formed Irish Free State side first played at the 1924 Olympic Games, and had a first home game against the USA shortly afterwards. Two years later, in March 1926, they travelled to Turin – a 3-0 defeat – and at a council meeting on 26 October invited the Italians back. The date was fixed for 23 April 1927, despite the association being aware that Italy had a game against France on 24 April. Perhaps there was some realism in this, and there were no official complaints when it was an Italy 'B' selection that made the trip to Dublin – the 'A' side were to draw 2-2 in Paris. Despite the quality of the visitors – although only three were debutants, only one of the team had played in the 3-0 win against Ireland in Turin – the FAI has always regarded this as a full international.

Running an international in Dublin was a long-forgotten art for Irish soccer officialdom and the FAIFS approached the IRFU for the use of Lansdowne, which they were granted for a guarantee of £150 and 10 per cent of takings in excess of £1,500. Admission – which was by ticket only – was set at 5 shillings and 4 shillings for the stands, 3 shillings for the touchline and uncovered stand and 1 shilling for the terraces.

CHAPTER 13

1927
First home soccer tie for the new state
Ireland v Italy, 23 April 1927

This newspaper advertisement notified the public of the historic fixture

There was some comment before the game that the fixture was styled 'Ireland v Italy', the contention being that only the Belfast-based IFA could put out teams called 'Ireland' in games under the aegis of the International Board (the rule-making body consisting of the FA, Scottish FA, Welsh FA and Irish FA). The Dublin press reported that this game was under FIFA regulations and that as the FAIFS had joined that body they could call the side 'Ireland'.

It was just the latest battle in an ongoing struggle between the associations which carried on for decades – the IFA team that played in the British home championship was always called 'Ireland', while going by 'Northern Ireland' in UEFA and FIFA competition. The FAIFS had struggled to gain international recognition and it was the Olympic movement that first opened the door with that invitation to the Paris games. Ireland's predominant Catholicism was reported to have been the factor that led to Italy granting the first fixture in 1926.

Another perennial difficulty for Irish soccer raised its head before the 1927 game. It was the first time the association had selected British-based players, and they were immediately faced with cry-offs due to club commitments. Goalkeeper Tom Farquharson couldn't play because his club, Cardiff City, were playing Arsenal in the FA Cup Final on the same day. It would have been a fond return to Dublin for the republican who was forced to flee his native city during the War of Independence. A friend of future taoiseach Sean Lemass, the pair were arrested for tearing down British Army posters in St Stephen's Green. As soon as he was out on bail Farquharson moved to Wales where he took up rugby and only returned to soccer when a local team were short of a goalkeeper. His consolation for missing the historic fixture in Dublin was to claim a winners' medal on the only occasion a non-English team won the FA Cup.

Former Celtic legend Patsy Gallagher (then with Falkirk) and Tony

Hunston (Chelsea) were also forced out through injury, so brought into the squad were Christy Martin of Scottish side Borrowstouness (unsurprisingly shortened to Bo'ness), who had scored a hat-trick against Clydebank the previous weekend, and another Irish soccer legend Billy Lacey (Shelbourne) who had a long and successful career with Liverpool. Enniscorthy man Lacey was first capped in the all Ireland days in 1909 and won his last for the Free State in 1930.

The official programme was distributed free by the *Irish Independent*

One of the stars of the selected team was Derby County centre-half Mick O'Brien, who had just moved from Hull for £3,000. O'Brien never played the game until he was eighteen when his family moved from Kilcock, Co. Kildare to the north-east of England. O'Brien played with seventeen clubs in a twenty-two year career, interrupted by service duties in the Royal Navy and Royal Flying Corps. Of the team that played in Turin, only captain Frank Brady and Bob Fullam survived in the selected squad.

> **ASSOCIATION FOOTBALL**
>
> **International Match**
>
> **IRELAND v. ITALY**
>
> **At LANSDOWNE RD.**
>
> **On Saturday, April 23, '27**
>
> KICK-OFF AT 3.30 P.M.
>
> This match marks a decidedly progressive step in the game in the Saorstat. It is the first time the Free State Football Association play as Ireland, and also is the initial representative game in which they have called on the services of players of Free State birth assisting Cross-Channel Clubs. This is the second match between the Countries, the first, last year at Turin, being won by the Italians by 3 goals to nil
>
> *This Souvenir Programme is printed and presented free by Independent Newspapers, Ltd., with the official sanction of the Football Association of the Irish Free State*

The Italian team arrived in Dún Laoghaire (Kingstown had been renamed in 1921) on the Thursday night, after a flight from Bologna to Paris and a connection to London. Train and ferry completed the arduous journey – but not as arduous as that suffered by the Irish players the year before when, because commercial air travel was in its infancy, they made the entire trip to Turin by land and sea.

The visitors were met on the pier by the Italian Consul-General, Signor Silenzi, and FAIFS officials including president Sir Henry McLaughlin and Osmond Grattan-Esmonde. Sir Henry was a Belfastman and former Cliftonville full back who took charge of demobilising the British forces in Ireland. Grattan-Esmonde was the first of several prominent politicians who were involved in Irish soccer over the years. A Cumann na nGaedhael TD for Wexford who learned his football at the Catholic public school Downside in England and at Oxford University, he was a direct descendent of Henry Grattan and son of Sir Thomas who was an independent senator until 1934. Sir Osmonde was also one of Ireland's delegates to the League of Nations.

The *Irish Independent* welcomed Dublin's first international visitors most effusively:

'In olden days, the landing of men from far lands on our shores would be the signal for flight on the part of our ancestors, "for they feared the Greeks even though they bore gifts" and the usual "present" in those days being a business-like battleaxe, or a broad Claymore, applied to the place that it would do the greatest good – for the striker. We have changed all that …'

The party was then taken by train to Westland Row and by charabancs to Jury's Hotel in Dame Street. After a runabout at Shelbourne's ground in Ringsend in the morning, the Italians were taken up to the Phoenix Park to meet the Governor-General Tim Healy at the Vice-Regal Lodge (now Áras an Uachtaráin). Healy gave them the guided tour, pointing out the fine Italian workmanship on his marble fireplaces, and remarked to the press, 'They are a powerful looking lot of boys. We will have some difficulty in beating them.' Healy also expressed his regret that he wouldn't be able to attend but Minister for Justice, Kevin O'Higgins (who was assassinated by republicans ten weeks later), promised he would be there. They spent the night before the game at the Theatre Royal where they saw the 9pm showing of *Pastimes*, a variety show starring Janice Hart and Frank O'Brian, Gipsy Woolf's Sixteen Charleston Steppers and the Martinis. Perhaps the last named made them feel at home.

Above: Bob Fullam, the local soccer hero with a deadly shot
Right: The Irish team that played Italy in 1927: BACK (players only) Billy Lacey, Frank Collins, Mick O'Brien, Bob Fullam; FRONT: Alec Kirkland, Christopher Martin, Harry Duggan, Frank Brady, Joe Kendrick, Sacky Glen, Tommy Muldoon

Italy was a very strong football nation and had put together a good series of results since it began playing in 1910. They missed the 1930 World Cup, but won the next two. A top English referee, Captain Prince-Cox, wrote a piece for the *Irish Independent* warning that the continentals should be respected. He had just refereed Italy's 5-1 win over Switzerland and was able to warn about these 'very efficient footballers' who were 'very fast and [had] wonderful stamina', singling out the outside-left as 'the fastest footballer I have ever seen'. He suggested however that 'if Ireland takes an early lead they will have a good chance of winning'.

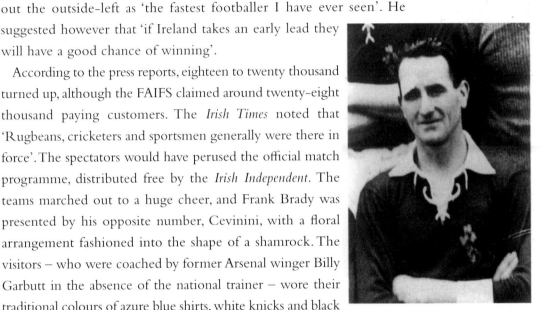

Frank Brady, Ireland captain

According to the press reports, eighteen to twenty thousand turned up, although the FAIFS claimed around twenty-eight thousand paying customers. The *Irish Times* noted that 'Rugbeans, cricketers and sportsmen generally were there in force'. The spectators would have perused the official match programme, distributed free by the *Irish Independent*. The teams marched out to a huge cheer, and Frank Brady was presented by his opposite number, Cevinini, with a floral arrangement fashioned into the shape of a shamrock. The visitors – who were coached by former Arsenal winger Billy Garbutt in the absence of the national trainer – wore their traditional colours of azure blue shirts, white knicks and black socks. Ireland wore green jerseys and white knicks.

The Irish trainer was Val Harris, top-rated southern footballer of the pre-war era who captained Shelbourne to the first Irish Cup to be won by a club from outside the north. Harris, from nearby Ringsend, also played with Everton. He won twenty caps for Ireland in the IFA days and also won an All Ireland senior Gaelic football medal with Ringsend club Isles of the Sea in the days before inter-county championships.

In a frantic opening, Pastore hit the crossbar for the visitors and Bob Fullam had a powerful header saved by Gianni. Irish soccer's first experience of the Lansdowne Roar took just six minutes, when a Christy Martin shot rebounded to Fullam who netted. It was Ireland's first goal in international football, but the roar that greeted it was destined not to be echoed for almost fifty years.

OGDEN'S CIGARETTES.

M. T. O'BRIEN.
HULL CITY.

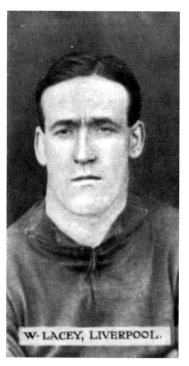

W. LACEY, LIVERPOOL.

Fullam was probably Irish soccer's first superstar. Another native of Ringsend, the village close to Lansdowne Road, he was a most versatile player possessed of the most famous left foot in the country until Liam Brady came along half a century later. His silky skills were allied to a hard-as-nails temperament honed on the Ringsend docks and he was well known to mix it when the going got tough. The catchphrase 'Give it to Bob' – a regular ploy by his Shamrock Rovers team mates – became part of the Dublin vernacular and is still uttered at screens showing televised matches in the pubs of his native village. Fullam spent a season at Leeds United, who won promotion to the first division, but made little impact on the English game and returned home to Rovers.

The Italians came back at Ireland and Pastore had a header kicked off the line by Brady. Ireland's powerful centre forward Martin tried time and again to break through, but was subdued by Italy's defence who towered head and shoulders above him. The pitch was firm and the ball lively on a bumpy pitch, but the Irish forwards struggled more to control it than the Italians.

Irish notions of sportsmanship were to prove costly. Substitution was not permitted in most soccer competitions of the time, even in case of injury, but friendlies such as this were more flexible. The Italians replaced full-back Zanello when he was knocked cold by a powerful Bob Fullam free kick – he recovered in hospital some hours later – but when Irish wing-half Muldoon was injured no substitution was made. Fullam was shifted back to left half and Muldoon limped out to left wing where he remained a passenger for the rest of the game.

The Italians were clearly chastened by the injury to Zanello and when Ireland were awarded a free kick later in the game the visiting defenders implored the referee not to let Fullam take it. There was also a suggestion that the Italians were subscribers to the dark arts, and that the tiny Christy Martin and Fullam received a few short-arm digs when the referee's back was turned.

After fifty-two minutes a move involving Rivolta, Pastore and Vojak set up Italian right winger Munerati to shoot and while Collins saved the Italian followed up to score. The winner came ten minutes from the end when Munerati saw his poorly hit shot from twenty yards slip under Frank Collins's body. Collins had fought in the Great War and a team-mate said a wound prevented him getting down low on his right as quickly as he had before the war.

It was a disappointing defeat for Ireland, but there were several positives to be taken from the display. Playing despite a dose of flu, centre half Mick O'Brien won praise for his resolution at the centre of the Irish defence. Weekly newspaper *Sport* commented: *'O'Brien is one of those players who can be labelled great. What magnificent grace and ease he introduces into his football. His display was a treat and still one got the impression that he held something in reserve.'*

The daily newspapers were critical of several of the Irish players, Sacky Glen being slammed for 'displaying but a crude idea of half-back play', while Collins was 'guilty of errors of judgment which no first-class goalkeeper would have been responsible for.' The Irish forwards were accused of having 'yet to learn how to trap a lively ball, to control it, and to shoot with power and precision'.

After the game the teams were treated to a banquet in the Royal Hibernian Hotel in Dawson Street, an event reported at greater length in *The Irish Times* than the match itself: 'the proceedings were marked with much enthusiasm, particularly when the orchestra played the Italian National Anthem, and later when the Italians rose and sang the Anthem of the Fascisti.'

Grattan-Esmonde asserted that the Italians and Irish had much in common, particularly the fact that both races had been stigmatised by their clichéd national characteristics, saying that 'They had exterminated the figure of the stage Italian just as they in Ireland were determined to exterminate the figure of the stage Irishman.'

The President of the Italian FA, Paolo Ingenere Graziani, presented his counterpart with an impressive bronze statue depicting Romulus and Remus, remarking that the figures were symbolic of the spirit of Rome

Opposite top: Mick O'Brien, who played despite suffering from the flu
Opposite bottom: Billy Lacey, Wexford native whose international career spanned twenty-one years
Top: Sir Henry McLaughlin, FAIFS president who had tried to have Kevin Barry spared from execution

The game was a delight for cartoonists, this from the *Dublin Evening Mail*

and 'represented the voice of the Italian people, and of the glorious Mussolini, speaking to the people of the Irish Free State (applause).' The FAIFS presented Signor Graziani with an ancient Irish urn.

The Italian consul-general said he was happy Italy had won, but sad for his hosts. He said he looked forward to the day 'when Ireland could beat all the champions of the world, except Italy (laughter).' There was also a presentation for referee John Langenus of Belgium, who was to go down in football history as the man who took charge of the first World Cup final in Uruguay in 1930.

The FAIFS chairman paid tribute to the IRFU for permitting the game to go ahead at their ground. 'It was a sportsmanship action by a sporting body, and I feel confident that it will be the means of banding the sportsmen of the country together.' Sealy Jeffares of the union replied that there was never any question about giving the ground once the representatives of the FAIFS had applied. 'The decision was unanimous'. The weekend ended in a handsome profit for the FAIFS of £251, after expenses of £1,409 had been deducted from the receipts of £1,660. The IRFU must have been delighted with the £302 they picked up from the game, while the Italians went home with £208. The Italian travel bill was £265 and the Irish £109.

The following day the Italians were taken on a motoring tour of the beauty spots of Wicklow before a reception at the Dublin Italian Club, *Fede e Patria*, in their premises at Fownes Street where the operatic tenor Signor Staffieri entertained them and the Fascist anthem '*Juvenza*' got another outing.

There was more saluting at the quay in Dún Laoghaire as the SS Hibernia 'steamed out to the strains of '*Juvenza*' and all gave the ancient gladiatorial and modern Fascisti salute, the right hand outstretched'.

IRELAND: Frank Collins (Jacobs); Alec Kirkland (Shamrock Rovers), Frank Brady (Fordson's, captain); William 'Sacky' Glen (Shamrock Rovers), Mick O'Brien (Derby County), Tommy Muldoon (Aston Villa), Bill Lacey (Shelbourne), Harry Duggan (Leeds United), Christy Martin (Bo'ness United), Bob Fullam (Shamrock Rovers), Joe Kendrick (Everton). Reserve: Foley (Shelbourne). Trainer: Val Harris (Shelbourne)

ITALY: Gianni (Bologna), Zanelli (Provercelli), Bellini (Internazionale), Genovesi (Bologna), Luigi Burlando (Genoa), Giordani (Bologna), Munerati (Juventus), Vojak (Juventus), Pastore (Juventus), Rivolta (Internazionale), Cevinini (Internazionale, captain). Referee: John Langenus (Belgium)

CHAPTER 14

1928
The Fatal
Scrum

The death of Lansdowne prop Brian Hanrahan, March 1928

It was the saddest episode in the long history of Lansdowne Road: a young man, at the start of his passage in life and just starting to become noted in his sport, felled by fate on a cold spring afternoon.

Bursting with anticipation for his first Leinster Senior Cup game, Tipperary man Brian Hanrahan pulled the black, red and gold jersey of Lansdowne over his head. He had trodden a well-worn path from the southern province to the Dublin club, and as he looked around the dressing room that day he would have seen at least three former schoolmates from his days at Castleknock College. When the time came he jogged out onto the international playing field to line out against the students of Trinity. But within a quarter of an hour he suffered a cataclysmic injury that would end his life.

Hanrahan was just twenty-two years old, a junior clerk who lived in South Richmond Street. Originally from Clonmel, where his father had been a solicitor, he was orphaned as a child. After school, he stayed in Dublin to work at the National Bank. His brothers had been excellent rugby players at Castleknock, playing for Leinster Schools, but the eldest, Edgar, had moved to Athlone and Charlie lived in Cork.

Charlie was a leading player with the Dolphin club in the southern capital, and had been prop-forward for Ireland since the 1926 championship. Brian had just started to make a name in the Lansdowne front row and there was some comment after his death that he could have followed his brother into a green jersey.

Brian Hanrahan, 'a fine and manly player', was first noted during Lansdowne 2nd XV's run to the Metropolitan Cup in 1927, when they beat the Railway and Steampacket Union 25-0 in the semifinal and Bective Rangers 21-12 in the final replay after a 0-0 draw. Hanrahan was 'the pick of the forwards' in that final, and was called up to the first XV for the last match of the 1926-27 season, when they beat touring side Headingley from Leeds by 11-0.

After a strong campaign by Lansdowne – only two games were lost – the Leinster Senior Cup promised to be a fine way of capping off the 1927-28 season for the club. The first round pitted it against Dublin University, itself a strong rival as the best in the province. The game was fixed to kick off at 4.30pm on Saturday 2 March after the undercard bout between Wanderers and Enniscorthy, the Wexford club making its first appearance in the competition.

Hanrahan had joined a star-studded team, with five internationals in Jack Arigho, Eugene Davy, Ernie Crawford, John Bermingham and Theo Pike. Three more were to be capped in the coming years, including one of Brian's school pals, Ned Lightfoot. Arigho had played in a strong Castleknock College team that fielded three other future caps, Michael Dunne (Lansdowne), Jimmy Farrell (Bective) and Charlie Hanrahan.

Trinity had hit a good run of form and were expected to give the home team a tough game. It was a cool, dry spring day with the ground hard under foot. The students started well, with their pack dominating the opening exchanges, but their backs failed to capitalise on a couple of clear chances.

On fifteen minutes, a scrum was formed about five yards from the touchline. The Trinity captain, Allan Buchanan, insisted later that 'the scrum got down in the usual way', but in those days the usual way was for opposing front-rows to run at each other. The scrum immediately collapsed. While the players stood up one by one, Brian Hanrahan lay on the ground, his neck damaged in the collapse. The young man told the referee, Thomas Bell, that he had no power in his body.

He was taken to the sideline and thence, by motor ambulance, to the nearby City of Dublin Hospital on Upper Baggot Street. He was admitted at five o'clock and was diagnosed, by Dr John C. Richardson, as suffering from paralysis. A friend visited him later in the evening when all Hanrahan wanted to know was who had won the game. (Lansdowne did, by 13 points to nil).

A Sad Accident.

MR. B. HANRAHAN.

All lovers of the game of Rugby in Ireland have been deeply shocked by the sad death of Mr. B. F. Hanrahan, the popular young Lansdowne forward, who met with a fatal accident during Saturday's Cup tie. Rugby, is, happily, very free from accidents of this kind. I happened to be present in the College Park some fifteen years ago, when the last fatal accident occurred on an Irish Rugby field. It was at the beginning of the season, and a trial match was being played between members of the Trinity Club. One of the players was Mr. C. V. McIvor, the old Portora wing three-quarter, who must have been one of the fastest "wings" that have played for Ireland in modern times. During a *mêlée* he sustained a nasty kick in the head, and although he recovered temporarily he died afterwards in hospital.

Poor McIvor was a member of that famous Portora team that carried all before it a few years before the war. It included George Wood, who afterwards played for Trinity; "Jimmy" Daniels, C. Clesham, R. V. Jackson, R. A. Lloyd, Scott, Gerald Bradsheet and R. Burgess. All these players reached international form, and but for the war, which claimed at least two of them as its victims, some of them might have made Rugby history. As it was, the name of R. A. Lloyd still is spoken with reverence by the younger generation of Rugby men, and it is as "Lloyd's team" that that great fifteen always will be remembered.

Brian Hanrahan, the Lansdowne prop who lost his life after an accident at the ground

W. E. CRAWFORD.

Ernie Crawford,
captain of the club

The young man's brothers were sent for: Edgar travelled up from Athlone, but Charles was on his way home from Limerick, where Dolphin had played Bohemians in a Munster Senior Cup match. It wasn't until he arrived in Cork that he heard the terrible news; a friend drove him up to Dublin.

Hanrahan remained conscious throughout Saturday, although paralysed from the neck down. At 9.30pm he told witnesses that his injury was due to a head-to-head collision. 'He attributed no blame to any person,' a doctor told a subsequent inquest, 'and considered it was purely accidental'.

On Sunday morning he slipped into a coma, and died around four o'clock that afternoon, almost twenty-four hours after the fatal incident. He is the only sportsman to die as a result of an injury received in Lansdowne Road.

An inquest was held on Monday at which successive witnesses testified as to the sporting nature of the game. 'I am satisfied that the game was played in an absolutely clean manner', said referee Bell, 'The incident came at a clean, ordered scrum.'

Edgar formally identified his brother, Brian Fitzgerald Hanrahan, and the coroner, Dr Mortimer Walters, ruled that the death was 'due to a fracture of the spine, accidentally received during the course of a football match'.

Edgar then thanked everyone for the expressions of sympathy and told the court 'the whole thing was a most unfortunate accident, of that I am satisfied'.

Hanrahan's funeral took place the next day, following 9am mass in Haddington Road church. His team-mates carried the coffin and the chief mourners were his brothers, and cousins D. and V. Fitzgerald. The attendance was 'enormous', with players from every club in the city and from all four provinces, especially Munster. There was also a strong turn-out of swimmers, a sport at which Hanrahan excelled, as he did at hockey and tennis. He was buried at Dean's Grange cemetery in Co. Dublin.

There was no stomach for sport that week. Several matches were postponed, and a shocked Charlie Hanrahan pulled out of the Ireland team that would play in Wales the following weekend. The Leinster v

Munster junior interprovincial, for which Brian Hanrahan had been selected to play against his native province, was called off.

A poem was published in the following weekend's *Sunday Independent*, penned by Kevin M Collins of Sandymount. Entitled '*In Memoriam*', it was dedicated 'to B. F. Hanrahan 3/3/28'

Jack Arigho (front row, right) appears in this 1925-26 photo of the Lansdowne 3rd XV

We know not when our threads shall snap
When we must cross the borderland
Yet know we well whate'er mishap
'Tis as the source of wisdom planned.
Though hearts may swell when virile youth
Is stricken down on sudden death
Forget not that emblazoned truth
'All sorrows cease, with carnal breath'
Age cannot set its servile zeal
Or sorrow blanch those youthful hairs
All human griefs no more to feel
Serene, he sleeps, secured from cares.

E. O. DAVY

Hanrahan's teammates went on to win the Leinster Senior Cup, and his brother Charlie – who had pulled out of Ireland's trip to Wales the following weekend – returned to become a regular member of the Irish front row for the next four seasons. He ended with twenty caps, was a selector of the successful sides of the late 1940s and IRFU president in 1954-55. The laws of rugby pertaining to the front row were changed to ensure front-rows came together in a controlled manner and have undergone several changes since to reduce the chance of catastrophic injury and death.

LANSDOWNE: W.E. Crawford; E.J. Lightfoot, G.P.S. Hogan, M.P. Crowe, J.E. Arigho; T.A. O'Reilly, E.O'D. Davy; J.C. Bermingham, F. Conroy, M.J. Dunne; J.D. McClelland, J.E. McEnery; B.F. Hanrahan, T.O. Pike, W.W. Rossiter

DUBLIN UNIVERSITY: H.E. Knott; M. Dee, J.C. Cherry, M.E. Cussen, J.C.D. Hewat; J.J. Grealy, C.E.G. Nunns; R.StJ Lyburn, A.McM. Buchanan, R.E. Pike; H.C. Dixon, J.B. McGuire; V.J. Pike, H.V. Tighe, J.R. McDonnell

PLAYER'S CIGARETTES.

C. J. HANRAHAN. IRELAND

Top: Eugene Davy, another member of the celebrated Lansdowne backline of the era
Bottom: Charlie Hanrahan, brother of Brian who made a frantic dash to be at his bedside

1922-1939

The
Bateman
Cup
creates
club
legends

After robbing the game of dozens of young players, the First World War had one positive impact on rugby in Ireland. Dr Godfrey Bateman had lost two sons on the Western Front, both of whom were keen sportsmen. Arthur was the most noted, winning two cricket caps before the war interrupted play, and was also a prominent rugby player at Trinity, where he studied medicine. He served in Flanders in the Medical Corps, but was shot and captured at the battle of Ypres and died in enemy hands. In memory of their sporting sons the Bateman family presented trophies to be competed for in swimming, football and rugby.

The Bateman Cup for rugby was a novel competition, originally played for by the winners of the senior cups in Munster, Leinster and Ulster, with Connacht joining in later. It became a highly prized trophy, although there were a couple of occasions when it proved impossible to fit the games in at the end of the season and it remained uncontested.

The first season saw the withdrawal of Ulster champions Instonians, but Lansdowne and Cork Constitution played out a good final in front of a large crowd at Lansdowne Road, with the home side winning 6-5. The tournament was usually seeded so the Leinster and Ulster sides avoided each other in the semi-finals, which were played on a Friday evening in early April, with the final the following day. For the first six years it was the preserve of the Dublin and Belfast clubs, with Bective Rangers winning twice.

In 1928 a new name was notified to headquarters as the Munster entrant for the competition: the Young Munster club from Limerick city. 'Munsters' were founded in 1901, and had only been awarded senior status in 1921. They won the Munster Junior Cup in 1927 and the Senior Cup by beating Cork Con the following March.

Once again, the Ulster champions, Instonians, had withdrawn, and there was much harrumphing in the press that this had 'robbed the Bateman Cup of much interest'. Instonians pulled out of the competition for several years, complaining bitterly that playing on consecutive days 'was not calculated to enhance the prestige of Irish rugby.'

By this time Connacht had joined in, and Galwegians played the Limerick side on the Friday night. In front of a tiny crowd Young Munster

The 1928 Young Munster team that won the Bateman Cup: STANDING: J. Gubbins (coach), G.J. Killeen, J.F. McNeice, M.J. King, C. St George, F Garvey, J.C. Casey, J.J. Connery, BM Nelson, MIDDLE: H. Raleigh, M. Cosgrave, M.J. O'Flaherty, A. Neilan (capt), G. Griffin, J. Brennan, P.J. Deegan, P. O'Callaghan, FRONT: M.D. Sheehan, J.J. O'Dea (INSET: unknown)

won 17-0, with their powerful pack giving a strong display, but *The Irish Times* regarded their backs as 'not as clever as those of Lansdowne'.

The final was an exciting game – 'about the best ever played in the competition', said the papers – and a deserved win for the visitors. 'In the success of the Southern team there was not a semblance of a fluke', said the *Times*, suitably contrite for its dismissive preview, telling its readers that it was a 'meritorious and highly deserving victory'.

Lansdowne were without Morgan Crowe in their star-studded backline, but still possessed enough firepower to repel these invaders. Early in the first half Lansdowne's Jack Arigho, playing out of position in the centre, kicked the ball across field, where Young Munster's Joe McNiece gathered and set off on a determined run. Cutting inside, he dodged internationals Ernie Crawford and Ned Lightfoot to cross for a try. Midway through the second half Mick O'Flaherty fielded a kick ahead and ran the ball back for the second Young Munster try. Crawford kicked a penalty for Lansdowne from an awkward angle, but despite frantic late pressure the game ended 6–3 to Young Munster. Godfrey Bateman, himself from Cork, was delighted to present the trophy to his fellow Munstermen.

The *Irish Independent* was also full of praise:

'*In winning the premier trophy of Irish rugby, the Limerick club have laid low the bogey of years standing. No longer can it be said that Munster rugby belongs* to the "Kick and Rush Order".'

The triumph was hailed by a parade and bonfires in Limerick, and a memorable ballad which is still sung lustily today. The fifteen men became folk heroes and names such as Charlie St George, Phonie Nealon and Danaher Sheahan are still spoken of reverently in the city:

Now there were Bohs in red, UCC,
Garryowen the boys in blue,
With Sundays Well, 'Twould be hard to tell
What the Dolphin boys would do,
And Cons all white made a right good fight
In the final well they showed,
But they all gave it up, for the Bateman Cup
Was won by the Yellow Road.

Perhaps smarting from the shock of defeat, Lansdowne went on to win the next three Bateman Cups as they completed an unprecedented five in a row Leinster Senior Cups. It was a glorious era for the club, the only sad note being the death of its founder H.W.D. Dunlop in 1930.

On two occasions in the 1931 season the club supplied Ireland with its entire three-quarter line of Jack Arigho, Eugene Davy, Morgan Crowe and Ned Lightfoot, a feat only matched by two other clubs worldwide.

Still performing at full-back was Ernie Crawford, Ireland's No.15 for most of the 1920s, while the half-backs of Sarsfield Hogan and Tommy O'Reilly were highly-rated too. O'Reilly would surely have been capped but for the fact his career ran alongside those of Mark Sugden and Paul Murray. Also squeezing into that side was Ham Lambert, who won Bateman medals in 1929 and 1931, and a couple of caps before a knee injury ended his playing career.

In 1938 Young Munster qualified for another crack at the cup. They had won the first Munster Senior Cup final to be played at the new Thomond Park, beating University College Cork by a drop goal to a try, and still had two survivors from a decade before, Danaher Sheahan and Tommy Hickey.

Munsters again beat Galwegians in the semi-final, by 11-0, but lost out by 13-6 to University College Dublin the following day. It was the third successive win by a different university and the fourth third-level team in all to win the competition.

The last Bateman Cup final was in April 1939, when Blackrock College from Dublin beat North of Ireland. The competition was not played during the Second World War, when petrol shortages made travel difficult and expensive, and was not restarted afterwards, despite several attempts to do so.

1928 BATEMAN CUP FINAL TEAMS

YOUNG MUNSTER: M. King; N.J. O'Flaherty, M.J. Cosgrave, P. Deegan, J. McNeill; J.J. O'Dea, M.A. Sheahan; C. St George, F. Garvey, A. O'Neill; H. Raleigh, T. Hickey; J.J. Connery, J. Killeen, J. Casey

LANSDOWNE: W.E. Crawford; E.J. Lightfoot, G.P.S. Hogan, J.E. Arigho, E. Taylor; E. O'D. Davy, T.H. O'Reilly; J.C. Bermingham, E. Conroy, M.J. Dunne; J.E. McEnery, J.D. McClelland; T.O. Pike, J.S. Synge, J.J. Winters

Referee: Mr W. Harland (Ulster)

BATEMAN CUP WINNERS

1922 Lansdowne

1923 Bective Rangers

1924 Queen's University

1925 Bective Rangers

1926 Dublin University

1927 Instonians

1928 Young Munster

1929 Lansdowne

1930 Lansdowne

1931 Lansdowne

1932 Queen's University

1933 not played

1934 not played

1935 North of Ireland FC

1936 University College Cork

1937 Queen's University

1938 University College Dublin

1939 Blackrock College

CHAPTER 16

1948 The Golden Age of Kyle and Mullen

The Grand Slam and all that

The funny thing about the 1948 Grand Slam was that nobody called it a Grand Slam for years afterwards. The only media reference to the term at the time would have been found in the Contract Bridge column, and it wasn't until 1966 that *The Irish Times* used it about rugby's international championship, when Paul McWeeney needed to explain that the term meant four victories in one season. It was more than twenty years after the event that Edmund Van Esbeck used the expression in the context of Karl Mullen's all-conquering team of 1948.

International rugby had resumed with a series of unofficial matches the winter after the Second World War finished, all of which Ireland lost. The programme notes for the Ireland XV v French XV game in January 1946 described a young Queens' student who was selected at out-half:

'The discovery of the season. He was on the Ulster Schools XV two years ago and proved himself to be in the top class by the great display for Ulster against the Kiwis in November, subsequently continuing that form against the Army. A particularly, straight, strong runner, he looks to have a brilliant future in the game. Aged nineteen.'

The youth was called John Wilson Kyle, although he preferred to be known as Jack. His name still evokes a sparkle in the eyes of old men and he was hailed as the greatest Irish rugby player of all-time in an IRFU poll in 2002.

His international career spanned the next eleven seasons, carving out a reputation as a magical fly-half as Ireland had its most successful spell of the twentieth century, with three championships, two triple crowns and that fabled Grand Slam. The Wales fly-half Cliff Morgan described his skills:

'He was so beautifully balanced and had this gift of lulling opposition into a false sense of security. You'd think he was doing nothing, and yet in an instant he'd pull the ball back, and there he was in a position to score or make a try.'

Kyle was decidedly modest about his talents. 'Like a model with all her good looks there was always a feeling you didn't deserve the praise. You were just fortunate to possess the genes to travel well over the ground – it was a gift,' he said. He told another interviewer: 'I was a bad passer of the ball. I didn't know this until I saw myself on film. Then it was too late to change.'

Kyle's last game, in March 1958, saw him become the most capped player in the world with forty-six Irish and six Lions appearances. He played all his senior rugby for Queen's, graduating from the university in 1951 and working as a GP in Belfast until 1962. He lived in the developing world for the next four decades, working as a surgeon in Indonesia and Zambia until he retired in 2000.

Kyle's first cap for Ireland was against France at Lansdowne Road in January 1947, alongside thirteen other debutants in a side captained by Con Murphy, the only survivor from the 1930s. Among those new boys were Karl Mullen, John Christopher Daly, Jim McKay and Barney Mullan, who would play important roles in the years ahead.

That game was lost, but a fortnight later England came to Dublin and were hammered. Mitchel Cogley of the *Irish Independent* later wrote that 'Ireland's staggering 22-0 win over England at Lansdowne Road in 1947 ... was really the start of Ireland's golden era. I can vividly recall the wonderful work of Ernie Keeffe in the lineouts, Kyle revealing his true greatness for the first time, and the fine play of two wings who are too often overlooked – Barney Mullan and Bertie O'Hanlon.' Until the 43-13 thrashing in 2007, it was easily Ireland's biggest win over the English (modern scoring values would have made the 1947 result 32-0).

JOHN WILSON KYLE

A Kyle-inspired win in Scotland gave hopes of a first Triple Crown for forty-eight years, but as usual Wales would prove an insurmountable barrier. In 1905, 1911, 1926, 1930, 1931, 1936 and 1939 Ireland had gone into the last game with a chance of the Crown. Each time they faced Wales, and each time they lost. Strangely, none were at Lansdowne Road. Ravenhill was the traditional venue for the Welsh game and would continue to be until the West Stand was built at Lansdowne Road in 1954, after which all Ireland's home games were played there for the next half century.

Cartoon tribute to the great Jack Kyle

Programmes from the 'golden era'

A 16-3 defeat to the Australian tourists gave no confidence to the Irish team that 1948 would be any better. The championship started with a New Year's Day game against France, at Stade Colombes. From 1891 until the late 1950s, the order of Irish fixtures was an unchanging rota of England, then Scotland, then Wales. The French fixture was played at the end of the season or, more usually, at the start. For a time it was played on New Year's Day, although 1948 was the last time the sides met on that anti-social date.

It was no easy jaunt to play rugby in the French capital, with many of the team taking three train journeys and two ferry crossings to reach Paris, and at the most difficult time of the year. Having set off on a Tuesday morning, the team arrived at their hotel late on Wednesday, merely dropping their bags before heading off into the Parisian night. 'We stayed at the Folies Bergeres into the wee hours', one recalled. With no discernible effect, too, as a 13-6 win set the campaign off to a fine start with tries from debutant flanker Jim McCarthy, centre Paddy Reid and winger Barney Mullan.

The IRFU took pity on the players when the next trip came around six weeks later – and for almost the entire party it was their first time on a plane. The selection committee of former internationals, Jack Siggins, Ernie Crawford, Charlie Hanrahan, Ned Lightfoot and Larry McMahon, seems to have been unimpressed with the win in Paris and made five changes to the team, dropping scrum-half Ernie Strathdee.

The latter decision created a vacancy as captain, which was filled by Old Belvedere hooker Karl Mullen, like Kyle a medical student. If some of the other selections puzzled many, the elevation of Mullen was inspired. A quiet, determined leader, he ensured his team was fitter than its opponents.

'I was a fitness fanatic. So were Kyle, Jim McCarthy and Bill McKay,' Mullen recalled sixty years later. 'It was terrific. I knew that every time we went on the field we would give 200 per cent. There was trust and mutual respect between us all. A natural bond. We became real friends, a family.' Mullen introduced a call to arms as his team walked through the tunnel onto the field of play: 'This is it boys!', to which the others would reply with the immortal phrase 'boot, bollock and bite'.

'We had a great feeling that we could achieve something that year,' Mullen said. 'We had real talent. It was well balanced and what set us apart was we had a very mobile pack of forwards. Everything was based on pace and movement. We were first to the breakdown, first to the lineout, and we were first to the scrum almost before the referee had blown his whistle.'

'Karl was a wonderful captain. His greatest gift was to let the men play to their full potential,' said Kyle.

On St Valentine's Day they took an 11-0 lead over England at Twickenham, through a try scored by Kyle and two others he created. But an untypical Kyle error let their opponents back in to the game and Ireland hung on for a 11-10 win.

'It was a real bogey ground for us,' said Mullen, 'After that win in London we felt we could beat anyone.'

Two weeks later came the only game at Lansdowne Road in the campaign, the visit of Scotland. Again the selectors made changes, dropping centre Paddy Reid and bringing back Dudley Higgins at full back. One of those brought in was Michael O'Flanagan, a member of a remarkable sporting clan. Only two men have played rugby and soccer for their country, anywhere in the world – and they were both from one Dublin household. Michael and Kevin played rugby for Lansdowne and

C. MURPHY (Lansdowne). One of the three pre-war internationals who retains his place on the Irish XV. Played in all three matches in 1939 and the five war-time "internationals" against the British Army at Ravenhill. At 31 still the soundest man at full-back in the country.

F. G. MORAN (Clontarf). In his ninth season of representative Rugby, he is playing better than ever before on the right wing. Played for Ireland in all international matches in 1937-38-39. At 31 has lost little of his pace and none of his dash.

H. GREER (N.I.F.C.). Played out-half for the Irish XV against the British Army in 1942, the first match of that series, and figures in the other four, either as out-half or centre. Always a great tackler, his attack was not up to the same standard until this season when he has shown a notice-able improvement in this respect. Age 26.

K. QUINN (Old Belvedere). May turn out to be one of Ireland's most brilliant attacking centres. Played on the 'cup-winning Old Belvedere teams in 1942, '43, '45; was injured before 1944 final. Was on the Irish XV against the British Army in the last two matches, and has a change of pace which can beat most defences. 22 years of age.

K. O'FLANAGAN (London-Irish). One of the finest all-round athletes of the present day. Has represented Ireland at soccer on many occasions, and, on going to London this winter, has proved a prolific scorer for Arsenal. Champion sprinter and long jumper, he did not take up Rugby until he had left school, and figured in two Leinster Cup finals for U.C.D.; played for Irish XV against British Army in Belfast in 1943. In addition to his speed, is

capable of kicking goals from the touch-line.

J. W. KYLE (Queen's University). The discovery of the season. He was on the Ulster Schools XV two years ago, and proved himself to be in top class by his great display for Ulster against the Kiwis in November, sub-sequently confirming that form against the Army. A particularly straight, strong runner, he looks to have a bril-liant future at the game. Age 19.

D. THORPE (Old Belvedere). Has had a curious Rugby career, for he played for several seasons at full-back for his club with brilliant success, yet had to take second place to C. Murphy in big matches. Succeeded G. J. Mor-gan as scrum-half, but has come to his best only now in that position. Is a cool, clever player, with a strong defence, and a valuable place-kick. 25 years of age.

J. BELTON (Old Belvedere). After figuring on all his club's cup-winning teams, gained his first representative honours last season against the Army, and has gone from strength to strength since. Ideal build for front row, he is an artist at getting the shove on at the right moment, and is also a grand worker and inspiring leader. At 31, is one of the best forwards in the game.

C. MULLEN (Old Belvedere). Has made a remarkably rapid advance since first attracting attention in last season's cup final by his successful hooking. Now he is far more than a specialist, being one of the keenest men on the ball in the pack. He is very solidly built and strong for his 19 years.

M. R. NEELY (Royal Navy). A surprise choice for the final trial. He was a member of the 1942 Irish pack abroad, has been playing well for the

BY TICKET ONLY

In connection with the Irish XV v. English XV Rugby match on the 9th February, it has been decided by the Committee of the I.R.F.U. to issue tickets for admission to the ground (as distinct from stand tickets), as it is felt that this will facilitate the flow of the crowds through the turnstiles and relieve congestion at Lansdowne road. No cash will be taken at the turnstiles under any circumstances.

These season tickets will shortly be on sale throughout the country and at the leading travel agencies in Dublin, and the public will be well advised to purchase their tickets at an early date.

5

Above: 1946 programme notes alert the rugby public to a brand new star
Bottom: The Ireland team that beat England at Lansdowne on 8 February 1947: BACK ROW: Jack Siggins (touch judge), D. Hingerty, C. Callan, E. Keeffe, J.W. McKay, M.R. Neely, J.C. Daly, M. Allan (referee), SEATED: J. Harper, J.D.A. Monteith, B. Mullan, C. Murphy, R.D. Agar, B. O'Hanlon, K. Mullen; FRONT: J. Kyle, E. Strathdee

football for Bohemians before Kevin joined Arsenal after the war. The Scotland game was to be Michael's only rugby cap, to go with the single one he earned for football two years earlier.

The teams trained the day before in Trinity, with selectors McMahon, Lightfoot and Crawford putting the Irish through their paces in those pre-coaching days. Kyle and Hugh de Lacy spent a lot of time working on establishing an understanding that had been weak at Twickenham.

The next day the Irish players made their own way to the ground, Mullen on the Number 11 bus from his parents' home in Drumcondra. On one international day he left his kit on the bus, but all was well that day.

President Sean T. O'Kelly was unwell, and no other government minister could be prevailed upon to perform the pre-match greeting of the teams, so the ceremony was dropped. There was a minor incident at the back of the East Stand at the Havelock Square end when two streams of spectators crammed into one gap, creating some crushing. Several supporters fainted and were carried to the touchline seats to recover.

Above: Barney Mullan goes over for a try against Scotland in 1948 **Right:** Paddy Reid, one of the characters of the Grand Slam team

The Irish team had a poor opening half, with the Scottish defence resolute and their forwards matching their powerful Irish counterparts. Mullen's pack weighed an average of thirteen-

The Irish team that
beat Wales in 1948

and-a-half stone, considerably heavier than previous sides – Horsey
Browne was considered a freak at twelve stones even as late as the 1920s.
They were a renowned scrummaging unit and masters of the tactical
wheel.

Ten minutes into the second half, McKee shook off a tackle and cut into
the Scots 25. The North centre threw a long pass to Barney Mullan,
missing out O'Flanagan, and the winger's speed saw him complete the
score in the corner

The Scots had a great chance to equalise from a penalty almost in front
of the posts, 35 yards out, but the chance was missed. Shortly afterwards
Karl Mullen got a lovely heel outside the Scots 25 and a little piece of
magic from Kyle completed the scoring, as writer Ulick O'Connor
recalled:

'.... almost as the ball left the scrum-half's hands to go into the scrum, Kyle's
feet twinkled into top speed. He took a crisp pass from Hugh de Lacy and ran in
between the fly-half and centre to place the ball under posts. There wasn't an iota
of a swerve or jink'.

Kyle loved playing at Lansdowne Road:

'There was something about the surface: I don't know whether you can talk
about springy turf or not but you could almost glide over it. I certainly liked that,
and the atmosphere. In the old days there were touchline seats so the crowd was
just a matter of a few yards away from you. And you could see the expressions on
their faces. It made for a terrific atmosphere that we all enjoyed.

The result ensured that Ireland won the championship – the first time
that had been secured at Lansdowne Road – and meant that victory in
the last game, against Wales at Ravenhill, would clinch the Triple Crown

Irish Rugby Review

1/-

TRIPLE CROWN SOUVENIR
1948 – 1949

The *Irish Rugby Review* annual celebrates more glory

too.

The selectors had taken note of the struggles in the backline, and Reid was recalled at centre for O'Flanagan and Ernie Strathdee back at scrum half instead of de Lacy. The Ulsterman had a better understanding with Kyle and his power and strength was adjudged more crucial against the Welsh than de Lacy's superior passing.

In front of a dangerously packed Ravenhill, Ireland and Wales shared the first half, with a try apiece by Barney Mullan and Bleddyn Williams.

Early in the second half, Wales had a scrum on their own 25, but the ball went loose and Bertie O'Hanlon kicked the ball ahead. Welsh full-back Frank Trott was unable to gather and the two London Irish forwards, prop J.C. Daly and flanker Des O'Brien charged ahead in a race for the ball as it bobbled through the in-goal area. Just short of the dead-ball line Daly won the race and touched down for an epic try. Legend has it that, as they trotted back, Daly turned to O'Brien and said 'Jaysus, if Wales don't score again I'll be canonised'.

Kyle talked with affection of the loose-head from Cobh: 'I changed next to him that game. He thumped one fist into another and shouted: "I'm mad to get at 'em." We all thought Jack was a bit mad.'

The Irish pack was utterly dominant and Wales never looked like scoring thereafter. At the final whistle Daly's jersey was rent from his back and torn to shreds. The teams had dinner together and went their separate ways, some to a dance at Queen's, after which a group were arrested after a late-night contretemps with an Orange flute marching band.

On their return to Amiens Street Station in Dublin next day, Daly was reputedly whisked away by a mystery woman in a sports car, and failed to appear for a week. It cost him his job. Reid and Daly never played for Ireland again, making the, at the time unforgiven, decision to play professional rugby league with Huddersfield.

The autocratic and strictly-amateur IRFU also clamped down on players talking publicly about their great achievement. 'We were not allowed to give interviews to newspapers or the radio,' said Kyle. 'It was frowned upon because you were a team, not an individual.'

The Grand Slam was to prove an elusive prize to recapture. 'We didn't realise at the time it was so special,' said Kyle many years later. 'We certainly didn't think we'd be the only Grand Slam winners last century, we thought plenty of other teams would do it, but we have been dining out on it ever since.'

● ● ●

Ireland took more than sixty years to do the Grand Slam again, but Mullen and Kyle's team collected a few more honours over the next three seasons.

The Triple Crown was claimed in 1949, again after losing the first game of the season in Lansdowne Road, this time to France.

The visit of England two weeks later saw a huge improvement, despite the selectors receiving a lot of criticism for making just one change. Ernie Strathdee, who had been dropped by Ulster, was recalled, a move that allowed Kyle to play to his strengths.

The team was arguably stronger than the Grand Slam fifteen; in the backs the loss of Reid was more than compensated by the arrival of Noel Henderson in the centre, while the brilliant Bective full-back George Norton was hailed as the best in his position in the championship that season, and a top class goal-kicker to boot.

In its essence however, it has the same: 'a great pack of forwards, a brilliant out-half and a remarkable spirit and stamina by the whole team', according to Paul McWeeney. Eight men – McKee, O'Hanlon, Kyle,

Scrum-half Ernie Strathdee formed a deadly partnership with Queen's team-mate Kyle

Mullen, Nelson, McKay, O'Brien and McCarthy – played in all six games of the back-to-back triple crowns

Uniquely, Ireland fielded two clergymen, Presbyterian minister Strathdee and Catholic priest Tom Gavin, and a photo of the pair together adorned the front pages of many newspapers at home and abroad.

The game was a grim affair, but the press hailed Ireland for having a plan and sticking to it to the end. Facing into a stiff breeze in the first half, Kyle kicked whenever he got the ball.

Ireland totally outplayed England up front, with McKay and McCarthy in the back row quick off the mark to smother any English possession. Des O'Brien was dominant in the line-outs, and won praise for his skill in being at the right place at the right time.

All but one of the scores came in the second quarter of the game. First Norton landed a penalty before Clive Van Ryneveld crashed through three tackles to score near the posts, to give England a 5-3 lead. Van Ryneveld was the son of a South African international and was in England as a Rhodes scholar. On his return home he played nineteen cricket tests for his native land.

Norton kicked another penalty, a tricky one in a swirling breeze. Ireland's first try came just before break, after Kyle started the attack with a break in midfield. He passed to McKee who made more ground before giving a long pass to McKay who sprinted along the left touchline. O'Hanlon, at his shoulder all the way, took the pass just short of the line and scored in the corner.

With a half-time lead of 9-5, the second half policy became even more kicking, this time to ensure the English were pinned back in their own half. It was conducted with such ruthless efficiency that England rarely got within range.

Barry Nolan in the *Irish Independent* reported that Kyle had 'one of his great days when every pass was taken at top speed, and the occasional cut through got the opposing defence into a tangle. He originated both the tries, and his kicking was most shrewdly done. His defence covering was masterly, for invariably he was in the right spot to save the occasional awkward situation with a tackle or a pickup from the feet of the English forwards.'

An attritional second half was almost devoid of incident, but just before the end Kyle created another opening for McKee to break through Holmes's tackle to score near the posts.

The Scotland game saw a glittering debut of another man destined to join the pantheon, Noel Henderson of Queen's. Two tries by McCarthy secured a 13-3 win. The Welsh were again the final barrier, and to claim the Triple Crown needed a win in Swansea, where Ireland hadn't prevailed since 1889. Again McCarthy scored a try, converted by Norton for a famous 5-0 victory.

The 1950 season saw just one win, over Scotland, but another championship was secured in 1951 after narrow wins over France (9-8) and England (3-0).

The victory over France was the first at Lansdowne since 1924, while the England game saw the ground attendance record broken when forty-four thousand people turned up. George Norton was carried off with a dislocated shoulder after thirteen minutes of the game in Murrayfield, forcing Ireland to play with fourteen men in those pre-replacement days. Another narrow win resulted, by 6-5. The final game, in Cardiff, finished in a 3-3 draw after a thrilling solo try by Kyle.

'There's never been a finer player,' Mullen said. 'He had everything.'

A souvenir of the Triple Crown

IRELAND v SCOTLAND 1948 TEAMS

(players in **bold** played in all four games)

IRELAND: J.A.D. Higgins (Civil Service NI); **B.R. O'Hanlon (Dolphin), W.D. McKee (NIFC)**, M. O'Flanagan (Lansdowne), **B. Mullan (Clontarf); J.W. Kyle (Queen's University)**, H. de Lacy (Harlequins); J.C. Daly (London Irish), **K.D. Mullen (capt., Old Belvedere), A.A.M. McConnell (Collegians); C.P. Callan (Lansdowne)**, J.E. Nelson (Malone); **J.W. McKay (Queen's University)**, D.J. O'Brien (London Irish and Old Belvedere), **J.S. McCarthy (Dolphin)**

SCOTLAND: W.C.W. Murdoch; T.G.H. Jackson, J.R.S. Innes (capt.), C.W. Drummond, D.D. Mackenzie; D.P. Hepburn, W.D. Allardice; S. Coltman, G.G. Lyall, I.C. Henderson;

H.H. Campbell, L.R. Currie; W.I.D. Elliott, W.P. Black, R.M. Bruce

Referee: C.H. Gadney (England)

IRELAND v ENGLAND 1949 TEAMS

(players in **bold** played in all three triple crown games)

IRELAND: G. Norton (Bective Rangers); M.F. Lane (UCC), W.D. McKee (NIFC), T.J. Gavin (London Irish), **B.R. O'Hanlon (Dolphin); J.W. Kyle (Queen's University), E. Strathdee (Queen's University); J.T. Clifford (Young Munster), K.D. Mullen (capt., Old Belvedere)**, A.A.M. McConnell (Collegians); C.P. Callan (Lansdowne), **J.E. Nelson (Malone); J.W. McKay (Queen's University), D.J. O'Brien (London Irish and Old Belvedere), J.S. McCarthy (Dolphin)**

ENGLAND: W.B. Holmes; D.W. Swarbrick, L.B. Cannell, C.B. Van Ryneveld, R.D. Kennedy; N.M. Hall (capt.), G. Rimmer; T.W. Price, A.P. Henderson, M.J. Berridge; J.T. George, G.R.D. Hosking, D.B. Vaughan, V.G. Roberts, J.M. Kendall-Carpenter

Referee: R.A. Beattie (Scotland)

RESULTS 1947-51
HOME GAMES IN CAPITALS, away in lower case, **Lansdowne Road in Bold**

Opponents:	England	Scotland	Wales	France	
1947	**WON**	won	lost	LOST	
1948	won	**WON**	WON	won	*Grand Slam*
1949	**WON**	won	won	**LOST**	*Triple Crown*
1950	lost	**WON**	LOST	drew	
1951	**WON**	won	drew	**WON**	*Championship*

CHAPTER 17

E ven after rugby became the sole occupant, the stadium that was conceived as primarily a running track continued to host small scale athletics meetings, although races were no longer run on a shingle path, but on grass.

The annual Garda sports and Boys Brigade sports day were regular events, while the likes of the Dublin Tramway Company and schools sports bodies also used the athletic facilities. A triangular international between Ireland, England and Scotland was held at Lansdowne in 1938.

In the period immediately after the Second World War, athletics was a popular sport in Ireland. Clubs organised attractive meetings and enticed foreign stars to come to Dublin. In 1946 the Clonliffe Harriers club brought over two West Indian sprinters, Arthur Wint and E. Macdonald Bailey to run at College Park. Clonliffe had an energetic secretary with an entrepreneurial streak, and he was soon a familiar figure at the big British meetings, carrying a large bag full of eggs, bacon and butter – rare commodities there at that time of rationing – as he cajoled the stars to run in Dublin.

His name was Billy Morton. He was a Dublin optician, and was to become a legendary figure in Irish sport over the next twenty years as he brought over the biggest names in track and field to his promotions at Lansdowne Road and, later, at Irish athletics' very own stadium.

A good athlete in his day – he set an Irish marathon best time of 2 hrs 48 mins 27 secs in winning the championship in 1936 – he was elected president of Clonliffe in 1941 and became secretary the year after, a post he held until his death in 1970.

Morton travelled with the Irish team to Paris in the spring of 1947, for the International Cross Country championships. On the way back he stopped off in London for a meeting with British team manager and BBC commentator Jack Crump. A deal was struck which would see Sydney Wooderson, a huge star of the sport before the war, race at the Clonliffe Harriers sports.

Wooderson had set an Irish two-mile record at College Park the year before, and his name was widely used in the advertising promoting the meeting, which would be held at Lansdowne Road. Tickets were offered

1947-1957
Morton's enchanted evenings

Track and field stars make a return

CLONLIFFE HARRIERS
(FOUNDED 1886)
"JUNE"
INTERNATIONAL SPORTS
UNDER THE RULES OF THE AMATEUR ATHLETIC UNION, 1881, AND C.E.I.

Nil Desperandum

I.R.F.U. GROUNDS, LANSDOWNE ROAD
MONDAY, 24th JUNE, 1957, at 7.30 p.m.

PROGRAMME · · · SIXPENCE

The Clonliffe Harriers promotions helped to pay for the building of Santry Stadium

at 2/6 for adults, one shilling for boys, while 'Defence forces in uniform are admitted free'.

In the event Wooderson travelled, but did not run due to injury, leaving John Joe Barry to beat Douglas Wilson over the mile. Wint was also ruled out, a disappointment to spectators hoping to see his duel with J.P. Reardon, a rising Irish star over the quarter-mile.

Macdonald Bailey returned to equal the Irish 100 yard record of 10.8 seconds held by rugby internationals Fred Moran and Denis Cussen. Imperial-measured distances such as the 100 yards and one mile were still popular in Ireland and Britain long after they were abandoned for the 100 metres and 1,500 metres distances run at the Olympic Games.

Bailey was a Trinidadian from the village of Hardbargain, who competed for Britain in the 1948 Olympic Games and, when he was past his best, in 1952 when he won a bronze. Wint won Jamaica's first Olympic athletics gold in 1948, over 400m.

Those London games produced a new superstar in women's athletics called Francina Blankers–Koen, better known as 'Fanny'. The thirty-year-old Dutch housewife's chances were pooh-poohed by Crump, but she stunned everyone by winning the 100m, 200m, 4x100m and 80m hurdles. Her haul of four athletics gold medals in women's events has never been equalled.

It was thus an extraordinary coup for Morton that Blankers–Koen agreed to travel to Dublin for a Clonliffe promotion less than two weeks after the games.

There was little women's athletics at the time, and Morton had to advertise in the newspapers for sportswomen to enter the races and take on the Olympic champion.

A Mr Duffy told a meeting of the County Dublin Board of the NACA that Ireland needed to encourage women to take up the sport.

'If athletics would bring the women from the jazz halls I would go "the whole hog" and provide athletics for them. These jazz halls are killing Irish athletics all over the country. Jazzing has become a mental disease, and before long many of our

athletes will be found in the asylum in Grangegorman.'

Women's sport was also strongly criticised by the authoritarian Catholic Archbishop of Dublin, John Charles McQuaid, who railed against women competing in cycling and athletics in his 1952 Lenten Pastoral. Future Olympic gold medallist, Mary Peters, recalled the atmosphere of those times:

'I think it was 1955, or 1956. Maeve Kyle brought a group of us down, and it was quite sensational. Women had never bared their limbs before. There is some RTÉ footage of me high jumping at those sports, with ladies in the stand in their flowery hats, and Eamon De Valera walking past, with his long cane and top hat.'

Blankers-Koen and the other eight members of the Dutch team arrived in Dublin the night before the races, and were entertained in the Mansion House the following morning. Seamus Kelly, writing in *The Irishman's Diary*, captured her vividly:

'A tall, wiry blonde woman with strong capable hands and a vigorous, almost boisterous manner. She was wearing a vivid blue blazer – without lapels and similar in cut to an Irish bawneen jacket – with a bright orange crest on the pocket, over a fawn sweater and grey flannel skirt.'

Her husband, Jan Blankers, was there too. A former police physical education instructor and now coach to the Dutch team, he told *The Irish Times* 'with a grin', that Fanny never allowed her practice to interfere with her housework. Kelly also puzzled at the various nicknames she attracted:

'Flying Fanny, the Flying Housewife, the Flying Dutch Ma, the Dutch Streak, the Blonde Streak, the Dutch marvel etc.'

The evening meeting was masterfully timed to coincide with the Dublin Horse Show, held at the nearby RDS grounds, which brought tens of thousands of people to that corner of the city every August. Such an important event was it that the lead story in that morning's *Irish Times* was that high winds had caused concern at the Horse Show, as ropes became uprooted and tents were in danger of flying away.

Morton got his enormous crowd – estimated at twenty-five thousand

The legendary Billy Morton

(the stadium capacity at the time was thirty-five thousand) – and the crowd got great value for its money. In austere, post-war Dublin, Blankers-Koen provided some rare female sporting glamour. Several reporters were clearly quite taken with her:

'(She is) A delight to watch … tall and slimly built. She has the long, controlled stride of the first-class male runner, yet she is more graceful than any man I have seen on the track. Her pace at the finish leaves her opponents a hopeless task', wrote Paul McWeeney in *The Irish Times*.

She won her heat easily ahead of British Olympian Audrey Williamson, and the final by five yards in 10.8 seconds, equaling her own world record. She got no assistance from the heavy grass track, while there was little breeze to assist her. Behind her trailed English sprinter Dorothy Manley, reprising her second place at the London Olympics; and Joan O'Reilly of Crusaders AC, who played on the wing for the Irish international hockey team. In the 200 yards Blankers-Koen went away at the bend to beat Williamson by ten yards.

The best of the men's races was the mile, won by Dutchman Willy Slykhuis, bronze medallist at 1,500m and 5000m in

London. Slykhuis was given a tough battle by the Irish champion and biggest star of the 1940s John Joe Barry, who stayed on his heels until the last twenty yards when he pulled away to win in 4 minutes 18 seconds.

Two of the field events that night were won by young men who went on to notable careers writing about the sport, among other things. Ulick O'Connor (Donore Harriers) won the pole vault with a mark of ten feet and David Guiney (Clonliffe) threw the javelin 172 feet 6 inches to beat a Dutch entrant.

The 1949 season was a lucrative one for the IRFU, as no fewer than five large meetings were held at their ground: Morton's two-day international meeting in June, and further events in August and September, while Dublin clubs Crusaders and Donore Harriers also got in on the act.

The June meeting again drew twenty-five thousand spectators, and saw one of the finest days in the career of Ireland's John Joe Barry.

Known as 'the Ballincurry Hare', Barry had moved to Dublin and joined Clonliffe after being pursued to a dance hall by Morton. A gifted natural runner, he never set much store by training and the best judges rated him as tactically naïve. His career was short but spectacular, setting world records but blowing his Olympic chance through lack of training and missing out on subsequent Games.

No less than three different US teams were touring Europe in the summer of '49, and Morton persuaded them to depart home from Shannon, calling in for one last meeting at Lansdowne. Other athletes came from Belgium, Norway, Holland and Britain.

There was much hilarity when the announcer asked that 'Miss Mary X report to the Wanderers pavilion, where Mr John Y of the American team, was anxious to meet her.' [the newspaper reports of the time were suitably discreet]. When the announcement was greeted with several thousand derisive whistles, Freddie Moran senior,

'in mildly pained tones, repeated his statement, with the addendum that Mr John Y was Miss Mary X's cousin, invoking a fresh tempest of whistles, as derisive as the first, but with a noticeable counterpoint of scepticism added.'

(The Irish Times)

Barry was entered for the three-mile race, a handicap event where he started at scratch alongside two top Americans, Fred Wilt and Curtis

Stone. The race went at a pace that was 'entirely new to me' wrote Barry afterwards, and stadium announcer Moran – owner of Moran's Hotel on Talbot Street – told the crowd that the two-mile mark had been passed in Irish record time.

The American pair vied for supremacy on the last bend, having dropped Barry six yards back, when Wilt moved out slightly. Barry saw the gap and darted through, and sprinted for the line. He won by twenty yards in a time of 13 minutes 56.2 seconds, thirty seconds faster than the Irish record.

Barry never seriously threatened the four minute mile barrier in his career – for all Morton's hype that he would be the first to do so – and an at times dissolute social life contributed to his early retirement in 1956. He settled in the US, where he had won an athletics scholarship to Villanova, and continued his carousing ways through three divorces. He returned to live in Ireland and died in 1994.

Morton was quoted as saying that 'a good Irishman against a good Englishman in the mile, and there's no stadium in Ireland big enough to hold the crowd'. He got his wish in the mid 1950s when a youngster from Sandymount called Ronnie Delany emerged to take on stars such as Brian Hewson and Derek Ibbotson.

John Joe Barry, known as the Ballincurry Hare

Delany was also on a scholarship in Villanova, and on 1 June 1956 became the seventh man to run the mile in under four minutes, at a US meeting. Three weeks later he was home for the summer holidays, but was carrying a foot injury after being spiked in an 800 metre race in Paris. Morton persuaded Delany to run at Lansdowne against Hewson and, despite a close, disputed, finish, Delany was placed second in 4 mins 7 secs. The pair faced up again in August in the Clonliffe Invitational when he tailed away 14 seconds behind Hewson.

The two defeats could have been disastrous for Delany as the Olympic Council was having one of its frequent spats with the athletics body and his selection for the Melbourne games was in the balance. Happily, Lord Killanin backed Delany and he was selected, and subsequently won the 1,500 metres gold medal – Ireland's only Olympic gold for athletics –

leaving Hewson back in fifth.

Delany was now the biggest name in Irish sport and Morton was all set to cash in. The promoter's dream was to build a track and field stadium at a site in Santry, to the north of the city. Profits from the Lansdowne Road promotions were crucial to the fund and Delany was signed up to run at four separate events there the following summer.

On 24 June 1957, a crowd of thirty-three thousand – the largest for an athletics meeting at Lansdowne – came to see his first appearance on an Irish track since his gold medal win. It produced £6,000 for the fund.

In front of the enormous throng, Billy Morton called out over the PA:

'Can everyone see me?'

'No', came the roar back.

'Because if you can't, I want you to come up to my shop on Monday and I'll fix you up with a pair of glasses.'

Some members of the Ophthalmic Association of Ireland got upset about this blatant breach of the advertising code before they were persuaded that it was a joke.

There had been some controversy before the race when the top English miler Derek Ibbotson pulled out late, but Morton secured Gordon Pirie, who had won the 5,000m silver in Melbourne.

At 8.10pm on a warm evening Fred Moran announced 'The Stadium Mile' and the athletes came out to a thunderous reception.

On the start of the second lap Delany lay fourth of the five contenders, but by the half-mile mark – reached in 2 mins 2 secs – he was last. With 3 mins 10 secs for three-quarters of a mile, a sub-four was clearly not on, with Welsh athlete John Davies leading Cameron (Scotland) and Hewson, followed by Delany and Pirie.

With the bell Delany moved up a gear and the crowd roared their approval. The Irishman moved into the lead, closely watched by Hewson and Pirie. Delany stretched his lead and, despite a brave sprint by Hewson, won by two yards in a time of 4 mins 9.7 secs.

A series of cycle races was also held as part of the programme, and Irish champion Jim McQuaid – father of several leading cyclists of the next generation – won the time trial.

Two days later, there were a mere two hundred spectators at the AAU championships, held in driving rain. The athletes were asked to vote on going ahead that evening or postponing the events for a week, and Delany duly won the 880 yards in a time of 1 min 56 secs.

On 19 July Delany and Ibbotson finally met, at White City in London. The Irishman was boxed in on the final lap, and the English runner broke away to take 0.8secs off John Landy's world mile record. Delany would get a chance to take on Ibbotson at home two weeks later, but first there was the Rehab Invitational at Lansdowne, where he won the 880 yards in 1min 55 seconds.

Twenty-five thousand spectators thronged Lansdowne Road for what would be Delany's last race at the venue, in the Clonliffe/Crusaders Invitational. The Yorkshireman, the only man to beat the Irish champion since Melbourne, shook Delany's hand before the race, saying 'The laddie that wins this race is a good laddie.'

Seven entrants lined up for the Santry Stadium Scratch Mile, with Roscrea College schoolboy Paul Toomey taking the pacemaking role until the half-way mark before being passed by Ibbotson, Delany and promising Englishman Peter Clarke.

Clarke led until the bell, but with the pace flagging, Ibbotson shouted at him three times to up the tempo. At the start of the final fifth lap Ibbotson passed Clarke, and then Delany joined him.

With sixty yards to go Delany made his move and sprinted off the last bend to breast the tape six feet in front in 4 mins 5.4 secs, the second fastest mile run in Ireland and the fastest ever run at Lansdowne Road.

Ibbotson complained the race was run too slowly, playing to Delany's fast finish: 'Coming up to the finish I felt very tired and when Delany came abreast of me he managed to get in front and stay there.'

The Yorkshireman later complained that Billy Morton had ensured the ground staff did not cut the grass too short so that he wouldn't be able to get away from Delany.

Twenty minutes after the race Delany lay prone in the dressing room with a bad attack of cramp, and had to go outside for fresh air, helped by his father and Captain Theo Ryan of Crusaders. 'I was always running confidently and felt in the last lap that I would win', said the Irishman.

In 1958 Morton fulfilled the dream he had nurtured through all the years at Lansdowne. Santry Stadium (it would later be renamed the JFK Stadium and subsequently Morton Stadium) hosted a gala opening, with Morton drawing the best milers in the world to his new track. The great Australian Herb Elliott demolished the world record by three seconds and the first five men all broke the four minute barrier, still quite a feat. The British athletics administrator Arthur Gold told of how he had quizzed Morton closely on rumours that he was paying athletes, contrary to the amateur code. 'Jaysus, no, Arthur', replied Morton, 'We couldn't afford that. I only pay the timekeepers.'

An insight into Morton's methods were given by an American distance athlete, Buddy Edelen:

'After the greeting, Billy got to the point. "Buddy, me lad," he said, "Are ya a betting man?" Buddy said that he was, so Billy explained the way things were. "Buddy," he said, "I can't pay you anything for this race because you're an amateur. But seein' as how you're a betting man," and he paused for effect before pointing to Buddy's suitcase on the floor, "I bet you a hundred quid you can't jump over that suitcase." As the meaning of Billy's wager struck home, Buddy quickly hopped over the suitcase. Morton exclaimed loudly at such a thing, "My God, Tommy, look at that, Buddy just took me for 100 quid!" but being a man of his word, he paid and left. Buddy was 100 quid richer, but he was still an amateur.'

John Joe Barry with American rivals Fred Wilt and Curtis Stone at Lansdowne Road, 1947

Morton died in 1969 after falling into a six foot deep hole dug by workmen for the telephone utility, near Cross Guns Bridge in Phibsborough.

His death robbed Irish athletics of its greatest promoter and Irish sport of its greatest showman.

CHAPTER 18

1958
No warm
welcome
for
Wallabies

Noel
Henderson's
epic try
heralds first
win over a
touring side

I reland of the Welcomes they call it. *Céad Mile Fáilte*. There may not have been the full hundred thousand welcomes for touring rugby sides at Lansdowne Road, but in the first eighty years of international rugby there, teams from the southern hemisphere had always enjoyed their visits and left with a win in their bag.

South Africa won in Belfast in 1906, and at Lansdowne in 1912 (a ten try, 38-0 thrashing), 1931 and 1951. The New Zealanders came first with the Native Team in 1888, and again in 1924, 1935 and 1954, collecting wins every time. Ireland still awaits its first win over the All Blacks.

A side calling itself the Waratahs and made up entirely of New South Welshmen beat Ireland 5-3 in 1927. Ireland awarded caps retrospectively, and almost sixty years later the Australian RFU decided to consider it a full international. Australia returned in 1947, and again won 16-3 against the team shortly to claim the first Grand Slam.

So by January 1958, Ireland was 10-0 down in games against touring opposition. Despite a reasonable season in 1957 (narrow defeats to England and Wales, wins over Scotland and France), the selectors opted to cap six new players against Australia. That three of those were to grow into future captains and major figures in the game shows how the Big Five occasionally got things right, as well as in their immediate mission of selecting a team to beat the Wallabies.

Ronnie Dawson was the new hooker, and marked the occasion with a try – the only one in his twenty-seven games for Ireland. He won the hooking duel with Brown by 18-13, leading the *Times* to report 'he is here to stay'. Bill 'Wigs' Mulcahy made a fine debut – the best scrummaging forward on the field said *The Irish Times*, while he won copious amounts of line-out ball. Noel Murphy had played brilliantly in the final trial and came into the back row. He would recall the game with slightly less fondness however.

It wasn't the greatest Australian side, from the controversial dropping of captain Dick Tooth before the tour began to the five defeats in the internationals. It lost 9-3 in Cardiff two weeks before the Irish game, and was clearly an unhappy party. In his memoirs, *A Life Worth Living*, senior player Nick Shehadie criticised the coach Dave Cowper, saying 'our training was devoid of variety which made it very tedious'.

There was a late change for Ireland as scrum-half John O'Meara was ruled unfit, with Andy Mulligan coming in to partner Jack Kyle, who was equalling Ken Jones's world caps record with his forty-fourth game for Ireland.

The Australians played into a strong, bitter wind in the first half, with the slippery surface also hampering the quality of play. The visitors took the lead in the twelfth minute when Saxon White sidestepped Hewitt and Jack Kyle missed a tackle, leaving left-wing Rod Phelps a clear run to the line. Ireland came back strongly, with chances for Hewitt and O'Reilly before Australia were penalised for offside under their own posts. Cecil Pedlow's kick was poor, but rattled over off an upright.

The score was 3-3 at half time, but just after the restart the game burst into life when Australian prop Shehadie punched Noel Murphy in the jaw. The wing forward was out cold and had to be helped from the field for treatment as the thirty-three thousand-strong crowd roared its disapproval. Henderson missed the penalty when the wind took it off target in the last few yards.

In the *Sunday Independent* next day, Australian journalist Phil Tresidder tried to nail the 'hysterical talk'. The Aussie's view was that Shehadie had 'dealt with' Murphy who had illegally 'worked' him by pulling him down by the jersey from the side of the scrum. 'Shehadie had tolerated this for twenty minutes and had issued due warning to Murphy'.

Shehadie, of Lebanese parentage, later became Lord Mayor of Sydney and was knighted by the Queen. He managed the Wallabies party that toured Britain and Ireland in 1981–82 and was one of the administrators behind the drive to start the Rugby World Cup in 1987. That year he also performed the unveiling ceremony in Sydney of the statue of Queen Victoria that had previously stood in Dublin.

In his autobiography he recounted the incident, and what it cost him:

Top: Irish team that beat Australia in 1958: STANDING: P. Lardner (touch judge), J.A. Donaldson, A.J.F. O'Reilly, P.J. O'Donoghue, W.A. Mulcahy, J.B. Stevenson, W.J. Evans (referee); SEATED: C. Pedlow, N. Murphy, R. Kavanagh, N. Henderson (captain), E. Crawford (IRFU president), J. Kyle, G. Wood, R. Dawson, P.J. Berkery; FRONT: D. Hewitt, A. Mulligan
Above: The match programme

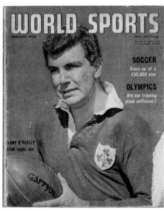

'I got mixed up in an awful incident, one I have never been proud of….

'Noel Murphy, the Irish breakaway, was constantly putting his hand over my eyes so that I couldn't see the ball being put into the scrum. Jim Brown, my hooker, said, "Hang one on him". As we broke up after one scrum, I warned Murphy that if he did it again I would deal with him. When he ignored my warning and did it again, I landed a punch that Muhammad Ali would have been proud of. It laid him out cold on the turf.

'Murphy came to and kept his hands away from my eyes during the rest of the match. However, from the penalty an "up and under" was taken by Ireland, aimed at me. With the forwards charging down, I stood my ground, waiting for the mighty hit, but it didn't come as one of my team-mates interfered illegally with the front-row charging down on me.'

'After the match Dave Cowper said it had been a vicious thing for me to do… He told me that I wouldn't be playing in any further test matches – and he didn't select me.

'One Irish newspaper said the two most hated men ever to come to Ireland were Oliver Cromwell and Nick Shehadie.'

The Australians regained the lead thanks to a fine try by Arthur Summons, who took a pass on the open side and wrong-footed the defence when he cut back to score in the right-hand corner.

The Australians led 6-3, and the Irish pack, with five new caps, looked beaten. But, with ten minutes remaining, they came bounding back. The spur was a fantastic sequence of passes across the back line –

with Tony O'Reilly and new cap David Hewitt to the fore – which went right across the pitch and switched back the other direction, only ending when Andy Mulligan was halted close to the line.

The tempo was upped and the first Irish try came after a scrum when the ball came out to Pedlow. His grubber kick was gathered by Phelps, who passed back to Terry Curley as he was nailed. Curley's clearing kick was blocked by Gordon Wood and Dawson, and the pair fell on the ball, with the latter awarded the score. There was disappointment that captain Noel Henderson's conversion hit the upright,

Shrugging off that setback, the Irish tore back into the game, and with five minutes left Hewitt made the brave call to nip between the centres to intercept a pass from out-half Arthur Summons at half way. Had he missed, a certain Australian try would have been the result. Hewitt ran up to half-way where he off-loaded the ball to Henderson, a pass that was judged forward by some Irish reporters. The captain had been a champion athlete as a young man, but this was the thirty-second of his forty caps and his declining pace had been widely commented on. Paul McWeeney in *The Irish Times* described the situation:

'The Irish captain has sharpened up his speed remarkably recently, but it seemed impossible for him to make fifty yards with the pursuit hot on his heels. With the roar of the crowd ringing in his ears he made forty-five of those yards, curving cleverly out towards the right corner to gain valuable distance and his weight in the final dive over the line did the rest.'

The incident spawned one of the most widely-told of Irish rugby anecdotes, involving the veteran *Irish*

Times photographer George Leitch. 'I took a photo of you as you got the ball from Hewitt on half way,' he told Henderson later, 'and then I ran along the touchline and around behind the dead-ball line with my camera focused on you when you eventually arrived to score'.

Henderson carried on for another season, playing at full-back and passing the captaincy to Dawson. He finished with forty caps, just six less than his brother-in-law Kyle. That was only his third try for Ireland, and he never scored another one. After he retired from playing he became a selector and administrator and was president of the IRFU in 1990-91.

Jack Kyle paid him this tribute: 'I was doubly blessed in that I also had Noel Henderson playing alongside me in the centre. He was a marvellous defender, performing many of my defensive duties and I am not saying that because he was my brother-in-law.'

IRELAND: P.J. Berkery (London Irish); A.J.F. O'Reilly (Old Belvedere), N. Henderson (NIFC, capt.), D. Hewitt (Queens University), C. Pedlow (CIYMS); J.W. Kyle (NIFC), A.A. Mulligan.(Cambridge University); P.J. O'Donoghue (Bective Rangers), A.R. Dawson (Wanderers), B.G.M.Wood (Garryowen); J.B. Stevenson (Instonians), W.A. Mulcahy (UCD); J.A. Donaldson (Collegians), N.A.A. Murphy (Cork Constitution), J.R. Kavanagh (Wanderers)

AUSTRALIA: T.G. Curley; K.J. Donald, S.W. White, J.M. Potts, R. Phelps; A.J. Summons, D.M. Connor; N.M. Shehadie, J.V. Brown, R.A.L. Davidson (capt.); A.S. Cameron, D.M. Emanuel; J.E. Thornett, P.T. Fenwicke, N.M. Hughes

The system of laws known as 'separate development', or *apartheid*, was adopted by the South African government in 1948. International opinion started to swing against the South Africans in the early 1960s when the full repressive horror of the system became obvious.

South Africa were expelled from FIFA in 1961 and from the Olympic Games in 1964 when they insisted on picking an all-white team, leading opponents of the system to the realisation that attacking the symbols of the sports-mad nation was an effective method of highlighting their cause.

The 1964-65 Springboks visit to Dublin was picketed by trade unionists and student groups. By the 1969-70 tour the mood had considerably darkened and the opposition was better organised. British students had been radicalised in the 1968 anti-Vietnam protests, while street protests had returned to Ireland north and south in housing and civil rights campaigns. A popular cause such as anti-apartheid drew wide support across the spectrum.

Other sports, too, were feeling the effects of apartheid. The South African refusal to allow black England cricketer Basil D'Oliveira into the country led to the cancellation of the 1968 tour, and saw future British Labour Party minister Peter Hain cutting his teeth as an activist. He organised a coalition of groups into the 'Stop the Tour' campaign, which targeted the 1969-70 rugby and 1970 cricket tours to Britain, leading to the cancellation of the latter. The rugby tour, however, went ahead.

From an early stage the tour was besieged, with hundreds of arrests of protestors inside and outside the grounds. Drawing pins were scattered on playing pitches and the players were confined to hotels for much of the time by widespread public disorder. At one stage they were smuggled into grounds early, spending up to three hours in the dressing room before the game; the players were reported as being under 'severe strain'. However, only one opponent, Welshman John Taylor, declined to play against them on moral grounds.

The game against Ulster, scheduled for early in the tour, was cancelled by the civil authorities, who had enough trouble at the time without hosting the 'Ambassadors of Apartheid'.

By early December, Chris Laidlaw, the All Black scrum-half, then

1969-1970 'A real ordeal' for The Springboks

Anti-apartheid demonstrators make life difficult for tourists

studying at Oxford, wrote in the *New Zealand Sunday Times*:

'The weirdest rugby tour in history may not last another match. The alien world of Britain is closing in on the Springboks in a variety of ways. The political and social implications of the tour are such that the whole of White South Africa is on trial in the dark mud of Britain's rugby fields.'

The Irish team to play South Africa is watched over by Gardaí on the barbed-wired wall on the railway line. BACK ROW: F. Slattery, R. Lamont, W.J. McBride, K. Goodall, E. Campbell, P. O'Callaghan; MIDDLE: K. Kennedy, B. McGann, M. Gibson, T. Kiernan (capt), S. Millar, R. Young, B. Bresnihan, FRONT: A. Duggan, B. Brown

On their previous tours of Britain and Ireland, South Africa had beaten Ireland five times, losing only in 1965, when they went down 9–6 at Lansdowne Road. That broke a run of twenty-two successive unbeaten tests in these islands: they had lost only one other international and seven club games on their six earlier visits. But by the time they arrived in Dublin in January 1970 they had lost four tour matches, including the test at Twickenham. Rugby writer Edmund Van Esbeck put their failure down to the rise in sophistication of coaches in northern hemisphere, combating the traditional Springbok and All Black trait of capitalising on opponents' error.

As the Lansdowne Road date approached, Irish opponents stepped up their opposition as the Anti-Apartheid Movement mobilised support from the trade unions and Labour Party. The Department of Defence withdrew the Army No 1 Band. Broadcasting unions threatened to black any coverage of the game, with Eoghan Harris, chairman of the RTÉ section of the Workers Union of Ireland, saying 'we have decided not to provide any services'. Other unions said they would ban phones and mail to anywhere that welcomed the tourists, and the Shelbourne Hotel declined the IRFU's booking. A standby arrangement with the non-union Royal Starlight Hotel in Bray ensured the visitors had somewhere to stay.

The match programme was a basic effort after printers had 'blacked' production of the usual edition

The newspaper letters pages were specially extended to include opinion of all shades on the controversial tour, with one teenage law student from Dublin, railing in the letters page of *The Irish Times* against the trade unions for their 'industrial blackmail':

> *'If this tyranny should continue unchecked, our right of freedom of speech and assembly, democracy and consequently the very existence of our society are jeopardised and most likely doomed … To surrender to this attempted totalitarianism is, in effect, to support oppression wherever it is practised and endured.*
>
> *Yours, etc, Michael McDowell'*

McDowell went on to become Minister for Justice, while another future political party leader, Gerry Adams of Sinn Féin, was in Dublin the same weekend and took part in the anti-apartheid protests.

The South African team flew in from Birmingham at 2.24 pm on the Wednesday before the game on flight EI265. Ironically the chairman of the Irish Anti-Apartheid Movement, Professor Patrick Lynch, was also chairman of Aer Lingus. Protests were muted, with barely sixty at the airport, and the few in Bray vastly outnumbered by a 'pro-tour' rally of a hundred schoolboys.

The following day the 'Boks trained at Lansdowne Road, and afterwards their manager, Connie Bornemann, remarked on how pleasant things were, with just two demonstrators, accompanied by a six-year-old boy, outside Lansdowne. Perhaps his ill-chosen comments riled their opponents, as he would not have used the word 'pleasant' about the rest of their stay. The Canadian writer Wallace Reyburn, in his book on the tour, *There Was Also Some Rugby*, started his chapter on the game with the line:

'The most vicious of all the demonstrations was undoubtedly in Ireland.'

The party returned to their hotel, where there was just one protestor, a seventy-two-year-old woman, who stuck her tongue out at the bus and gave it a Nazi salute. She told reporters the absence of other protestors was because 'Ireland was a racialist country'. The tourists later went on an excursion to the ancient Christian settlement of Glendalough in Co. Wicklow, encountering barely half a dozen people on a snowy day.

The papers reported that the IRA had issued a threat against the IRFU and its members:

"The IRFU have been notorious in the past for anti-Irish, snob attitudes, and we take their current action as a blatant insult to the historic Irish nation". However the Provisional Army Council swiftly denied it said any such thing and said the threat was "false and highly irresponsible".'

Protestors marched to Ballsbridge before the game

The Irish political establishment were opposed to the tour, with Taoiseach Jack Lynch and Fine Gael leader Liam Cosgrave speaking out against it, and President de Valera declining an invitation to attend. However, one TD, Dublin North West Fine Gaeler Hugh Byrne, invited Borneman and five Springboks to lunch in Leinster House. As the nakedly opportunist politician posed for photographs, outside a crowd of about sixty threw eggs and sang 'We Shall Overcome'. Other protests saw pickets at the Killiney home of IRFU secretary Bob Fitzgerald, the sawing down of the rugby posts at UCD, and an attempt to set fire to the press box at Lansdowne Road.

The South African journalist A.C. Parker, in a book on the tour, described the mood in the Springbok group:

'*The visit to Ireland, however, was a real ordeal and Dawie de Villiers, in an interview with the veteran rugby journalist Roelf Theunissen of Die Beeld was to admit the things had come close to "breaking-point".*

'*Members of the team were pelted with eggs and cream cakes outside the Dáil and the team's bus assailed after they left their hotel in Bray. During their stay a group of protestors kept up an unholy chant outside the team's hotel which prevented players getting any sleep until 1am.'*

The main protest was held on the day of the game, when between six and ten thousand people marched from Parnell Square on the north side of the city, to Ballsbridge. Many church and political figures spoke at the rally, as did Alec Foster, then seventy-nine years old, who won seventeen caps on either side of the First World War and was also an IRFU selector. Another rugby notable to join the protestors was UCD captain Peter Sutherland.

If you could see their national sport, you might be less keen to see their cricket.

Anti-Apartheid Movement, 89 Charlotte Street, London W.1.

A rare light moment occurred before the game when comedian Spike Milligan, a rugby-fan and well-known opponent of apartheid, was spotted walking towards the game by the protestors. He was asked to join the parade and given a megaphone. The Goon marched along, bellowing 'I'm a fascist bastard! I'm a fascist bastard!' before he was relieved of the bullhorn.

They arrived at Lansdowne Road where 1,200 gardai and 350 stewards were deployed, twice the usual requirement – and that for a crowd of twenty-four thousand, half the size of that which usually turned up for internationals.

Irish Anti-Apartheid Movement chairman Kader Asmal, a law lecturer

at Trinity College, thanked the demonstrators for their orderliness, but that seemed to be the cue for an element to charge the No.1 gate. A couple of protestors climbed the wall and unfurled the Starry Plough, emblem of the Connolly Youth Movement, but Gardaí were on battlements inside and swiftly ended their protest.

The terraces behind the goals were closed, and barbed wire was erected around the pitch. To the consternation of many, the Wanderers clubhouse bar was closed until after the game. The usual match programme was unavailable, having been 'blacked' by union printers, but a single folded A4 sheet, poorly produced, carried the bare details of the teams and no advertising. At the last minute RTÉ decided to show the game on television.

South Africa dropped out-half Piet Visagie and with centre Eben Oliver out injured, Mike Lawless got his first test start for six years. Ireland made a late change when Mick Molloy (who had played a 'storming game' for the Combined Services against the tourists) was injured, and Eric Campbell of Old Wesley came in for what would be his only cap.

The teams changed in the old Lansdowne pavilion behind the North-West Stand, posing for the official team photograph in the tiny garden with Gardaí sitting on the high, barbed-wired wall behind them that ran alongside the railway track. The facilities were starting to show their age, as Willie John McBride remembers:

'We changed in the old wooden hut at the end of the west stand with big old heaters on the wall. We changed there into the one jersey and the one pair of socks we got for the season – if it got torn you got it sewed, and if you lost your socks they charged you 2/6 for a new pair. Nothing changed during my time there. I think they used to give us a cup of tea under the stand before we'd go off.'

The game kicked off and the tourists quickly gained the upper hand over what Parker's tour book called 'an ageing Irish pack', although only Syd Millar (aged thirty-five) was over thirty. Among the three new caps was a twenty-year old UCD wing forward called Fergus Slattery who was to become one of the greatest players in the history of the game, starring on the two epic Lions tours to New Zealand (1971) and South Africa (1974). When he retired in 1984 he was Ireland's most-capped player with sixty-five appearances.

Ireland was forced to defend with grit, with centres Mike Gibson and Barry Bresnihan tackling like demons and No 8 Ken Goodall standing out in a struggling pack.

Inside the ground there were minor scuffles and sporadic protests by those demonstrators that got into the ground. Ireland hooker Ken Kennedy was hit in the back by a bottle thrown from the East Stand while throwing the ball into the line out, although the perpetrator later insisted he was aiming for the South African No 2. The bottle-thrower's protest was at 'certain aspects of his play', not his country's racial policies.

Against the run of play Ireland took the lead in thirteenth minute. Gibson intercepted a rash pass inside his own half and passed to Lansdowne right wing Alan Duggan, who scored at the posts. Almost immediately Henry De Villiers landed a forty-yard penalty to cut the lead to 5-3.

That was still the score with ten minutes to go, when Ireland were awarded a scrum five yards from their own line. Charlie Cockrell won the strike against the head and as the pack wheeled to the left, Piet Greyling fell on the ball for a try and de Villiers' conversion gave the Boks an 8-5 lead.

Deep into injury time, Springbok centre Mannetjies Roux had possession on half way, but was tackled and threw a hospital pass out to the left wing. Duggan 'joyously intercepted' and ran into the opposition 25 before cross-kicking. Flanker Jan Ellis was first to the ball and a ruck formed in front of the posts. When the ball didn't emerge, Scottish referee Eric Grierson awarded a penalty in front of the posts. Kiernan (who had missed from thirty yards a few minutes earlier) landed the kick to tie the scores at 8-8, and Grierson immediately blew the final whistle.

There was sympathy from all sides for the tourists, who were 'only deprived of victory by sheer robbery', according to Paul McWeeney in *The Irish Times*. Welsh rugby reporter J.B.G. Thomas agreed the 'Boks were 'robbed', while Barry Glasspool in the *Johannesburg Sunday Times* insisted there was no more than three minutes to be added:

'To have had the game snatched form their grasp in this "long-playing" second half of unbearable tension is in keeping with the incredibly bad luck that has dogged the Sixth Springboks in this tour of Britain.'

The Springboks' sense of grievance would not have helped their mood when they were confronted with more demonstrations that night at the Royal Hibernian Hotel in Dawson Street, where the IRFU hosted the traditional post-match dinner for both teams.

There was a bomb scare at the hotel when a brown paper parcel was found to contain a loudly-ticking alarm clock, and the atmosphere worsened as a large crowd gathered. That weekend in Ballsbridge, Sinn Féin was holding the famous *ard-fheis* at which the party split into 'official' and 'provisional' wings. Its activists boosted the crowd in the city centre.

Dublin-based protestors complained later that the trouble was caused by northerners who came prepared by wearing helmets. Some of these were members of the People's Democracy, a socialist republican grouping whose leaders included MP Bernadette Devlin. *The Irish Times* complained that the march 'brought a whiff of the northern air to the politics of the capital, and not a few of the more experienced practitioners of marching'.

Devlin wasn't impressed with the IAAM's tactics, and told reporters that she had come down to Dublin, 'because these fucking demonstrators aren't being tough enough with these fucking Springboks.'

The MP went on to *The Late, Late Show* on RTÉ television that night to protest about a garda baton charge and what she described as the force's brutality. She read aloud an individual garda's badge number and he later successfully sued her and RTÉ for libel.

At the hotel a petrol bomb was thrown, hitting a lamp-post. Inside an IRFU official told the guests that the protests were not really representative of Irish society.

After the dinner the crowd shouted abuse as the South Africans left.

One Irish player was reported to have said to a Springbok mate 'If this crowd of weird bastards touch us I'll tear them to pieces' as they left arm-in-arm.

The Gardaí had to seal off Molesworth Street so the team bus could make the two hundred-yard trip up to the Shelbourne Hotel, and it was rained on with bottles, stones and eggs. By now having had several drinks, some of the Springboks grew angry and shouted abuse back in Afrikaans.

There were more ugly scenes outside the Shelbourne, where they spent their last night in Dublin, with chants of '*sieg heil*', 'apartheid out' and 'IRFU – FU' splitting the air. Some of the players came out on to a balcony to sing 'go home you bums' to the tune of 'Auld Lang Syne'.

The Springboks left for Limerick by train the next morning, and were given a warm welcome, with two hundred members of the city's rugby clubs turning out, in contrast to the twenty protestors. After Dublin, the Limerick leg was a respite for the 'Boks, who enjoyed sight-seeing and a banquet at Bunratty Castle before beating Munster 25-9. An anti-apartheid march, led by rugby international Fr Marnie Cunningham, drew 350 protestors.

Perhaps due to the pressure the players were under, it was a dismal tour for the South Africans, losing two internationals and drawing the other two. Of the twenty-five games, fifteen were won, four drawn and five

There was a strong northern nationalist element to the protest, with MP Bernadette Devlin among the throng

Alan Duggan went over for the Ireland try

lost, with the Ulster fixture cancelled. According to A.C. Parker, sports editor of the *Cape Argus*, 'It was something of a minor miracle that the tour went the full distance'.

The week in Dublin was one of the most difficult the tourists endured, wrote Parker, 'yet the crowds in Lansdowne Road and Thomond Park were among the most sporting encountered and in Limerick the 'Boks actually encountered warm friendliness.'

Even so, the tourists were clearly glad to get out of Ireland. Springbok back-row Tommy Bedford said, 'When I got out of the plane at Edinburgh I jumped up and down a couple of times, to feel the good, sane soil of Scotland under my feet.'

The South African rugby team was never able to tour Ireland again until the end of apartheid, but the issue of sporting links with the pariah republic was to rear its head several times through the next two decades. Irish rugby figures and players were to the fore on Lions tours in 1974 (when Syd Millar coached and McBride captained the tourists to a 3–0 series win) and 1980 (managed by Millar, coached by Noel Murphy), sparking debate once more back home. The most vigorous protests took place in 1981, when the IRFU accepted an invitation to send an Ireland touring party. Protests were widespread and the Garret FitzGerald-led coalition expressed its disapproval, reflecting the wider public opinion. Rugby opinion was divided, with strong objections raised by the *Irish Times* correspondent, Edmund Van Esbeck:

'I remember a few of us tried to visit a township in Port Elizabeth in 1980. England captain Bill Beaumont was with us too. But someone at the hotel tipped off the authorities after we left and by the time we got there, each entrance had been sealed off by policemen.

'We were told there would be multi-racial rugby and there wasn't any. There couldn't be because of the laws of the land? The Group Areas Act and the Separate Amenities Act in themselves precluded multi-racial rugby. So instead you had this cosmetic exercise in '81, when Ireland played against the President's Trophy XV or the South African Mining XV. It was a joke. I bitterly opposed that tour and nothing I saw convinced me I was wrong.'

Four Irish players – Donal Spring, Moss Keane, Hugo MacNeill and Tony Ward – opted out on moral grounds, while five others were unable to secure leave or co-operation from their employers. Two quit their jobs so they could join the tour.

After England toured South Africa in 1984 the stream of opponents dried up, and South African rugby was isolated until the end of apartheid in 1992. When the first cabinet of the new republic sat down together, among them were two men who had been in Dublin a quarter of a century earlier: IAAM chairman Kader Asmal and Springbok captain Dawie de Villiers.

And, having been excluded from the 1987 and 1991 Rugby World Cups, the hosting – and winning – of the 1995 event was a powerful signal that South Africa was back in world rugby.

IRELAND: T. Kiernan (Cork Constitution, capt); A. Duggan (Lansdowne), B. Bresnihan (London Irish), M. Gibson (NIFC), B. Brown (Malone); B. McGann (Cork Constitution), R. Young (Collegians); S. Millar (Ballymena), K. Kennedy (London Irish), P. O'Callaghan (Dolphin); E. Campbell (Old Wesley), W.J. McBride (Ballymena); R. Lamont (Instonians), K. Goodall (City of Derry), F. Slattery (UCD)

SOUTH AFRICA: H.O. de Villiers; S.H. Nomis, O.A. Roux, F.D. Roux, A.E. Van der Watt; M.J. Lawless, D.J. de Villiers (capt); J.L. Myburgh, C.H. Cockrell, J.F.K. Marais; F.C.H. du Preez, I.J. de Klerk; P.J.F. Greyling, T.P. Bedford, J.H. Ellis

Referee: T.F.E. Grierson (Scotland)

CHAPTER 20

1968-1971
Soccer
returns

AFTER the 1927 game against Italy, the football authorities decided Dalymount Park was sufficient for their needs, and all home internationals were staged there for the next four decades. There were periodic attempts to bring soccer south of the Liffey, notably after the gates at Dalymount gave way, leading to a crushing incident in November 1952 when Ireland played France. Thirty-five spectators were injured, and further embarrassment was caused to the FAI when the plaster fell off the ceiling in the showers, raining down on the visiting players.

The *Irish Times* soccer writer, Frank Johnstone, came straight to the point:

'Dalymount Park will not do for international soccer matches. This was all too obvious on Sunday ... and it was only the level-headedness of the crowd; the magnificent police work; and sheer good fortune, which prevented a repetition of the 1946 Bolton disaster, in which many people lost their lives'

Johnstone urged the FAI to switch their games to Lansdowne. The soccer body had attempted to so in the past, but the IRFU had refused to allow games to be held on Sundays, which was the traditional day for Ireland's international soccer matches. The original lease from the Pembroke Estate forbade Sunday sport, and the union had to secure permission to eventually lift the ban for some Leinster Senior Cup rugby games in April 1975.

Nothing came of Johnstone's suggestion, and it wasn't until September 1968, forty-one years after the last game, that soccer eventually made its return.

It was the provincial clubs that opened up Lansdowne to soccer, and who would continue to utilise the ground over the next decade. In 1968, Waterford were League of Ireland champions; their home ground, Kilcohan Park, was a modest venue, so when they were drawn to play the European champions, Manchester United, a larger ground became essential. Waterford chairman Don Kennedy liaised with UEFA, the FAI, IRFU and United manager Sir Matt Busby before he was able to announce that the game would take place at Lansdowne Road.

Most European competitions were played at night, but with no floodlights at Lansdowne, the game was fixed for 5.45 pm. United turned up with nine of the team that had won the European Cup at Wembley four months before. Missing were Shay Brennan – who later ended his career with Waterford – and John Aston; their replacements were Francis Burns and Denis Law.

Waterford wanted to charge five shillings admission, but the FAI stepped in and ordered them to charge the going rate of four shillings. The stand seats were priced at ten and twelve shillings. The Waterford gamble in hiring the enormous ground was amply rewarded with a sell-out all-ticket crowd of more than fifty thousand packing the stadium. Hundreds more gained admission by scaling the walls and clearing the barbed wire fence, and at times the crowd threatened to spill out onto the pitch.

Waterford were a talented side, but were no match for United. Law netted his first in the eighth minute, while George Best had 'a perfectly good goal' disallowed in the twenty-fourth. Law rose to head home a Brian Kidd cross after forty minutes, and again eight minutes after the

Above: Waterford was the first soccer club to venture back to Lansdowne Road
Below: Waterford v Man United, 1968 (from *The Irish Times*)

THE IRISH TIMES, THURSDAY, SEPTEMBER 19, 1968   3

EUROPEAN CUP SOCCER SPECIAL

DISAPPOINTING NIGHT FOR THE IRISH

IT WAS a bad night for the Irish clubs in their five-pronged assault on the European Cup competitions last night.

Two League of Ireland and three Irish League clubs were engaged, but only Crusaders managed to avoid defeat when they managed a 2-2 draw with Kamraterna (Sweden) in the first round of the European Cup-win-

ners' Cup at the Oval, Belfast.

League of Ireland champions, Waterford, crashed 3-1 to the holders, Manchester United, in the European Cup at Lansdowne Road, where a capacity crowd of 48,000 saw Denis Law score a hat-trick.

Shamrock Rovers went down to a goal scored two minutes from the end of their Cup-winners' Cup tie

against Randers Freja in Denmark, a deficit, however, they should wipe out in the second leg.

Irish League champions, Glentoran, fell to the Belgian champions, Anderlecht, in the European Cup tie in Brussels, while in the Inter-Cities' Fairs Cup, Linfield had a fruitless trip to Setubal (Portugal) and carry a 3-0 deficit into the return leg.

Hat-trick by Law meant Waterford were never in with a chance

WATERFORD 1   MANCHESTER UNITED 3

IT WAS AS EASY AS THAT! Manchester United, the European champions, came to Lansdowne Road last night; they saw and they conquered a Waterford team that, for all the skill and courage of players like Alfie Hale, Al Casey, Jackie Morley, Peter Bryan and Peter Thomas, were never in this European Cup tie with a chance.

On the lush carpet of grass that was Lansdowne Road, the Red Devils, not quite showing the teamwork that had won them this trophy last May, were sufficiently skilled individually to secure a comfortable first-leg lead and to make their Old Trafford meeting with the League of Ireland champions on October 2nd a mere formality.

It was much more than a Lansdowne road sell-out. The huge all-ticket crowd, swelled considerably by many hundreds more who scaled walls and risked injury on the barbed wire, threatened at times to overflow onto the playing pitch; but somehow or other the referee, Mr. W. I. Mullan, of Scotland, managed to play out time in spite of several encroachments.

Waterford weren't altogether disgraced. Though their limitations were obvious they managed to play some splendid attacking football, particularly in the second half. They did not, however, possess a Jackie Charlton, a Georgie Best or a Denis Law, and try though he might! Alfie Hale just could not pot it alone.

LAW THE MATCH-WINNER

It was the incomparable Law who really settled Waterford's hash. In the eighth minute, after Best had sweeled an unlikely tackle by Vinny Maguire and opened the gap, Law ran through, brushed off

— By —
SEAMUS DEVLIN

Jimmy McGeough were completely out of touch. At all events they contributed little to the well-being of the Waterford side generally and this fact, coupled with Maguire's fatal errors of judgment, left the League of Ireland champions struggling, at least until the second half when, it appears, they decided to have a

out for a corner. But in the eighth minute Law put the visitors in front and the Waterford goal bore a charmed life subsequently.

Best was brilliantly supporting Law; but was himself deprived of this Manchester United trio, Foulkes, Law and Stiles, at Lansdowne Road, last night.

go at Waterford and bore a charmed life subsequently.

shot to the roof of the net. Unfortunately it seems that Kidd was offside.

Thomas saved magnificently from a Law header just on the half-hour; but in the 40th minute was beaten by another headed effort from the same player, who then went on to complete his hat-trick in the 53rd minute. Maguire tried to beat both Law and Best; was swivelled to send a right-footed

Bryan was penalised for an attempted foul on Best almost in the next minute; but Law's shot hit the upright and went wide. Matthew's goal came in the 63rd minute when he picked up after Casey's shot had been blocked and beat Jimmy Rimmer (a substitute for Stepney after 50 minutes).

Hale was unlucky not to have scored six minutes from the end when his header came back off the crossbar with Rimmer hopelessly beaten.

best effort came in the second half. Thomas displayed the odd bit of brilliance but generally the Manchester United defence, with Tony Dunne and Francis Burns outstanding, were well on top and little was seen of John O'Neill or Shamie Coad.

Thomas saved magnificently from

Hale, the Waterford inside-forward, on extreme right, beat a formidable task in trying to beat

One late slip but Rovers must still be fancied to eliminate Danish cup-holders

SHAMROCK ROVERS 0   RANDERS FREJA 1

AFTER A FINE DISPLAY of disciplined and, at times, courageous defence, Shamrock Rovers finally capitulated with only a minute to go at the Municipal Stadium, Randers, last night, when a lucky goal by Gaardsoe gave the latter victory in this European Cup-winners' Cup first leg game.

Judged by any standard, however, the result was an unqualified triumph for the Irishmen's superbly executed defensive methods, and on the evidence of this performance, they must have an outstanding chance of reaching the second round of the competition when the return game is played at Daly-mount park in a fortnight's time.

Even the most partisan Danish supporters, in an attendance of 13,000, must have been pleasantly surprised when, after 89 minutes of fruitless endeavour, they finally succeeded in speeding that all-important late goal. And, typical of the Danes' performance, on a night when they enjoyed 80% of the play territorially and still failed to produce no more than three real chances, the score had a

Round-up of the results

EUROPEAN CUP

First round—First leg—Waterford 1, Manchester United 3; Floriana Valletta 1, Lahden Reipas (Finland) 1; Nendeln 1, A. Ajax Amsterdam 2; A.S.K. Aarhus 1, Le Jeunesse D'Esch (Luxembourg) 0; Dinamo Bucharest 3, Spartak Trnava (Czech) 2; Manchester City 0, Fenerbahce 0; Reipas Lahti 1, Real Madrid 2; Ferencvaros (Hungary) 3, Milan 1; Rosenborg Trondheim (Norway) 1, Rapid Vienna 3; Anderlecht (Belgium) 2, Glentoran 0; B. Eintracht (Austria) 2, Celtic (Scot.) 0; Zurich 1, A. K. Copenhagen 0; Real Madrid 4, Limassol (Cyprus) 0.

EUROPEAN CUP WINNERS' CUP

First round—First leg—Randers Freja 1, Shamrock Rovers 0; Cruzeiros 2, Kamraterna Metselgoep (Sweden) 2; Dunfermline Athletic 10, Apoel (Cyprus) 1; Cardiff 0, Porto (Portugal) 2; U.S. Rumelange (Luxembourg) 0, Slavia Sofia 2; Brann (Norway) 2, Lyn Oslo 1; Parizan Trnava 1, A.C. Turin 0; Slovan (Belgium) 3, Setubal (Portugal) 0.

INTER-CITIES FAIRS CUP

First round—First leg—Olympic (Yugoslavia) 0, Hibernian 3; Basel (Swit.) 2, Hvidovre (Denmark) 1; Juventus (Italy) 3, Stal Mielec; Goztepe Izmir (Turkey) 2, Olympique Marseilles (France) 0; Hamburg 1, Slovan Bratislava (Czech) 0; Hanover 96 (Germany) 3, O.G.C. Nice 0; Sportclub, Vienna 1, Slavia Prague 2; Lingfield 0, Vitoria (Portugal) 3; Standard Liege 0, Leeds

— By —
PETER BYRNE

into operation, that Randers were never able to come up with an effective answer.

You could, perhaps, fault the Danes for not varying their game when it quickly became apparent that the high, speculative cross into the goalmouth cut no ice against a formation in which Smyth was once again at his brilliant best in goal, even after taking the winner's lack of imagination into consideration, however, the Irish men could still claim this as something of a moral victory, for it produce no more than three real chances, the score had a

Those sentiments just about summed up a game which did little to boost the image of Danish football but, the format of present-day European football is such, that any team escaping only a goal down from their away tie has acquitted itself well. And Rovers, despite one or two shortcomings, did just that last night.

The pattern of the game was set early with Rovers bringing back as many as seven players into their penalty area when danger threatened. Lykke, Vonyld and Bodker ranged through virtually unopposed to test Smyth, who was equal to all demands during these early opening minutes. One save from a 20 yard shot by Gardsoe, brought appreciative cheers from the

Professional boxing

COOPER REGAINS TITLE

HENRY COOPER, at the ripe age of 34, fought like a 20-year-old in winning back the European heavy-weight championship for Britain at the Empire Pool, Wembley, last night.

Cooper beat the reigning champion, Karl Mildenberger, of Germany, on a 8th round disqualification. The German was ruled out by the Italian referee, Nello Barovecchio, after Cooper had come away from a clinch with blood streaming from a bad cut over his right eye.

It was the first disqualification in his 62-fight career of the German, and provides an unhappy blot on his record. But the manner in which the fight ended was equally unfortunate for Cooper. He was robbed of the satisfaction of stopping the German on merit or even knocking him out, for, make no mistake, Mildenberger could scarcely have survived the ham-

Soccer: European championship game at Lansdowne Road

IRELAND UNLUCKY IN 2—1 DEFEAT

IRISH ATTACK REPULSED

Lack of penetration lets Italians off the hook

REPUBLIC OF IRELAND ... 1   ITALY ... 2

By
SEAMUS DEVLIN

Rugby

Best international series for decades

JACKLIN, THOMSON ENTER FOR GALLAHER ULSTER

Golf

VICKERS SLUMP

By
PAUL MacWEENEY

HARD STRUGGLES IN SOCIETIES CUP

BRISBANE WORKOUT UNDER LIGHTS FOR LIONS

Ireland not geared for intensive competition

Tennis

interval following some more magic from Best. Law missed getting his fourth when he hit an upright from the penalty spot. Johnny Matthews got a consolation for Waterford when he followed up a shot from Al Casey that had been parried by sub keeper Jimmy Rimmer. The brilliant Alfie Hale could have reduced the deficit to one with eight minutes left when his header came back off the crossbar.

At one stage the United and Ireland full-back Tony Dunne clashed with the tiny Al Casey. The Waterford player lay on the ground in agony. 'Get up, you're OK,' said Dunne, standing over him.

'It's alright for you to say that,' replied Casey, 'but I'm on the 4-to-12 shift in the paper mills tomorrow while you will be out playing golf.'

There was a pitch invasion of local United fans when Law completed his hat-trick. Sir Matt Busby said: 'It was remarkable to see the crowd mob Denis ... a wonderful sight to see one of our players given this reception on a visiting ground.'

Law managed four in the second leg in Manchester, which United won 7-1, while Waterford returned to Lansdowne the following season and lost 3-2 to Turkish side Galatasaray. They were again gifted a fabulous draw in the 1970-71 European Cup, when Glasgow Celtic came out of the hat alongside them.

European Nations Cup

REPUBLIC OF IRELAND versus ITALY

Official Souvenir Programme

PRICE 10P

Monday 10th May 1971 : Lansdowne Rd., Dublin

KICK·OFF 7pm

The fixture was marred by crowd trouble before kick-off, when different factions of the Celtic support clashed behind the goal on the South Terrace, but it was rapidly quelled.

The game was barely a contest, with Willie Wallace scoring from a

Bobby Lennox cross within twenty seconds. Lou Macari scored with a cheeky back-heel after eleven minutes and Celtic were 4-0 up at half-time through two more goals scored by Bobby Murdoch. Wallace completed his hat-trick before being substituted, while Macari scored with a shot from the edge of the area shortly before the end. The 7-0 deficit was insurmountable, although Waterford took a 2-0 lead at Parkhead before losing 3-2.

Other clubs hired Lansdowne for European fixtures over the next thirty-five years, most notably Limerick United in 1980 when they were drawn to play Real Madrid. The League of Ireland side, under manager Eoin Hand, gave the Spaniards – the eventual finalists – quite a fright. Des Kennedy gave Limerick the lead before a disputed penalty allowed Juanito to equalise. The part-timers eventually ran out of steam and Pineda scored the winner towards the end. Switching venue to the other side of the country was highly unpopular in Limerick, and the game proved a spectacular failure at the gate. Just 6,500 fans paid in, and the losses discouraged other clubs from hiring the ground. UEFA competition made a return in the 2004-05 season, when Shelbourne became the first Irish club to reach the third qualifying round of the Champions League. Lansdowne Road was the only suitable ground for their game against Deportivo La Coruña of Spain, and twenty-five thousand fans came along to watch a 0-0 draw.

The FAI first hired the ground for its showpiece domestic fixture, the FAI Cup Final, in 1990. The final was a fairytale affair, with non-league Dublin side St Francis pitted against second division Bray Wanderers, and the biggest crowd seen at a local game for decades – more than thirty-thousand – turned up at Lansdowne to see Bray win 3-0 thanks to a hat-trick by John Ryan. The final continued there until 1997, and again from 2003 to 2006. The last ever soccer game in the old stadium was the 2006 FAI Cup Final, when Derry City beat St Patrick's Athletic 4-3 after extra time.

By the time the ground closed for rebuilding later that year, Lansdowne Road was long-established as the home of the Irish football team, but the FAI had been slow to follow the clubs in hiring the stadium almost forty years earlier. In 1970 Ireland were drawn in a difficult European

Opposite top: Coverage of the 1971 Ireland v Italy match (from *The Irish Times*).

Opposite bottom: Official souvenir programme of the Ireland v Italy match, May 1971.

Championship group with Austria, Sweden and reigning champions Italy, who had also finished runners-up in the Mexico World Cup.

Six months before the game the FAI had already received eighty media applications from Italy, which seemed to provoke debate on moving the game out of Dalymount. FAI general secretary Peadar O'Driscoll told the press:

'*As I understand the position, Lansdowne Road is out as far as Sunday sport is concerned. But, if that is not so, and we can also overcome the problems of our commitment to the Bohemians club in respect of the agreement in relation to Dalymount Park, I have no doubt the council would consider the matter …*'

There was a financial reason, too, to move south of the river. The total gross receipts for the previous ten years' internationals at Dalymount came to £60,000. With twelve thousand seated capacity at Lansdowne that one game could be expected to yield more than £30,000. Even with the rent and other expenses the FAI expected to clear its overdraft of £7,000 and have more than £10,000 surplus.

In January 1971 the FAI met Bohemians to discuss the six-year contract, and came to an 'amicable' – presumably financial – agreement that Lansdowne Road could be used. The difficulty with the Sabbath could not be overcome, so the game was fixed for Monday 10 May with a 7pm kick off. The FAI also booked the ground for a fixture two weeks later to celebrate the association's golden jubilee.

The Italians named a squad of seventeen players, seven from league champions Internazionale of Milan. Two of the players who lost that epic final to Brazil the previous summer were missing – Luigi Riva was nursing a broken foot and midfielder Gianni Rivera had been injured the week before.

The English league season was over, so the Irish squad, almost all of whom played for English clubs, gathered in an end-of-term mood. They stayed in the Montrose Hotel, and trained in the nearby university, UCD, on the Friday before heading off to play golf in Milltown. The *Irish Independent* complained about fifty UCD students who came to watch the training, 'who had nothing to do except give some of the players "the bird".'

There were injury concerns about Tony Dunne (Manchester United), John Dempsey (Chelsea) and Eamon Rogers (Blackburn). Rogers hated flying and got the ferry over on the Friday night, while the new star Steve Heighway also delayed his arrival. He had one more club game that Saturday – the FA Cup Final at Wembley.

Dempsey pulled out on Saturday morning before the team trained at Lansdowne, which was when many of the players got their first sight of the stadium. They returned to the hotel to watch Arsenal beat Liverpool 2-1 after extra time, with Heighway scoring his team's only goal.

The day of the match saw a one-day bus strike in Dublin, adding to FAI concerns about the less-than-expected advance ticket sale. Irish coach Mick Meagan had his own problems, and not just the injuries that had taken out Dempsey and Terry Conroy. It had been seventeen games since Ireland had actually won a match and achieving the dream of qualifying for a tournament was nearly twenty years in the future.

Italian coach Ferruccio Valcareggi was able to name eight of those who played in the 1970 World Cup final, with two more on the bench. In goal was Dino Zoff, who would lift the World Cup himself as Italy's captain in 1982.

The visitors got off to a cracking start, scoring after sixteen minutes through Roberto Boninsegna after a quickly taken free. Ireland recovered well, with a superbly-flighted Eamon Dunphy free kick headed home by Jimmy Conway. Ireland came to dominate the game for long periods, but

Republic of Ireland players singing the national anthem before the European Championship tie against Switzerland in 1975. Left to right: Johnny Giles, Don Givens, Ray Treacy, Paddy Roche, Terry Conroy, Mick Martin, Liam Brady, Eoin Hand, Joe Kinnear, Paddy Mulligan, Tony Dunne.

lacked penetration in the box where the Italians formed a dense blue blockade.

Ireland were also badly served by the West German referee who turned down two penalty appeals in the first five minutes of the second half. Writing in *Irish Press*, Séan Diffley had this to say: 'Hans Gerhard Schulenburg, without the slightest shadow of a doubt, has grievously missed his vocation. I'm certain he would be far more at home in some stentorian Wagnerian Opera, preferably hamming the heavy chester'.

'I thought we had the winning of the game at half time', Meagan said afterwards, 'but the second Italian goal was a real killer.' The goal came on the hour, when Boninsegna nodded down a cross to Pierino Prati who slotted the ball past Alan Kelly in the Irish goal.

According to Tom O'Shea in the *Evening Press,* 'Johnny Giles was the outstanding player on the field', but he was closely attended by the Italians and Ireland's eighteenth game without a win was duly ended.

'We should have won that match,' recalled Paddy Mulligan many years later, 'We just didn't take our chances.'

'Italy were very strong,' said the defender, who won a European Cup Winners Cup medal with Chelsea ten days later. 'Their first touch, awareness, movement and quick thinking were tremendous. We were certainly playing well enough to beat them. They were there for the taking that night. But although we rattled them, Italy were able to regain their rhythm and their passing game.'

The Italian press was unhappy with its own side. Alberto Ghirelli wrote in *Corriere della Sport*:

'Italy did not show a clear superiority over Ireland, who based their play on rhythm and enthusiasm … Many of the key men needed to be replaced, even if we won over the highly modest men of Mr Meagan …'

There were headaches for the FAI as the attendance of twenty-five thousand fans was a long way short of their expectations, although the bus strike and live transmission on RTÉ were widely blamed.

Mitchel V. Cogley, in an *Irish Independent* piece headlined 'Soccer Crazy, how are ye!', wrote

'The wide open spaces on the terraces and in the stands at Lansdowne Road last evening would seem to indicate that even the appeal of the World Cup runners-

up in the European Championships, Italy, in a fully competitive match against the strongest (on paper) team that the Republic of Ireland have been able to muster for quite a number of years, just hadn't got the appeal.

'[The bus strikes and TV ...] didn't account for the thousands of unsold stand tickets which one will have thought would have been collectors' items long before transport trouble and TV had entered the situation.

'Soccer football at this level has lost spectator appeal, and for most of last night's exercise the reasons were painfully and boringly obvious ...

'There was no big match atmosphere – with a more than half empty ground; and there was no big match performance, except perhaps by the over-marked Johnny Giles.'

The immediate result of the game was a backlash against Meagan by FAI officials. One selector resigned, complaining he wasn't being listened to, and several other officials attacked the coach. 'I am sick of all the favourable newspaper comments about the manager,' said Charlie Liddy of the Junior Committee. Meagan believed his position had been undermined, and resigned.

He stayed on for the prestige friendly against England two weeks later, although the visitors sent a distinctly third-class selection with none of the big stars of the day. The crowd of eighteen thousand reflected this.

Until the late 1980s the FAI flitted between the two Dublin stadia, staging the biggest games at Lansdowne, although the ground was not always available to the association. The largest crowd seen there was the fifty-three thousand that crammed in for the World Cup qualifier in 1981 when Ireland beat France 3-2. It was also notable as the first soccer international for fifteen years attended by the serving Taoiseach.

Kevin Keegan made his debut for Southampton against Shamrock Rovers in 1980

However, some potentially disastrous crowd incidents when crushing forced fans onto the pitch at friendlies with Italy and France at

Dalymount persuaded the association that the Northside stadium was no longer a fit and safe venue for international football. From 1990 to 2006, besides two games against Wales staged at Tolka Park and the RDS, all Ireland's home games were played at Lansdowne Road.

1968 EUROPEAN CUP MATCH

WATERFORD: Peter Thomas; Peter Bryan, Noel Griffin; Vinny Maguire, Jackie Morley, Jimmy McGeough; Al Casey, Alfie Hale, John O'Neill. Paddy Coad, Johnny Matthews

MANCHESTER UNITED: Alex Stepney; Tony Dunne, Francis Burns; Pat Crerand, Bill Foulkes, Nobby Stiles; George Best, David Sadler, Bobby Charlton, Denis Law, Brian Kidd. Sub: Jimmy Rimmer for Stepney

1971 INTERNATIONAL MATCH

IRELAND: Alan Kelly (Preston North End), Joe Kinnear (Tottenham Hotspur), Paddy Mulligan (Chelsea), Tony Byrne (Southampton), Tony Dunne (Manchester Utd), Eamon Dunphy (Millwall), John Giles (Leeds United, capt), Eamonn Rogers (Blackburn Rovers), Steve Heighway (Liverpool), Don Givens (Luton Town), Jimmy Conway (Fulham)

Sub: Al Finucane (Limerick) for Rogers 45 mins. Unused subs: Eoin Hand (Portsmouth), Ray Treacy (Charlton), Mick Kearns (Oxford)

ITALY: Dino Zoff; Tarcisio Burgnich, Roberto Rosato, Pierluigi Cera, Giacinto Facchetti; Mario Bertini, Giancarlo De Sisti, Mario Corso, Piero Prati; Roberto Boninsega, Sandro Mazzola

IRISH sport has had an at times uneasy relationship with politics. In the nineteenth century the foundation of the Gaelic Athletic Association was linked to the national liberation movement and over its first two decades administrators introduced rules that drew other sports into the struggle. What became known as 'The Ban' drew a line that put Gaelic Games on one side and the 'garrison games' on another. Members of the GAA would be banned if they were to play, or watch, a game of football, rugby, hockey or cricket.

Cricket was a sport very closely identified with the British rulers, and the games played on the ground at the Vice-Regal Lodge in the Phoenix Park were an important element of the social scene surrounding the Dublin Castle administration. While that sport withered in the south in the years after independence, football and rugby continued to flourish in the capital and other cities. In the north, all three remained strong, particularly in Protestant communities.

While two associations governed football on each part of the island after independence, almost all other sports continued as thirty-two county bodies, with the Ireland side being picked from both sides of the border and all creeds. There were periods when the sensibilities of the times strayed into the sporting arena – some southern players almost mutinied over the playing of 'God Save the King' before internationals at Ravenhill in Belfast – but by and large the Irish rugby team played together in a harmonious atmosphere. Ireland captain Willie John McBride made that very clear in his autobiography, *Willie John*:

'In the green jersey of Ireland, the northern Protestants stood shoulder to shoulder with the southern Catholics. Nor did anyone in the squad give a thought to a man's background. He was a colleague, a team-mate ...'

The advent of the Troubles in 1969 threatened all that. The situation escalated alarmingly and in 1972 there were 472 people killed. In January that year thirteen men were shot dead by the British Army after a march in the city of Derry, and a week later the British embassy in Dublin was burned to the ground by an angry mob. Three weeks later an IRA bomb killed six people at an army base in Aldershot.

This was the background to the most serious disruption of the international championship over its 130 year history.

1973 'At least we turn up'

Ireland 18 England 9, 10 February 1973

Ireland began the 1972 Five Nations with a fantastic 14-9 over France at Stade Colombes. It was the eve of the day that would be remembered as Bloody Sunday, when thirteen people were shot dead by the British Army at a civil rights march in Derry.

Two weeks later Ireland beat England 16-12 at Twickenham thanks to a memorable try by Kevin Flynn, and looked strong contenders for a first Grand Slam for almost a quarter of a century, with home games against Scotland and Wales to come.

Sadly, those two nations' rugby boards decided not to travel to Dublin because of their fears about the political situation a hundred miles to the north.

The Scottish union expressed their concerns to the IRFU two weeks before the game, and a high-powered Irish delegation travelled over to Edinburgh to attempt to reassure them. The Scots expressed fears that their supporters might be set upon after the game and were especially concerned as some Scottish regiments were particularly unpopular north of the border at that time.

Nine days before the game the SRU secretary, John Law, telephoned his Irish opposite number, Bob Fitzgerald, to tell him they would not be fulfilling the fixture. The executive decision to cancel had been passed by one vote.

'We are very disappointed', was Fitzgerald's typically understated response. There were stronger emotions flying around however, not least because the income from international matches – around £65,000 at the time – was by far the main contributor to IRFU funds.

'This is desperate news,' said captain Tom Kiernan, 'I am amazed. They seem to have been swayed by press and television coverage.'

The Welsh union had similarly cold feet one week later when a letter was received threatening reprisals against the players and allegedly signed by Dr Roy Johnston, a former secretary of Official Sinn Féin. Johnston denied he wrote the letter, but the hoax seemed to have disconcerted the Welsh sufficiently and they pulled out too.

Ireland captain Willie John McBride was furious:

'Those gentlemen who took the decision to abandon their matches with us that year failed Ireland, failed their own countries and failed the game of rugby football.'

'We were let down by the administrations. It was not the players from Wales and Scotland who were to blame, but their governing bodies.

'It sickened me because we in Ireland had kept rugby football strong through the dark days. That others could not recognise that and stand alongside us by fulfilling their fixtures saddened me immensely. Our friends had let us down.'

Luckily for the IRFU their French friends came to the rescue and played a non-championship international at Lansdowne Road in April, which Ireland won 24-14.

As the year went on the slaughter continued and rugby fans eyed the 1973 fixture list with some nervousness.

On New Year's Day it was reported that the Middlesex rugby union – the largest body in the RFU – had proposed that England pull out of the game. Elements in the London media, most notably the *Telegraph* writer, John Reason, were arguing strongly that it was too dangerous to travel, painting outrageous pictures of snipers in the grandstands.

On 4 January the RFU met at the Hilton Hotel in London, at which the motion to withdraw was 'overwhelmingly rejected', with just 'one or two abstentions'. The RFU president was a resolute Yorkshireman called Dickie Kingswell and he insisted that England would come, even if they had to bring a third choice XV.

The New Zealanders arrived in early January, and were held to a 10–10 draw thanks to a thrilling Tom Grace try. It is still Ireland's best result against the All Blacks, and led to raised expectations that the dashed hopes of the previous season would be converted into silverware.

However, the charged atmosphere led to serious pressure on individual

Opposite top:
Match programme for the game
opposite bottom:
Dick Milliken's debut try made the front page of *The Irish Times*

players, and in late January Moseley clubmates Sam Doble and Nigel Horton, a policeman, pulled out.

David Duckham was the golden boy of English rugby at the time, a free-scoring three-quarter with a shock of blond hair. He had just got married and rang his old Lions colleague, Willie John McBride to voice his doubts.

'David had got married three months earlier. He said that his wife Jean was not at all happy about him going to Dublin and he feared he would have to cry off. I said to him "for God's sake, David, you are the one guy England keeps picking. If you cry off, the others will too and the game will be off," wrote McBride.

'I suggested to David that he bring Jean over with him, and that the wives of the Irish team would look after her and make sure she had a great time.'

Mr and Mrs Duckham agreed to travel and the England squad that travelled some weeks later was virtually at full strength. Jean Duckham had a great weekend, although McBride recalls that the RFU committeemen 'looked down their noses, disapproving of a player bringing along his wife for the weekend.'

However, despite Duckham's decision, just eight days before the opening Five Nations game, some England players still held doubts, and most notable among these was captain John Pullin.

The English RFU secretary announced that the deadline had passed for players to make themselves available; Pullin said he had not made a definite decision but would do so over the weekend.

Willie John McBride, who won his fiftieth cap against England

Pullin drove to Cardiff for the final curtain call on the New Zealand tour. There he met up with McBride, Fergus Slattery, Ray McLoughlin and Mike Gibson who were named alongside him in the Barbarians side. It was one of the most celebrated games of rugby ever played, with the selected side winning an epic by 23-11. But just as important was the work put in by the Irish quartet off the field, helping to convince Pullin to travel to Dublin.

'I didn't have many reservations,' Pullin said thirty years later. 'After all, a lot of us had been under a fair bit of pressure when we went to South Africa the year before. We went then, so were used to threats. But we did have a few letters before we went to Dublin, some were hate mail, others offered support.'

On the Monday the political atmosphere was heightened further when Taoiseach Jack Lynch called a general election, to be held on 28 February. On the Wednesday before the game there were serious riots in Belfast after a one-day strike called by Loyalist workers. 'Five Die As Loyalists Rampage in Belfast' ran the *Irish Times* headline; 'Mob Fury' screamed the *Irish Independent* in an exceptionally large headline run across the full width of page one.

Before the England squad assembled there were two more withdrawals, scrum-half Jan Webster and lock Peter Larter, a serving officer in the RAF.

The team usually met up on the Thursday for the flight to Dublin, but security advised against it. Tony Neary had a law exam on Friday morning so didn't join up with the squad until they had a final run out at Twickenham that afternoon. The party then travelled on a charter flight to Dublin.

For hours before the team arrived anyone entering the arrivals building was searched and scanned. The airport was packed with gardaí, both in and out of uniform. When the plane touched down a bus screamed across the runway to collect the players, with escort from two garda vans and motorcyclists. The players were driven around the back of the terminal

The Irish team that played France in the extra game in 1972: BACK R.F. Johnston (referee), F. Slattery, S. McKinney, M. Hipwell, J. Lynch, W.J. McBride, C. Feighery, R. McLoughlin, J. Moloney, T. Kearns (IRFU), FRONT: B. McGann, M. Gibson, K. Kennedy, T. Kiernan, K. Flynn, A. Duggan, W. McMaster

where they switched to another coach and, as the *Irish Independent* reported, 'the usual customs regulations were waived'.

The party stayed at the Shelbourne and Majestic hotels, again on security advice as their city location made for shorter journeys than the hotel in Bray the Springboks had used three years before. Armed gardaí were stationed in the hotel lobby and on the corridors leading to the players' rooms.

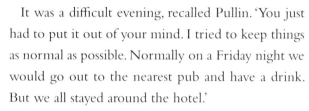

It was a difficult evening, recalled Pullin. 'You just had to put it out of your mind. I tried to keep things as normal as possible. Normally on a Friday night we would go out to the nearest pub and have a drink. But we all stayed around the hotel.'

Those English supporters that travelled found it hard to buy a drink in Dublin that weekend – not because of any reluctance of bars to serve them, but because Irish supporters were so delighted to see them that they plied them with stout in the pubs along Baggot Street where fans met up.

On the day of the game the gardaí sealed off roads surrounding and leading to the ground. The city centre was closed to traffic from 10pm on Friday night until Sunday morning. Army roadblocks had been set up on the border from Friday morning and cars were searched three or four times on the road from Belfast to Dublin.

At lunchtime on match day the England team were given a garda escort to the ground, less than a mile away, where 550 members of the force were on duty. The plan was for the two teams to walk out side by side in a show of unity, but as the teams waited to go out there was a swelling roar like no-one had ever heard before.

'When the English team ran out the spontaneous standing ovation seemed to go on and on and on,' recalled Ollie Campbell, then an eighteen-year-old spectator.

'I was up sitting on the steps of the West Upper and as long as I live I will never forget the applause once the English team ran out. It really

John Pullin, captain of England

does to this day give me goosebumps on the back of my neck and down my spine nearly forty years later. I also remember how Willie John McBride, sensing what was happening, held back his team from running out so that the applause rang out even more.' McBride, who was winning his fiftieth cap, had been given the honour of leading the team out by captain Kiernan.

Roger Uttley, later to become one of England's rugby greats, was winning his first cap that day. 'As a young bloke I was just pleased to be playing for my country. The reception we got proved that it was the right decision. The standing ovation when we ran on to the pitch made the hairs on the back of your neck stand on end.'

The man of letters Ulick O'Connor wrote, 'I can never forget that incredible moment as the roar went up when the English team came on the field for that match. The crowd clapped for five minutes and there were tears in a number of eyes. If ever sport could have been said to have begun a bonding, it was this moment. I simply had to stop at the Shelbourne Hotel on the way home to leave a note for Dicky Kingswell to thank him for coming here and putting sport above politics.'

John Pullin wasn't overjoyed at the delay and having his team stand for the anthem. 'You didn't want to spend too much time standing still, you felt very vulnerable. But a lot of the players were nervous. We kept on the move.'

Eventually, the game kicked off, and England were 3–0 up inside three minutes when Tony Jorden landed a penalty.

It was a game graced by two fantastic front rows, with Ireland's Lions trio of Ray McLoughlin, Ken Kennedy and Sean Lynch having the upper hand on Fran Cotton, Pullin and Stack Stevens. The *Irish Independent*'s Mitchell Cogley was moved to write that the first half was the best forty-minute stint he had seen by an Irish team:

'*England were the ancient enemy again, the chips were down, the knives were*

Mike Gibson, one of Ireland's greatest players

A 40p ground admission ticket for the 1973 game

out, and for the rest of a tremendously spirited first half it was evident, as events were to prove, that the English team, who defied all sorts of pressures in honouring their engagement, lacked protection only where it was needed – on the pitch.'

Ireland were playing into a stiff breeze in that first half, but were still comfortably 12-3 ahead at the break thanks to two fabulous tries by Tom Grace and the debutant Dick Milliken. Barry McGann converted both and smoothly sent over a dropped goal early in the second half to give home supporters hope that they might see the Irish record score over England broken. That mark, just 22, was set in the first post-war season of 1947.

Ireland's control of the game was such that Kiernan didn't get to touch the ball in the second half. However a Neary try brought England back into the game before McGann scored a final penalty for an 18-9 scoreline.

It continued a dismal sequence for England, as debutant Uttley discovered: 'I said to Chris Ralston, my second-row partner that day, that I felt a bit sick at losing my first game in an England shirt. He told me not to worry, and added, "It's my tenth, and I'm still waiting for a win".'

After the game the chairman of England selectors, Sandy Sanders, restated his union's attitude: 'We were determined to come. We said we would come and we are delighted we came. The reception we got was nothing short of fantastic and we are grateful for it.'

The teams met up later that evening for the post-match dinner in the Shelbourne Hotel, where Pullin received yet another ovation when he opened his speech with the immortal phrase, 'we may not be much good, but at least we turn up.'

Pullin explained many years later about one of sport's most enduring one liners:

'I hadn't thought about what I was going to say. At the time it didn't strike me as anything out of the ordinary. But it seemed to fit the moment.'

'It was a great occasion, and the craic afterwards was extraordinary,' said Uttley. 'I remember drinking with Fergus Slattery and going to bed at about three in the morning before catching an early flight back to London. When I came downstairs

at 6am, he was still in the bar where I had left him, and he offered me a drink. It was great hospitality and great camaraderie.'

England No. 8 Andy Ripley also greatly enjoyed his weekend:

'Ireland was just brilliant, and Dublin is a place that steals people's hearts, and quite rightly. We got a really big cheer, and then for the next eighty minutes the Irish kicked shit out of us.'

The extraordinary game lit up an odd season in which all ten games were won by the home side, resulting in a five-way tie for the championship, a unique conclusion to the tournament.

IRELAND: Kiernan (Cork Constitution); Grace (St Mary's), Milliken (Bangor), Gibson (NIFC), McMaster (Ballymena); McGann (Cork Constitution), Moloney (St Mary's); Moore (Highfield), Buckley (Sunday's Well), Slattery (Blackrock); McBride (Ballymena), Mays (UCD); Lynch (St Mary's), Kennedy (London Irish), McLoughlin (Blackrock).
ENGLAND: Jorden (Blackheath), Duckham, Preece (both Coventry), Warfield (Rosslyn Park), Morley (Bristol), Cowman (Coventry), Smith (Sale); Ripley (Rosslyn Park), Neary (Broughton Park), Dixon (Gosforth); Ralston (Richmond), Uttley (Gosforth); Cotton (Loughborough Colleges), Pullin (Bristol), Stevens (Penzance-Newlyn).

CHAPTER 22

1973 United Irishmen

3 July 1973 -
The day an all-
Ireland soccer
team played
World
Champions
Brazil

In June 1972, Liam Tuohy took a badly-depleted Ireland squad on a summer tour to the Brazilian city of Recife; they were there to play in a fifteen-team mini-World Cup tournament celebrating 150 years of Brazilian independence. Despite being without his two best players, John Giles and Steve Heighway, neither of whom were let go on the trip by their clubs, Tuohy's side held their own and more in the unrelenting heat. They beat Iran and Ecuador in their opening two matches before going down to a pair of hard-fought 2-1 defeats to Portugal and Chile. It was the first time an Ireland soccer team had ever played in South America and, apart from a few bad cases of sunburn, the whole adventure was deemed quite a success.

But probably the most notable achievement by an Irishman in Brazil that June – and certainly the one that would last longest down the ages – had nothing to do with any of the matches that took place. Louis Kilcoyne, one of three brothers who owned Shamrock Rovers and who would in time become the FAI's Honorary Life President, had organised the trip and decided to stay behind after the team was knocked out because he had a mission to pursue.

Kilcoyne knew that Brazil had planned an eight-game tour of Europe for the summer 1973, in preparation for the 1974 World Cup in West Germany. He knew also that Joao Havelange had been president of the Brazilian FA (or the CBD as it is known) for almost thirteen years at that point and had his eye on the top job at FIFA, the elections for which would be taking place in Frankfurt in 1974 and the politicking for which had long since begun. FIFA presidents had always been European, right back as far as Frenchman Robert Guerin in 1904. If Havelange was to break that streak and become the first South American head of world football, he would need European votes. Kilcoyne had an Irish one to offer.

So he went and sat in Havelange's office and waited. And waited. Eventually, his persistence paid off and he got himself the meeting with Havelange in which he asked that a match at Lansdowne Road be added to the Brazilian itinerary the following summer. It would be a charity match, with half the proceeds going to Unicef and the other half to the Irish Cancer Society. Havelange agreed, on the basis that Brazil would be playing an all-island Ireland team, with players drawn from north and south of the border.

This was a delicate area to tiptoe into. For one thing, relations between the FAI and the IFA had historically swung between frosty and furious. They were two very young associations in their current form – they had only split from each other in 1921 – and in 1972 could best be described as still learning how to live peaceably with each other. But less than a quarter of a century before that, they were at loggerheads over many issues, most obviously the right claimed by both to call on players from all over the island to play on their respective sides.

In September 1950, for instance, Sligo-born Celtic defender Seán Fallon was named in a Northern Ireland squad to play against England in a friendly. Fallon had made his name at Glenavon the previous season and, were he to take up the offer of playing for the North, would have been in line for a £1,000 cheque and a gold watch. But as soon as the FAI got word that he'd been selected, they sent him a letter calling on him to declare for the Republic.

Above:
An unofficial programme for the Shamrock Rovers XI v Brazil match in 1973 showing the Brazilian team.

'My father was in politics in Sligo and this was a very hot potato at the time,' said Fallon some years later. 'I very reluctantly pulled out. I was the last player from the Republic to be selected by the IFA and I felt I had let them down because I had said I would play.'

Although more and more middle ground had been found between the two associations as the years had passed, there was still suspicion and ill-will on both sides. Kilcoyne knew the Brazil game in Dublin wasn't an idea that would go down particularly well with Harry Cavan, the long-serving head of the northern association and a particularly powerful figure in European and world football politics. He knew most of all that any attempt to select Northern Ireland internationals to play for a team named 'Ireland' would meet with stern resistance from the IFA president. The distinct fear in the North was that the fielding of an All Ireland team could be the first step along the road to a permanent reunification, although this was always denied.

The wider context, of course, was that this was a time of ferocious political and social upheaval in Northern Ireland, as detailed in the previous chapter. The notion of a representative soccer team drawn from both sides of the border was so dramatically out of sync with the events of the time as to make the fixture seem quite astonishing in hindsight. It's true that the national rugby team was struggling on manfully with players and officials from both sides of the divide, but that was because the sport in Ireland had been run under a single IRFU umbrella since 1880 and everyone made a conscious effort to keep politics out of it.

The same didn't apply in soccer. It wasn't just that the IFA was in Belfast and the FAI in Dublin. The prevailing culture meant that northern Catholics wouldn't support the Northern Ireland soccer team, choosing instead to follow the Republic. With a united Ireland the ultimate aim of an IRA that was waging a vicious war both in the North and in England, putting together an all-island team just then was dipping sport's toe in very sensitive political waters. Kilcoyne knew it would have to be handled subtly and skilfully and that even then, there was no guarantee it would come off.

He enlisted the help of Giles who, as well as being Ireland captain, was also his brother-in-law. Giles in turn contacted Derek Dougan, the thirty-five-year-old Wolves striker who was still nominally captain of Northern Ireland, though age was restricting his playing time. Outspoken and charismatic, Dougan had always supported the idea of an all-island team, even though he came from a solid east Belfast Protestant background – his autobiography in 1972 was called *The Sash He Never Wore*. He was also chairman of the Professional Footballers' Association in England at the time, which would help in putting a squad together.

'I had no problem getting players because of the PFA thing,' Dougan said before his death in 2007, 'but the reality is that everybody wanted to be involved because of the opposition. I'd worked for ITV through the whole of the 1970 World Cup finals and this was definitely the best side I'd ever seen. I mean people talk about Hungary with Puskas, but the reality is that they weren't even in the same league. So of course the players were interested to take part and for the supporters it was this great Brazilian side against a team drawn from the whole of Ireland, which hadn't happened in maybe twenty years. So it was a spectacle, like Frank Sinatra or Elvis or Barbra Streisand coming to town. It was something you desperately wanted to see.'

Dougan was right. Although Pele, Gerson and Tostao had retired, the bulk of Brazil's wondrous 1970 team were still involved three years later. Havelange had agreed to bring the Brazil of Jairzinho and Rivelino, of Piazza and Clodoaldo to Dublin. Lansdowne Road would be hosting easily the most high-profile soccer match in its history. Not only would Brazil be the first reigning world champions to play in the stadium, they'd be the first South American team ever to turn out there as well.

But before all that could happen, however, Dougan had to convince Cavan to give his blessing to the game. Or at the very least, persuade him not to make any attempts to stand in the way of it. He was unsuccessful on both counts.

'I put the idea of north and south coming together to play Brazil at a meeting in London with the two senior officials of the IFA – Harry Cavan the president and Billy Drennan the secretary,' he later wrote. 'My hands were wet with the sweat of nervous tension. I thought we were talking about history in the making, talking and building bridges. Then came the moment I will remember for the rest of my life. Mr Cavan received the news as if a bomb had hit him. I was confronted by a stony silence. Cavan informed me tersely that he would put the matter to the IFA. Drennan was enthusiastic, but I never heard from either again.'

In interviews down the years, Dougan never spared Cavan when it came to recounting his efforts to stop the game being played. He often told of how, after sharing a TV studio with Sir Stanley Rous, then FIFA President, in the run-up to the game, he got buttonholed by Rous and scolded for upsetting Cavan with this all-Ireland team nonsense. But once Kilcoyne deftly suggested naming the team 'Shamrock Rovers XI' instead of 'Irish XI' and promised to fly only the Brazilian flag over Lansdowne Road and play only the Brazilian anthem on the day of the game, not even the most powerful man in world football could stop it in any official way. And given that Havelange was on his way to becoming the next man in Rous's seat, he couldn't very well lean on the Brazilian president either.

'Harry Cavan tried to get the match cancelled purely and simply because he felt, stupidly, it was going to be a landmark game,' said Dougan. 'That the north and south was going to come together after that. That day, however, there was no hidden agenda as far as I was concerned. I just felt it would be a unique chance for us to play the best team in the world. Cavan was trying to stop progress, but why should he interfere with me? He may have changed the team name, but what he couldn't do was take away that memorable day.'

Liam Tuohy was asked to coach the team and between him, Dougan and Giles, they came up with a squad of twenty-one players, which Tuohy announced at a press conference on 7 June. There was some surprise that Heighway's name was on the list, given that he'd been pulled from World Cup qualifiers against France and Russia by Bill Shankly the previous month. Kilcoyne conceded that nobody had yet spoken to the Liverpool manager. When the final squad was whittled down to fifteen, Heighway's name was gone due to a training injury.

For some of the squad, the chance to play Brazil was enough. 'First and foremost, we were football people' said Bryan Hamilton, who back then was an Ipswich midfielder and who, in later years, would go on to manage Northern Ireland. 'And when someone said, "Would you like to play in an all-Ireland side against Brazil?", I've got to say that it was Brazil that stuck in my head.'

For others in the squad, however, it was impossible to divorce themselves from the political subtext of the match. 'I was brought up Presbyterian,' said Allan Hunter, then a rugged centre-half with Ipswich. 'But I went to a mixed school and all my friends were Catholics. I felt that I had to play in this game, to show those friends that I wasn't going to be part of all the nonsense that was going on. I thought by me coming down to Dublin to play this game, I was reaching across the political divide in some way.'

The game was fixed for Tuesday, 3 July. Since it was a close-season match, the players would have to get used to something that wouldn't normally have exercised them – mid-summer training. 'I was staying down in Wexford that summer,' said Giles, 'and I was running on the beach to stay fit. The last thing I wanted was to be out of condition taking on Brazil.' When Tuohy got them together, he built the side around Giles. Figuring that the Brazilians would be coming to play, he didn't see any point in not trying to do the same thing. 'I thought John Giles was one of the best passers of the ball in the world,' he said, 'and I would have been anxious for him to get enough possession to run the game'

Predictably, it rained in Dublin on the day of the game. Equally predictably, however, the rain wasn't enough to keep the crowds away. Close to thirty-five thousand turned up to watch these two unique teams play the last game of Brazil's European tour. Oddly, considering all the careful steps that had been taken in the build-up not to tweak the tails of the IFA any further than was necessary – along with the name change and the lack of flags, the team played in the green and white hoops of Rovers instead of the generic green jersey that would have been common to both countries – the St Patrick's Brass and Reed Band struck up 'A Nation Once Again' as the pre-match build-up came to a close.

As the teams posed for their photographs, the sun came out and Kilcoyne was able to look out onto the Lansdowne turf and see his vision made flesh. Brazil, in their world-famous yellow and blue, fielded four of the side that had started the World Cup final in Mexico three years previously. Two more – Paulo Cesar and Marco Antonio – had featured in the bulk of Brazil's games, with the latter the youngest player in the tournament.

Their European tour hadn't been quite the stroll they'd perhaps expected, with only five wins from eight games, a draw against Austria and defeats against Italy and Sweden. They'd had massive rows with their travelling press corps over some of the tales of excess they'd been sending home and had withdrawn all co-operation. They could have been

Derek Dougan scores against Brazil

forgiven for just wanting to get Lansdowne Road over with, to go through the motions and go home. But they came to play, mindful at least a little of the place they were in and what the game represented. 'We were aware of the political situation in Ireland regarding the game,' said Jairzhino in 2007, 'but football is a powerful force that can unite nations and cultures.'

And in the green and white hoops of Shamrock Rovers stood six players from the north and five from the south. The great goalkeeper Pat Jennings was the reigning Football Writers' Player of the Year in England. In front of him was a back four of David Craig, Paddy Mulligan, Hunter and Tommy Carroll – who was only called in as a late replacement when future Arsenal assistant manager Pat Rice had to get his tonsils out. Midfield was made up of Giles, Mick Martin and a twenty-one-year-old Martin O'Neill playing behind a front three of Dougan, Terry Conroy and Don Givens.

Brazil started in classic mode, passing and moving the ball around with ease. They won a penalty after just twelve minutes when Carroll made a rash tackle on Jairzinho on his own endline when the danger seemed slight and Paulo Cesar slid spot-kick to Jennings's right. But the Shamrock Rovers XI gradually found their feet and they were on terms by the half-hour, Mick Martin scrambling home from three yards in a chaotic Brazilian goalmouth. That came only a couple of minutes after Dougan crashed a header against the crossbar from a Giles corner.

The home side were enjoying their day and when Givens hit the crossbar again five minutes before half-time, anything seemed possible. But a beautifully-taken goal from Jairzinho right on half-time sent Mario Zagallo's side in 2-1 at the break. They swiftly made that 3-1 and then 4-1 through goal from Valdomiro – easily the strike of the day from 22 yards – and Paulo Cesar again. With sixty-one minutes gone, Brazil looked home and hosed.

Tuohy made a double substitution shortly afterwards and sent on Hamilton and Liam O'Kane for Givens and Carroll. It had an immediate effect, with Hamilton haring down the wing to start the move that led to Dougan pulling one back. And ten minutes from time, Dougan flicked on a cross from Mulligan and Conroy came flying in unmarked to head into

the bottom corner and make it 4–3. But although the crowd screamed for an equaliser, Brazil held possession for the rest of the game and even had time to miss a penalty, Paulo Cesar drawing a fine save from Jennings after late substitute Miah Dennehy handled.

When the final whistle went, the hunt began for shirts to swap. O'Neill was delighted to get that of Clodoaldo, the silky defender whose soft-shoe dribble had started off the most famous team goal of all time in the 1970 final. Hamilton came away that of the great Rivelino, one of the all-time top ten Brazilian players. Afterwards, both sets of players went off to a reception in the Gresham Hotel.

A second goal for Ireland!

The sad postscript to the day has always been the fact that Dougan remained convinced for the rest of his life that his involvement in organising the game is responsible for ending his Northern Ireland career. Those who deny that any pressure was brought to bear from on high in the IFA always point out that Dougan hadn't been named in the squads running up to that game and that he was thirty-five years old when it was played. The truth is likely somewhere in between – whatever chance he had of extending his international career certainly wasn't done any favours by going against Cavan's wishes on such a grand scale.

Dougan didn't particularly care anyway. He always had grander plans for himself. Before he died, he became an author, saved Wolves from going out of business, did a stint as chairman and chief executive at Molineux, stood for election in East Belfast, went on the BBC show *Question Time* as a member of the United Kingdom Independence Party and carried

George Best's coffin. The man lived a life.

'After it,' he said in an *Irish Times* interview in 2005, 'I probably had a couple of my best years at Wolves but I never played for Northern Ireland again. I finished up with forty-three appearances, seven short of my second gold watch. After fifteen years I had no complaints.

'But you lot down south owe me a watch!'

SHAMROCK ROVERS XI: Pat Jennings (Tottenham/NI), David Craig (Newcastle Utd/NI), Paddy Mulligan (Crystal Palace/RoI), Alan Hunter (Ipswich/NI), Tommy Carroll (Birmingham City/RoI), John Giles (Leeds Utd/RoI), Mick Martin (Manchester Utd/RoI), Martin O'Neill (Nottingham Forest/NI), Terry Conroy (Stoke City/RoI), Derek Dougan (Wolves/NI), Don Givens (QPR/RoI). Subs: Liam O'Kane (Nottingham Forest/NI) and Bryan Hamilton (Ipswich/NI) for Carroll and Givens (66 mins); Miah Dennehy (Nottingham Forest/RoI) for Conroy (88 mins).

BRAZIL: Leao, Ze Maria, Luiz Pereira, Piazza, Marco Antonio, Paulo Cesar, Clodoaldo, Rivelino, Valdomiro, Jairzinho, Dirceu.

Referee: Dominic Byrne

Ollie Campbell's record points total helps Ireland to their first Triple Crown since 1949

By 1982, Ireland's long-standing lack of success in the Five Nations was an embarrassment. Generations of Irish rugby players had soldiered through their careers without ever having come close to emulating the heroics of Jack Kyle, Karl Mullen and the rest of the men who won the Grand Slam in 1948 and the Triple Crown the following year. Indeed the prince of the 1982 side, Ollie Campbell, would often tell of having been brought up on stories of those men of the 1940s, their achievements the stand-out successes in Irish rugby history and the benchmark against which all subsequent generations were to be judged.

Certainly for so apparently straightforward a task – a Triple Crown involves winning just three matches, after all – the wait was becoming interminable. When Ireland sealed their third Five Nations Championship in four years on 10 March 1951 with a 3-3 draw against Wales, few would have believed that it would be another twenty-three years before they finished on top of the table again. When they did, in 1974, they were denied the Triple Crown by another draw against Wales, this time a 9-9 affair at Lansdowne Road in early February. That draw, followed by another depressingly barren spell – they didn't manage a single win over Wales in the whole of the 1970s – meant that by the time the 1982 Five Nations dawned, Ireland had gone a whole thirty-three years without winning a Triple Crown.

There was precious little indication that this was going to be the year it all turned around either. They came into the championship on the back of a run of seven defeats and one draw – and even that was against lowly Romania – in their previous eight matches. Ireland had been whitewashed in the 1981 Five Nations, finishing dead bottom of the table with no wins and no points. True, it had been what Moss Keane, the big second-row from Kerry came to refer to as 'Ireland's greatest ever whitewash', since each game had only been lost by a single score. They had actually led all four matches that year, but ended up being pipped on each occasion – twice by a solitary point, at the hands of Wales and Scotland.

Even so, it was hard to see where they were going to draw any putative reversal of fortunes from. Most of the forwards had been around so long

Ciaran Fitzgerald
leads the Ireland
team out followed
by Ollie Campbell

by that stage the press had begun to refer to them as 'Dad's Army'. Phil Orr, Gerry 'Ginger' McLoughlin, Keane, Willie Duggan, Fergus Slattery and John O'Driscoll had packed down together more or less uninterrupted since the mid- to late-seventies. By the start of the '82 campaign all six had beaten off challengers for their places and were back in harness, with new captain Ciaran Fitzgerald at hooker and Donal Lenihan alongside Keane in the second row.

Those players might have had a few miles on the clock but they were canny with it. Ireland had gone on tour to South Africa the previous winter and, despite bringing what was largely a development squad, hadn't disgraced themselves at all. They'd lost the two tests by respectable margins − 23-15 in Cape Town and 12-10 in Durban − and in those days, respectability was about as much as anyone asked for from them. On the flight home, the wily Duggan had convinced Slattery that Ireland were worth a bet at 14-1 for the Triple Crown. It was a punt, though, entered into more in the spirit of adventure than with any degree of confidence.

The one member of the party who would certainly have had the Triple Crown in mind from before the beginning of the season was also the last man you would have heard declaring it in public. Tom Kiernan was a coach who very much advocated lying in the long grass and preventing public expectations becoming unduly great. It was an approach that had come off spectacularly four years earlier when he masterminded Munster's famous victory over the All Blacks at Thomond Park.

Few men thought as deeply about the game or devoted as much of their life to it. Kiernan had played fifty-four times for Ireland, had captained the Lions, would go on to usher in the move to professionalism and be the driving force behind the Heineken Cup. As a nine-year-old boy, he'd been smitten by the exploits of Mullen and Kyle and had carefully tended to scrap-books detailing their Grand Slam and Triple Crowns. He never lost those scrap-books or threw them away, keeping them in a safe place in his Cork home where they remain to this day, some sixty years later.

The Triple Crown was an abiding passion for him and the 1981 whitewash tore at his soul. Later that year, he called the whole squad to a team meeting in the Shelbourne Hotel in Dublin and warned them all that they would need to train harder if they were to achieve anything the following season. Sitting down the back of the room were Keane and Duggan, 'trying to make ourselves look as small as possible in case Tommy started asking hard questions,' remembered Keane years later. Neither man was in any doubt who Kiernan was especially directing his exhortations towards – the two old lags down the back. 'We'll see that man out, Moss,' whispered Duggan to his cohort at one point.

Come the beginning of the championship, however, both men were present and ready for duty. Keane had spent the winter trying to overcome an ankle injury picked up in an interpro game against Ulster at Halloween. Conventional methods hadn't worked and, on advice from a then unknown herbalist from Co. Meath called Seán Boylan, he'd been paddling every day in Dollymount Strand with a green and gold scarf up over his face in case anyone recognised him. And Duggan was still sucking down his pre-match cigarette ten minutes before walking out on to the pitch. To say they were an unlikely bunch of heroes would be putting it mildly.

Certainly nobody expected them to end up as heroes going into the opening match against Wales. They needed a win – any win – to halt the wretched slide of the previous season. Although Ireland had managed to take the corresponding fixture in 1980, Wales still carried an aura passed on from the great teams of the seventies.

The first match of the 1982 championship was to take place at Lansdowne Road on Saturday 16 January, but as the game loomed, it became clear that Mother Nature had other ideas. In the opening weeks of that year, northern Europe found itself held in the grip of the worst weather in over five decades. Whole countries came to a standstill as temperatures plummeted and blizzards swept across the continent, causing hundreds of deaths. In Ireland, villages were cut off from the outside world by snow drifts that reached fifteen feet in height.

There were bread riots in Howth, queues for milk in Templeogue, food parcels dropped from helicopters to help out communities trapped in the Wicklow mountains. Over ten thousand homes countrywide had no power and every school in the state closed down. One man in south Dublin was even able to build an igloo in his back garden and live in it for a weekend.

Through it all, sport was more or less wiped out across the country, with even competitions that had been due to take place indoors called off because of road closures. It was assumed from early on that the Wales

The great Tom
Kiernan

game would go the same way, but as it happened, Lansdowne Road was actually in a passable enough state. The worst of the weather had missed Dublin 4 and although there were a few inches of snow on the pitch, it was nothing that couldn't be shifted to allow a game to go ahead. The iced-over terraces were of greater concern, but again they wouldn't have presented an insurmountable problem had the decision been taken to go ahead with the fixture.

In the end, it was actually a confluence of factors that put paid to the game, not the least of which was the severe difficulty the Welsh squad had in assembling in Cardiff to fly to Dublin. No less than in Ireland, the blizzards had wreaked havoc in the Welsh countryside. All off-duty soldiers in the principality had been called into service, handed shovels and sent to literally dig-out villages that had been cut off by the snow. The touring Australian team that had been due to play the Barbarians in Cardiff had been airlifted by helicopter from their Porthcawl base and flown to

London because the roads were impassable. And the Welsh squad, which drew heavily from the famed valleys which were now blanketed in snow, would face huge logistical obstacles just to meet up together at the airport.

All of which led to the first Lansdowne Road international match to fall victim to the weather since 1933, when a clash with Scotland had similarly fallen by the wayside. The only other internationals at the venue to have been called off in that time were the Wales and Scotland matches in 1972, which as an earlier chapter has explained, were lost to the dreadful political situation that year. This time around, with what was ultimately a convenient three-week break before Ireland's second match of the championship, the Wales game was put back for just a week, going ahead instead on 23 January.

It was the beginning of what would become eternally and appropriately known as 'Campbell's Triple Crown'. Ollie Campbell had, for the best part of the previous few years, been one half of the most gripping head-to-head ever to play itself out between two Irish rugby players. Himself and Tony Ward were a couple of spectacularly gifted outhalves, jointly

Left to right: Willie Duggan, Robbie McGrath, Donal Lenihan, Ollie Campbell (background) and Moss Keane (No 4)

cursed to have been playing in the same era as each other. Kiernan had attempted to fit them in the same team, on occasion trying Campbell out at centre, but to no avail. It boiled down to a simple either-or and for that year's championship, Campbell got the nod. It would prove an inspired decision.

Ireland beat Wales 20-12 that day, with Campbell untouchable at outhalf. The Irish team, which had been characterised as a grizzled old pack and not a whole lot more, actually ran in three tries by their speedy wings, Trevor Ringland and Moss Finn. It was the first time in seven years that two Ireland wings had scored in the same game, albeit that Finn didn't remember anything about his as a concussion early in the game wiped the action from his head. The first he knew of his two tries was when he saw them on the BBC programme *Rugby Special* from his bed in St Vincent's Hospital the following afternoon.

Finn wasn't the only Ireland player to take a battering in the match. David Irwin, the Belfast centre, broke his leg early on and had to be stretchered from the pitch. He was carried under the West Stand and into an ambulance, which was about to leave for the hospital when the driver was radioed and told to come around to the East Stand to pick up a supporter who had taken a fall and needed help. When they got there, the door was opened and the medical staff ushered in a middle-aged man with blood pouring from his head, very obviously liquored up to the

eyeballs. The man took one look at Irwin, laid out in his full Ireland gear with his leg broken and slurred, 'Were you at the game?'

The Wales game was also notable for the first recorded appearance of streakers at Lansdowne Road. Or maybe that should read 'streakers'. Streaking at sports events hadn't really taken hold as a craze just yet, as it was seen more as a phenomenon particular to college campuses in the US during the previous decade. But once Erica Roe flounced topless onto the pitch at Twickenham at half-time in the England v Australia match on 2 January 1982, streaking was in the public consciousness in a way never before imagined. So much so that three weeks later, a couple of terrace wags at Lansdowne Road came up with Ireland's answer to the craze. Sadly, they were not quite as comely as the fair Erica.

'The game's only sideshow was a colourful streak by two burly "ladies" wearing wigs and festooned with pendulous plastic bosoms,' reported *The Irish Times* the following Monday. 'Even the dark pagans of the valleys were moved to guffaw as Lansdowne's answer to Twickenham's bare-breasted exhibitionists baffled the Dublin stewards, family men who hardly knew what to grab as the streakers ran across the pitch at half-time.'

Ireland were up and running now and a fortnight later, they pulled off a rousing win 16-15 over England at Twickenham. The game is best remembered for Ginger McLoughlin dragging half the England team over the line with him for a try that, in this era of Television Match Officials almost certainly would not be awarded nowadays since there was no way of telling whether or not McLoughlin had grounded the ball. But it was good enough for Scottish referee Allan Hosie. Incidentally, in an odd little quirk of fate, Hosie would become chairman of the Five Nations just over fifteen years later. His predecessor in the role? One Tom Kiernan.

And so Ireland went back to Dublin with the scent of a first Triple Crown in thirty-three years in their nostrils. It was also a chance for them to allow Lansdowne Road in on the act, as each of the country's previous four Triple Crowns had been clinched away from the old ground and, indeed, away from Dublin altogether. The 1894 and 1948 successes were completed in Belfast while the other two, in 1899 and 1949 were finished off in Wales.

In fact, this would be the first time that Lansdowne Road would host even a potential Triple Crown match. On the previous eleven occasions where Ireland had won the first two legs, they had been beaten by Wales in the third match each time – twice in Belfast and nine times in Wales. It seemed a travesty that this stadium, which was such an integral part of the history of Irish rugby, had never been treated to a day of days such as would arrive if they were able to beat Scotland on 20 February 1982. It added an extra element to an already pressurised situation.

'It was a very nervous time,' recalled McLoughlin. 'The most nervous time of our lives. None of us had ever experienced anything like it ... It had been so long. The build-up for a couple of weeks beforehand was huge, enough on its own to put the nerves into anyone. It hadn't happened for so long, you knew if you lost it you were never going to get the chance again.'

The country went into overdrive. There was a general election the week of the match, brought about by the fall of the Fine Gael government who had proposed a tax on children's shoes in the budget. 'Ollie For Taoiseach' posters appeared in places and a country that was deep in the mire of a desperate recession and angry with the politicians who had landed them

Ollie Campbell avoids the tackle of Scotland's Jim Calder as David Johnston (12) and Andy Irvine (15) look on

there voted the government out on the Thursday (although they would vote them back in within nine months) and turned its attention to Lansdowne Road on the Saturday. The black market was flooded with what Gardaí estimated to be around ten thousand forged tickets. Whatever the accuracy of the figure, there is no doubt that the ground was filled well beyond capacity.

The match belonged to Campbell. The day after the England game, one in which he had played well but had missed a couple of kicks that annoyed him terribly, he had gone on his own down to Angelsea Road and practised kicking for two hours from this one spot out on the right hand side. He later said he'd kicked maybe three hundred shots at goal from there, before eventually being moved on because the Old Belvedere seconds had a game against Drogheda. It would pay off in spades against Scotland, a match in which he kicked what was then a world record twenty-one points. The very first of his six penalties that day was from exactly the spot he'd been practising and he would kick two more from there as the afternoon wore on. By the end of the day, he had scored all of Ireland's points in a 21–12 win.

It was one of the greatest days in Lansdowne Road's long history. For the first time in 107 years of internationals, the Triple Crown had been secured in the heart of Dublin 4. The massive crowd which had spent the last twenty minutes singing 'Cockles And Mussels' on what had seemed like a continuous loop took to the pitch afterwards and engulfed their heroes. Campbell himself took an age to reach the dressing room, as every man, woman and child in the ground wanted to congratulate him personally.

When he got there, he found a team basking in the glow of having proven everyone wrong. They had been genuinely annoyed by the 'Dad's Army' tag and had felt grievously wronged by the previous season's whitewash. It hadn't been a proper reflection of their worth. This, they felt, was more like it. As they sat in the dressing room beneath the West Stand, Moss Keane hit on an idea.

'Hey, Fitzy,' he shouted over at his captain. 'I'm the oldest so I'm taking the cup to Currow next weekend. No more about it – my mind is made up.'

'But Moss,' replied Fitzgerald, 'there is no trophy. The Triple Crown is a mythical trophy.'

'Is there a medal?'

'No, Moss.'

'You mean to say we went to all this trouble and they won't even give us a shagging medal?'

'Sorry, Moss.'

Their only chance of a trophy would come in Paris a month later when they went to the Parc des Princes needing a win to seal the Grand Slam. But with the best will in the world, that trip turned out to be an afterthought. They celebrated the Triple Crown with the same amount of gusto they'd put into winning it and by the time Paris came around, they were pretty much a busted flush. Ireland hadn't beaten France in France since 1972 and wouldn't do so until Brian O'Driscoll came along in 2000. The men of 1982 fared no better, going down 22-9. It didn't bother them unduly, however. 'The celebrations probably cost us the Grand Slam,' recalled McLoughlin, 'but the Triple Crown was the big thing at the time.'

CHAPTER 24

1985
Giving it a lash!

Michael Kiernan's late drop goal seals a second Triple Crown in four seasons

With the distance of time, Ireland's pair of Triple Crowns in the 1980s invariably tend get coupled together, as though one followed the other like night after day. In reality, they were markedly different phenomena. Despite the two triumphs being separated by only three years, Irish rugby's time-honoured propensity for riding the rollercoaster between success and failure at dizzying speed meant that not only was the 1985 team significantly different from the 1982 one, but in-between times the national team managed to finish both top and bottom of the Five Nations table. Consistency has never been a particularly strong point.

The historic Triple Crown of 1982 was followed by a share of the championship alongside France a year later and then the wooden spoon by way of whitewash in 1984. Indeed, so bad were things in '84 that Ireland's one and only try in the whole of the tournament came at Lansdowne Road in the final game, with Michael Kiernan scoring in a 9-32 drubbing at the hands of Grand Slam winners Scotland. The crowd that day in Ballsbridge had already given up on another year by the time Kiernan crossed the line, the match and the season long lost.

That campaign saw the sun set on a slew of legendary Ireland careers. No longer could the national side call on the class of Ollie Campbell and Fergus Slattery or the nous of Moss Keane and Willie Duggan. Back-row forward John O'Driscoll was gone too; his influence on Irish rugby not to be seen again until his nephew Brian thrillingly arrived on the scene fifteen years later. Most significantly of all, however, was the exit of coach Willie John McBride after just one season in charge and the entrance in his place of one Michael Gerard Martin Doyle.

Mick Doyle had been on the selection committee under McBride and while his elevation to the top spot hadn't taken the smoothest course, he wasn't the type of man to be restricted by either modesty or caution. No sooner was he in the job than he made a point of laying down a marker. The Irish rugby team would be changing and the style of play long associated with the national side – grinding, rumbling, unapologetically forward-based – was to be thrown aside. His Ireland would run the ball; his Ireland would involve the backs as well as the forwards.

'We will not get involved in any macho scrums,' he said. 'The talent at

our disposal now is good enough behind the scrum to adopt an open approach. As far as I am concerned the scrum is no more than a means of restarting the game.' They would, in Doyle's famous phrase, 'Give it a lash.'

Ireland were due to open their 1985 campaign against England at Lansdowne Road. By then, Dick Greenwood was in his third and ultimately final season in charge of a not terribly good England side and was under pressure from the beginning. The father of future World Cup-winning centre and Sky rugby pundit Will Greenwood, for one reason and another he'd never had a lot of luck in games against Ireland. Capped five times as a player back in the late 1960s, he hadn't beaten the Irish in two attempts.

Indeed, on the occasion of his only match as England captain in March 1969, Ireland welcomed Greenwood and his men to Lansdowne Road and beat them 17–15 on a day so cold the English team were given thermal vests and pants to wear by the RFU. Sadly for them, the pants came down to their knees and so couldn't be worn under their standard issue shorts. Greenwood never played for England again.

If his representative playing career was less fun than he had hoped, Greenwood's three years as England coach weren't all that enjoyable either. In the two Five Nations Championships he'd overseen before 1985, England had only posted one win in eight games (he'd finally broken his

Nigel Carr faces up to England's Rory Underwood duck against Ireland with a 12-9 win at Twickenham in 1984). England as a rugby nation was going through quite a barren spell, with only one outright championship win in a quarter of a century. All of which makes it tough to fathom what he was thinking when he gave one of the all-time great hostages to fortune before the start of the 1985 campaign; told of Doyle's plans to make Ireland into a team that would play a fifteen-man game, Greenwood harrumphed at the thought. 'You can't give a whole country a brain transplant overnight,' he said. Doyle, who twenty years previously had taken Greenwood's spot at openside flanker on the Cambridge team at Christ's College, filed the insult away. But by no means did it go unnoticed.

As it happened, he would have to file it away for longer than he'd expected because for the second time in four seasons, Ireland's first match of the championship was postponed because of the weather. While the snowfall that week wasn't nearly as apocalyptic as the one that had nixed the Ireland v Wales opener in 1982, it was still enough to close Dublin

Airport for the morning on the day before the game. By that stage, the England team was already in Dublin which meant that even though the game was called off, competition rules saddled the IRFU with hotel and transport costs for the whole English travelling party.

At the time, the official party line was one of sadness that the game had been postponed. Had it gone ahead, the match would have been the 150th international to be played at Lansdowne Road and because England had played in the first one back in 1878 and had provided opposition on more occasions than any other nation down the years, it was felt that their presence for such a milestone would have been fitting. As it was, the 150th international would come a month later against France.

The newspapers of the day reported that Mick Cuddy, chairman of selectors, carried a great burden of sadness for the players involved once it was known the match wouldn't go ahead. 'We are obviously very disappointed. You build up for such a fixture and the build-up was considerable and had gone extremely well. I feel particularly for the players.' The truth of the matter, revealed a few years later by Doyle himself in his autobiography, *Doyler*, was, shall we say, a little less sombre.

'All the players and selectors adjourned to O'Donoghue's Pub on Merrion Row and had the best preparation for the season we could have had – a genuine Irish piss-up with sandwiches and soup as soakage. It built up a grand spirit and camaraderie among the whole group and it was time well-spent. We beat the living bejaysus out of England about ten times during the course of that afternoon, as well as Scotland, Wales and France for good measure. We had New Zealand on their knees by the time we were ejected.'

And so, team spirit present and correct, Ireland began their Five Nations a fortnight later than planned, against Grand Slam champions Scotland in Edinburgh. Trevor Ringland, the bookish Queens University winger, had by now become obsessed with a video that had been sent to Doyle by the former Welsh great Cliff Morgan. *Wales – The Crowning Years* contained passage after passage of thrilling Welsh running rugby from the seventies with Barry John, Gareth Edwards, J.P.R. Williams and the rest making the game sing. Ringland kept persuading the rest of the squad sit down and

Ciaran Fitzgerald breaks from an English line-out

watch parts of it with him and they all agreed that this was how they wanted to play under Doyle. The Scotland game would be their first opportunity to try it out.

These were the days before professionalism had largely robbed rugby players of opportunities to smell the roses. The day before the match, the whole squad killed time by going to the cinema to see the new Eddie Murphy film *Beverly Hills Cop*. Anyone familiar with the movie will remember the effete LA art gallery employee named Serge who Murphy's character Axel Foley meets and chats to when he first arrives in town. Told by Serge that one of the pieces in the gallery had sold for $130,000, Foley responds with a high-pitched, disbelieving 'Get the fuck outta here!'

As soon as the light went up in the cinema, the Ireland team turned around to find the whole Scotland squad seated just three rows behind them. A massive popcorn fight ensued and the Friday night movie-going public of Edinburgh were treated to the sight of two groups of giggling rugby players ducking behind seats and shouting, 'Get the fuck outta here!' at each other. The following afternoon, when Scottish flanker John Jeffrey nailed Paul Dean with an early tackle and pinned him to the ground, he couldn't resist whispering his Axel Foley impression into the Ireland outhalf's ear.

True to Doyle's word, Ireland played running rugby throughout the game. They should have had two tries inside the opening ten minutes, but full-back Hugo MacNeill couldn't finish either of them off. Despite playing well, however, they were still 12-15 behind with five minutes to go. Doyle later said he would have been delighted with the performance regardless of the result – out on the field his team were anything but.

And so it was that in injury-time at the end of the game, outhalf Paul Dean took a low pass from scrum-half Michael Bradley up from his ankles, looped around inside centre Michael Kiernan, dummied to pass, straightened, offloaded to outside centre Brendan Mullin who passed to MacNeill who sent Ringland in for a brilliant try in the corner. Every Irish back apart from left wing Moss Finn was involved for what will forever be remembered as one of the great Irish tries. Doyle's grand running plan might have seemed pie in the sky to many people – and there was obviously no guarantee it would work every time – but for that afternoon at least, it looked like he was on to something.

'You need someone to be the catalyst,' MacNeill later recalled. 'You need someone to say, "You can actually do this." Mick Doyle caught the spirit of an already confident group, he lit the touchpaper. You couldn't say he coached the side in the strictest sense, but he was very important in that liberating aspect.'

Next up, Ireland faced France at Lansdowne at the beginning of March. The elation brought about by the late win at Murrayfield hadn't worn off, despite the month-long wait for a second match. Notes of caution were being sounded, of course, the key one being Ireland's lack of a place kicker. With Tony Ward once again frozen out of the Ireland team (over the seven-season period from 1981 to 1987, Ward appeared in an Ireland shirt at least once a year apart from the Triple Crown years of 1982 and 1985) and Dean anything but a typical kicking outhalf, it fell to Kiernan to assume kicking duties.

Kiernan had a solid sporting pedigree. His father Jim had been good enough to make a final trial for Ireland as a player and in later years had been a selector. His mother Ann had played camogie for both Cork and

Munster. He even had uncles from either side of the family who had played for the Lions – Ann's brother Mick Lane had appeared twice on the 1950 tour to Australia and New Zealand and Jim's legendary brother

Tom had toured South Africa twice as a Lion and was captain in 1968. Kiernan himself had been on the 1983 tour to New Zealand, but had endured just as bad a time as the rest of the travelling party, playing and losing all three tests.

He was more or less dragooned into becoming Ireland's place-kicker by Doyle once Dean had been made the Ireland outhalf. Few outside the team had much confidence in him. He had filled in for Ollie Campbell on occasion without any great success and after he'd missed three kicks at goal in the opening half of the Scotland game, it looked like confirmation of everyone's worst fears. Nobody could have imagined then that Kiernan would go on to pass Campbell as Ireland's record points-scorer, a record that would stand for eleven years after his playing career ended in 1991.

At Lansdowne Road on 2 March, 1985, Kiernan kicked five out of seven penalties to secure a 15-15 draw against France in a game that is mostly remembered for two utterly different reasons. Firstly, for the French side, which was guilty of some pretty brutal and savage play at times, with Brian Spillane left needing eight stitches in his lower lip and back-row partner Philip Matthews suffering an early shoulder injury that he had to carry through the whole of the game. And secondly, for a now famous banner in the crowd that day extolling the virtues of Irish lock Willie Anderson over French counterpart Jean Claude Condom. *Our Willie Is Bigger Than Your Condom* …

Opposite:
Donal Lenihan and
Ciaran Fitzgerald

Ireland were unbeaten and on a high now and headed to Wales for the third match, knowing they hadn't won in Cardiff since 1967. Typically, Doyle brushed off any suggestion that this was a statistic that meant anything – little wonder, since he had played openside flanker on the Ireland team that had won 3-0 in Cardiff Arms Park that day. When some Welsh journalists put it to him that the long spell without a win would weigh heavy on Irish minds, Doyle answered as only he could (or would). 'The lads don't give a fuck about what's happened to the Irish team in Cardiff for the past eighteen years. They don't give a bugger about the reputation of the Arms Park, its history and all that stuff.'

How right he was. Ireland blew Wales away that day, running in two excellent tries by Keith Crossan and Ringland in a 21-9 win. Kiernan was a revelation with the boot again, his five successful kicks from five attempts easing Ireland clear. The back row of Nigel Carr, Matthews and Spillane were untouchable all game as well in what was, by common consent, the finest performance of the Doyle era. So thrilled was the Ireland coach that he declared an unchanged team for the next game before they had even left Wales.

The Triple Crown was up for grabs now and would all rest on a showdown at Lansdowne Road a fortnight later, the refixed match against England. Just as with three years previously, the nation became gripped. With a whole generation having emigrated over the previous five years because of the terrible economy, a massive Irish population lived and worked in England. Aer Lingus had to schedule fourteen extra planes from London, Bristol, Manchester, Liverpool and Birmingham for the weekend to keep up with demand.

Hotel owners in Dublin were up in arms because the refixed match clashed with the Fianna Fáil Ard Fheis. The Ard Fheis running order, incidentally, was changed that Saturday so as to allow a three-hour recess in the afternoon during which delegates could watch the match. No such luck at the GAA Congress in Ballina, however, as recess there was kept to a tight seventy-five minutes. There was a television installed in the room set aside for the press at the event, but it was officially only to allow the

GAA writers watch the Grand National. Actually, it seemed for a day or so that even this concession might be rendered obsolete, as a pay dispute in RTÉ threatened a TV black-out, but all was well by the morning of the game.

Because of the almost two-month delay between the original date of the England match and the day it actually went ahead at Lansdowne Road, there were widespread fears that ticket forgers would have a field day (since they had ample time and originals to work off if they were so inclined). Mindful of the overcrowding that had occurred at the stadium for the Triple Crown in 1982, a special team of detectives spent the two days before the match going undercover from pub to pub in the south of the city looking to buy black market tickets. By match day morning, they hadn't found even one. A couple of days well spent, then.

Sadly, there were more sinister forces to keep the Gardaí occupied that weekend. The political situation in the North, while not quite as relentlessly dangerous as it had been just four years earlier during the IRA hunger strikes, was nonetheless still unresolved and provided ample opportunity for subversive organisations to make their mark. In the weeks running up to the match, dark echoes of the dog days of the 1970s returned as a series of death threats to the English team were delivered to newspapers in London, with warnings of what would happen to their players if they turned up for the match. One letter contained a bullet.

The general public didn't know about the letters until after the match had been played as the newspapers concerned agreed not to publicise them. The English team ignored the threats and travelled to Dublin anyway – just as their counterparts had done thirteen years earlier. Security around the players and officials was tightened severely and the decision was taken to house the travelling party at the Killiney Castle Hotel for the weekend as its location – far from the city centre and right at the top of a hill – made it easier for Gardaí to patrol. Plainclothes and uniformed officers protected the hotel throughout and the England players weren't allowed to leave the grounds unaccompanied at any time.

When they moved into the city the night before the game, car-parking was prohibited all around the Shelbourne Hotel. It was grim, but those were the times. And while there was no widespread knowledge of the

death threats before the game, the reception afforded the England team as they took the pitch at Lansdowne on Saturday 30 March spoke volumes for the public's regard for them at what was still a very delicate time politically. 'Let's welcome England!' roared the PA announcer that day. 'Our oldest friends in rugby, who played Ireland when no other team would!' And roar them the crowd duly did.

Michael Kiernan celebrates the drop goal that won the Triple Crown with Michael Bradley (No. 9)

The scene was set. Ireland were led out by Ciarán Fitzgerald, captain again after having been controversially dropped for the 1984 season in the wake of his nightmare stint as Lions captain in New Zealand in 1983. Fitzgerald had famously been coursed by the British – in truth, predominantly English – media for his captaincy during that tour and had spent much of the 1985 season brushing off the notion that media criticism affected him. As an army man – and a quite prominent one, since he was President Patrick Hillery's aide-de-camp at the time – his leadership skills had been long taken as a given. Returning to lead Ireland to another Triple Crown would seal his legacy forever.

That legacy was by no means assured as what turned out to be a flat, disappointing game entered its closing phase. Heavy rain on the morning of the match had made sticky going of the Lansdowne pitch and a cloudburst just in time for kick-off made the ball dreadfully slippy. The game became a lottery at times, the scoreline a measurement of which side could make the fewer handling errors. It was one of those days when the famous Lansdowne Road wind played havoc with the kickers, as both Kiernan and Rob Andrew were made to look fools from placed balls.

The only Irish try of the game was a scrappy affair, Mullin scoring from a charge-down on an attempted clearance by England full-back Chris Martin. The English reply was better-crafted, Rory Underwood latching beautifully onto a lovely chip-through by their captain Paul Dodge. And when an Andrew penalty put England 10-7 ahead with just twenty minutes to go, all the great hopes for another Triple Crown looked in real danger. Even when Kiernan managed to pull Ireland back level with ten minutes to go, a restless crowd weren't especially confident that Ireland could eke out the required score to win the day.

In that crowd, incidentally, was a nine-year-old boy from Cork who went to all the matches with his brother and his father. Sadly, being from Cork meant needing to make the 4.50pm train from Heuston Station and so, along with hundreds of other men and boys of his county, Ronan O'Gara had to leave Lansdowne Road with the score at 10-10. What he missed with his eyes he had to imagine with his mind, as DART carriages full of supporters shushed each other to hear Jim Sherwin's radio commentary describe the closing stages of the match.

The most famous passage of play he missed came with thirty-five seconds left on the clock. But the second-most famous sight little Ronan didn't see was Fitzgerald, in a break in play with just five minutes to go, going round as many of his players as he could get to exhort them and ask them straight out and in full view of the TV audience one simple question. 'Where's your fucking pride?'

'I don't even like repeating it,' Fitzgerald later admitted. 'Very rarely would I repeat it. I just knew my own thought processes at the time. I really felt we were backed into a corner. We were trying to keep the tide out because, physically, they were a much bigger team and the game was played in wet, heavy conditions. We were getting outmauled in the second half, smothered nearly. Guys were getting tired and you could see it. I don't know where it came from. It might have been out of pure desperation. There was nothing else there to think of. And that's about it.'

What followed passed into legend. Brian Spillane called a quick line-out on himself and fed Donal Lenihan who drove forward. Lenihan gave it to Bradley and all of a sudden, the whole ground could see what was on the cards. Kiernan had dropped back into position and all that was needed was a good pass from Bradley and the centre would have the choice between a three-man overlap on his right or a simple kick at the posts to win the Triple Crown. He chose the latter and the convoy of Corkmen rammed together on Ronan O'Gara's DART carriage heard Jim Sherwin describe one of their own do the needful. 'Drop goal on ... Drop goal taken ... DROP GOAL GOOD!!'

Kiernan had done it. His drop goal won the match 13-10 and took his personal tally for the championship to forty-seven points. 'That drop goal has been replayed more times than The Angelus,' he would joke in time. It meant that every last one of Ireland points in the 1985 Five Nations had been scored by their backs, a thumping endorsement of Doyle's insistence on playing fifteen-man rugby. And it meant that Dick Greenwood's words had come back to haunt him, a fact which wasn't lost on the Irish supporters of course. They took great delight in the banner that was held aloft on the South Terrace afterwards advertising *Dr Doyle's Transplant Clinic*.

Of course, Ireland being Ireland, success was but a passing fad. The win in Edinburgh that had kicked the season off was to be their last of the century and that city would become a graveyard for Irish teams until Eddie O'Sullivan's men won there in 2003. The draw with France would be the closest an Irish side got to their Gallic tormentors until 2000. And for all Doyle's success in his first year, Ireland were whitewashed again in 1986.

'It still irritates me greatly that we didn't go on to achieve more,' said Philip Matthews in 2004. 'The harsh truth is that we underachieved and should have been a real force throughout the Eighties. The 1985 Triple Crown should have been a launching pad to greater things.'

Still, it was the most tremendous fun while it lasted.

CHAPTER 25

1986
'Go Home Union Jack'

A cool reception for Jack Charlton's first game in charge of the Ireland soccer team

Lansdowne Road has seen some epic days. Days when they sold every seat in the place but the people only used the edges of them. This chapter does not deal with any of those days. Indeed, the game featured here was among the most laboured, humdrum events ever inflicted upon the watching public in the long and storied history of the place. But it was the start of something. Nobody knew it and nobody predicted it, for if they had they'd have been shouted down by an Irish soccer public that had long despaired of ever seeing success on an international stage. But the match against Wales in March 1986 was the first domino to fall in what would become one of the greatest stories ever in Irish sport – the Jack Charlton era.

In the spring of 1986, Irish soccer was at as low an ebb as it had ever been. A generation of high-quality players had flourished in the early eighties, the likes of Liam Brady and Mark Lawrenson, Ronnie Whelan and Frank Stapleton, Kevin Moran and David O'Leary. Top players enhancing the fortunes of the Liverpools, the Arsenals and the Manchester Uniteds and yet, through combinations of bad planning, bad play and often sheer bad luck, the country had still never made the finals of a major tournament.

The latest one they'd missed out on was the 1986 World Cup, the qualifying campaign for which had ended with barely a whimper the previous November as just 15,154 fans – approximately six thousand of them supporting the away team – had seen Ireland lose 4–1 to Denmark. It was the lowest ever recorded attendance at an Ireland qualifier at Lansdowne Road, a sad, shuffling, awkward end to Eoin Hand's reign as national team manager. The Football Association of Ireland had been unable even to find a sponsor for the match.

Not that this should surprise anyone, given the condition the association was in at the time. These were truly the bad old days of the FAI, when finances were a mess and the organisation of the place even worse. Stories were legion of delegates falling asleep at council meetings, of the Ireland team being checked into tumbledown hotels on away trips, of small acts of official pettiness that gave the association a bad name far and wide.

One particularly hapless unedifying incident came about when Hand asked that a chef be brought to Moscow for the away qualifier against the

USSR in October 1985. The FAI refused him on the basis that it would cost too much, leading Hand's wife to step into the breach by offering to travel and prepare meals for the squad without asking for a penny. Even at that, when Hand went to FAI headquarters on Merrion Square to sort out the travel details with FAI treasurer Charlie Walsh and secretary Peadar O'Driscoll, the two men ignored him and had a blazing row with each other over who would get to travel with the official party. As Hand looked on uncomfortably, Walsh and O'Driscoll stormed out of the building, leaving him to lock up and turn out the lights. In retrospect, it's a grimly appropriate metaphor.

Into this world breezed Charlton, although he was initially an unlikely choice to be Hand's successor. A World Cup winner as a player, he had walked out on the Newcastle United job a week before the start of the 1985/86 season and hadn't picked up any managerial work in the interim. But as early as the day after Hand's last game, he was denying that he had any interest in taking the Ireland job. 'It's utter nonsense,' he said. 'It brings a smile to my face. I don't know anything about the position. I didn't even know it was vacant. Has Eoin Hand been sacked?'

That was in November 1985. By the following February, however, he was the FAI's chosen one. But only after a drawn-out and typically

Jack Charlton's first press conference, surrounded by FAI officials

Charlton and his
assistant Maurice
Setters

convoluted committee meeting during which the FAI managed to alienate John Giles forever and almost award the job to ex-Liverpool manager Bob Paisley. The most successful manager in Liverpool's history, Paisley had only allowed his name go forward on the condition that he was guaranteed to get the job – a guarantee which Giles was also led to believe he had – but they were both trumped after four ballots and a last-minute change of heart shunted Charlton into the job almost by accident. When association president Des Casey sat down for a press conference after that meeting, he admitted he wasn't sure whether or not Charlton would accept the job because the telephone at his Newcastle home kept ringing out.

Across town, Gay Byrne looked into the camera on *The Late, Late Show* and said off-handedly, 'I've just been handed a piece of paper here which says that Jack Charlton has been appointed manager of Ireland.' And as he put the slip of paper aside, he muttered, 'Whatever that means ...' There came a single whoop of support from the audience. Gay carried on with the show, quite unmoved by the news.

Charlton and his assistant Maurice Setters

Charlton was eventually located by an English journalist who told him he'd got the job and within a week he was in Dublin to thrash out the details with the FAI. When he sat down with association officials in Merrion Square, they cagily asked him what he would want to be paid. Charlton replied he wasn't in this for the money and whatever Eoin Hand had been getting would be good enough for him. They told Hand had been on £15,000 a year. 'Well I'll want a bit fucking more than that!' Charlton said. He got a bit more.

Next up was a date with the press, a comical encounter in the Westbury Hotel at which Charlton sat in the centre of a nineteen-man top table, told all and sundry that the Irish team had a bright future ahead of it and generally charmed everybody in the room. Everything was going swimmingly until the man from *The Irish Times* asked Des Casey to explain what had happened in the committee meeting at which Bob Paisley's fortunes had risen and fallen so dramatically. Casey demurred, saying this wasn't the time or place, which led Eamon Dunphy (then of the *Sunday Tribune*) to tell Casey that it was in the public interest to answer the question.

This, in turn, inexplicably and hilariously, got Charlton's hackles up and led him to offer to take Dunphy outside for a fight. 'I know you,' he said. 'You're a fucking troublemaker, you are. I'm not going to argue with you. I'm bigger than you. If you want to step outside, I'm ready now.' And with that, he grabbed his cap, stood up from the table and walked out, saying he had a match to watch. He even got a round of applause from the rest of the press pack.

Six weeks passed between Charlton's appointment and his first match on 26 March 1986, during which Ireland's putative opponents changed twice. On the day he took the job, it was intended that Brazil would be coming to Dublin for the first time in thirteen years as part of their European tour. Tele Santana's side were down to play Austria on 12 March and West Germany on 16 March and were happy to come to Lansdowne Road to face Ireland on 19 March.

However, it was a measure of the lowly standing of the game in Ireland at the time that this suggestion was dismissed out of hand because the stadium was already booked for the day by the Leinster Branch of the

IRFU; Blackrock College were down to meet St Michael's in the final of the Leinster Junior Cup so if Brazil wanted to come to Dublin, they'd have to do it the following Wednesday, the 2 March. They passed, preferring instead to go and train at altitude in preparation for the Mexico World Cup.

Hungary were then announced as the new opposition, a development welcomed by Charlton who figured that having drawn Bulgaria in the qualifiers for Euro '88, it would be better to get experience playing an eastern European team anyway. But within forty-eight hours of confirmation the Hungarians had cancelled as well, citing an unwillingness to disrupt club matches. The FAI were left in limbo, frantically ringing around to find an association willing to take up an invite. Fortunately, it turned out that Hungary had also cancelled on Wales that week and so the Welsh FA signed up to a trip to Dublin.

In the meantime, Charlton set about making his mark on his new land. Starting as he meant to go on, he wasn't at all shy about ruffling feathers. In fact, it seemed that he positively craved confrontation. Having already put FAI officials and the press on notice that he would be doing things his way or no way at all, he critically undermined Liam Tuohy, manager of the national youth team and the man who most people expected to become his assistant.

The Lansdowne Road crowd are less than welcoming to their new manager

At half-time in a youth international against England at Elland Road on 26 February, Charlton walked into the away dressing room, breezed past Tuohy who was about to launch into his half-time team talk and started giving out to the Ireland team who were trailing 2-0. Charlton wanted them to get the ball forward at every opportunity, to get the England defence turning and chasing back towards their own goal. When one of the players piped up and asked, 'Are we not to pass the ball anymore?', Charlton cut him down. 'You'll do what I tell you,' he growled.

Tuohy, outraged at what he saw as rank bad manners and a lack of respect, resigned immediately on his return to Dublin. 'I don't believe I was allowed to act as manager,' he said. 'Taking all things into consideration, I had no choice but to resign. The position I'm in was forced upon me and the stand I took was the only one any person of integrity could take.'

By now, Charlton was becoming deeply unpopular in his adopted country. A general public already not especially well-disposed to an Englishman being in charge of the Ireland team was coming to the realisation that Charlton could be a boor and a bully when he wanted to be. And a soccer public that could just about swallow the notion of an English manager so long as he behaved himself, saw his treatment of so sacred a cow as Tuohy as an abomination.

Brian Kerr and Noel O'Reilly – Tuohy's assistants in the youth set-up – quit in solidarity. Limerick City's chairman Pat Grace – the League Of Ireland's main sponsor – resigned from the FAI Executive in an effort to 'publicly dissociate myself from the humiliation of Liam Tuohy'. The poisonous atmosphere that had characterised the end of the Hand era – and from which Charlton's time was supposed to represent a clear departure – hadn't gone away at all. If anything this was worse, since Charlton's Ireland hadn't even kicked a ball yet.

But the big Geordie didn't care. Indeed, he further antagonised people within the game in Ireland by appointing another Englishman, Maurice Setters, as his assistant, ignoring the claims of such home-grown luminaries as Billy Young, Jim McLoughlin and Turlough O'Connor. The notion of two Englishmen running the Ireland team without any input from the locals was not a popular one. Jimmy Meagan, writing in the *Irish Press*, branded the state of affairs both 'ludicrous' and 'appalling'.

And if annoying Irish football people wasn't enough, Charlton then drew ire from beyond the national border when he named two uncapped Oxford United players in his first squad, beneficiaries of the increasingly notorious Granny Rule that allowed players whose Irish links stretched back two generations to declare for the country. John Aldridge and Ray Houghton were by no means the first players with English and Scottish accents to be parachuted into an Ireland squad, but they were the latest in what was becoming a long line and the practice was beginning to irk observers in other countries.

Certainly, Wales manager Mike England did little to hide his irritation as the match approached. So suddenly did the names Aldridge and Houghton spring up that there wasn't time to process their claims for Irish passports before the game and so Charlton had to rely on England's goodwill to allow them tog out. He gave it, grudgingly.

'What the FA of Ireland do is their business but they must be careful they don't get into hot water,' he said. 'The rest of the world considers the Irish system as something of a joke. If you've been to Dublin for a fortnight's holiday, you can apparently qualify for an Irish cap. The youngsters playing in Ireland are entitled to feel upset. What future have they got when they bring in players with the most tenuous qualifications to represent the country? I don't mind who Ireland pick – my concern is for Wales. But it doesn't seem like the best way to go about encouraging Irish players.'

All of which meant that if the FAI thought they were going to drum up a bumper crowd full of fervent hope for the future on the occasion of Charlton's first outing, they were to be sorely disappointed. A Wednesday afternoon kick-off didn't help either – floodlights would not be a feature at Lansdowne Road for eight years yet so winter evening matches weren't a runner - led to a crowd of just over sixteen thousand paying through the turnstiles. The FAI would lose £15,000 they could ill-afford on the match. Those who did turn up did so out of curiosity. And not everybody welcomed the new man – one banner in the crowd said: 'GO HOME UNION JACK'.

'I think a lot of the players were surprised that an Englishman had been appointed to the job,' said Paul McGrath later. 'That was first and foremost. But he came in and introduced himself and took to it straight away. and we actually took to him as well after a couple of early training sessions.'

Charlton didn't pick the team for that first game, leaving that task instead to the team's physio, Mick Byrne. 'I didn't know the players, I didn't know who we had,' he said. 'I didn't know anything about the structures within the team. So I got Mick Byrne to do it and let them go out and play. All along, I felt that my job would start after that first game, after I had seen what I'd got.'

The game itself was terrible and suffered badly from a barely-playable pitch. The FAI's renting arrangement with the IRFU covered certain types of matches but not others, meaning that they could expect a soccer-standard pitch to be prepared for big qualifiers, but not necessarily for friendlies. The pitch had had three rugby matches played on it inside the previous eleven days, including Ireland's final match of the Five Nations campaign against Scotland. The surface was bare in some places and dangerously pockmarked with holes in others.

This was to prove especially detrimental to the Wales goalkeeper Neville Southall. Collecting a long ball under pressure from Aldridge midway through the second half, he caught his ankle in a divot and went down in agony. He ended up having to be stretchered off and taken to St Vincent's Hospital with a broken ankle. Both managers were scathing about the pitch afterwards, although Charlton would come to use the unwelcoming surface to Ireland's advantage many times in the years that followed. In one particularly famous home win over Spain in 1989, the pitch could almost have been voted man of the match.

Even that kind of success felt a lifetime away in March 1986, however. Wales won the game 1-0 that day, courtesy of an Ian Rush header from a corner early in the game. In a lapse that would end up costing him a couple of years in the international wilderness, David O'Leary lost Rush at the corner and Charlton could be heard swearing as he left the pitch that O'Leary would never play for him again. Aldridge hit the post twice and would take until his fifteenth match in an Ireland jersey – against Tunisia two-and-a-half years later – to score his first international goal. He and Houghton would go on to play 131 times for Ireland between them.

John Aldridge, Charlton's newest recruit

'Obviously,' laughed Mick Byrne years later, 'Jack blamed me for the defeat.'

The media were very certainly unimpressed by this new dawn. 'IT'S NOT ALRIGHT, JACK!' roared the the *Irish Press* the following day. *The Irish Times* didn't spare the new administration either. 'Very often, one felt like one was watching a second division game on a sub-standard pitch,' read their report. 'At least Jack Charlton is starting right from the bottom. We really cannot get any worse, although the performances of Aldridge and Houghton were crumbs on an afternoon of dull mediocrity.'

It was no surprise then that even fewer turned up for his second match at Lansdowne Road – a crowd of just fourteen thousand deigned to come to a 1-1 draw against Uruguay the following month. But at the end of the season, Charlton took his squad to Reykjavik to play in and win a triangular tournament against Iceland and Czechoslovakia and the rest, well, the rest you probably know. He would go on to manage Ireland for just short of a decade and lead the country to two World Cups and a European Championships.

His team would generate an interest in soccer unheard of in the country up to then, one that would echo down the generations. Lansdowne Road would never again see such sparse crowds for international matches and, in time, the scruffy pitches would disappear too. The FAI would eventually smarten itself up and haul itself to a point where it could generate enough revenue to join with the IRFU and build a new stadium, the one that sits on Lansdowne Road today.

But nobody was dreaming that big on 26 March, 1986. Nobody would have dared to.

I n 1980s Ireland, one topic of conversation consumed all others. The thick grey cloud of recession hung over the country like a fire blanket, ready to cut off the oxygen supply to any and all sparks of ideas for at the future. Emigration siphoned off a generation, splitting families and pouring the best and the brightest out of a hole in the national bucket which seemed for the longest time like it would never be patched up. The unemployment rate among those who remained came close to touching 20 per cent. The ashen economy was the prism through which just about everything else that happened in the country was shot.

Lansdowne Road was by no means sheltered from the storm. It was costing the IRFU close to £500,000 a year in rates, insurance, wages and upkeep and, in truth, was beginning to show its age in places. At a time when the Ulster branch could draw crowds to interpro matches under lights at Ravenhill and Old Belvedere were running a hugely popular floodlit cup on midweek nights at Anglesea Road, the home of Irish rugby was still only fit for afternoon matches because floodlights were too expensive to install. Beyond that, the stadium's internal lighting was weak, the PA system had long been in need of an overhaul and, in those pre-Hillsborough days, an entire new perimeter fence was being planned as part of a wide-ranging security review. If the IRFU was to modernise the stadium, it would need more revenue than was coming from half a dozen or so rugby and soccer internationals it was hosting each year.

Jim O'Brien wasn't to know any of this when he arrived in Dublin in 1985. A tall, well-appointed Boston businessman in his late forties, he'd made his money selling class rings and yearbooks to high schools and college students in the US. He was in Dublin because he'd taken some of that money and invested it in the burgeoning Irish basketball scene, putting a small interest into the Jameson St Vincent's club in Glasnevin. In time, he would come back and trace his roots – his people were from Co. Clare – but this, his first visit to Ireland, was for the purpose of checking in on St Vincent's, courtesy of a friend of his at the club by the name of Pádraig McLoughlin.

They caught a game and afterwards, as per St Vincent's tradition, they went back to Hedigan's pub on Prospect Road for a drink. As the pints and conversation flowed, O'Brien noticed that there was an American

CHAPTER 26

1988
A whole
new ball
game

American
football at
Lansdowne
Road

Jim O'Brien and IRFU official Harry Booker

football game being played on the pub's television and, even more strangely, that people were actually watching it. He knew Irish people had their own sports that they loved, he knew they liked rugby too and soccer. But American football? Really?

He soon found out that the country was going through what would be a short-lived, but nonetheless entirely real, period of fascination with the game. In those pre-Sky Sports days, it was rare enough to see much foreign sport at all on terrestrial television and yet RTÉ was broadcasting an hour-long NFL highlights show on Thursday nights throughout the season and even had live coverage of the Super Bowl each January between 1986 and 1991. Indeed, by 1989, O'Brien himself would be part of the RTÉ Super Bowl programme, along with Tony Ward and presenter Myles Dungan.

But that was all far away in the future on that Thursday night in 1985. Sitting in Hedigan's – or The Brian Boru as it is also known – O'Brien was just tickled at the notion that Irish people would be interested in this most American of games at all. Because never mind basketball, gridiron was really his sport.

He had played to a high standard back in the late fifties and early sixties and had come within a hair's breadth of properly making it big. At Boston College, he was a brilliant offensive and defensive tackle and won the award for Outstanding Lineman at the 1959 All-American Bowl Game. In 1960, he was drafted by the Detroit Lions and looked a cert to have a long career ahead of him. But in his first ever game in the NFL he suffered a dislocated elbow and that was more or less the end of him. He spent a long time injured and never got back to the big show, although he would be inducted into the Boston College Hall of Fame in 1993. That he found himself sitting in a Dublin pub a quarter of a century after he finished playing, watching Irishmen watching NFL highlights on a rickety old TV made him laugh at fate more than anything.

'And so we got to talking about football,' he said later, 'because it was becoming such a popular sport in Ireland at the time and one of the guys said, "Well, why don't you bring a game over to Dublin?" And I went, "Right. Sure. Just like that, right?" But it planted a seed in my mind.'

O'Brien stayed in the Berkeley Court Hotel in Ballsbridge that night and the following day, as he waited on the lift in the hotel lobby, he caught sight of what was obviously a stadium of some description down the street. When he asked at reception, he found out that he was looking at Lansdowne Road and so he decided to take a wander over for a closer look. He found an open gate and strolled into the ground and was drinking in the place, noting that its location, among a cluster of neighbourhoods and side-streets, must make for quite an atmosphere on a big day, when he had an encounter that would shape the next three years of his life.

Lansdowne from the air

Cheerleaders at the game

'I ran into a gentleman who was on the IRFU committee and he showed me around we got talking about different sports. It came up that I was a graduate of Boston College and that I had played a little and actually, it was him who asked me what I thought the possibilities were of bringing an American football game to Dublin. Well now, this was the second time it had been mentioned to me in a couple of days by two completely unconnected people so I thought to myself that maybe there was something in the idea.

'So the fella said, "We're actually having a meeting tomorrow of the committee – would you be interested in coming to it?" "Sure," I said. "I'm an American businessman – I love to meet people." So I meet that IRFU committee the next day and we talk it out and by the time I leave, we're pretty much decided that we'll try and see where we go with it. The Dublin Millennium celebrations in 1988 were an obvious thing to target because it would give us a few years' planning time and it all just came from that.'

O'Brien got a letter of intent from the IRFU, granting him permission to stage one game a year in their stadium for the next decade. For the enterprise to work, O'Brien knew he would need to supply not only the teams and the razzmatazz, but a decent proportion of the crowd as well. He hit upon the idea of making the game into a homecoming opportunity for the US-based diaspora, the people who like him had Irish names, but hadn't ever done very much about finding out where those names had come from. If he could bring, say, ten thousand Americans to Dublin for the game, then The Emerald Isle Classic (for that's what it came to be called) might turn out to have legs.

There was no chance of staging an NFL game outside the US – that wouldn't happen until a game in Mexico City in 2005 – but college games had been held semi-regularly on foreign soil, so often in fact that the NCAA had introduced a rule saying that each college could only play abroad once every four years. O'Brien knew that his *alma mater* Boston College had played in Japan in 1984 and so they would be available for Dublin in 1988.

The Boston College Eagles were the obvious choice for the game, the college having long-standing Irish links going right back to its founder in 1863, a Jesuit priest from Fermanagh by the name of Fr John McElroy. O'Brien still had close ties to the school and knew the athletic director Phil Flynn would probably be up for it. 'He was a Flynn, I was an O'Brien,' he said. 'This was happening.' The army college at West Point made most sense as a choice of opponent, since they had a constant supply of servicemen in Europe who could provide a ready-made audience.

O'Brien got things moving quickly. He set up a promotions company called Brian Boru Marketing in honour of the pub where the idea first came up. In Boston, he organised for a travel company to start selling the game to BC graduates. West Point organised for the game to be shown in US Army bases in thirty countries throughout the world.

In Dublin, the IDA and Bord Fáilte got involved. He knew that getting enough people interested in the game to make any money, he would need Irish businesses on board to create a buzz. The game would be shown live on ESPN in the US, giving Irish companies opportunities to advertise to a huge audience both during the game and in preview shows the night before and highlights packages later on the day. Almost by accident, O'Brien had stumbled upon the perfect selling point for his game – never mind the action, feel the marketing opportunity.

By November 1986, they were ready to present the idea to the world and the Emerald Isle Classic was leaked to a few

Boston College tailback Mike Sanders enjoying the day

Irish newspapers to test the waters. It was reported that O'Brien's company was willing to underwrite the cost of installing floodlights at Lansdowne Road, but that was never that case, which was a pity since it meant that game would have to kick off at 7.30am on the American east coast. However, floodlights would cost somewhere in the region of £100,000, a sum neither party had to hand. O'Brien had become so consumed by the project that he'd sold his half of his jewellery company to his business partner.

'My whole idea was I wanted to make it successful for the colleges and for Ireland and for all the people who would be going over,' O'Brien recalled. 'I never really did it to make money. It became a passion of mine more than anything. I was always of the attitude, "Well hey, if I make some money along the way then fine, so be it." But I wasn't really doing it for that purpose. And it's a good thing I wasn't, that's for sure. By the time we paid for everything, for the insurance, the TV costs, the hiring of the stadium and all the other things that go into an event like this, there isn't a whole lot left over.'

Meantime, in Ireland, politicians desperate to be involved in anything remotely outward-looking and optimistic-sounding climbed aboard O'Brien's bandwagon. He made up over twenty trips to Ireland in the three years between the St Vincent's basketball game and the BC Eagles-West Point match and each time he came, he could hardly move for people looking to get into a picture with him. The Minister for Sport Frank Fahey was there at the official launch, along with US Ambassador Margaret Heckler (a Boston College graduate) and the Garda Commissioner of the time, Eamon Doherty. The Minister for Industry and Commerce Albert Reynolds attended a lunch with a hundred invited American guests linked to the game. All that could be done to wring every last dollar out of the event was done.

By the time gameday came around on Saturday 19 November 1988, a massive buzz had been created with events planned all across Dublin for the weekend. The National Arthritis Foundation held a ball in a huge marquee behind the stadium the night before the game and the Point Depot, which had opened for gigs earlier in the year, was booked for a Marty Whelan-hosted Touchdown party on the Saturday. A parade

through St Stephen's Green was organised for the Friday afternoon, led by the Garda Band and including both college's marching bands. O'Brien even got on to *The Late, Late Show* two Friday nights in a row.

Dublin was flooded with visitors for the weekend, with an estimated twelve thousand coming over for the game. The Boston travel company signed up by O'Brien chartered planes and block-booked seats on five different airlines to get to Dublin. He rented out 150 buses to take tourists around the country in the week leading up to the game. All in all, it made claims on being the biggest ever single influx of Americans into Ireland for one event – the average St Patrick's Day only ever attracted a couple of thousand each year. In the end, the weekend was estimated to have been worth somewhere in the region of £10m to the Irish economy.

Boston quarterback Mark Kamphaus thrills the girls

The stadium itself had to be adapted for the occasion. Americans were used to concession stands and hotdog vendors at their games, but you couldn't buy so much as a bar of chocolate inside Lansdowne Road in the 1980s. Extra toilets were needed since the game would last over three hours as opposed to the usual eighty-minute rugby international. The fifty-four thousand capacity had to be lowered by about eight thousand because the sport's tradition of having teams standing up on the sidelines meant people in the first few rows of seats wouldn't be able to see the action. Quarantine regulations had prevented Army from bringing their famous mule mascot over to Ireland with them so a replacement was sourced from a breeder in Armagh.

The teams arrived in Dublin three days before the game, drawing crowds of curious onlookers to their practice sessions in UCD. They were whisked around radio stations to drum up publicity and the newspapers gloried in photos of the players, one particularly excitable writer describing BC lineman Joe Wolf as 'a tidal wave of rippling muscle'. Wolf would go on to be drafted by the Phoenix Cardinals the following year and play out a decent NFL career, a starter in ninety-four games over the following decade.

Wolf was far from the only future star to appear at Lansdowne Road that Saturday. His friend and right guard Doug Widell would go on to a stellar career as well, joining the Denver Broncos in the 1989 draft and lodging 139 starts for four different teams in a nine-year NFL career. Indeed, only fourteen months after playing in Dublin, Widell was a rookie starter for the Broncos in the 1990 Super Bowl in New Orleans, although his team did sadly go down to a record 55-10 defeat.

On the Army side, half-back Mike Mayweather was on his way to becoming one of the all-time legends of West Point football. By the time he finished his college career, he held the college's career rushing record of 4,299 yards and finished tenth in the voting for the 1990 Heisman Trophy (awarded to the most outstanding college footballer in America each year), an almost unheard-of achievement for an Army footballer in the modern era.

On the day, Mayweather scored a touchdown in the game against Boston, but his team were outplayed in front of a Lansdowne Road crowd of 44,525. BC's junior full-back Ed Toner scored three touchdowns, all from just a yard out. Boston led 17-10 at half-time, but worked their way clear in the second half to finish up comprehensive 38-24 winners. The result was actually something of an upset, as Army had come into the game in much better form than the Eagles and went on to finish their season with a much better record.

The event was a roaring success. Despite the stop-start nature of the game, the virtually sold-out crowd enjoyed themselves immensely in the crisp November cold, with the BC cheerleaders proving an especially popular diversion. Pubs, hotels and restaurants throughout the city were jammed all weekend. O'Brien's gamble had paid off in spades. He hadn't made a fortune out of the event, but he'd covered himself, with enough left over to prompt him to go again in 1989.

But things didn't work out as well the following year. The NCAA's four-year rule meant that Boston College and West Point were ruled out as options so O'Brien was forced to look elsewhere for teams willing to travel. But whereas he was able to give the 1988 teams the best part of three years' notice, uncertainty over whether or not the first game would be a success meant he was forced to find the 1989 teams at short notice. In the end Rutgers University, New Jersey played the University of Pittsburgh and the vast battalion of graduates that bolstered the crowd in 1988 couldn't be sourced the second time.

Only around two thousand Americans signed up to the travel packages in 1989 and there were no servicemen stationed in Europe to call on either. Combined with a lower-key build-up – the novelty had worn off for the Irish media who barely covered it except to say there wasn't as much buzz as the previous year – and the awful December weather, the lack of a significant American element kept the crowd down to around twenty-thousand and effectively sounded the death knell for the series. O'Brien lost a lot of money and the ten-year IRFU letter of intent wasn't going to be required.

'If the second year had been the first year and the first year the second, everyone would have thought it was great,' he said. 'We had two thousand Americans over the second time around and the game drew a crowd of twenty thousand or so. But because it paled in comparison with the first year, everybody was down on it. We had it too late in the year as well and the weather was really bad I remember. It was in December and that meant it was too close to Thanksgiving and Christmas and that turned a lot of Americans off coming over a second time. But if that had been the first year and we'd fixed it all for the second year, everybody would have thought it was great. We hit a home run with our first swing of the bat and when you do that, people expect the same every time to step to the plate.'

O'Brien went on to become a regular visitor to Ireland and got heavily involved in the Irish-American scene in Boston, eventually becoming chairman of the Irish-American Chamber of Commerce (later renamed the Boston Irish Business Association). He did a lot of work with the Special Olympics movement too and led the Massachusetts delegation when the World Games were held in Ireland in 2003.

But whatever else he did in his life, he was forever delighted that a chance observation in a Glasnevin pub one night led him to feel the warmth and buzz of those neighbourhoods and side-streets he'd seen out the front window of the Berkeley Court and to eventually to reconnect with the country of his forefathers. 'It didn't make me rich obviously,' he said over twenty years later, 'but it enriched my life beyond words.'

Ireland come within minutes of a World Cup semi-final only to be denied by Michael Lynagh and Australia

W hen plans to hold the first ever Rugby World Cup were announced in early August 1985, to say that Ireland were reluctant supporters of the idea would be to severely understate the case. The World Cup was an enterprise on which France, Australia and New Zealand made all the running and for the IRFU, it was a massive step into the unknown. They feared that a World Cup would not only disrupt touring schedules worldwide (and kill off the Lions), but would also take too great a physical toll on amateur players and could only therefore hasten a rush to professionalise the sport.

The IRFU weren't alone in their reluctance to accept the invite to play in what was officially titled, with classic International Rugby Board pomposity, The International Tournament For The Webb Ellis Cup. Indeed, so squeamish were the likes of the Irish and Scottish unions about the whole idea that when it was announced it had to be put forward as a stand-alone event. While it was generally thought that the exercise might be repeated in the northern hemisphere in 1991 if the 1987 version proved a success, nothing of substance was on the table. Given the opposition from most within the home unions, it seemed an unlikely runner.

In the end though, everybody signed up to play in the 1987 tournament, the IRFU figuring it would be better to row in with the rest of the world than to sit on the sideline as conscientious objectors to whom nobody paid much heed. The union even awarded full caps to the players taking part, although they only arrived at the decision to do so five months before the tournament kicked off. Once there, Ireland beat Canada and Tonga as expected in their pool, but lost to Wales before exiting at the quarter-final stage in Sydney at the hands of Australia. No worse than had been expected and certainly no better.

On the eve of the tournament, the outgoing chairman of the organising committee Dick Littlejohn was quite bullish about the future. 'The first Rugby World Cup will certainly set a precedent for the second one and we truly believe that it will contribute significantly to the development of the sport,' he said. And by the time New Zealand had beaten France in the final in Auckland, the Argentine, French and home unions were all

elbowing each other out of the way to present their bids to host the 1991 version.

If anyone pondered the irony of the original opponents of the tournament, the home unions, being so keen to take it to their own turf, they didn't get to ponder it for long. The IRB awarded Britain and Ireland the World Cup in March 1988, but instructed that they had to share this lucrative new adventure with France. It was a classic case of pleasing nobody by pleasing everybody and it led to nineteen venues being used to host matches in the tournament, a full ten more than in 1987, a record number that is unlikely ever to be beaten. The stadiums ranged in size from the mighty seventy-five-thousand-capacity Twickenham to tiny Cross Green, home of Otley RFC in Leeds that could take a mere five thousand.

Whatever behind-the-scenes manoeuvring was carried out by the IRFU paid off too as, after a long and tortuous process, it was announced that five games would be held on the island during the tournament – Japan versus Zimbabwe in Ravenhill and four matches in Lansdowne Road. Were Ireland to finish second in their pool, they would most likely play a World Cup quarter-final in Dublin 4 against Australia, the odds-on favourites to finish on top of Pool C. In theory, it was an enticing prospect.

In practice, however, the Ireland rugby team was going through one of its troughs at the time. In the six seasons since the glorious Triple Crown triumph of 1985, they'd played twenty-four Five Nations matches and only managed to win five. They were going into the World Cup off the back of another winless championship in which they were only saved from a whitewash by a 21-21 draw with a Wales team that was in a similar funk to them (and one which would go on to lose to the unheralded Western Samoa in the tournament itself).

Ciaran Fitzgerald was the coach at the time and a flavour of the state of flux that surrounded the squad can be found in his team selection for the opening match of that Five Nations against France. Fitzgerald named five new faces, one of whom was even made captain to widespread astonishment. Rob Saunders, a twenty-two-year-old scrum-half who had not yet even played for Ulster, took on the mantle after it had been turned down by Philip Matthews in the absence of the injured Donal Lenihan. It was the first time in thirty-five years that an Ireland player making his first appearance in a green jersey had been handed the captaincy and Saunders was on a hiding to nothing in many ways, charged with marshalling a young and not particularly organised side. Despite his best efforts, he never won a game as Ireland captain. Indeed, in his twelve-cap career, he was on the winning side only twice.

But in their own unique ways, each of the other four new caps against France in Lansdowne Road that day left their mark. Brian Robinson was a big-boned school teacher from Belfast who had been in and around the fringes of the squad for a while and who would go on to play twenty-five times in Ireland's back row, mostly at number eight, but sometimes as flanker towards the end of his career. Later that year at Lansdowne Road, he would become the first Irishman ever to score four tries in an international when Zimbabwe were put to the sword.

Ahead of him in the second row was the twenty-four-year-old former All Ireland-winning Gaelic footballer from Kerry, Mick Galwey. Despite ceding his place to Lenihan by the time the World Cup came around that year, Galwey would go on to have the longest career of any of the debutants and was the only player in that team whose playing days extended well into the professional era. Long after many of his contemporaries were settled into a life of media punditry, Galwey was wet-nursing the next generation of Ireland internationals into their careers.

The other two debutants against France in 1991 would both go on to become cult heroes. Simon Geoghegan was a young trainee solicitor from London Irish who, in another age and with better luck, would surely have been one of the greatest of all Irish rugby players. He arrived that year in a blond blaze of glory, scoring tries against Wales, England and Scotland and offering hope amid the gloom. In time, injuries would curtail his career, but back then there was no brighter hope for the future.

The final freshman was a twenty-six-year-old wing-forward from junior club NIFC (Northern Ireland Football Club) by the name of Gordon Hamilton. He'd been a dogged part of the Ulster set-up for a couple of years at that stage – himself and a young Peter Clohessy had had a serious set-to in an interprovincial match the year before and had needed to be separated in the bar afterwards – and his elevation had come at the expense of his provincial colleague Denis McBride. The dividends weren't immediate – France's 21-13 set a grim trend for the year – but Fitzgerald's selections would be vindicated in time.

Despite not winning a game in the championship, there were definite straws to clutch at in Ireland's performances in early 1991. At the very least there had been some scoring to get excited about. Whereas the 1990 campaign had provided a wretched return of just thirty-six points and four tries, Fitzgerald's side had run in ten tries on their way to scoring sixty-six points this time around. True, they hadn't managed a win, but they hadn't been disgraced either and had finished with their best points difference in five seasons. Okay, that points difference was still minus-twenty, but these were bad times and Irish rugby supporters hung onto whatever little hope there was.

The all-consuming mania of the previous year's soccer World Cup had thrown the fortunes of the national rugby team into sharp relief. If Jack Charlton's side could make it to the last eight in the world in the planet's most played sport, the onus was now squarely on the rugby team to follow suit. In a Euro '92 qualifier in October 1990, Ireland beat Turkey 5-0 at Lansdowne Road in front of a Wednesday afternoon full house, the biggest win at the stadium since soccer had returned.

As the popularity of that sport went orbital and Charlton's side outplayed England in Euro '92 qualifying matches at both Lansdowne and Wembley, many within rugby feared for the future. Even the previous year's FAI cup final between St Francis and Bray Wanderers had unexpectedly drawn a crowd of thirty thousand to Lansdowne Road, the most for a domestic final since 1968. Soccer was a juggernaut now and there was a real worry that rugby could become a sideline interest, kept going in a few die-hard pockets of the country, but a niche pursuit elsewhere. Heading into the World Cup, a World Cup Ireland would play largely on home soil, the game here badly needed the boost of the unexpected.

Robinson's four tries against Zimbabwe in the opening game on 6 October were a good start and the 55-11 win was notable for other reasons too. Ralph Keyes, the Cork out-half who was playing at Lansdowne Road for the first time as a full international, kicked twenty-three points and passed Ollie Campbell's record from the 1982 Triple Crown clincher over Scotland along the way. The game was also the first international match ever to be played at Lansdowne Road on a Sunday.

Three days later Ireland faced Japan who, like Zimbabwe, were playing their first ever international against Ireland. Japan were coached by the inimitable Shiggy Konno, whose favourite claim to fame was that he was a failed kamikaze pilot in World War II. 'My commanding officer refused to send me on missions because I was considered more dangerous to my fellow pilots that I was to the enemy,' he said. His team put up a more than spirited resistance against Ireland, eventually going down to a 32-16 defeat at Lansdowne.

David Campese
tackled by Brendan
Mullin

Neil Francis brings the Irish fight to Willie Ofahengaue

By now, the World Cup and Ireland's progress in it was starting to grab the attention of the public at large. Their final pool match was against Scotland in Murrayfield on Saturday, 12 October, a fixture for which an estimated fifteen thousand Irish people made the trip to Edinburgh. Because tournament rules stipulated that an equal number of tickets for each game should go to both nations involved, this was a three times the amount of travelling supporters that would have been the norm for a Five Nations match. The Irish public had no problem taking up the extra supply.

They were to be disappointed, however, as Ireland went down to a 24–15 defeat in a game best remembered for a savage high tackle on Ireland full-back Jim Staples by Scottish wing-forward Finlay Calder when Ireland were 15-9 ahead. A game that had hung in the balance swung definitively Scotland's way thereafter as in the very next play, a plainly groggy Staples attempted to catch a high ball, but only succeeded in causing the ball to bounce off his shoulder and into open play where it was gathered by Scotland wing Tony Stanger and recycled for substitute Graham Shiel to score. Within ten minutes, another Scotland Garryowen rained down on Staples and in the ensuing melee, scrum-half Gary Armstrong won the game for the home side.

All of which put Ireland, as predicted, into a quarter-final against Australia the following Sunday. Nobody gave them a prayer facing a side that had already beaten England and New Zealand earlier that year, but nevertheless, they had huge public support after the Scotland game and the controversy over Calder's tackle. Whereas the World Cup organisers were forced to advertise tickets for the early pool games at Lansdowne

Road, £20 tickets were changing hands for £150 this time around.

It didn't hurt that the Aussies had made themselves at home in Dublin. With a squad sprinkled with names like Lynagh, Horan and Kearns – not to mention a coach called Dwyer and a team manager called Breen – they were comfortable and popular from the minute they arrived. A win over Ireland would mean their semi-final would also be in Lansdowne Road so they figured they were settling in for a fortnight's stay once they arrived. At a training session on the Tuesday before the game, the Australian ambassador Terence McCarthy met the Irish press corps and was asked if he'd like to be addressed as 'Ambassador' or 'Your Excellency'. 'Fuck, no,' he replied. 'Call me Terry.'

For Ireland, there was no expectation so there was little pressure. Fitzgerald took the squad off for a few days' downtime in Kerry after they got back from Edinburgh and allowed the rest of the world to pass them by. 'We weren't overly successful at that time,' said Hamilton, 'but we were never easily beaten. So in all truth the attitude was just to give it a rattle. It wasn't much more scientific than that. We had planned all week that we'd attack that game with a view to knocking them over.'

Hamilton was by no means a cast-iron selection going into the game. He'd had a reasonable World Cup, but there were worries that he wasn't abrasive enough to annoy the Australians and some had called for Pat O'Hara to come in for him. But Hamilton had impressed the selectors with his attitude and work-rate. In the run-up to the tournament he, along with Robinson, Steve Smith and Keith Crossan had done specialist plyometrics work in Belfast with a thirty-two-year-old fitness coach called Eddie O'Sullivan in a bid to improve his sprinting speed. That fitness coach would go on to win three Triple Crowns in four years as overall Ireland coach in the first decade of the 2000s, but in the shorter term, the work he did with Hamilton would pay off in spades.

Despite a disrupted build-up that day – the Ireland team bus got stuck in traffic on the way to Lansdowne and the team went on to the pitch with no more than a rudimentary warm-up completed – Ireland turned in a performance of utterly unexpected ferocity and brilliance. From the props Nick Poppelwell and Des Fitzgerald (whose then four-year-old son Luke would go on to star for Leinster, Ireland and the Lions) through the

Gordon Hamilton scores arguably Lansdowne's most famous try

outstanding Neil Francis and Matthews and Robinson, Ireland's pack pushed and hustled throughout. Keyes continued the brilliant kicking streak that would see him end the tournament as its top scorer and Staples recovered from his Murrayfield ordeal to shine at full-back.

But the day would be forever remembered for Hamilton. With six minutes to go, Ireland trailed 15-12 having stayed in touch through the boot of Keyes as the wondrous David Campese had run in two tries for Australia. But from a scrum just outside their own 22, Saunders fed Keyes who dished onto centre David Curtis. Staples joined the line then and once he drew a tackle he kicked ahead for winger Jack Clarke to battle with Campese for the ball. Clarke's desire hooshed Campese out of the way and in one slick movement, he picked the ball up and flicked it inside to Hamilton who was coming through on his shoulder like a train.

Suddenly the whole of Lansdowne could see the possibilities. Hamilton had run the most perfect line imaginable and had built up a head of steam while everyone else on the pitch was flat-footed and weary. Campese realised instantly that he'd messed up and went to chase, but gave up again within ten yards of the line. Australia's last hope was covering winger Bob Egerton who dived full-length at Hamilton and brought him to the ground a yard short of the line. Such was the Ulsterman's momentum, however, that with one bounce on the Lansdowne turf, he was free.

The place went haywire. Ireland fans spilled onto the pitch to swarm around Hamilton and congratulate him. All of a sudden, Ireland were 16-15 ahead with a possible conversion to come from Keyes and just five minutes left to hold out for a place in the World Cup semi-final. Most of the Aussies assumed they were beaten. Centre Tim Horan remembered thinking that he'd sent his clothes to the laundry that morning and now they'd be wet all the way to Australia. Bummer.

But as Keyes lined up the conversion – which he stroked through the post from the left touchline to a cheer almost the equal of the one that greeted the try – Australian stand-in captain Michael Lynagh gathered his team under the posts and laid it out for them. 'I had to come up with a plan or we would be on the plane back home to Australia the next morning wrapped in failure,' he said later. 'I just said, "If you get the ball,

hold on to it." I intentionally wanted to avoid, at all costs, any negative talk. I wanted to give players things to do rather than tell them what not to do. I kept saying to myself, "Do *not* use the word 'don't.'" I wanted to keep the instructions as simple as possible.'

Meanwhile, Ireland's players were huddled on the halfway line. They knew the pressure was going to come and stressed to each other that the one imperative was that when they got the chance, the ball was to be kicked high into the stands. If they kept their heads, they'd shock the world.

But when the key play came, the unfortunate Saunders got over-excited and went for distance instead of safety with a clearance kick. His intent was sound in that he wanted to pin the Aussies back in their own half, but his execution was poor. The ball didn't make touch and from there, Australia came at Ireland in waves. From a scrum seven metres out, they worked a backline move that send Campese flying for the line and although he was stopped just short, the ball popped up into Lynagh's hands and that was that. Lynagh missed the conversion, but it didn't matter. Australia's day, 19-18.

'We were awfully close,' said Hamilton, 'but Lynagh sneaked in for a try

Michael Lynagh breaks Irish hearts

almost from the kick-off. Any defensive coach watching that clip now might throw themselves off a cliff. It certainly wasn't textbook defending by any means. In hindsight, if we were a little smarter and maybe a bit more advanced in our defensive systems, we would've won that game.'

When it was over, Fitzgerald and Matthews walked into the press conference to a round of applause from the rugby media. Everyone knew they'd seen something special and for a team that had been criticised from all quarters for most of the previous six years, the irony here was that while the public and press were lauding them, they were furious with themselves for giving away the late try. 'People are constantly asking me to relive the try,' said Hamilton, 'but to be honest, the thing I remember most about that game is that we lost.'

Sadly, there was no fresh dawn off the back of that day. Australia went on to beat New Zealand in the semi-final at Lansdowne the following Sunday and then England a week later to lift their first World Cup. And Ireland went on to endure the 1990s, as wretched a rugby decade as they'd ever known. They finished dead last in the Five Nations another four times before the decade was out and actually won more championship games in Cardiff than at Lansdowne. The officials had been correct – the World Cup did hasten the onset of the professional game and by the time the next one happened in South Africa in 1995, the rest of the world had gotten the jump on Ireland. It was to take the best part of a decade for them to catch up.

But none of that could have been foreseen in October 1991 when for one afternoon – and one five-minute spell in particular – Lansdowne Road convulsed with the giddiness of forty thousand believers.

IRELAND: Jim Staples; Simon Geoghegan, Brendan Mullin, David Curtis, Jack Clarke; Ralph Keyes, Rob Saunders; Nick Popplewell, Steve Smith, Des Fitzgerald, Donal Lenihan, Neil Francis, Philip Matthews (capt.), Gordon Hamilton, Brian Robinson
AUSTRALIA: Marty Roebuck; David Campese, Tim Horan, Jason Little, Bob Egerton; Michael Lynagh, Nick Farr-Jones (capt.), Tony Daly, Phil Kearns, Ewen McKenzie, Rod McCall, John Eales, Simon Poidevin, Jeff Miller, Willie Ofahengaue. Sub: Peter Slattery for Farr-Jones (17 mins)
Referee: Jim Fleming (Scotland)

CHAPTER 28

1993 Beautiful, Beautiful Munsters

The biggest AIL attendance ever watches Young Munster beat St Mary's in a final-day decider

When the All Ireland League (the AIL) came kicking and screaming into the world in October 1990, it was initially treated with some suspicion among many of Ireland's rugby clubs. It was no accident that Ireland was the last of the British and Irish nations to set up its own countrywide domestic league – Irish rugby clubs had historically settled into a comfortable routine of playing local competitions and senior cups with occasional away-day weekend trips filling out their seasons and the notion of shaking things up with a nationally-organised competition met with resistance from the start.

Indeed, so ingrained was the status quo that when a survey of the clubs in the mid-1980s asked if they might consider signing up to a national league, not even the fact that just over half of them said they would was enough to get it going. The closeness of the vote made the IRFU shelve the idea for another few years. This reluctance would in time come to appear futile and wrong-headed, however, as the AIL's popularity grew quite spectacularly once it got up and running in 1990. The initial competition was made up of two divisions, comprising the team that had performed best in the provincial leagues over the previous two seasons and by the end of the first season, all the other clubs were angling to get involved. In time, there would be four divisions.

Crowds flocked to games, the rugby press got behind the idea and for most of the 1990s, the AIL went through a golden age. And while the achievements of the all-conquering four-in-a-row Shannon side can't go without mention, there is really no competition for the greatest AIL afternoon in Lansdowne Road's history – Young Munster's final day victory over St Mary's in February 1993.

Munsters were the copybook Cinderella story that year. In a survey of the AIL club captains before the start of the season, only one – Kenny Andrew of Ballymena – predicted that they'd even finish in the top three in the table. To everyone else, they were hardly mapped. Only a couple of years previously, they'd had a last-gasp battle with Highfield for the right to play in Division Two of the AIL and had just about scraped through thanks to a Miko Benson drop goal as the clock ran dead. In the meantime, their tough, uncompromising brand of rugby had bought them

Young Munster's legendary prop Peter Clohessy

respect in spades, but imagining them as overall league champions was fanciful to say the least.

Despite acquitting themselves better than most had expected, they were still among the also-rans in most people's minds as they headed into their sixth match of eight that season. Coming off the back of a 3-3 draw against title contenders Greystones, they faced an away fixture against Cork Constitution on 23 January in which it was assumed their season would effectively come to an end, albeit a typically spirited one. Con, the inaugural AIL champions two years earlier, were unbeaten up to that point and played a free-scoring, attacking game that looked on paper to have too much class for the Limerick team. And when Con winger Kenny

Murphy kicked the home side into a 13-9 lead just past the hour mark, the pre-match predictions looked reasonably safe.

But from that point until the end of the match, Young Munster reached out and grabbed their destiny with both hands. Playing into the teeth of a gale, they laid siege to the Con line, sending forward after forward crashing relentlessly into the home side's defence. 'I remember asking the referee how long was left when we started in their corner,' said captain and flanker Ger Clohessy. 'And he said, "Seventeen minutes." We hardly gave them a touch of the ball after that.'

It was remarkable rugby, a quarter-hour passage of play that typified everything that made the AIL such a draw for the public through that era. Surge after surge of Young Munster play was repelled by the Con defence, mostly on the try-line. Con gave away ten penalties and countless scrums, but still held on as the game went into injury time. But right at the death, with the Cork Con defence out on its feet and anticipating another forward-heavy rumble, Munsters finally spun the ball to the backs, through out-half Aidan O'Halloran and centre Francis Brosnahan who fed a long pass out to Niall McNamara on the right wing. He crossed to make it 14-13 and when O'Halloran's conversion gave Munsters an epic 16-13 victory, it cracked the top of the league wide open.

'They were incredible, that pack,' said Paul O'Connell, who was thirteen at the time and rising through the Young Munster ranks. 'They were everything that rugby can be about. You could look at some teams that would throw the ball around and that's one way of winning rugby games, but they were sheer physicality and intimidation.'

Having ground Cork Con to dust in that final quarter, Young Munster were viable contenders for the title now, along with Con and St Mary's. Greystones were in there too, although they would finish the season meekly and fade away. But with two matches to go, Con faced St Mary's on the same afternoon as Young Munster took on the previous year's champions, Garryowen. Their city rivals had had a poor season in defence of their title and were actually in danger of being relegated. Young Munster were only too delighted to take advantage of their poor form, beating them 13-6 thanks to another awesome forward performance on 6 February.

When the result filtered through from Temple Hill soon after the final whistle to say that Mary's had beaten Con, the massed ranks of Tom Clifford Park rubbed their hands together in anticipation. Whoever had put the fixture list together back in the autumn had hit paydirt – Young Munster's final match of the league season was down for the following Saturday against St Mary's. Both teams would go into the game on eleven points, meaning whoever won the game took the title. A draw would mean the league was decided on points difference, in which case the Dublin club would come out on top. It was a delicious prospect.

But almost immediately, there was a snag. St Mary's home ground at Templeville Road in Templeogue had a capacity of six thousand – perfectly serviceable in the normal run of things, but likely to be woefully inadequate given the certainty of at least that amount travelling from Limerick alone for the title decider. When it was suggested that St Mary's might move the game to accommodate the bigger crowd, the club instinctively bucked against the idea. 'I am quite positive that will not happen,' said club spokesman David Maloney. 'There is no way we would be prepared to surrender the chance of playing this match on our own ground.'

That was on Sunday, 7 February but by the following afternoon it was becoming clear that, while it was understandable that St Mary's would want to play the match on their own ground, they had underestimated the extent of the frenzy Young Munster's assault on the AIL title had created in Limerick. Quite apart from their own band of die-hard supporters, there was a wider subtext at play in that Munster clubs had already won the first two instalments of the AIL: Cork Con in 1991 and Garryowen in 1992. The thought that Young Munster could carry on the streak – and in the heart of leafy south Dublin to boot – energised more than just that one club. Two special trains were booked from Limerick to Dublin for the day above and beyond the normal services, as well as an estimated three dozen coaches. There would be a lot of disappointed people come Saturday if St Mary's didn't move the game.

The Templeogue club weren't for moving, however. By hook or by crook, they were intent on playing the game on their own turf. They vowed to erect special temporary terracing to increase the ground's

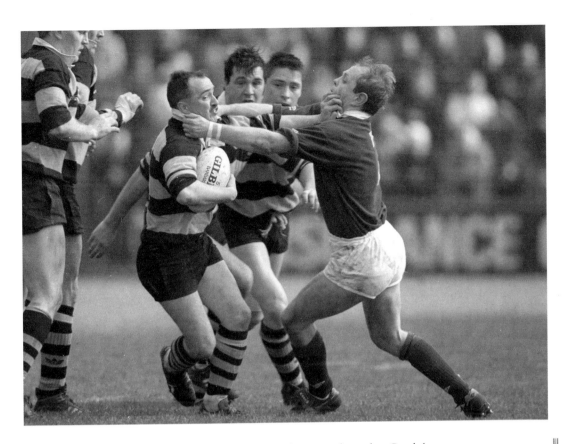

capacity if it meant getting their own way. And even when the Gardaí and Fire Brigade nixed that idea on health and safety grounds on the Wednesday and declared that the allowable capacity of the ground would be a mere 5,500 people, they still tried to hold firm.

There was a back-story to their unwillingness to move the game, in particular to accommodate Young Munster. Relations between the two clubs had been frosty since the previous season when St Mary's scrum-half John Muldoon had been the victim of a very nasty ear wound in their league encounter. Muldoon had dived on the ground to retrieve the ball from a botched line-out early in the game and had emerged from the ensuing melee with his left ear partially severed. He left the pitch and went straight to hospital for extensive stitchwork, leaving behind him an ill-tempered game that simmered with rancour for the rest of the afternoon.

Young Munster officials and players repeatedly emphasised afterwards that while they regretted the injury Muldoon had received, there had been no deliberate attempt to harm him. While extremely careful not to throw any accusations around in public, St Mary's had sent a letter to the

Derek Tobin of Young Munster breaks Ciaran Devlin's tackle

AIL champions
Young Munster lift
the cup

league committee in protest at 'the manner in which the game was played'. If Young Munster were expecting much leeway from them now, eighteen months later and with the league title on the line, they had another think coming.

And anyway, it was perfectly understandable that St Mary's didn't want to move. Home advantage in the most important match of the season would surely have been worth a try at least to them and it seemed unfair that every other team in the league had been allowed its full allocation of home matches while they were effectively being asked to pay a price for their success. Two years previously, when the self-same scenario had presented itself with Garryowen drawn against Cork Con in the final game of the season and both teams vying for the title, nobody had asked Garryowen to give up playing at Dooradoyle. St Mary's also had club sponsors to keep happy and staff to employ. What, they wondered, was the point of tending assiduously to their own patch if they weren't allowed to put it to its intended use?

But the league had moved onwards and upwards even in the short two years since Garryowen v Cork Con and the longer the week went on, the clearer it became that Templeville Road simply couldn't cope with the numbers looking to get into the match. Gardaí genuinely feared that the Templeogue venue could become overwhelmed with traffic – both motorised and human – come Saturday. By Thursday afternoon, the IRFU stepped in and declared they were moving the match to Lansdowne Road. St Mary's were predictably appalled.

'We feel a precedent has been set which will have far-reaching implications for the competition,' they said in a statement. 'The principle appears to have been established that demands of a visiting side can influence the outcome of where the match can be played, dismantling the long tradition of the "draw" system. The capacity of St Mary's compares favourably with all clubs in the league and having offered Young Munster over 50 per cent of the tickets, we are most disappointed that this has been unacceptable to the visiting team.'

St Mary's weren't the only party with a grievance to air on the back of the IRFU's decision. With the national side due to play France in the Five Nations the following Saturday, it was normal practice to leave the Lansdowne pitch free of use for a fortnight in preparation. As a result, Wanderers had already been told to move their AIL Division Two match against Dolphin to Merrion Road. When they heard that the pitch would, in fact, now be used, they weren't best pleased. 'All it takes for Wanderers to be summarily dismissed from the use of the main pitch at Lansdowne Road is a shower of rain,' mused Wanderers president Harry Jackson.

For all the fire and fury, however, the match was set and on Saturday 13 February, Lansdowne Road hosted the highest ever attendance for a club match in Ireland, a record unlikely ever to be beaten. No precise figure was taken, but the lowest estimates from all sides put the crowd at a minimum of seventeen thousand, with many reports claiming there were up to twenty thousand spectators there that day. Late in the day and inadvertent though it was, the switch allowed the AIL to showcase itself beyond just the supporters of the two teams.

Neutrals at a loose end on an unseasonably mild Saturday afternoon dropped in to watch the game and there was a genuine feeling among the crowd that the AIL's day had come. At a time when the national side appeared in constant crisis mode – they'd been whitewashed in the previous year's Five Nations and the World Cup quarter-final against Australia seemed a distant memory now – this was a phenomenon worth getting excited about. There was colour and atmosphere in the ground and in a pair of teams who had previous together, you had the perfect ingredients for a final to remember.

It was predictable, therefore, that the game wouldn't go long without a punch-up and the teams duly obliged inside the first minute. It took Cork referee Dave McHugh a few minutes to calm everyone down and the general warning he issued to the two captains would come to have a bearing later in the game when Brent Pope, the St Mary's number eight who would in time become famous as a rugby analyst on RTÉ, was sent off for punching veteran Young Munster centre Brosnahan and fracturing his cheekbone. St Mary's played the whole of the second half without Pope, who had been their talisman for most of the season.

Still, the Dublin club hung in there, helped by the fact that Munsters were down a couple of their best men also. Brosnahan was unable to carry on after being poleaxed by Pope and captain Ger Clohessy had limped off after just four minutes thanks to a hamstring tear. In Clohessy's absence, two men in particular stood up – his brother Peter, a week short of making his Ireland debut against France and club legend John 'Paco' Fitzgerald.

Munsters had forged a 14-6 lead thanks to an intercept try from flanker Ger Earls (whose then five-year-old son Keith would go on to star for Munster, Ireland and the Lions) but when Mary's winger David Wall squared the ledger at 14-14 with just over ten minutes to go, the stadium erupted.

The endgame was as tense as anything the old ground had experienced down the decades. With six minutes to go, Young Munster were awarded a penalty fully 40 yards out and into the wind. As O'Halloran stepped up to it, he knew this was what the whole season boiled down to. Just eighteen months earlier, he'd been reduced to playing junior rugby with Thomond after becoming disillusioned with the game while sitting on the bench for Garryowen and playing a few games of soccer (a game he was good enough at for the Young Munster lads to call him 'Gazza'). Yet here he was, the second highest points-scorer in the league for the season lining up the kick that could win it all. As he held the ball in his hand, Fitzgerald shot him a look. 'This one for me, Gazza,' he said. The draw was no good to Young Munster – this had to go over.

It did. By a couple of revolutions of the ball and no more. But the celebrations were cut short almost immediately as referee McHugh awarded St Mary's a penalty only two minutes later. It was around five or six yards further out than O'Halloran's had been, although the Mary's kicker Aidan White had the wind behind him. But White was neither the first nor the last kicker to rely on a Lansdowne Road gust of wind that either suddenly wasn't there or that decided at the last second to switch direction and his kick, while long enough, came agonisingly back off the right-hand post. The most unbearable, incredible AIL final imaginable finished 17-14 to Young Munster.

They sang 'Beautiful, Beautiful Munsters' from the podium as IRFU president and Munsters clubman Charlie Quaid presented the cup to Ger Clohessy. The repeated warnings to stay off the pitch ahead of the France game were roundly ignored and the area in front of the West Stand thrummed with the excitement of thousands of Limerick people revelling in a moment few could have foreseen in their lifetime. When the train made it back west, an open-top bus was on hand to carry them through the streets of the city. It was a carnival, an awakening in a way.

And not just for Young Munster, it seemed. That day in Lansdowne Road gave everyone involved in club rugby a glimpse of what the AIL might be capable of. The sport was coughing and spluttering its way through its final days as an amateur endeavour and in the cloudburst of excitement that February, the possibility of a nationwide thriving domestic scene that could feed into the national team hung in the air.

It proved to be a mirage, though. The game went professional in 1995 and although this took a while to filter properly through to the Irish game, the decision to make the provinces the engine of the national team rather than the clubs was always going to denude the club scene of its best talents. By the time the thirteen-year-old Paul O'Connell whose heroes played that day became the twenty-two-year-old Paul O'Connell, his bread and butter was Munster red rather than Young Munster yellow and black. As Munster's love affair with the Heineken Cup started to gather pace in 2000, the club scene soon became an afterthought in the media and with the public.

The dominance of the Munster clubs carried on in the AIL until finally, in 2000, St Mary's became the first club from outside the southern province to take the title. Despite the league changing its structures to provide for play-offs and a Lansdowne Road final each year, nothing approaching the crowd or atmosphere of that day in 1993 was ever replicated. It stands alone, the day club rugby stuck its chest out on the national stage and looked for all the world like the future made flesh.

Not bad for a game the stadium wasn't even hosting forty-eight hours before kick-off.

YOUNG MUNSTER: G. McNamara; N. McNamara, N. O'Meara, F. Brosnahan, J. McNamara; A. O'Halloran, D. Tobin; J. Fitzgerald, M. Fitzgerald, P. Clohessy, P. Meehan, R. Ryan, Ger Clohessy (capt.), D. Edwards, G. Earls. Subs D. Mullane for Ger Clohessy; M. Benson for Brosnahan

ST MARY'S: A. White, A. Gillen, G. Lavan, V. Cunningham, D. Wall, N. Barry, M. Thorne, B. Keane, M. Corcoran, D. Dowling, S. Jameson (capt.) T. Coughlan, K. Potts, B. Pope, K. Devlin

Referee: D. McHugh

1995
Riot Acts

England soccer
fans trash
Lansdowne's
West Stand
and cause an
Ireland friendly
to be
abandoned

On an arctic night in Liverpool in mid–December 1994, England beat Ireland in a B international in front of around 7,500 shivering customers at Anfield. It had been a nothing game, really – a snatched mid-season opportunity by Jack Charlton and Terry Venables to give some fringe players a chance to put their hand up for selection and have it seen rather than overlooked. Goals from Newcastle striker Andy Cole and a nineteen-year-old crowd favourite called Robbie Fowler earned England a 2-0 victory that would have been forgotten by the time everyone had left the ground had it not been for a conversation between the managers after the game.

As they exchanged the usual pleasantries, Charlton and Venables each declared themselves happy enough with the night. Around that time, Charlton was keen to get more games organised as he tried to bring through a fresh generation of players to replace the ones who'd been to two World Cups already and were beginning to show their mileage. Between them, he and Venables cooked up the idea of England coming to Dublin for a friendly the following February. Within a week, the FAI announced the fixture.

To many ears, it sounded like an idea whose time had finally come. The two countries hadn't played a friendly in Dublin in thirty years and England had only ever played soccer at Lansdowne twice, during qualifying campaigns for the 1980 and 1992 European Championships. When you consider that the England rugby team provided the opposition for more of Ireland's Lansdowne Road rugby internationals than any other nation, it should have been an embarrassing anomaly that the soccer team were such infrequent visitors.

That's not how it was though. England's absence was never particularly lamented by the Irish soccer-going public, who knew that if you brought the England team over to Dublin, you brought English fans along with them. The scourge of hooliganism that had been such a blight on the sport in the 1980s had fizzled out to some extent by the mid-1990s, but their reputation was still pretty tawdry even then. At the 1992 European Championships in Sweden – the last major tournament for which England had qualified – English fans had rioted in Malmö and Stockholm,

leading to over two hundred arrests for public order offences. It was a measure of just how bad things were in the 1980s that despite the arrests, the general consensus was that some progress was being made.

By late 1994, English football had gradually taken on a different face for itself. The indefinite European ban imposed on English clubs by UEFA in the wake of the Hysel Stadium tragedy in 1985 had ended after five years. The Taylor report that followed the Hillsborough disaster in 1989 had led to the modernisation of football stadia, chiefly in the instalment of seats throughout the grounds and the consequent demise of terracing. The launch of the FA Premiership in 1992 and the dawn of Sky Sports had glamourised soccer and the authorities had come to realise that there was money to be made in attracting a new, family-orientated constituency to the game. While some lifelong followers grumbled that this was sanitising football, not everybody necessarily thought that sounded like such a bad idea.

And so by the time the friendly at Lansdowne Road was announced, the notion of inviting hordes of England fans to Dublin didn't appear as distasteful as it would have done even a couple of years beforehand. With England in line to host Euro '96 – another step along the road to presenting a less threatening demeanour to the outside world – and pubs the length and breadth of Ireland filling up on winter Sunday afternoons to watch live action from across the water, it seemed like the right time to bring the cream of English football over. The fixture was broadly welcomed that Christmas week.

Broadly but not universally, however. Garda Chief Superintendent Patrick Doocey had experienced this fixture before. In November 1990, England had played Ireland in Dublin in a qualifying match for Euro '92 and Doocey had liaised with the FAI and the English authorities on the security arrangements. The game itself had passed without much by way of incident inside the stadium (on or off the pitch, as it happened, the teams playing out a dreary 1-1 draw) but the lack of floodlights at Lansdowne Road back then had been a huge help. The game had kicked off at lunchtime on a Wednesday and the English fans were transported in through Dún Laoghaire port and out again, mostly without any of the anticipated mayhem.

That said, the B&I ferry company refused to leave Dún Laoghaire after the match unless a dozen Gardaí came aboard to keep the peace. But all in all, most of the trouble that occurred in Dublin that night came from Irish fans. While nothing major happened in and around Lansdowne Road, there were huge disturbances in O'Connell Street later in the evening. Of 110 arrests, only eleven were Englishmen. Some troublemakers had come down from Belfast spoiling for a fight, but in the main, it was locals who caused the most trouble. FAI Chief Executive Seán Connolly blamed Dublin's 'gurrier element'.

As he sat down to plan the arrangements for the 1995 match, then, Chief Superintendent Doocey knew that while bringing England to Dublin undoubtedly posed more security problems than a run-of-the-mill soccer international would, it was by no means impossible if handled the right way. As soon as the fixture was announced on 20 December 1994, Doocey contacted Connolly who was still the head of the FAI. Early in their series of

Gardaí head for the West Stand to confront the rioters

meetings, Doocey asked that the game be fixed for midday to allow the orderly shipping in and out of English fans through Dún Laoghaire that had worked so well in 1990.

Key to this idea was the fact that a noon kick-off would curb the amount of drunkenness in the city and would mean that overnighting would be kept to a minimum. Visiting fans would arrive and leave Dublin in the same day and, if at all possible, be kept out of the city centre. But the FAI and FA insisted on an evening match and were originally set on a 7.30 kick-off, which would have worked best for television. In the end, they compromised and moved it to 6.15. Doocey wasn't particularly happy with this either as it added rush-hour traffic to the mix of factors that had to be taken into account, but agreed to make the best of it.

In early January 1995, he got in contact with Detective Chief Inspector Bryan Drew, the head of the Football Intelligence Unit (FIU) in England. Doocey and Drew had worked together to contain the hooligan threat for the 1990 match and were happy to do so again. Drew agreed to supply Doocey with ongoing intelligence and travel information on potential troublemakers in the run-up to the match, an offer that was gratefully

Jack Charlton leaves the pitch

received.

Disastrously, however, the offer of a member of the FIU to help the Gardaí out in the days before the game was declined as was the offer of members of the English police force who could act as spotters. Despite the obvious expertise of the English in dealing with decades of the worst soccer hooliganism in Europe, the Gardaí decided against accepting their help in an effort to keep a 'low-key' police presence in the stadium. This would later be pinpointed as one of a plethora of mistakes made in the security arrangements for the game.

Three weeks before the game, the Gardaí received written warning that hooligan elements from various clubs were intending to travel to Dublin. These would include members of the National Front and Combat 18, virulent right-wing groups that had long been associated with the darkest days of football violence. National Front paraphenalia had been left at Hysel Stadium on the night of the awful tragedy there in 1985 and throughout that decade, the group had targeted football fans in an effort to swell its numbers.

When Ireland had played at Wembley in 1991 – the return match of the 1990 fixture at Lansdowne – a National Front mob had attacked the Black Lion pub in Kilburn. An estimated two hundred England fans had gone on the rampage up Kilburn High Road, knocking over litter bins and smashing windows. Police and ambulance services had to be called as buses containing Irish fans were pelted with stones and bottles. In all, sixty-eight arrests were made, the vast majority of them English. The violence had been orchestrated by National Front and Combat 18 members.

Both groups had a massive presence among the estimated 1,800 English fans who came to Dublin that February. In the clean-up at Lansdowne Road that followed the game, calling cards for such organisations as the Cheltenham Volunteer Force were found in the stands with the slogan, 'Invasion of Dublin 1995 – Ulster Is British, God Save The Queen' written on them. Others proclaimed the plight of a group called the National Alliance – 'The Earth's Most Endangered Species – The White Race. Help Preserve It.' Scores of skinheads with 'Made In The UK' tattooed above their ears in blue ink were part of the travelling party. All hallmarks of fascistic, right-wing groups.

The FIU in England passed on names and travel details of known hooligans who were intending to make the trip, some of whom would be coming to the stadium without tickets. On the evening before the game, the English Travel Club – through whom the tickets for the visiting fans had been sold – furnished the Gardaí with a list of names and seat numbers of their members making the trip. Eighty-seven of those names had asterisks beside them to indicate people who at one point or other had been involved in minor incidents at away matches, incidents that had not been deemed serious enough for them to be thrown out of the club.

The Gardaí decided that for confidentiality reasons, none of these names could be passed on to the FAI. Indeed, they decided it wasn't necessary to inform the FAI that such a list existed or that what the FIU called 'known trouble-makers' were at the game at all. The Finlay Report into that night would later find that many of the fans who caused the worst trouble inside the ground got their tickets through the English Travel Club and English officials at the game were astonished to be able to pick out faces on security screens of hooligans they could identify by name off the top of their head.

The FAI's head of security that night, Bernard O'Byrne – who would go on to become the association's chief executive – admitted that the first he knew of a known hooligan presence at the game was when he was told about it by a senior Garda officer five minutes before the start of the game. That lack of knowledge was to become a huge embarrassment for the FAI in the days and weeks afterwards. 'I think the FAI and the Gardaí learned a lesson that such information should be given to everyone involved in organising such a match,' said Connolly some years later, with some understatement.

The worst mistake was yet to come, however. As if allowing known hooligans into the ground in the first place wasn't bad enough, as if foregoing the help of specialist English police units in the run-up to the game wasn't a serious enough error, the placement of the English fans on the upper deck of the West Stand took the biscuit. Much was made by the Gardaí afterwards of the fact that at checkpoints outside the ground, they'd confiscated eight barrels worth of potential missiles – glass bottles, flag poles, even some knives. But this was all for nothing in the end as the rickety wooden seats in the Upper West Stand made for an ample supply of perfect throwing implements.

Worse still was the fact that by kick-off, some Irish fans were finding out to their horror that their tickets put them right in the centre of what was by now a very loud and aggressive English crowd. Because the English FA had only managed to get rid of around half of their full complement of 3,300 tickets, the FAI had sold on the returns to Irish fans without making sure the two sets of supporters were properly segregated.

'They started spitting at us,' said Brian Kane, an Irish fan who was caught up in the worst of what was becoming a very nasty atmosphere. 'And then this big fat guy came across and started throwing punches. I started calling out to the stewards for help but none of them did anything to save us. We were kicked down the stairs. We could have been killed.' Eventually, the Irish fans made a break for it and ran, heads down, dodging missiles.

'That was deplorable,' Connolly later admitted. 'It was a big oversight by the FAI and people like myself. It was extremely dangerous for those Irish fans to attempt to leave and was a serious error on the FAI's behalf.'

By 5.30 that day, with kick-off three-quarters of an hour away, there was

The English fans were kept in the ground for three hours aferwards

growing chaos inside and outside the ground. With eighty fewer Gardaí on duty in and around the stadium than had been the case for the 1990 match, the crowd became increasingly difficult to contain. At one point, a group of around 150 English fans stormed the turnstiles all at once, prompting Gardaí to baton charge them to protect the stewards. Around sixty ticketless fans made it into the ground during this surge, only around a dozen of whom were subsequently found, caught and thrown out.

When the teams came out on to the pitch, the English fans were in full voice, making Nazi salutes and singing 'No Surrender To The IRA (Scum)'. Irish supporters in the south terrace were booing them and exchanging increasingly vicious taunts. Both anthems were booed by opposing sets of fans. Once the game kicked off, the barrage of abuse from the West Stand continued unabated, completely unconnected to the ebb and flow of the play.

Down on the pitch, a below-strength Irish team was doing okay against an England side containing seven of the team that would narrowly miss out on the final of Euro '96 almost eighteen months later. Charlton had never lost a game against England in his time as Ireland manager and despite having to do without Roy Keane, Ray Houghton, John Aldridge, Phil Babb, Gary Kelly and Jason McAteer, his team wasn't ranked ninth

The aftermath

in the world at the time for nothing. They got about the English in typical style and, after a fine passing move that began in their own penalty area, went 1-0 up through David Kelly after twenty-one minutes.

It would be wrong to say that this sparked the worst of the violence from the English fans in the West Stand, as there is little doubt they came to Dublin intent on causing mayhem and trying to get the game abandoned no matter what happened on the pitch. But soon after Kelly's goal, England had one disallowed when David Platt was caught offside. And soon after that, pieces of wood and metal and plastic came raining down from the Upper West Stand.

'In retrospect the English fans obviously shouldn't have been put up there and the same trouble wouldn't have arisen if English fans were on the lower tier as well,' said Connolly. But down in the Lower West Stand, there were indeed further pockets of English fans and they entertained themselves by ripping up the plastic seating and throwing them onto the pitch and at Irish supporters further down.

Scores of people looked to escape onto the pitch at this point and were allowed to by stewards on whom the horror of what was developing was beginning to dawn. Shortly afterwards, Dutch referee Dennis Jol brought the game to a halt and took the players off the pitch. Stadium security and Gardaí went to the Upper West Stand to try to restore order and sixty back-up Gardaí arrived at the ground as reinforcements.

But in a scene reminiscent of the worst slapstick comedy, they were delayed at the entrance to the stadium because stewards told them they weren't allowed to come in that particular gate. Some of them stood and argued the toss, others simply climbed over the gate and ran to where the trouble was. A severe lack of functioning walkie-talkie units in the ground coupled with the sheer noise of the riot made communication between Gardaí, security and stewards close to impossible.

For all the glaring errors made by the FAI and the Gardaí, the evacuation of the stadium went according to plan. Despite having to keep at bay a crowd of furious Irish supporters who were attempting to force their way into the Upper West Stand to confront the English fans, Gardaí and stewards had cleared that stand of everyone bar the troublemakers inside thirteen minutes. The missile-throwing had also been contained by then, as riot police moved in. The English fans were kept in the stadium for almost three hours as Lansdowne Road was cleared of Irish fans looking to gather outside.

Charlton by now was on the pitch as well, trying to appeal to his countrymen to behave themselves. They responded to him by screaming taunts of 'Judas! Judas!' To see this happening in his adopted country broke his heart, as much for the reaction it prompted from the Irish people as the English.

'I grabbed one of our lot,' he said, meaning an Irish supporter. 'He was throwing a bottle back into the stand. He just grabbed a bottle they had thrown. I was pushed and I was shoved. I saw a guy throwing a bottle into the crowd and I shoved him away. I lost my temper. There were tears of frustration in my eyes. I was embarrassed because the people behaving so badly were from my country.'

With the game abandoned, Lansdowne Road found itself the centre of news coverage across the world. This was the first time in history that an England international had been shut down due to crowd violence and straight away there were calls for the country to be stripped of the European Championships. The Irish embassy in London was inundated with phonecalls that evening and the next day from English people apologising for what had happened and distancing their country from those who were responsible.

In all, sixty-two people were injured in the violence, ranging from cuts and bruises to severe concussion. One of the worst injuries happened to a Roscommon inter-county Gaelic footballer by the name of Eamon McManus, the Garda whose duty it was to escort Charlton to safety once the trouble started. As he went back out on to the pitch, he was hit in the head by plastic seat with a metal bar attached and was knocked unconscious. He was taken to St Vincent's Hospital with a fractured skull.

Almost three years to the day after the riot, Judge Cyril Kelly imposed a £5,000 fine, a two-year suspended jail sentence and a twenty-year ban from the State on Jerome Lindlay of Newport-Bagnell in Buckinghamshire, the last of the eighty-six Englishmen to be convicted of public order offences in the aftermath of the riot. His wasn't an untypical punishment – for the most part, Irish judges didn't see the point of jailing them and having to spend £100 a day to keep them in their cells. Lindlay had been in the Lower West Stand and was captured on film – in what became an iconic photograph – giving a Nazi salute. 'You have shamed your flag, disgraced your nation and scandalised all true sports supporters,' Judge Kelly told him in court.

The episode remains the darkest night in Lansdowne Road's history. But the authorities learned their lesson, at least in the short term. When the two countries next met – in an under-21 international at Dalymount Park six weeks later – there were more Gardaí than spectators. On a deathly quiet afternoon in north Dublin, the only sound to be heard was the horse bolting off into the distance long after the stable door had been locked.

TEAMS
IRELAND: Alan Kelly; Denis Irwin, Alan Kernaghan, Paul McGrath, Terry Phelan; Eddie McGoldrick, Andy Townsend, John Sheridan, Steve Staunton, David Kelly, Niall Quinn
ENGLAND: David Seaman; Warren Barton, Tony Adams, Gary Pallister, Graeme Le Saux; Peter Beardsley, Paul Ince, David Platt, Darren Anderton, Alan Shearer, Matt Le Tissier
Referee: Dennis Jol (Holland)

CHAPTER 30

1999 Ulster says yes!

A team made up of part-timers and professionals wins Ireland's first European Rugby Cup

Few Irish sports stories came wrapped in so unlikely a bow as Ulster winning the European Cup at Lansdowne Road in January 1999. Just five months previously, their newly-appointed coach Harry Williams prefaced the province's intentions for the season by telling reporters that his hastily-cobbled together squad were well aware of their targets. 'The players have agreed that we only have one objective this season,' he said, 'which is to qualify for next season's European Cup by finishing in the top two in the interpros. That's our sole objective.'

This wasn't just your usual case of a coach lowering expectations ahead of the season. Williams genuinely had a massive job on his hands in August 2008. The whole of the rugby world was in flux at the time; professionalism was dawning and the game in Ireland was still trying desperately to work out how best to tackle it. The IRFU had been slow to decide on whether a provincial structure or club structure would put Ireland's best foot forward and, as a result, lots of players had left to play in Britain. Only that summer had some shape been put in the sport here and although Ulster had managed to claw back a host of prodigal sons to rejoin their squad, the notion that come January they might be the champions of Europe wasn't far short of laughable. The fact that the final was to be held in Lansdowne Road was irrelevant just then.

And anyway, it wasn't at all certain that there was going to be a European competition to play in. In those early days of professional rugby, nobody knew for certain where it was all headed and there was a lot of jockeying for position in order to grab every last available pound on offer. Everyone was going into the unknown, nobody could tell where the money was to be made in this new world.

Thus, when the English clubs pulled out of the tournament that year and left the threat of a British League – incorporating the two top Welsh clubs Cardiff and Swansea – hanging in the air, there was a chance that the whole tournament might be scrapped.

Indeed, it was only a week before Williams had announced his meagre ambitions for the season that the French clubs confirmed that they would in fact be taking part, English clubs or no English clubs. For all their bravado, however, the inclusion of the French teams wasn't enough for the

The Ulster pack crouches, ready for action

Heineken to commit to stumping up for the 1998/1999 season and so no English clubs meant no sponsor. It remains the only time in its history that the tournament everybody in Europe knows as the Heineken Cup (apart from in France, where it's called the H–Cup due to advertising restrictions) went sponsorless.

So chaotic were the preparations for that season's tournament that once the draw for the pool stages was made, the European Rugby Cup (ERC) authorities kept it under wraps for a full three weeks as they waited on Cardiff and Swansea and the English clubs to change their mind, which led naturally to bouts of fevered speculation and a general sense of farce. Not that Williams could concern himself with it all. He had enough problems of his own to worry about.

Reintegrating the group of players who had returned *en masse* from playing their rugby in England was his first job. There was no doubt that the players coming back were talented, but getting them to gel was going to be difficult. David Humphreys, Mark McCall, Jonathan Bell, Justin Fitzpatrick and Allen Clarke were all Ireland internationals and in addition to them, former Ireland full–back and specialist place-kicker Simon Mason was joining too. But they were coming into a set–up that, while elite, was nonetheless still predominantly amateur.

'At the start of the season, none of us would have envisaged where we'd end up,' said Bell. 'Obviously the professional attitude and abilities of the players coming back to the province was going to make a difference. People tend to overlook the talent that was already there though.

Andy Matchett, one of the few part-timers in the Ulster squad

'We started out with a two-year plan, but things just accelerated. The priority was to win the interprovincials and we ended up finishing second. We also looked for a decent performance in the European Cup. The transformation in our fortunes during the season coincided with a change of regime. Training was switched from the evenings to during the day time to facilitate the professional players and that definitely made a difference.'

It seems quite incredible, considering how ultra-professional the game became as the years passed, but back in 1998 this was a real problem for Bell and the returning professionals. Right up until the start of October that season, the team had been training at the crack of dawn and in the evening time to facilitate the amateur players in the squad. Players like scrum-half Andy Matchett, an insurance salesman who spent most of his days in his car. Matchett had been repeatedly called up to Ireland A squads, but had never quite risen high enough in the game to earn a full-time contract anywhere.

Ulster's indifferent start to the season led to some none-too-subtle grumbling in the dressing room. And so, after a 31-9 trouncing at the hands of Munster in Musgrave Park in October, Williams announced that things were going to change. Training sessions would be mid-morning and mid-afternoon from there on out.

'It just hadn't been working out and that was a very, very big decision for Harry to take,' said McCall. 'We had been talking about it and then Harry came up with the idea without us even mentioning it. For a couple of days afterwards, the boys couldn't believe it. We London-Irish boys were used to it, but to the home-based players this was unbelievable. It [the new regime] was more like a nine-to-five job and a not very demanding nine-to-five job.'

'Our season was weird. Early on, quite a lot of the time a load of players wanted to give their tuppence worth. It wasn't necessarily a case of dressing room unrest, but it was noisy. As everyone saw the merit of Harry's ways it became a lot quieter.'

Quiet and simple would always have been Williams's way. A career school-teacher, he carried with him the preternatural calm that years of calming classes of rowdy schoolboys brings. 'Harry's the same all the time – he pisses ice cubes,' was the way his players put it. For his part, Williams very rarely saw the point in losing his temper.

'Once you start screaming and yelling,' he said late in that season, 'you lose your reason, you lose your logic. You stop thinking and it's a matter of getting rid of your own frustration rather than trying to be clinical with the players. So when I lose my temper it's something serious.

'I am the boss, but to be the boss you don't have to be rude or crude or arrogant to other people. I look on these guys as my surrogate sons and I try to treat them as intelligent, grown men. And you don't treat intelligent grown men badly by shouting at them. There's no need to be abusive. So my idea is to try and draw the best out of my players. If you can talk to them on an even keel, cajole them, push them, I don't see any reason why you have to fall out with them over it.'

If Ulster's prospects were minimal going into their first game against

Edinburgh, they were positively invisible in the opening stages as they found themselves 14-0 down after just four minutes. Official records of the crowd in Ravenhill that night have been lost to the ages, but there can't have been more than four thousand in the ground. Those who were there were treated to a madcap game that eventually ended in a 38-38 draw. When Ulster got torched 39-3 away to Toulouse in their next game, Williams did lose his temper – apparently for the one and only time all season. 'It made me feel a lot better but it didn't do a hell of a lot for anybody else,' he'd say later.

It was soon after this that Williams switched the training times and saved Ulster's season in the process. Soon, they were beginning to mould into a formidable outfit. McCall was lost with a neck injury after the Edinburgh game but Bell more than compensated at centre and the Kiwi vice-captain Andy Ward was brilliant at openside flanker. Humphreys was finally realising his potential at outhalf and Mason almost never missed a kick. This all combined to turn Ravenhill into an impregnable fortress and Ulster went unbeaten through the rest of the pool to qualify for the knock-out stages. 'We didn't have a very good team, but we got on a roll,' was how Humphreys summed it up.

A consequence of getting on that roll was that support for the team spread through the province, gradually at first and like wildfire the further they progressed. At a time when peace in Northern Ireland was looking like a more feasible prospect than ever – the Good Friday Agreement had been signed earlier that year and there had been universal revulsion and condemnation across all communities when the Real IRA had bombed Omagh – people who had never watched a rugby match in their lives were latching onto this unlikely success story.

It helped that the team had characters and personalities that the public could warm to. From second-row Gary Longwell who was nicknamed 'Boat' because of his prow of a nose to Humphreys who the rest of the squad would try to annoy by calling him 'Jackie' after Jack Kyle, they were a bunch who didn't take themselves all that seriously and who forged a connection with their supporters.

When Ward was substituted early in the second half of their quarter-final against Toulouse, he got a thundering reception from the crowd, all

Ulster fans on the pitch, with the East Stand in the background

of whom knew that he was leaving the game because McCall – who had been holding Ward's mobile phone all through the game – had just got the call saying Wendy Ward had gone into labour. The warmth of that moment let everyone know that something special was afoot.

And when Ulster followed it up with another brilliant win over French opposition in the semi-final – Stade Français left Ravenhill with a 33-27 defeat behind them – it became clear even to their opponents. 'For the first time in my life,' said Stade prop Serge Simon, 'I can say that the winner on this day was rugby. The conditions were marvellous and the public support was extraordinary. I am very happy for all these people because we have been able to understand how much this victory meant for all the people.'

It was after that game too that Williams voiced what had hitherto been a delicate and unapproachable notion. He wanted his team to take up where Barry McGuigan had left off almost fifteen years previously, to become a team that stood for everybody, from all communities and all backgrounds.

'We have tried to emphasise the importance of this and the chance that the players have to make history. No other Irish team can ever do what we've done. We want to be the first team to win it for Ireland. It's not just for us, we're a very tight bunch and we're very aware that this is not just for Ulster, this is for Ireland. We're all under the IRFU umbrella.'

Between then and the final against Colomiers three weeks later, Williams's sentiments began to take hold. Ulster got faxes of support from Linfield FC, from GAA clubs in Monaghan, Cavan and Donegal, from all

Three of Ulster's spiritual leaders (l-to-r) David Humphreys, Tony McWhirter and Andy Ward

over the world. The Ulster Branch were going through five rolls of fax paper a day in the week running up to the game. One player went to pay for his lunch in a restaurant early in the week of the final and was told his money was no good. Another ordered a pint the Saturday night before the game and was refused. 'I can't serve you, you've got a big match next weekend.' This was a new, new world for everyone.

'There were just a few hundred people at our first match,' said Humphreys, 'but our success struck a chord, initially across the province, but then across the whole of Ireland. When we were driving down to Dublin for the final all the flags of support for us really inspired us. All of Ireland got behind us because we were bidding to become the first Irish side to win the competition. I suppose it was all the sweeter for me as I was the captain. Mark McCall was the captain for the opening match but he got injured and the captaincy fell on my shoulders by default. The whole day was an incredible experience.'

President Mary McAleese gave the team a reception in Áras an Uachtaráin the evening before the game and sitting in the Berkeley Court hotel that night, Humphreys was passed a hand-written note of support from Prime Minister Tony Blair, telling him the whole province was behind him. But it was what happened as the team walked through the lobby of the hotel on the way to their bus on the day of the final that stuck with many of the players afterwards.

'For me, that was the moment of the day,' said Gary Longwell. 'There was this great roar as we walked to the bus. There were hundreds of Ulster fans and people from Limerick and Cork and all over Ireland. There were Gaelic players, everything, patting us on the back, screaming and singing. It was a special moment for all of us getting on the bus. It totally took my breath away.'

On another landmark day for Lansdowne Road, the stadium hosted forty-nine thousand people – officially the first time the stadium was filled to capacity for a non-international rugby match. It was also a record crowd for a European Cup game up to that point, although the record only lasted until the following year when Munster helped fill Twickenham with a crowd of 68,441 people.

The old ground had rarely seen such a sea of fervent support as on that day. The absence of the English clubs made no impression whatsoever on the occasion, as both stands and both terraces teemed with Ulster white. Whether by design or pure serendipity, Ulster took to the pitch just as 'We Are The Champions' by Queen was playing over the tannoy. Humphreys very deliberately walked his men around all four corners of the pitch to soak up the crowd, 95 per cent of whom were behind his team.

The game itself turned out to be a stinker, a nervy, dreary, tryless slugfest in which referee Clayton Thomas was far too prominent. No Ulsterman was inclined to complain, however, as the majority of Thomas's decisions went the way of Williams's side and Mason simply kicked Colomiers out of the game. By the end, his six penalties and a Humphreys drop goal were enough to put the French side away and a famous 21–6 victory went the way of the Northern Irishmen. With three minutes to go and the game in the bag, back row forward Tony McWhirter was substituted and walked off the pitch in tears, setting off the Ulster bench as he did so. 'We all started crying,' said McCall. 'It really was an amazing day.'

Afterwards, Williams railed against questioning from English journalists pondering whether it meant as much to win the competition without the English clubs taking part. 'I consider it disrespectful in the extreme to suggest we've only won this title because the English clubs chose to boycott the competition,' he said. 'We'll play any English club that cares to come to Ravenhill or anywhere else for that matter.' By the following season, the English clubs were back and one of them, Northampton, took the title.

But that didn't really matter to Harry Williams as he sat in the little bandroom between the West Stand and the North Terrace on 30 January 1999. He was mostly just marvelling at what had happened to him and his little Ulster team. 'Three months ago, I would never have believed this could happen,' he said quietly. 'In fact, I still can't believe it.'

In that, he was by no means alone

2001
Dutch Gold

Jason
McAteer's goal
beats Holland
and sends
Ireland on their
way to the
2002 World
Cup

For all the success of the late 1980s and 1990s, Lansdowne Road had never hosted one of the truly momentous Irish soccer days. While the stadium had witnessed the occasional against-the-odds victory over a powerful nation – beating the Soviet Union in Eoin Hand's time and Spain in Jack Charlton's, for instance – those wins had always come early on or in the middle of qualifying campaigns. The win over Brazil in 1987 had made for a fine day out and would stand forever as a testament to Liam Brady's genius, but it was nonetheless just a friendly. The planets had never quite aligned to provide a crucial win over one of the blue chip countries right when it most mattered. Not until September 2001, that is.

Mick McCarthy went into the qualifying campaign for the 2002 World Cup knowing it was make or break time for him and the Ireland job. It was accepted by most people that taking over from Charlton was bound to be a thankless task for the first few years, but by now he was four seasons and two campaigns into his own era. His team had missed out on both the 1998 World Cup and Euro 2000 by losing out cruelly in play-offs, in the latter case only after a Macedonia goal in the last minute of the last group match had deprived Ireland of a place that had seemed assured.

The first failure to qualify was put down to the inexperience of what was a young and evolving side, but McCarthy wasn't spared by either media or public after the second. The Macedonia goal had been leaked thanks to chaotic organisation at an injury-time corner, precisely the sort of situation McCarthy the player would have relished. That it went wrong for McCarthy the manager when it most mattered ruined what had been a decent campaign and it was taken as read that if Ireland didn't make it to the World Cup in Japan and South Korea, he would be thanked for his time and asked to step aside.

His prospects looked fraught from the outset when the draw landed Ireland in a group containing Holland and Portugal. Not since they'd drawn France, Holland and Belgium in an attempt to qualify for the 1982 World Cup had the road to a major tournament looked so daunting. Holland and Portugal had lit up that summer's European Championships, both sides exiting unluckily at the semi-final stage – after extra-time in Portugal's case and on penalties in Holland's. Indeed on the day of Ireland's opening match in Amsterdam on 2 September 2000, Portugal stood at number seven in the FIFA World Rankings and Holland at eight. Ireland were thirty-ninth.

But despite the plethora of world-class players they had to face – over the course of the campaign Portugal captain Luis Figo would win both the Ballon D'Or and FIFA World Player Of The Year awards – McCarthy's side came through the early skirmishes with their heads held high. An opening 2-2 draw away to Holland was followed by an equally credible 1-1 draw in Lisbon the following month. Having picked up points in the two toughest fixtures in the group, they went on a run of four wins against Estonia, Cyprus and Andorra twice. A home draw against Portugal in June 2001 followed by a 2-0 win in Estonia four days later sent Ireland unbeaten into the business end of the campaign.

Holland arrived in Dublin needing a win and needing it badly. The damage done by Ireland's draw in September 2000 had been compounded by a home defeat to Portugal a month later and their campaign had never properly recovered. Like Ireland and Portugal, they made mostly short work of the three minnows in the group but they were unable to earn any more than a point in Porto in March 2001.

And so, when 1 September dawned, the three nations were well clear at the top of the group, with Ireland on eighteen points, Portugal on fifteen and Holland on fourteen. Ireland had played a game more than the other two, but by now this was almost an irrelevant statistic because of the likelihood that each team would polish off their remaining games against

Roy Keane tackles Marc Overmars in the opening minute

the also rans. The permutations were gloriously simple – win or draw and Ireland would eliminate Holland from the running and guarantee themselves at least a play-off spot.

For all the peril in their situation, the Dutch came to Dublin with their usual swagger. 'Of course, we are very confident,' said their manager Louis Van Gaal. 'A World Cup without the Dutch would be very hard to take.' He even went so far as to suggest that true football fans among the Irish support would rather see his team than their own go to Japan and South Korea. Needless to say, his comments only served to fuel an already growing fire within the Irish public.

Such was the excitement level in the run-up to the game, the FAI knew that demand for tickets would outstrip supply by multiples of the 33,500 capacity of Lansdowne Road. In an effort to put even a small dent in the shortfall, the association's chief executive of the time Brendan Menton hit on the idea of installing touchline seats along the lines of those regularly used by the IRFU for rugby internationals. Oddly, touchline seats had never been used for soccer matches, apparently for the simple reason that nobody had ever thought to suggest it.

It was perhaps typical of the FAI that when they decided to install the 1,500 extra seats they could fit around the touchlines, not only did they charge premium prices for them (the IRFU had always sold them as the cheap seats) but they deliberately didn't tell the authorities of their plans to change the capacity of the stadium. 'There was no reaction from UEFA after the match,' Menton would later say. 'I doubt if the match delegate realised we had made this significant change.' From that day until Lansdowne Road closed five years later, the extra touchline seats were a feature of every soccer international.

It was the sort of day where every voice in the crowd would matter. Ireland's history with Holland over the previous couple of decades had not been a happy one. The Dutch had put Jack Charlton's side out of both the 1988 European Championships and the 1994 World Cup and had also denied them a place at Euro '96 in a play-off at Anfield in Charlton's last game in charge.

In McCarthy's playing days, he'd twice played against them, but had never beaten them. Not that he hadn't let them know who he was; when he was asked before their 1988 encounter about the balletic grace of the supreme Dutch striker Marco Van Basten, he gave notice of the type of battle the AC Milan forward could expect, 'He'll find it hard to pirouette with a limp,' he said.

For all their famed differences, on that note at least McCarthy chimed with his captain at Lansdowne thirteen years later. The game was barely a couple of minutes old when Roy Keane came flying into a tackle on

the back of Dutch winger Marc Overmars' ankle, giving away a free, but escaping a yellow card. It stirred an already fervent crowd into even greater voice. Patrick Kluivert instantly went close to giving Holland the lead, but his shot trickled wide of Shay Given's post.

The game quickly assumed the expected pattern. Holland's players were quite patently better than Ireland's and they should have been three goals up by the twentieth minute, but the Irish goal led a charmed life. Misses by Kluivert, Bolo Zenden and Ruud Van Nistelrooy kept the score at 0–0 and while the Irish team weren't making very many inroads in attack, their high-pressure defence was keeping them in the game. Roy Keane was magnificent, like a chess grandmaster playing three different games at a time and winning them all. And in defence, Richard Dunne was having the game of his young career.

Ireland got to half-time unscathed. Holland had controlled the game, had retained a huge proportion of the possession, but couldn't break Ireland down. After their initial spurt had been quelled, they had been reduced to hoofing long, high balls in on top of Van Nistelrooy and hoping for the best. Afterwards, they would claim they were forced into this because the Lansdowne Road grass was too long and surprisingly dry. Long grass was a complaint many visiting teams had made before when they'd been beaten at Lansdowne. Dry grass? That was a new one.

Just over ten minutes into the second half, the game looked to have swung even further in Holland's direction when Ireland full-back Gary Kelly was sent off for a second yellow card after a clumsy tackle on

Overmars. Straight away, McCarthy sent Steve Finnan on for Robbie Keane as Ireland set their stall out to try and hold on for the draw that would send the Dutch out of the World Cup. To any objective eyes, it seemed a forlorn hope. Most eyes in the ground that day were anything but objective, however.

'The intensity of the crowd really came through when we went down to ten men,' said Steve Staunton, who was playing centre-half alongside Dunne. 'I know they've been brilliant down through the years but I'd never experienced anything like that before. It was like another hundred thousand people had walked through the gates.' Sub goalkeeper Alan Kelly felt the same. 'When Gary was sent off, it definitely went up a level,' he said. 'The sound was absolutely amazing. I think the crowd thought, "We need to get behind these lads. We need to make a difference."'

Some days fortune decides it likes the look of you and this was one of those for McCarthy and his side. Within ten minutes of Kelly's sending off, Van Nistelrooy went straight through on Given, slipped the ball past him and was blatantly fouled by the Ireland goalkeeper as he went to collect. But referee Helmut Krug – who, as disgruntled Dutch journalists would later note was German – waved play on, to the general amazement of just about everyone in the ground.

'You could see that he was fouled to stop him getting there,' said Niall Quinn. 'We couldn't have argued with a penalty there. You could look at it over and over again, it was a penalty.' Kelly was even more forceful. 'If mine's a sending off, that's a penalty,' he said. 'Would I have given it? Definitely. And if you gave the penalty, you'd have to send him off. Maybe the referee said, "I can't send two of them off, I'll be fucking lynched!"'

Whatever the reason, Ireland had an escape to revel in. And revel they did. Five minutes later, Roy Keane lifted a siege in his own penalty area and surged forward to try to get his team playing in the Dutch half of the pitch. Holland had four strikers on the pitch by this stage and were thoroughly unbalanced so that when the ball found its way to Finnan wide on the right, he had time and space to turn back inside and hoist a crossfield ball to the equally unfettered Jason McAteer in the Dutch box. With one sweep of his right boot, McAteer caught the ball first time and sent Lansdowne into rapture.

That it was McAteer who got the goal was an especially glorious twist in the story. He had come to Dublin that week without having kicked a ball at club level all season. He'd been frozen out at Blackburn Rovers and had feared for his place in the Ireland side as a result. But McCarthy had always liked him and he was hugely popular with the public too. He was never surly as seemed to increasingly be the case with young millionaire footballers and was forever telling stories against himself and glorying in his own self-deprecation. For him to score the most important Ireland goal since Ray Houghton's in New Jersey seven years previously was sweet indeed.

'I was just jogging in and didn't have a clue what was around me,' he said. 'Could have been a man on me for all I knew. Then the ball went out to Finn [Steve Finnan] who turned back on himself. It was instinctive. The ball bounced up and I've just got a whip on it. I could do it again ten times and not hit the target again. But it just went in.'

The goal had come completely against the run of play and now Holland were in real trouble. They needed to score twice or they were finished. But Van Gaal's substitutions – bringing off Overmars and Zenden and sending on Jimmy Floyd Hasselbaink and Pierre Van Hooijdonk – had left them completely without width and subtlety. They just kept sending the ball long and Dunne and Staunton kept clearing it.

'For the last twenty minutes, it was onslaught after onslaught,' said Given. 'There was one save in the end, a weak header from Van Nistelrooy, and it was just a basic dive to my left. But I remember the ball going away from me by a yard and being hard to grip because I was sweating so much. My gloves were just drenched in sweat.'

With ten minutes to go, the stadium announcer came on the tannoy system and asked stewards to move to their end of match positions. Never in the history of the stadium had such a prosaic public safety request been met with such a raucous reaction from the crowd. Mobilising the stewards meant there were less than ten minutes to go and the whole stadium just wanted the game over now. The tension inside the ground was past unbearable. When the final whistle came, the scenes were unlike any ever experienced at a soccer match in the stadium.

'One memory from the day?' said Given. 'The final whistle. It was

immense. The best atmosphere I've ever known in an Irish shirt by a mile. I could have stayed on the pitch for a couple of hours, but emotions were running so high that a lot of what happened is a blur.'

The scenes in the dressing rooms below the West Stand were unforgettable. While in the corridor outside Edgar Davids was in tears at his country missing out on the World Cup for the first time since 1986, the Ireland dressing room was a jubilant sight, captured in an epic piece of sportswriting by Paul Kimmage in the *Sunday Independent* the following month. Team physio Mick Byrne, who had been in the dugout for all those defeats in 1988, 1994 and 1995 could hardly contain himself. 'We've done it!' he roared. 'We've beaten them fucking Dutch. Thirteen years we've waited! We've waited for thirteen years and youse fuckers have done it!'

Mick McCarthy and Roy Keane share an iconic handshake

They had indeed and it was as good as life got in the McCarthy reign. The iconic photograph of the day is of the strained handshake between himself and Keane after the final whistle, McCarthy stretching to reach him and Keane not even looking him in the eye as he walks off the pitch. It hinted at the rift between the pair that would explode so dramatically in the Pacific island of Saipan the following summer.

Ireland ended up finishing second in their qualifying group behind Portugal and came through a two-legged play-off against Iran to make it to the World Cup. McCarthy was voted Philips Manager of the Year and also took the RTÉ Sports Person of the Year award that December. The following summer he managed Ireland to a second round exit from the World Cup, only going out on penalties to Spain after a highly creditable tournament performance given the ructions caused by his row with Keane and the chaos that ensued. In truth, he never recovered from that and when Ireland lost their opening two matches in the qualifying campaign for Euro 2004 the following autumn, he resigned.

But regardless of how bitter it got by the end, he and Keane and the rest of country will always have that September day at Lansdowne Road. That day was special.

IRELAND: Shay Given, Gary Kelly, Richard Dunne, Steve Staunton, Ian Harte, Jason McAteer, Matt Holland, Roy Keane, Kevin Kilbane, Robbie Keane, Damien Duff. Subs: Steve Finnan for Robbie Keane, 59 mins; Niall Quinn for Duff, 88 mins; Andy O'Brien for McAteer, 93 mins

HOLLAND: Edwin van der Sar, Mario Melchiot, Jaap Stam, Kevin Hofland, Artur Numan, Boudjwein Zenden, Marc van Bommel, Phillipe Cocu, Marc Overmars, Patrick Kluivert, Ruud van Nistelrooy. Subs: Jimmy Floyd Hasselbaink for Zenden, 56 mins; Pierre van Hooijdonk for Numan, 64 mins; Giovanni van Bronckhorst for Overmars, 72 mins

Referee: Helmut Krug (Germany)

CHAPTER 32

2003 Red carpet, red faces

England captain Martin Johnson refuses to budge

When Martin Johnson came to Dublin as manager of the England rugby team during the 2009 Six Nations, he took his seat at the traditional pre-match press conference and set about explaining the poor run of form his team was going through at the time. He tried to talk about a young team that was still evolving into what he wanted it to be and how his players were learning all the time, just as he was himself in a job he'd been in for a mere six months at that stage.

But it was to no avail. All the gathered press corps wanted to talk to him about was what had happened at Lansdowne Road six years previously, when his refusal as England captain to move his team to its allotted spot for the pre-match handshake with President Mary McAleese sparked a diplomatic incident. His wry smile when he was asked about what kind of reception he'd received since he arrived betrayed the fact that he'd been fully expecting 2003 to be brought up.

For all the furore it caused, the incident itself was almost laughably small and mercifully brief. It was over in seconds and a huge proportion of the crowd in Lansdowne Road that day didn't know what exactly had happened until after the game. And yet it nonetheless prompted letters of apology from both the English and Irish rugby unions to be sent to Áras an Uachtaráin and was talked about for years afterwards as a heinous breach of protocol. It led to a flood of letters to newspapers and a barrage of tut-tutting from columnists and opinion-writers in both Ireland and England. On the flipside, it was also hailed as one of the greatest pieces of captaincy the old ground had ever seen.

To set the day in context, it is necessary to go back four years to Wembley Stadium in London on 11 April 1999. On that day, Johnson and his England teammates lost the last ever Five Nations match to an injury-time try by Welsh centre Scott Gibbs, dramatically losing out on the Grand Slam and championship on a 32-31 scoreline. It was the beginning of a cruel run of desperately close calls that saw them just miss out on three successive Grand Slams, all on final-day defeats away from Twickenham. The following year, they lost 19-13 at Murrayfield and then in 2001 they came to Lansdowne Road and got beaten 20-14.

That defeat in Dublin had hurt England most of all. The championship

The two teams line up, with Ireland past the red carpet

had been disrupted by an outbreak of foot and mouth disease and it was October by the time they got around to wrapping it up. England were ambushed in Lansdowne Road that day, Keith Wood scoring an iconic set-piece try off a line-out move in the first half. 'Of all the teams we played in Grand Slam deciders, I think that Ireland one was probably the best one,' Johnson said.

All those defeats proved character-building and went much of the way to creating the side that would go on to win the World Cup in 2003. England became expert at storing up grudges and using them as inspiration. When they set their sights on you around that period, you knew about it. The year after the Wood-inspired defeat at Lansdowne, they handed Ireland an unmerciful 45-11 hiding at Twickenham in Eddie O'Sullivan's second game in charge. When O'Sullivan went into the dressing room afterwards to congratulate them, he saw a big sign scrawled on their dressing room white board saying simply, 'REMEMBER DUBLIN'.

The confluence of this succession of disappointments and gradual build-up of bitterness meant that England were a huge, gnarled and intimidating team in the 2003 Six Nations and it was no real surprised that they'd swept all before them by the time they reached the final match in Dublin. They'd beaten France by eight points, Wales by seventeen, Italy by thirty-five and Scotland by thirty-one. They were in no mood to be denied again by Ireland.

But Ireland were no also-rans, at least not before kick-off anyway. O'Sullivan's tenure was turning into quite a successful one and after winning three games in his first Six Nations, they'd won each of the first four in his second. A first victory at Murrayfield by an Ireland side for eighteen years had kicked the championship off in style and was followed up by a convincing 37-13 win in Rome. A rare home win over France – the only one of O'Sullivan's entire reign as it turned out – and a thrilling 25-24 affair in Cardiff meant that Ireland would be welcoming England to Lansdowne on the last day for a Grand Slam decider.

Martin Johnson lays down the law

This had never happened before in all the years rugby had been played there. Ever since the Home Nations Championship had expanded to include France in 1910, Ireland had arrived at their final fixture having won all their games on only four occasions. For three of those, they had to travel abroad on the last day – to Swansea in 1926, to Cardiff in 1951 and to Paris in 1982 – and the one they got to play as a home fixture famously took place in Belfast in the immortal Grand Slam season of 1948. So however the match played out, another little kernel of history would take place at Lansdowne Road on 29 March 2003.

In truth, few expected an Ireland victory. O'Sullivan's team was talented, but still fairly young at that point and the manager himself admitted later that they weren't far enough advanced to be able to compete on a level footing. By contrast, England were the best team in the world and before they went to Australia for that year's World Cup, they simply had to get the monkey of last-day Grand Slam meltdowns off their backs. They came to Dublin with their hackles up,

their paranoia in overdrive and prepared as a group to use every slight – perceived or actual – to their advantage. Johnson was especially primed for combat, as the following passage from his eponymous autobiography makes clear.

'I remember Will Carling,' he wrote, 'talking about how, after Scotland had beaten England in 1990, he and the other players had used the Scottish dislike of England and the English to their advantage, using it to fuel the aggression and power that would win the Grand Slams in 1991 and 1992.

'Will said, "When we play these guys at rugby they hate us and they make no bones about it. But if we tell them we hate them they're shocked. Somehow that isn't in the rules. The English are the hated, not the haters. I just tell them, you hate me so I'll hate you and let's leave it at that." I follow the same path. Everyone hates the English and likes to see us lose and in Dublin that day everyone around the world would have been rooting for the Irish. My response is, "Fuck you all. We are going to beat you and we don't give a fuck."'

The hordes of Irish fans who swarmed the England base at the Four Seasons Hotel in Ballsbridge on the morning of the game just wound Johnson and his teammates up tighter and made them more determined. Johnson later claimed that the crowds tried to intimidate the England players that morning by coming up to them and shouting. 'Come on Ireland!' in their faces and flicking V-signs at them. And when they got to Lansdowne Road, his mood wasn't helped any by an Ireland official approaching him with thirty minutes to go until kick-off asking him to sign a jersey.

'The tension was there,' he said. 'That half an hour immediately before a game is always a very pressurised period and that was magnified in Dublin, with all the Grand Slam history. I am not at my most approachable at this point. Ridiculously little things rile me up. Afterwards, when all the tension is released you can laugh at yourself and it all sounds so petty. With the hatred fairly bubbling in my veins, I led the guys out for the anthems.'

Clare McNamara was RTÉ's sideline reporter on the day and witnessed at close quarters the brooding intent on the faces of Johnson and his England squad as they emerged from the tunnel. 'I was just a few feet away from him and you could see straight away that they came to set their stall out. It was, "We won't be bossed around. We won't be told where to go or where to stand."'

What happened next was, depending on your viewpoint, an awful lot of fuss about nothing or the epitome of ugly boorishness from a team that was starting to revel in the role of schoolyard bully. To this day, Johnson claims it was all a misunderstanding and that he merely took his team to the South Terrace end of the red carpet because that was the side they'd be defending in the first half. But many, including O'Sullivan, believe it was a deliberate move on Johnson's part to seize the initiative of the day and make an early statement of intent.

O'Sullivan was sitting in the manager's box in the West Stand when over the intra-squad radio came the voice of Ireland's Operations Manager, Martin Murphy. In time, Murphy would go on to become the stadium director at the Aviva Stadium when Lansdowne was rebuilt but on this day, he was the middle man in conveying Johnson's intransigence to the Ireland coach.

'He won't move,' said Murphy.

'Did you tell him he's on the wrong side?' asked O'Sullivan.

'Three times.'

'And?'

'And he told me to go fuck myself!'

Johnson's England and Leicester Tigers teammate Neil Back was standing next to him. Back was already pretty unpopular with Irish supporters having just the previous year denied Munster at the death in the Heineken Cup final by snagging a ball illegally out of a late scrum and had been asked earlier in the week about how he might react if he came under crowd pressure during the Grand Slam decider. 'No amount of intimidation from any fan in any stadium in the world has affected my performance in a negative way,' he declared. Like Johnson, he was beginning to enjoy the situation as by now, the crowd could see what was going on and was jeering and booing the England players. 'No, Johnno,' he kept saying to his captain. 'You can't concede on this. Don't concede, don't concede.'

Brian O'Driscoll had led his Ireland team over to their mark only to find Johnson and his men standing there instead. This left O'Driscoll with a quandary. If they moved down the red carpet to where the England team was supposed to have been standing, it would have been seen as a capitulation – and the older members of O'Driscoll's squad made it clear to him that this wasn't an option. O'Sullivan toyed with the idea of sending a message down to O'Driscoll to tell him to go and line up two feet in front of the England team. But that could have led to mayhem.

'Personally,' said O'Driscoll, 'it had never occurred to me to give any thought to which side we were supposed to stand on. That wouldn't have affected me to be honest. But some of the lads as we were walking over said, "They're standing on our side. Let's either stand in front of them or stand beside them." Well, we couldn't stand in front of them – you'd be liable to get a box in the back of the head. So we just went down the far end of them.'

By now it was clear to everyone in the ground that something was amiss but only those sitting in the West Stand could see Johnson repeatedly refuse to move his team. He sent Murphy away with a flea in his ear and even had a hint of a smile playing on his face while he did so. This was a hostile atmosphere and he thrived on hostile atmospheres.

'If they'd been clever about it,' he said later, 'they'd have got the referee to ask us to move. I would never have refused to do it for the referee because that's before the game starts. They sent someone else out and told me I had to move and I said, "I'm not going anywhere, just get on with the game." People thought I did it deliberately, that I should know well what side we usually stand on. But I hadn't played there since 1999 and it was an honest mistake. There is apparently a four-page document somewhere outlining the etiquette for visiting teams on matchdays. I've never seen it and if I had, I wouldn't have read it.'

The upshot was that President McAleese would have to walk on the Lansdowne Road turf instead of the red carpet when shaking hands with the Ireland team. She met Johnson and the England team first before moving on to O'Driscoll, in whose ear she quite pointedly spoke before he introduced her to his players. While she never made any comment about the incident, the sight of a head of state having to leave a red carpet

Mike Tindall scores a try with Brian O'Driscoll in his wake

England players celebrate winning the Grand Slam

was at the very least unedifying. 'Can you imagine the hullabaloo if we behaved like that with the Queen at Twickenham?' wondered O'Sullivan.

In a rugby sense, however, it was a masterstroke by Johnson. O'Driscoll later said that, 'In a funny kind of way, you'd almost have to respect him for it.' O'Sullivan went further in his autobiography. 'With hindsight,' he wrote, 'I could admire Johnson's pig-headedness. In fact I would almost go so far as to say he was dead right. To blow another Grand Slam decider would almost certainly kill off any pretensions they had of winning that year's World Cup. So he brought them to Dublin on a war footing and Martin Murphy just happened to be directly in the line of fire. You could see it in their body language. They were strutting their stuff, all but inviting our lads outside.'

The whole incident was over within minutes, but the tone was set. Although Ireland opened the scoring with a David Humphreys penalty after three minutes, England scored the first try on eight minutes. They ended up winning 42-6 and if the scoreline was a little flattering – Ireland were only 13-6 behind with twenty minutes to go – the result was never really in doubt. England came, saw and conquered. Within six months, they would go unbeaten on a tour of the southern hemisphere and become the first ever northern hemisphere side to win the World Cup.

In the meantime, however, Johnson took a lot of flak for his refusal to budge. The IRFU issued a letter of apology to the President for the lack of respect shown to her on the day. The English RFU did likewise, a move that drew criticism from some of the English players, most notably scrum-half Matt Dawson. Some English newspapers got after Johnson as well, with notable *Independent* columnist James Lawton calling him, 'not so much a leader as a yob'. Plenty of sportspeople admired him for it though. Former All Ireland-winning Clare manager Ger Loughnane called it 'the finest piece of captaincy I've seen all year'.

One funny coda to the whole incident came after the match, as the England players prepared to leave Lansdowne Road to go to the banquet in the Berkeley Court Hotel. As anyone with any knowledge of the area will be able to confirm, the Berkeley Court was no more than a hundred-yard walk from the dressing rooms below the West Stand and the obvious thing to do on a lovely spring day was to walk up the street.

But Johnson, mindful that he'd riled the crowd before the game and silenced them during it, didn't fancy walking *en masse* through a street full of Irish fans who'd just lost out on a first Grand Slam in fifty-four years. So he told his men to get on the team bus. 'Off we drove, up a totally empty street,' he later wrote, 'looking for all the world like big-timers who were determined to arrive in style. Should have walked, Johnno.'

Judging by the outrage that followed – Joe Duffy's *Liveline* radio show was predictably thunderous the next afternoon – it wasn't the only time that day that taking his own advice would have bought him a quiet life. But then, a quiet life wasn't really Johnson's style.

IRELAND: Geordan Murphy; Justin Bishop, Brian O'Driscoll (capt.), Kevin Maggs, Denis Hickie; David Humphreys, Peter Stringer; Marcus Horan, Shane Byrne, John Hayes, Malcolm O'Kelly, Gary Longwell, Victor Costello, Keith Gleeson, Anthony Foley. Subs Paul O'Connell for Longwell, 57 mins; Ronan O'Gara for Humphreys, 64 mins; Alan Quinlan for Costello, 69 mins; Justin Fitzpatrick for Horan, 76 mins; Girvan Dempsey for O'Driscoll, 80 mins

ENGLAND: Josh Lewsey; Jason Robinson, Will Greenwood, Mike Tindall, Ben Cohen; Jonny Wilkinson, Matt Dawson; Graham Rowntree, Steve Thompson, Jason Leonard, Martin Johnson (capt.), Ben Kay, Richard Hill, Neil Back, Lawrence Dallaglio Subs: Trevor Woodman for Rowntree, half-time; Danny Grewcock for Kay, 45 mins; Dan Luger for Tindall, 69 mins

Referee: Jonathan Kaplan (South Africa)

CHAPTER 33

2004 Elation once again

Ireland's golden generation beat Scotland to win a first Triple Crown in nineteen years

The young squad that Eddie O'Sullivan brought into the 2004 Six Nations championship would, in time, back-bone the most successful Irish rugby generation in history. No fewer than fifteen of that panel would eventually win Heineken Cups with their provinces and ten would still be around six years later to bridge a sixty-one-year gap by winning the Grand Slam. But that all seemed a long way away in early 2004 as Ireland went into the championship more, it seemed, in hope than in expectation.

Having been emphatically put in their place at Lansdowne Road the previous March by Martin Johnson and friends, Ireland had gone to Australia for what was ultimately a disappointing World Cup in the autumn of 2003. Despite running the hosts close in their pool match, their quarter-final against France was over within the first twenty minutes. With it went the career of Keith Wood, Ireland's inspirational captain and O'Sullivan's right-hand man, who retired at the end of the game.

Other factors contributed to a sense of foreboding as Ireland faced into the Six Nations that year. There had been some controversy shortly after the World Cup when the team's fitness coach Mike McGurn declared in a newspaper interview that the Ireland team had only been operating at around 70 per cent of the fitness levels they should have had during the tournament and called for 'a fitness revolution in Irish rugby'. Speaking out of turn like that had not gone down well with the IRFU.

There was another personnel wrinkle to contend with in the run-up to the championship when O'Sullivan had attempted to get his assistant coach Declan Kidney eased aside. Kidney had been appointed to the role when O'Sullivan had taken the top job as much out of recognition for his work with Munster as anything else. Sadly, they had just assumed that he and O'Sullivan would click as a coaching ticket, but by the end of the World Cup, O'Sullivan could see that they hadn't and weren't going to. Kidney was offered a contrived position within the IRFU looking after elite underage talent, but turned it down in favour of continuing to work with O'Sullivan through the championship. It made for a distinctly uncomfortable dynamic.

On top of everything, Ireland were facing into a Six Nations where they would be playing England and France away from home. In the

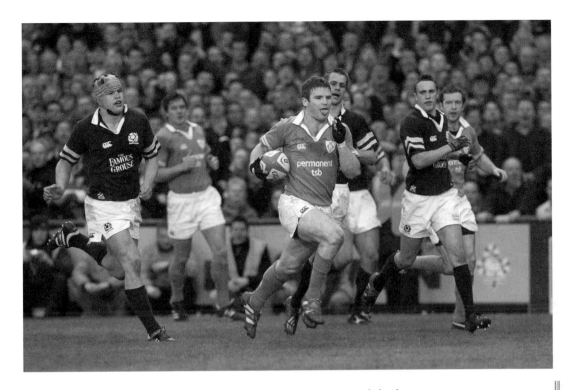

seventy-four runnings of the championship since France joined the home nations, Ireland had only twice won the competition outright when having to travel to Paris and London. The omens were anything but good and when it came to light that new captain Brian O'Driscoll would miss the season-opener against France through injury, it seemed Ireland were doomed to another unfulfilling season. One French newspaper called them 'Les Irlandais Orphelins' – the Irish orphans who would be lost children without Wood and O'Driscoll. The absence of both Geordan Murphy and Denis Hickie surely wouldn't help either.

And so it proved. Ireland came home with the sound of a 35–17 beating ringing in their ears. Coupled with the behind-the-scenes stories that were doing the rounds and the fact that they'd now lost their last two Six Nations games by a total of fifty-six points, it made for grim prospects for O'Sullivan and his team. But in the face of extreme media criticism, they stood firm and swore there were green shoots to be seen in their performance. 'This wasn't like the bad old days,' said Shane Byrne, Wood's replacement at hooker. 'We were actually angry with ourselves because we could have won that game. Silly mistakes cost us. We let France get some easy scores, we let ourselves down. So it wasn't the same old story. Not by a long shot.'

That may have been the case for the players, but beyond the squad the

Gordon D'Arcy was the Player of the Tournament

general public was going to take plenty of convincing. And the general feeling of doom around the place was only deepened by the imminent arrival at Lansdowne Road of Wales who had looked scintillating against Scotland in their opening match. The Welsh had just endured a desperate couple of years in which they'd won only one Six Nations game out of ten but this win over Scotland was being hailed as the beginning of a revival.

O'Sullivan wasn't especially worried, however, and nor were the players. They were well used to beating the Welsh players with their clubs in the Heineken Cup and Celtic League so they didn't hold any great fears now.

On top of that, they had been genuinely encouraged by the performance in Paris and became convinced that with a bit of a harder shell, they'd be a formidable force. When the Monday training session in Naas became cranky and physical – with a couple of fights breaking out along the way – O'Sullivan was delighted. The conditions for an ambush couldn't have been more perfect.

The return of O'Driscoll prompted a little lateral thinking from O'Sullivan when he chose to drop Kevin Maggs instead of Gordon D'Arcy as most had presumed he would. D'Arcy had mostly been a wing or a full-back and had played a little in the centre for Leinster, but having made a couple of decent breaks in Paris, he got the nod ahead of the more combustible Maggs. The other change saw Donncha O'Callaghan come in for Malcolm O'Kelly to partner Paul O'Connell. Nobody predicted it then but for the rest of the decade, the partnerships of O'Connell and O'Callaghan at second row and O'Driscoll and D'Arcy at centre would be more or less set in stone when each player was fit. The Wales game at Lansdowne in February 2004 was where that all began.

David Wallace scores for Ireland

Ireland simply blew them away. Byrne got a try on the board within fifty-three seconds of the kick-off and even managed to add another later on. Ireland sailed away from Wales, beat them up and left them in a state. At one point the scoreboard on the East Stand read 36-3 to the home side.

A couple of late Tom Shanklin tries left it 36–15, but the point had been made. The Welsh revival could wait.

'We pretty much stuffed them I have to stay,' said Reggie Corrigan. 'There was a lot of talk beforehand, about Welsh rugby being back and all this kind of stuff. We had to endure that and listen to it all week, which isn't easy when you're playing in your home town. It was hard to take.'

Just like that, the mood around Irish rugby changed. One win over a fellow home nation side and already there was loose talk about a possible Triple Crown. All of a sudden, it was taken as an article of faith that England were vulnerable, that the fog of their post-World Cup hangover hadn't cleared yet and that they might be ripe for the picking. Initially, it seemed fanciful thinking – after all, Ireland had won just one match at Twickenham in twenty years and Clive Woodward's side were unbeaten at the ground since 1997. But without the retired Martin Johnson and the injured Jonny Wilkinson, England were missing the heart of the team that had won them the World Cup the previous October. Ireland had a chance, certainly.

They would be helped along by a combination of little x-factors. For one thing, they were still smarting over the previous year at Lansdowne Road – not so much the red carpet incident as the 42–6 hiding that followed. For another, the fact that this would be England's first game back at Twickenham since being crowned world champions appealed to the Irish sense of mischief. The place would be bedecked, with the whole of English rugby expecting a performance. To spoil the party would be delicious.

When the Irish team arrived at Twickenham for the traditional captain's run, they found a location dedicated to the all-powerful might of English rugby. On the frame of a dressing-room door, there had been twenty-two plaques affixed, one to mark each of the games in their seven-year unbeaten run at the ground. England did not look as though they would be wearing their success lightly. There was an arrogance about them that could very easily set them up for a fall and Ireland decided to use this to their advantage. They hit on the idea of clapping them onto the pitch before the game, to puff them up and fuel their sense of their own immortality. Then Ireland would launch into them.

That was the plan anyway. But the night before the game, O'Driscoll came to O'Sullivan and told him some of the players thought clapping England onto the turf was taking deference and respect a little too far. The consensus was that a guard of honour would be plenty. O'Sullivan said that was no problem and asked if there had been anyone in particular against the idea. 'Maggsy,' replied O'Driscoll, referring to the Bristol-born centre. 'He nearly went fucking crazy!'

The day went better than O'Sullivan could have dreamed it would. Ireland welcomed England onto the Twickenham grass and then leathered them off it. Without Johnson and Wilkinson, England were indeed ponderous and leaderless and the Irish forwards ground their pack into dust. In the backs, D'Arcy was a revelation and it was his break that set-up the move for Girvan Dempsey's match-winning try. In the end Ireland walked away with a 19-13 victory, the largest winning margin by an Ireland side at Twickenham since the day Mike Gibson made his debut in a green shirt in 1964. And by God, they made sure to enjoy it.

'I think when we walked into the dinner was the best moment,' said Corrigan in Peter O'Reilly's account of that season, *The Full Bag Of Chips*. 'There were about seven hundred people at this dinner and it was very much set up as a World Cup celebration. You had the Webb Ellis trophy here, a string quartet there. We arrived in and suddenly noticed it went a bit quieter.

'You could see all these old lads sitting around sipping glasses of wine. You knew you hadn't just spoiled a party, you had ruined it. Maggsy was hilarious. He was straight up to the bar in the middle of the room, ordering beers all round in his loudest voice. He was really rubbing it in – he was loving it obviously. You just sat down and looked around. They were very quiet. It had hit home.'

What had also hit home by now was the possibility, for the first time in nineteen years, of an Irish Triple Crown. Not only that, but the chance to close it out at Lansdowne Road as well. Only Scotland stood in their way now and they would surely make for beleaguered opponents having lost to Italy earlier in the afternoon. The scene was set for three weeks of Ollie Campbell and Ciaran Fitzgerald and Michael Kiernan stories, three weeks of a monkey on the back of Irish rugby that needed to be thrown off.

First though, Italy would be coming to Lansdowne Road. In many ways, it was a welcome distraction for an Irish team that hadn't won anything yet and could well do without having to spend a full three weeks hearing the phrase 'Triple Crown' at every turn. All questions could be deflected until after Italy had been dealt with. In the end, Italy were duly beaten 19-3 on one of those rotten Lansdowne days where the main objective was to get in out of the weather as quickly and efficiently as possible.

The following seven days dragged interminably. Wise old heads with bitter experience of Irish rugby's propensity for walking into open manholes warned against complacency, newspapers compared the teams of the 1980s with O'Sullivan's of 2004 and every player who came within a yard of a microphone was asked about his memories of Triple Crowns past. David Wallace, who was brought into the side for his first appearance of the championship in place of Keith Gleeson who broke his arm against Italy, was one who played along obligingly.

'I was nine years old and was living in Cork at the time,' he said, 'and I suppose we always had a few rugby balls in the house and a few broken window panes. We spent a fair bit of time playing rugby in the garden. If

I imagined myself as one of that Ireland team, it was probably Michael Kiernan – he was working with my dad and he was probably one of my idols. For me to be back, with a chance of emulating that team by helping Ireland win a Triple Crown, is unbelievable really.'

And yet, despite all the reminiscing, there was certainly a sense that the prize of a Triple Crown wasn't quite the bonanza a lot of people made it out to be. By the end of the decade, of course, Ireland would win Triple Crowns as a matter of course, but even then, there were dissenting voices that said perhaps everyone should be dreaming bigger dreams. Writing in *The Irish Times* on the morning of the game, columnist Donal Spring questioned just how relevant an achievement a Triple Crown would be in the modern era.

'In a political sense the continuation of the Triple Crown up to Irish independence or even to the end of our membership of the Commonwealth made sense,' he wrote. 'But we are now very much Europeans and the only special tie with England, Scotland and Wales is our use in common of English as a main language.

'During the amateur era, it was without doubt a coveted prize but it probably contributed to an Irish inferiority complex when it came to playing the French. Great progress has been made in overcoming this

Brian O'Driscoll and Eddie O'Sullivan

complex in recent years, particularly by winning in Paris [in 2000]. The quarter-final of the World Cup, however, was a major setback and we definitely seemed to be lacking in confidence and self-belief when we played France in Paris in February. I believe if we were to meet them again at this stage of the season it would be a better contest.'

And although in time, most of the Irish rugby public would come to agree with Spring as the team achieved more and set their sights higher, on 27 March 2004 he was something of a lone voice. The vast majority of patrons in south Dublin that day just wanted to see the Scots routed and history made once again. They didn't even seem to mind very much that local businesses were making a killing out of the whole thing – the Director of Consumer Affairs later found that six pubs in the Baggot Street/Haddington Road area of the city hiked their prices by up to a euro on the day of the game.

It wasn't plain sailing at Lansdowne either, just as O'Sullivan had spent the week drilling into everybody's head that it wouldn't be. With half an hour to go, the score stood at 16-16 and it was the visitors who were in the ascendancy, having scored the first try of the second half through flanker Ally Hogg. For a moment, the dreaded notion of Scotland wrecking the party raised its head. But a trademark David Wallace try in which he wriggled through a bank of blue defenders and squirmed over the line to touch down sent Ireland on their way five minutes later before first Peter Stringer and then Player of the Tournament D'Arcy ran up the total. It finished 37-16 and Ireland had won their sixth Triple Crown, their third successive one to be secured at Lansdowne Road.

Earlier in the week, 1985 veteran Donal Lenihan had texted fellow Corkonian Ronan O'Gara saying that at least this time around he'd do him the courtesy of staying until the end, unlike the nine-year-old O'Gara the year Lenihan had won his. He wasn't the only one who stayed. Although there was no trophy presentation – the tournament sponsors Royal Bank of Scotland eventually commissioned an official Triple Crown plate in 2006 – the crowd lingered and demanded a lap of honour. After years of heartache, Irish rugby finally had something to celebrate. Not just the achievement but the promise of more to come as well.

However, that day will always be remembered with a tinge of sadness.

At various points in the game, the PA announcer at Lansdowne Road had asked if there was an Ian McCall in the ground and if there was, that he make himself know to the stewards. As it happened, Ian McCall was sitting at home watching the game on TV and by the time the IRFU finally got hold of him, it was half-time. The news he received was the worst imaginable – his son John had died that afternoon playing for Ireland in the under-nineteen World Cup in Durban, South Africa. He'd had a cardiac arrest arising from swollen heart muscles, an ailment more commonly known as Sudden Adult Death Syndrome. He was nineteen years old.

The players got the news in the dressing room straight after the game, quelling their jubilation. Brian O'Driscoll's cousin Cillian Willis had played scrum-half for Ireland in Durban that afternoon so the sense of how small the Irish rugby world is was lost on nobody. The champagne in the corner remained there, unopened.

Within a few short years, the lap of honour at Lansdowne in 2004 would come to look almost quaint. Having gone into that Six Nations with only six Triple Crowns won in 105 years, Ireland went on to win three more on top of it in the following five seasons.

Memorable as those days were, though, each of them had their climax

Scoreboard announces Ireland's seventh Triple Crown win

IRELANDS CROWN

EXIT

EXIT

away from Lansdowne Road. In 2006, Shane Horgan's last-minute try to clinch the Triple Crown was at Twickenham (where Ireland became the first team to hoist the newly-minted trophy). In 2007, Ronan O'Gara scored all the points in a 19-18 win over Scotland in Murrayfield to complete Ireland's first back-to-back Triple Crown double since 1949. And in 2009, the Grand Slam was famously finished off in the Millennium Stadium in Cardiff, with O'Gara's immortal drop goal and Welsh out-half Stephen Jones's dropped-short penalty attempt. Great journeys all, started at Lansdowne Road in the spring of 2004.

IRELAND: Girvan Dempsey; Shane Horgan, Gordon D'Arcy, Brian O'Driscoll (capt.), Geordan Murphy; Ronan O'Gara, Peter Stringer; Reggie Corrigan, Shane Byrne, John Hayes, Malcolm O'Kelly, Paul O'Connell, Simon Easterby, David Wallace, Anthony Foley Subs: D. O'Callaghan for O'Kelly; M. Horan for Corrigan; F. Sheahan for Byrne; V. Costello for Wallace; G. Easterby for Stringer; D. Humphreys for O'Gara; K. Maggs for D'Arcy

SCOTLAND: Chris Paterson (capt.); Simon Danielli, Tom Philip, Andrew Henderson, Simon Webster; Dan Parks, Chris Cusiter; Allan Jacobsen, Gordon Bulloch, Bruce Douglas, Scott Murray, Stuart Grimes, Jason White, Cameron Mather, Simon Taylor Subs: G. Kerr for Jacobsen; J. Petrie for Taylor; N. Hines for Grimes; M. Blair for Cusiter; B. Laney for Henderson; R. Russell for Bulloch; D. Lee for Danielli

Referee: Nigel Williams

2006
The
Donnybrook
in Dublin 4

Munster meet
Leinster in the
quarter-final of
the Heineken Cup
and a nation
stops to watch

On 2 May 2004, Kerry and Galway played out an entertaining National Football League final in Croke Park in front of 28,072 people in Croke Park. Two years later, give or take a week, the two counties met again at the same stage of the competition, this time at the Gaelic Grounds in Limerick. But instead of the usual throw-in time of 3.30, this game started at 5.30 and unlike the 2004 final, this one only saw 7,598 punters pay through the stiles. As referee Pat McEnaney threw the ball in the air, the main reason for that discrepancy had just finished up 125 miles away at Lansdowne Road.

The final truly memorable day at the old stadium had a build-up like none that had gone before. There had certainly been times in Lansdowne's 134-year history when what had taken place down by the Dodder had grabbed the nation by the throat and made it impossible to look away, but you would be hard pushed to name a day when the planets had aligned as perfectly as this one. The weather was picturebook, the stakes were sky-high and the hype that had been building for three full weeks made Lansdowne feel like the centre of the universe for a couple of hours as Munster faced off against Leinster for place in the 2006 Heineken Cup final.

Context is everything. By 2006, the appetite for rugby right across Ireland would have seemed utterly alien to the folk who attended the first games at Lansdowne Road. Never mind that, it was barely credible to the people who had frequented the stadium in the latter part of the twentieth century. To anyone who'd sat through the flux and drudgery of the 1990s, the notion that so many people would have paid in to watch a Munster versus Leinster match that you could have filled the place at least three times over would have caused them to choke on the contents of their hipflasks.

And while the sudden success of the national team was the most obvious driver of the game's popularity – Eddie O'Sullivan's side had just completed its second Triple Crown in three years thanks to a last-minute Shane Horgan try at Twickenham the previous month – many would argue that the real engine was the Heineken Cup. Europe's premier club rugby tournament had grown exponentially since Ulster's fabled win at

Lansdowne Road just seven years before. The English teams had returned in 2000 and proceeded to win four of the next six tournaments. Toulouse had flown the flag for the French clubs, winning twice in three seasons and prompting their fellow countrymen into taking it more seriously than had been the case.

Attendances had exploded across the continent. The official total number of people through the stiles in the season of Ulster's success was 322,340, but by the end of the 2006 competition that number had trebled, with 964,863 paying in to see what was now the most popular rugby tournament on the planet. And the Irish provinces had more than done their bit to support it. When Leinster got on a roll in 2003 for instance, their quarter-final and semi-final matches at Lansdowne Road had created tournament records for non-final games, with over forty-three thousand spectators twice filling the stadium inside in a fortnight.

But it was Munster who had given the Heineken Cup its most compelling narrative. No other club had dragged so many supporters across so many lands for so many epic matches and to a soundtrack of such constant heartbreak. They'd been to two finals and had come up just short in both. They'd lost two semi-finals by a single point and another by five to Wasps at Lansdowne in 2004 in what came to be accepted across the board as the best match of the decade at any level. By 2006, they had strapped a whole region to their shoulders and earned admiration and respect beyond it.

What they hadn't done, of course, was actually win the thing and by the 2005/2006 season, there were plenty outside the squad who'd started to believe they possibly never would. The first generation of professional players had passed through by now and if the likes of Mick Galwey, Peter Clohessy and Keith Wood could retire without a Heineken Cup, then it was far from inconceivable that the likes of Ronan O'Gara, Paul

Leinster fans queue for tickets

O'Connell and Anthony Foley might have to settle for a similar lot. They'd gone three seasons without making the final and had even fallen short of the semi-final for the first time in six years. If something wasn't done soon, it might not be done at all.

'Coming into the new season, there were issues we needed to rectify,' said Foley. 'Like dealing with the hype around big games. There comes a point where you either take the lessons fully on board or you leave the class. There comes a time when you just have to go out and win the thing.'

That was all very well, but by the turn of the year, Munster looked to be in trouble. They'd lost their first pool match away to English high-flyers Sale and had been playing catch-up ever since to reasonable, but not spectacular, effect. They were still in with a shout, but they needed a lot to go right for them and needed most of all to change the mood that surrounded them that Christmas. They needed people to stop declaring that they'd gone as far as they were going to go. What they did not need was a trip to Dublin on New Year's Eve to play an up-and-coming Leinster team at the RDS.

Leinster had none of the back-story or romance associated with their country cousins. Their Heineken Cup record was best described as patchy – they'd twice been semi-finalists and twice more gone out at the first knock-out stage without threatening to make a final. They'd built up a reputation for flightiness best exemplified by the rapid rate at which they picked up and discarded out-halves. In the five years up to and including

2004, they'd gone through no less than ten number 10s, each of varying abilities but all ultimately to similar effect. That merry-go-round ended with the signing of twenty-five-year-old Argentine Felipe Contepomi from Bristol in late 2003. Even at that, they'd initially overlooked registering him for the Heineken Cup.

But by late 2005, they were beginning to get their act together. A new Australian coach – Michael Cheika – had come in; along with a quixotic assistant, fellow Aussie David Knox, he got Leinster moving in the right direction. Already feted for the slickness of a three-quarter line that read Denis Hickie, Gordon D'Arcy, Brian O'Driscoll, and Shane Horgan, Leinster's pack was starting to assert itself to boot. They'd leaked a couple of games in the Heineken Cup, but were at a stage in their development where results weren't quite as important as progress. And nobody could deny that they were making progress.

So when Munster came to Dublin on New Year's Eve, Cheika and his men were ready for them. Contepomi was outstanding in a 35-23 win in which he equalled Munster's total for the day all by himself. He scored two tries and after the second one that sealed the win he gestured to the

Ronan O'Gara scores the try that sealed the win

crowd by cupping his hands behind his ears. The picture appeared in all the Sunday papers and didn't go down well with the Munster players.'[It was] as if to say, "What have you got to say about that?"' said Foley. 'That wasn't the only time he got up our noses that season. He was making a good living in Ireland. He should mind his manners.'

Munster left Dublin that night in almost the perfect mindset; they were hurt and they were bitter and they had a grudge to file away for later. They were angry at themselves for not measuring up and at a few of the Leinster players who they felt overdid the celebrations. O'Gara later described it as the night they won the Heineken Cup.

Within a fortnight, they went to France and minced Castres in the fifth-round match of their pool. The next day, a rejuvenated Leinster torched Glasgow at home and set up a final pool weekend of complicated maths and high drama. The day after a last-minute David Wallace try gave Munster a famous bonus-point win over Sale, Leinster went to Bath and achieved a victory that not only put them into the quarter-finals, but also handed Munster a home draw due to the byzantine structure of the competition.

Paul O'Connell and Brian O'Driscoll after the game

It was a weekend of outrageous bravado from both sides, one that cemented for good the tournament's place in the Irish public's heart. Munster's win over Sale on the Saturday evening had garnered the highest television audience up to that time for a Heineken Cup match, with close on half a million people tuning in for the heart-stopping finale. It was the last pool match RTÉ ever got to broadcast live, as Sky Sports commandeered full rights from the following season on.

After the Six Nations break (which brought that Triple Crown to an Ireland side made up predominantly of a Munster pack and a Leinster backline), the two provinces provided another day of days in the quarter-finals. First Leinster went to Toulouse and played the game of their lives, running in four tries to beat the French giants 41–35 on their own ground. It was scintillating stuff, their third try an especially wonderful, length-of-the-field effort that finished with Hickie diving over in the corner. No sooner was it over than Munster kicked off in Lansdowne Road, putting together a more subdued but equally merited 19–10 win over Perpignan. By the final whistle, the whole of Ireland was salivating. The semi-final would be between Munster and Leinster at Lansdowne Road three weeks later.

The country lost the run of itself completely for the next three weeks. Tickets sold on eBay for up to €900. Every newspaper put together colour supplements, every radio station ran competitions giving away tickets to the game. At one point, the mayor of Limerick was forced to take to the airwaves to plead with Munster supporters to return to the city after the game because that Sunday night was census night across the land. 'Many thousands of Limerick people will be in Dublin and this could well result in the population of Limerick, as recorded in the census, being reduced by several thousand from the real figure,' he said. 'This could have serious implications for Limerick in terms of government and European funding over the next five years. Put simply, the smaller our population, the less funding we will receive.'

For the players, it was torturous. Their every move was catalogued, their every utterance parsed. The hype was impossible to ignore and it had its effect too. On the Wednesday before the game, Munster lock Donncha O'Callaghan found himself throwing a perfectly well-cooked piece of fish in the bin for fear that he'd make himself ill if he ate it – and this with a full four days to go! It was a perfect example of just how far off the axis the country had spun in anticipation of the game.

The key to the madness really had little enough to do with rugby in the end. It was the age-old clash of cultures and clichés, country versus city, hard chaw versus pretty boy. Former Leinster coach Matt Williams – an Aussie who'd been in Ireland on and off for the guts of a decade – observed the prevailing mood pretty well in his *Irish Times* column the Friday before the game.

'Munster are Ireland's team, loved by the nation. They are considered to engender all the qualities that Irish people love in their sporting heroes;

valiant, hard-nosed, uncompromising with a never-say-die spirit and the mental strength to defy the odds. Even when Munster don't win a match, it's a failure that's regarded as heroic.

'In contrast, Leinster are considered as moneyed, slightly prima-donna-ish and don't command anything like the same affection with neutrals. When they lose a big game they are seen as flaky and weak, castigated mercilessly, something I discovered when Leinster lost that Heineken European Cup semi-final against Perpignan at Lansdowne Road [in 2003].'

Like all clichés, there was more than a hint of truth in everything Williams wrote. The perception was abroad that Munster would go to the ends of the earth for a Heineken Cup and if that meant taking out the good people of Dublin 4 along the way, well so much the better. That Leinster would field players from Wexford, Louth, Wicklow and Kildare was largely ignored. 'We were hearing from people all the way through the build-up, people at home telling us how important it was that we beat them,' said Peter Stringer. 'Munster people living in Dublin letting us know just what it felt like up there. They were telling us this was much more than just a rugby game.'

By kick-off, the Munster support didn't have to tell the players anything. The sheer strength of their numbers inside the ground said it all. Nominally, twenty-two thousand tickets apiece had been made available to Munster and Leinster, but on the day, it was clear that around three times as many Munster supporters were in the ground as Leinster ones. Munster back-row forward Denis Leamy described approaching the stadium on the team bus as like something from Munster hurling final day in Thurles.

Although set in the heart of Dublin 4, Lansdowne Road was officially a neutral venue for the day as it was a Heineken Cup semi-final game. When Munster coach Declan Kidney walked past the Leinster dressing-room and saw they had a 'HOME' sign up on their door, he found an ERC official and insisted that the two teams toss for home advantage. Leinster lost the toss and had to take the sign down. A small thing, but Munster weren't going to let anything go that day.

And so it proved for the rest of the afternoon. O'Gara kicked off and

Munster fans
thrilled in victory

the ball fell between Jamie Heaslip and Malcolm O'Kelly, but neither listened to the other's call and the ball was spilled right from the off. The tone was set. For all the hype and all the build-up, the game itself turned out to be a one-sided affair. Contepomi had a nightmare all day and was outplayed by O'Gara who performed like a man with a point to prove.

The Munster outhalf had spent five days in hospital between the quarter-final and semi-final after getting an infection in a cut he picked up against Perpignan. He been hooked up to a drip and had needed a crutch when he got out. But he played as if nothing had ever happened and scored the iconic try of the day, handing off O'Kelly before touching down and vaulting the advertising hoarding in front of the South Terrace. In the end, Munster ran out easy 30-6 winners. One of those results that seemed inconceivable beforehand suddenly looked inevitable in hindsight.

'Munster were a solid, experienced side with two finals under their belt already,' said Contepomi. 'Leinster were nowhere. We'd beaten Toulouse out of the blue and suddenly we were facing Munster. You can't even compare one team with the other in terms of maturity.'

When it was over, the Munster players shook hands and were careful not to rub the win in Leinster faces. And afterwards on RTÉ, O'Connell brought everyone thumping back to earth with a post-match interview of touching humility and honesty, one that reminded everyone that for all the madness of the previous three weeks we share a very small island when you take a little time to think about it.

'There are guys there on the Leinster team who I would have died for a couple of months ago and they would have done the same for me,' he said. 'It's a great win for us and I can understand their predicament. It's going to be a tough couple of weeks for them. I don't think you saw many of us jump around the place at the end. It wouldn't be right.'

The following month, he and Foley and O'Gara and the rest of them finally made the promised land when they beat Biarritz in the final in Cardiff. They'd go on to repeat the feat in 2008, also in the Millennium Stadium.

And when Leinster finally emulated them in 2009, it felt apt that they had to go through their oldest rivals along the way. That rematch came at the semi-final stage and happened a few miles to the north, in Croke Park in front of 82,208 people. It was a world record attendance for a club rugby match, made possible by the opening up of the home of the GAA to other sports while Lansdowne Road was being rebuilt.

Even by the very fact of its temporary obsolescence, Mr Dunlop's old patch of land in Dublin 4 was contributing to history.

LEINSTER: Girvan Dempsey; Shane Horgan, Brian O'Driscoll, Gordon D'Arcy, Denis Hickie; Felipe Contepomi, Guy Easterby; Reggie Corrigan, Brian Blaney, Will Green, Bryce Williams, Malcolm O'Kelly, Cameron Jowitt, Keith Gleeson, Jamie Heaslip Subs: Ronan McCormack for Corrigan, Eric Miller for Jowitt
MUNSTER: Shaun Payne; Shane Horgan, John Kelly, Trevor Halstead, Ian Dowling; Ronan O'Gara, Peter Stringer; Federico Pucciariello, Jerry Flannery, John Hayes, Donncha O'Callaghan, Paul O'Connell, Denis Leamy, David Wallace, Anthony Foley. Subs: Frank Roche for Foley, Rob Henderson for Kelly, O'Leary for Henderson
Referee: Chris White (England)

1873-2010
Evolution-
ary Road

The life and
times of the
stadium at
Lansdowne
Road

Right from the beginning, Lansdowne Road was in a state of constant evolution. From its first incarnation as a sporting complex that included a cinder track, a cricket square, tennis courts and a rugby pitch, it went through myriad regenerations through the years. The road travelled from there to the stunning glass structure that grabs the eye on any trip through Dublin 4 these days took turns and passed through phases that Henry Dunlop couldn't possibly have conceived of back the late nineteenth century.

Originally, the pitch ran at right angles to the one that generations of spectators would come to know, but it suffered badly from being at too low a level in relation to the River Dodder. Dunlop once found himself paddling a canoe through a foot and a half of water one especially wet winter as sheep grazed on an island in the centre of the pitch. He eventually decided this must be remedied; three hundred carts of soil were taken from beside the railway line near where the West Stand would in time be built, and the pitch level was raised by two feet.

The West Stand would go through a few incarnations as the decades passed. Once the IRFU had secured tenancy on the ground in January 1907, they went about building two stands on that side of the pitch. By the time Scotland came to play the following year – on 29 February, as it happened, the only time in history Ireland played a test match on the extra day of a leap year – patrons could choose between a large covered stand and a smaller uncovered one.

The covered stand lasted just under forty years and was replaced by a two-tiered structure that straddled the railway line behind it in 1955. The new stand was a source of huge pride to the IRFU at the time as the newspapers reported breathlessly on the 'splendid new committee rooms, tea rooms and reception rooms' underneath the seats. They also boasted that the new dressing rooms, constructed from the shell of the old committee rooms, were 'the most luxurious in the country'.

But as demand for international rugby tickets grew over the years, so did the IRFU's ambitions for the stadium and consequently the decision was taken in 1976 to upgrade further. The bottom tier of the covered stand was taken out completely and refitted and the small uncovered stand was

The Old and the New —
a matter of 10 months, in 1955

A 1955 photograph
of the old stand

knocked to make way for an extension of the North Terrace. The result
was an extra 1,600 seats in the stand and the wholesale replacement of
those luxurious dressing rooms and reception rooms.

On the opposite side of the pitch, the only structure to stand on the
high grassy bank in the early decades of the twentieth century was the
press pavilion. That changed in 1927 when the first East Stand went up,
a doughty building that stood for over half a century until it was replaced
in 1984. *The Irish Times* reported that on the occasion of the first
international in front of the East Stand, on 27 February 1927, the weather
was so bad that several players from both the Ireland and Scotland teams
had to be helped from the pitch suffering from exhaustion. The first of its
kind in Ireland, the East Stand was built on concrete pillars with standing
room underneath and would provide a template for the building of the
first incarnation of the Cusack Stand in Croke Park just under a decade
later.

After it was demolished and rebuilt at a cost of £5m in 1983/84, the
capacity of the East Stand went from 3,400 to 13,400. It was initially
called the 'Triple Crown Stand', but the name never stuck, despite Mick
Doyle's Ireland team achieving the fabled trifecta within a year of its

unveiling. The 52,720 who watched Ireland lose 18-9 to Wales on 4 February 1984 was the biggest crowd ever to watch a rugby match in the country up to that point.

The world was moving fast, however, and Lansdowne Road struggled to keep up. Floodlights weren't installed until 1995, causing games to be played in the afternoon or not at all. And while the likes of Twickenham and Murrayfield were modernising by the year and expanding their corporate hospitality facilities, Lansdowne could do no better than marquees on the back pitch on match days. Media facilities were from another age too – wooden benches in the Upper West Stand packed tightly together and electrical sockets that called for an adapter if a reporter wanted to use a modern three-pin plug (an inconvenience that continued right up until the stadium's final day on New Year's Eve 2006).

Every once in a while, the spectre of a serious crush happening on one of the terraces would raise its head. At the Five Nations game against France in February 1981, crowds poured into the South Terrace for fifteen minutes after kick-off, eventually causing the St John's Ambulance staff to open the gates in the perimeter fence and allow people onto the side of the pitch. Similar scenarios arose in 1983 (France in the Five Nations again), 1984 (Wales) and 1990 (Scotland) and each time the complaints from spectators were the same – overcrowded terraces (often due to people getting in with no tickets or forged ones), which led to panic, to people being carried off their feet with arms pinned by their sides and no route of escape or relief. Serious injury was avoided, but the dangers were obvious to all.

World events brought them into sharper focus as the years went by. In the summer of 1989, FIFA announced that it was to ban standing accommodation at all international venues by 1992 in response to the Hillsborough tragedy. With the terraces at either end of the pitch making up more than 50 per cent of Lansdowne's capacity, this meant that the FAI faced a future with only around twenty-one thousand people at their home matches – a disastrously low figure at any point, but especially so as Jack Charlton's Ireland team came to tighten its hold on the nation's affections. While an accommodation was reached in time with FIFA and UEFA over the use of temporary seating on the two terraces, it became increasingly clear that the stadium needed to be modernised.

By the mid-1990s, the IRFU was giving serious thought to the future of the stadium and set up a committee chaired by Tom Kiernan to assess its options. The union bought a ninety-five-acre site at Newlands Cross in 1994, but didn't particularly want to move international matches so far out of the city centre if they could avoid it. A putative move to a new development in the Phoenix Park actually received full IRFU backing at one point, but it never came to fruition – local opposition to a casino that was to come as part of the development caused Fianna Fáil to nix the idea ahead of the 1997 general election. But one way or another, everyone agreed that something needed to be done with the old place.

'The reality,' said Kiernan in 1998, 'is that Lansdowne Road as it stands is no longer adequate. Every option has to be examined. That includes the redevelopment of Lansdowne Road, moving to another location or the possible development of the site the IRFU purchased in Newlands. I am well aware and fully understand the emotional attachment to Lansdowne Road. The big decision is to build a new stadium or redevelop Lansdowne Road. There are financial and other considerations to be weighed.'

One such consideration was to gauge the future plans of the FAI. The annual rent from the national soccer team's annual half-dozen or so matches was always a welcome addition to the IRFU coffers and any prospect of it drying up would necessarily affect the union's ability to redevelop the stadium. When the FAI announced in January 1999 that they planned to build a forty-five-thousand-seater stadium of their own on a fifty-acre in Citywest Business Park off the Naas Road, the IRFU issued a short statement wishing them every success with their venture, while firmly pointing out that they had their own stadium plans with which to concern themselves. The notion that they might reverse roles with the FAI and become their tenants was dismissed.

Meanwhile, the Bertie Ahern-led government of the day was formulating its own plans to build an eighty-thousand-seater national stadium. Like the FAI's stadium – putatively named Eircom Park after the national communications company announced it was coming on board in a deal worth £11m – it would be built in west Dublin, a few miles to the north in Abbotstown. It would be known as Stadium Ireland and would be the centrepiece of Sports Campus Ireland, a sprawling, multi-sport project situated just off the M50. The IRFU broadly welcomed the plan, but while they didn't rule out the notion of playing internationals at the new stadium, they didn't sign up to any binding agreements either.

Ireland at the dawn of the new century was therefore a mad and maddening place to be when it came to the stadium question. For a couple of years, you had the very real prospect of a city of just over one million inhabitants with no major professional sports team to speak of being home to four stadiums whose capacity would be above 45,000 each. Lansdowne Road, Croke Park, Eircom Park and Stadium Ireland would, if all went to plan, be part of the Dublin skyline by 2005, despite the fact that it made no sense from a revenue point of view to have any more than two of them.

In time, the options were whittled down. Bertie Ahern was determined to make Stadium Ireland a reality, a monument to the Celtic Tiger years of plenty that would stand long into the future. In the spring of 2001, the government promised the FAI £165m in funding over the following thirteen years on condition it drop its plans for Eircom Park and then another £60m to the GAA to keep the gates of Croke Park closed to soccer and rugby. All the while, the actual cost of the new stadium sky-rocketed, from an initial estimate in 1999 of £281m to an eye-watering £704m in 2002. In the end, political pressure from Fianna Fáil's coalition partners the Progressive Democrats forced an embarrassing climb-down – in the face of mounting public pressure about the health service and other public services, an exorbitantly-priced stadium was beginning to look unwise – and the project was scrapped.

Lansdowne Road on its last day

All of which left the IRFU and FAI still hosting international matches at Lansdowne Road, which was crumbling more with each passing year. As every other option fizzled out, the two associations came together and

finally decided to redevelop Lansdowne Road as a joint venture. Partly funded by National Lottery money, plans for the new stadium were announced in January 2004, bringing an end to one of the most drawn-out and tedious sagas in Irish sporting history. Well, almost to an end – the granting of planning permission took until March 2007 to secure.

But secured it was and on New Year's Eve 2006, Leinster played Ulster in the Magner's League, a reprise of the first rugby match to be played on the ground 130 years beforehand. Even in its final hours, the stadium set a record – the forty-eight thousand who turned up constituting the largest ever crowd for that competition. They weren't really there for the game, more the occasion which, for the record, Leinster won 20-12.

And in May 2007, the diggers moved in and demolition began. The fourteen-acre site took three years to redevelop, with almost a thousand workers on-site daily. Over four and a half thousand people were employed through the three years it took to knock and rebuild a stadium that reaches eleven storeys high and takes up almost 730,000 square feet. Each of the fifty thousand seats in the ground has an unobstructed view, thanks to the six huge steel towers that hold up the crisp-shaped roof. In February 2009, it was announced that the insurance company Aviva had won the naming rights for the first ten years of the stadium's life.

The Aviva Stadium is light years removed from the cold, dreary old edifice that Lansdowne Road had become in its latter years. Gone are the small, damp dressing rooms that had been built for teams of fifteen players (substitutes were not a regular feature when they were built in the 1950s, backroom teams even less so) and in their place are massive, U-shaped changing facilities with room for twenty-eight players and separate office space for team management including video analysis suites. The home dressing room also comes equipped with hydrotherapy facilities – hot and cold pools that allow players to rehab immediately after the final whistle. There are four medical treatment rooms, an on-site x-ray room down the hall and an artificial-turfed warm-up area with a high roof for teams who want to practise line-outs before a match.

Away from the playing side of things, the ancient, cramped press box has been replaced with a two-hundred-seat media centre (with modern plug sockets!) and four television studios. There are thirty-six corporate boxes that can hold up to 1,300 people, sixty catering kiosks and conferencing facilities for up to eight hundred people. Two large screens relay the action to the crowd.

Eco-friendliness that would not have been a huge consideration in the earlier incarnations of Lansdowne Road is to the fore in this one, even going so far as to have had a consultant ecologist involved throughout. The East Stand has a rainwater-harvesting system that funnels the rain that falls from the Dublin sky into large storage tanks underneath the pitch to provide natural irrigation for the sod. The pitch itself is grown from the soil of the old one, which was kept in cold storage for the three years of redevelopment and contains sand and fibre-elastic material as well as grass. There's even a car park underneath the back pitch with space for two hundred vehicles.

It took €410m to build and filled rainforests-worth of newspapers along the way; a government almost fell and Croke Park saw rugby and soccer matches played because of it; it waded through the treacle of the planning process and came out the other side with local residents for the most part onside. And on Saturday 7 August 2010, a Munster/Connacht selection took on a team from Ulster/Leinster on the first day of the rest of Lansdowne Road's life.

A stadium for all our futures on a site from all our pasts.

BIBLIOGRAPHY

NATIONAL NEWSPAPERS

The Irish Times
Irish Independent
Freeman's Journal
Sunday Independent
Sunday Tribune
The Star
Irish Daily Mirror
Evening Herald
Irish Press
Sunday Press
Evening Press

INTERNATIONAL NEWSPAPERS

The Sunday Times
The Times
The Daily Telegraph
Daily Mail
The Independent
Observer
London Gazette
Bell's Life
Illustrated London News
New Zealand Sunday Times
Corriere della Sport

LOCAL AND SPECIALIST NEWSPAPERS

Sport
Irish Sportsman
The Dublin Penny Journal
Dublin Evening Mail
News 4
Irish Field
Cork Examiner
Tipperary Free Press
Munster Express
Limerick Leader
Belfast Telegraph

MAGAZINES

Irish Rugby Review
Munster Rugby News
Irish Rugby
Rugby Ireland
Leinster Rugby News
Rugby Ireland International
You Boys in Green
Soccer Reporter
World Soccer
Irish Soccer Magazine
When Saturday Comes
British Medical Journal (Aug 1880)
Irish Runner

BIOGRAPHY/AUTOBIOGRAPHY

RUGBY

Willie John by Edmund Van Esbeck (Gill & Macmillan, 1976)
Doyler by Mick Doyle (Gill & Macmillan, 1991)
Martin Johnson: The Autobiography by Martin Johnson (Headline, 2003)
A Life Worth Living by Nicholas Shehadie (Simon & Schuster Australia, Sydney, 2003)
Willie John, My Autobiography by Peter Bills (Portrait, 2004)
Rucks, Mauls & Gaelic Footballs by Moss Keane and Billy Keane (Merlin, 2005)
'David Gallaher, 1873-1917' by Denis McLean (*Dictionary of New Zealand Biography*, 2007)
Never Die Wondering by Eddie O'Sullivan and Vincent Hogan (Century, 2009)

ATHLETICS

Recollections of a Veteran Irish Athlete: the Memoirs of Pat Davin, the World's All-Round Athletic Champion by Pat Davin (Juverna Press, Dublin 1938)
The Ballincurry Hare by John Joe Barry (Athletic Publications, Dublin, 1986)
Michael Cusack and the GAA by Marcus de Burca (Anvil Books, 1989)
A Cold Clear Day: The Athletic Biography of Buddy Edelen by Frank Murphy (Wind Sprint Press, 1992)
Maurice Davin by Seamus Ó Riain (Geography Publications, 1994)
Staying the Distance by Ronnie Delany (O'Brien Press,

Dublin, 2007)

FOOTBALL

The Sash He Never Wore by Derek Dougan (Allison & Busby, 1972)

Jack and Bobby by Leo McKinstry (Harper Collins, 2002)

Niall Quinn: The Autobiography by Niall Quinn and Tom Humphries (Headline, 2002)

Keane by Roy Keane and Eamon Dunphy (Michael Joseph, 2002)

Back From The Brink by Paul McGrath and Vincent Hogan (Century, 2006)

The Doog: The Incredible Story Of Derek Dougan by Steve Gordos and David Harrison (Know The Score Books, 2008)

MISCELLANEOUS BIOGRAPHIES

Stories of Old Ireland and Myself by Sir William Orpen (1924)

A Cavalier Irishman: Diaries 1970-79 by Ulick O'Connor (2004)

GENERAL SPORTING HISTORIES

RUGBY

Football: the Rugby Union Game edited by Rev. F. Marshall (London, 1892)

The Complete Rugby Footballer by David Gallaher & Billy Stead (Methuen & Co, 1906)

The Rugby Football Internationals Roll of Honour by E.H.D. Sewell (1919)

Rugger – The History, Theory and Practice of Rugby Football by W. W. Wakefield, H. P. Marshall (London, 1928)

Irish Rugby Football Triple Crown Souvenir (Dublin, 1949)

Ireland's Golden Rugby Years, 1947-1952 edited by Barry S. Nolan (Dublin, 1952)

Great Rugger Clubs by J.B.G. Thomas (London, 1962)

Men, Matches and Moments by J.B.G. Thomas (Pelham Books, London 1970)

Springboks 1891-1970 by A.C. Parker (Cassell, 1970)

There Was Also Some Rugby: the Sixth Springboks in Britain by Wallace Reyburn (Stanley Paul, 1970)

The Men in Green by Sean Diffley (Stanley Paul, 1972)

One Hundred Years of Irish Rugby by Edmund Van Esbeck (Gill & Macmillan, 1974)

The Story of Irish Rugby by Edmund Van Esbeck (Gill & Macmillan, 1974)

Ireland's Triple Crown by Karl Johnston (Gill & Macmillan, Dublin 1982)

Irish Rugby Scrapbook by Edmund Van Esbeck (Souvenir Press, 1982)

Centenary: 100 Years of All Black Rugby by R.H. Chester & NAC McMillan (Moa Publications, Auckland 1984)

The Encyclopedia of New Zealand Rugby by R.H. Chester & N.A.C. McMillan, 2nd ed. (Moa Publications, Auckland, 1987)

New Zealand Rugby Legends by Terry McLean, (Moa Publications, Auckland, 1987)

The Phoenix Book of International Rugby by John Griffiths (London, 1987)

The All Blacks by T.P. McLean (Sidgwick & Jackson, London 1991)

Forerunners of the All Blacks by Greg Ryan (Canterbury, New Zealand, 1993)

The Murphy's Story of Munster Rugby by Charlie Mulqueen (Cork, 1993)

The Daily Telegraph *Chronicle of Rugby* (1996)

Rugby's Golden Year: the Unique Grand Slam of 1948 by Sean Diffley (Blackwater, Dublin, 1998)

Irish Rugby 1874-1999: A History by Edmund Van Esbeck (Dublin 1999)

The Five Nations Story by David Hands (Tempus, 2000)

150 Years of Trinity Rugby by Trevor West (ed.) (Wordwell 2003)

The Full Bag of Chips, Ireland and the Triple Crown by Peter O'Reilly (O'Brien Press, 2004)

Legends Of Irish Rugby by John Scally (Mainstream, 2005)

Belvedere's Rugby Heroes by Oliver Murphy (ed.) (Belvedere Museum, 2006)

Lansdowne Through The Years by Edward Newman (Hodder Headline, 2006)

The Ireland Rugby Miscellany by Ciaran Cronin (Vision Sports, 2007)

From There To Here: Irish Rugby In The Professional Era by

Brendan Fanning (Gill & Macmillan, 2007)

ATHLETICS

Athletics and Football by Montague Shearman
(Spottiswode, London 1887)

Athletics by D.G.A. Lowe and A.E. Porritt (Longman,
London 1929)

Fifty Years of Irish Athletics by 'Carbery' [PD Mehigan]
(Dublin, 1943)

Seventy Years of Irish Athletics by 'Carbery' [PD Mehigan]
(Dublin, 1945)

The Politics of Irish Athletics, 1850-1990 by Padraig
Griffin (Ballinamore, Co. Leitrim 1990)

*The Irish Championships 1873-84, the ICAC and the
DAC Championships* by Colm Murphy (2003)

Irish Championship Athletics 1873-1914 by Tony
O'Donoghue (Dublin, 2005)

FOOTBALL

The History of Irish Soccer by Malcolm Brodie (Arrell,
Glasgow, 1963)

The Bass Book of Irish Soccer edited by Sean Ryan
(Dublin, 1975)

100 Years of Irish Football by Malcolm Brodie (Belfast,
1980)

The Book of Irish Goalscorers by Sean Ryan and Stephen
Burke (Irish Soccer Co-Op, 1987)

Ireland on the Ball by Donal Cullen (Elo Publications,
1993)

The Team That Jack Built by Paul Rowan (Mainstream,
1994)

Football Association of Ireland – 75 Years by Peter Byrne
(Sportsworld, 1996)

The Boys in Green: the FAI international story by Sean
Ryan (Mainstream, 1997)

The Garrison Game by Dave Hannigan (Mainstream,
1998)

Mick McCarthy's World Cup Diary by Mick McCarthy
and Cathal Dervan (Townhouse, 2002)

Association Football and society in pre-partition Ireland by
Neal Garnham (UHP, 2004)

Freestaters by Donal Cullen (Desert Island Books, 2007)

Futebol: The Brazilian Way Of Life by Alex Bellos

(Bloomsbury, 2008)

OTHER SPORTS

Bill James Historical Baseball Abstract by Bill James
(Chicago, 1985)

The Bold Collegians by TT West (Lilliput Press, Dublin
1991)

Baseball: A history of America's Game by Benjamin G.
Rader (Chicago, 1992)

A Brief history of Croquet in Ireland by Clive Martin &
Simon Williams (2004)

Green Days, Cricket in Ireland 1792-2005 by Gerard
Siggins (Nonsuch, 2005)

*Spalding's World Tour: the epic adventure that took baseball
around the globe – and made it America's game* by Mark
Lamster (PublicAffairs, 2006)

100 Greats of Irish Cricket by Gerard Siggins and James
Fitzgerald (Nonsuch, 2006)

History of Irish Tennis by Tom Higgins (3 vols, Sligo,
2006)

Cooperstown Confidential by Zev Chafets (Bloomsbury,
2009)

GENERAL SPORT

Sport is My Lifeline by Ulick O'Connor (London, 1984)

Laptop Dancing and the Nanny-Goat Mambo by Tom
Humphries (Townhouse, 2003)

More Than A Game by Con Houlihan (Liberties, 2003)

Giants Of Cork Sport by Dave Hannigan (Evening Echo,
2005)

ANNUAL PUBLICATIONS

Lawrence's Handbook of Cricket in Ireland, various editions
from 1866-1882

Football in Ireland by R.M. Peter, 1880

Rothman's Rugby Annual, various editions

Fred Cogley's Irish Rugby Annual, various editions

CLUB PUBLICATIONS

Wanderers FC centenary brochure (Dublin, 1970)

Lansdowne FC centenary 1872-1972, Gary Redmond
(ed.) (Dublin 1972)

Dublin University Harriers & Athletic Club: a centenary

history 1885-1985 by Alan Gilsenan (ed.) (Dublin, 1985)

Old Wesley RFC 1891-1991 by Edmund Van Esbeck (Dublin, 1991)

The Story of Young Munster by Michael O'Flaherty (Limerick, 1996)

Farewell to Ormeau (NICC, Belfast, 2003)

Various IRFU and FAI match programmes

Minute Book of the Irish Champion Athletic Club 1872-74

LOCAL HISTORY

The Neighbourhood of Dublin, Weston St John Joyce (Dublin, 1912)

The Rivers of Dublin by Clair L. Sweeney (Dublin 1991).

The Old Township of Pembroke 1863-1930, by Jim Cooke (CDVEC, 1993)

The Ogham Stone: an anthology of contemporary Ireland, by Michael Mulreany and Gerald Dawe (eds.) (IPA, Dublin 2001)

Four Roads to Dublin by Deirdre Kelly (O'Brien Press, Dublin 2001)

Old Limerick Journal, various editions

Dublin Historical Record, various editions

GENERAL REFERENCE BOOKS

University of Dublin War List (Dublin, 1922)

Dictionary of New Zealand Biography Vol.2 1870-1900 (1993)

Dictionary of Irish Biography by James Quinn and James McGuire (eds.) (CUP, 2009)

GENERAL HISTORIES

The Glories of Ireland edited by Joseph Dunn and P.J. Lennox (New York, 1914)

The Pals At Suvla Bay: Being the Record of 'D' Company of the 7th Royal Dublin Fusiliers by Henry Hanna (October 1916; reprinted Naval & Military Press Ltd, 2002)

Sport in the Making of Celtic Cultures by Grant Jarvie (1999)

Fields of Glory by Gavin Mortimer (London, 2001)

ACADEMIC JOURNALS

'They Stooped to Conquer: Rugby Union Football 1895-1914' by James W. Martens (The Journal of Sports History, Vol 20, No.1, Spring 1983)

'Rugby and the Forging of National Identity' by Scott A.G.M. Crawford (Sporting Traditions, The Journal of the Australian Society for Sports History, 1999)

ACADEMIC PAPER

'For the Sake of Sport and Human Decency: Sport and the Irish Anti-Apartheid Movement, 1964-74' by Kevin O'Sullivan (Sports History Ireland Annual Conference, 2007)

GOVERNMENT REPORTS

Violence at Lansdowne Road by Thomas A. Finlay (Stationary Office, 1995)

FILM

Resistance by Ruth Power (Students of DIT Aungier Street, 2008)

FICTION

Ulysses by James Joyce (Faber & Faber, 1939)

WEBSITES

www.scrum.com (ESPN rugby)

www.irishrugby.com (IRFU)

www.rsssf.com (The Rec.Sport.Soccer Statistics Foundation)

www.cricketarchive.com (Cricket Archive)

www.cricketeurope.org (CricketIreland)

www.greatwarforum.com (Great War Forum)

www.irishwarmemorials.ie (Irish War Memorials)

www.Limerickpride.com (Limerick Pride)

www.rugbymuseum.co.nz (New Zealand Rugby Museum)

http://nifootball.blogspot.com (Northern Ireland's Footballing Greats)

CLUB WEBSITES

www.lansdownerugby.com (Lansdowne)

www.wanderersfcrugby.com (Wanderers)

www.cliftonrfc.com (Clifton RFC, Bristol)

www.bohemians.ie (Bohemians AFC)

www.bceagles.cstv.com (Boston College)

www.army.rivals.com (Army American football team)

APPENDIX 1
RUGBY INTERNATIONALS AT LANSDOWNE ROAD 1878-2006

DATE	OPP	RESULT	SCORE	SCORERS
11.3.1878	ENGLAND	lost	(nil – 1T 2G)	
30.1.1880	ENGLAND	lost	(1t – 1G 1T)	Cuppaidge T
28.1.1882	WALES	lost	(nil – 2G 2T)	
6.2.1882	ENGLAND	drew	(2T – 2T)	Johnston T Stokes T
4.2.1884	ENGLAND	lost	(nil – 1g)	
6.2.1886	ENGLAND	lost	(nil – 1T)	
5.2.1887	ENGLAND	won	(2g – nil)	Tillie T, Montgomery T, Rambaut 2C
3.3.1888	WALES	won	(1g 1dg 1t – nil)	Warren T, Shanahan T, Rambaut C
1.12.1888	NZ NATIVES	lost	(1g 1t – 4g 1t)	Woods T, Waites T, Stevenson C
				(point scoring system introduced in 1890)
1.3.1890	WALES	drew	3-3	Dunlop T
7.2.1891	ENGLAND	lost	0-9	
5.3.1892	WALES	won	9-0	Walsh 2T, Davies T, Roche C
4.2.1893	ENGLAND	lost	0-4	
24.2.1894	SCOTLAND	won	5-0	Wells T, JN Lytle C
2.2.1895	ENGLAND	lost	3-6	Magee T
15.2.1896	SCOTLAND	drew	0-0	
14.3.1896	WALES	won	8-4	JH Lytle 2T, Crean T, Bulger C
6.2.1897	ENGLAND	won	13-9	W Gardiner 2T, Bulger T, GM
4.2.1899	ENGLAND	won	6-0	Allen T, Magee P
24.2.1900	SCOTLAND	drew	0-0	
9.2.1901	ENGLAND	won	10-6	P Gardiner T, Davidson T, Irwin C
8.3.1902	WALES	lost	0-15	
14.2.1903	ENGLAND	won	6-0	Ryan T, Colley P
27.2.1904	SCOTLAND	lost	3-19	Moffat T
25.11.1905	NEW ZEALAND	lost	0-15	
24.2.1906	SCOTLAND	lost	6-13	Robb T, Parke T
9.2.1907	ENGLAND	won	17-9	Caddell 2T, Tedford T, Thrift T, Parke C, GM
29.2.1908	SCOTLAND	won	16-11	Thrift 2T, Beckett T, Thompson T, Parke C, Hinton C
13.2.1909	ENGLAND	lost	5-11	Parke T, Pinion C
20.3.1909	FRANCE	won	19-8	Thompson 2T, O'Connor T, Gardiner T,C, Parke P,C
12.3.1910	WALES	lost	3-19	McIldowie
11.2.1911	ENGLAND	won	3-0	Smyth T
24.2.1912	SCOTLAND	won	10-8	Foster T, Lloyd P,D
30.11.1912	SOUTH AFRICA	lost	0-38	
8.2.1913	ENGLAND	lost	4-15	Lloyd D
28.2.1914	SCOTLAND	won	6-0	Quinn T, McNamara T
14.2.1920	ENGLAND	lost	11-14	Lloyd T,P,C, Dickson T
3.4.1920	FRANCE	lost	7-15	Lloyd D, Price T
26.2.1921	SCOTLAND	won	9-8	Cussen T, G Stephenson T, Cunningham T
11.2.1922	ENGLAND	lost	3-12	Wallis T
8.4.1922	FRANCE	won	8-3	G Stephenson T, Wallis C,P
24.2.1923	SCOTLAND	lost	3-13	Cussen T
10.3.1923	WALES	won	5-4	Cussen T, Crawford C
26.1.1924	FRANCE	won	6-0	G Stephenson T, Atkins T
1.11.1924	NEW ZEALAND	lost	0-6	
28.2.1925	SCOTLAND	lost	8-14	H Stephenson T, Crawford P,C
13.2.1926	ENGLAND	won	19-15	Cussen 2T, G Stephenson T,P,2C, F Hewitt T
26.2.1927	SCOTLAND	won	6-0	Ganly T, T Pike T
12.3.1927	WALES	won	19-9	G Stephenson 2T,2C,P, Ganly 2T
12.11.1927	AUSTRALIA	lost	3-5	Ganly P
11.2.1928	ENGLAND	lost	6-7	Arigho T, Sugden T
23.2.1929	SCOTLAND	lost	7-16	Arigho T, Davy D
8.2.1930	ENGLAND	won	4-3	Murray D
28.2.1931	SCOTLAND	won	8-5	Sugden T, V Pike T, Murray C

DATE	OPP	RESULT	SCORE	SCORERS
19.12.1931	SOUTH AFRICA	lost	3-8	McMahon P
13.2.1932	ENGLAND	lost	8-11	Murray P,C, Waide T
1.4.1933	SCOTLAND	lost	6-8	Murray T, Crowe T
10.2.1934	ENGLAND	lost	3-13	Morgan T
23.2.1935	SCOTLAND	won	12-5	Bailey T, Ridgeway T, Lawlor T, O'Connor T
7.12.1935	NEW ZEALAND	lost	9-17	Beamish T, Beamish P, Siggins P
8.2.1936	ENGLAND	won	6-3	Bailey T, Boyle T
27.2.1937	SCOTLAND	won	11-4	Morgan T, McMahon T, Alexander T, Bailey C
12.2.1938	ENGLAND	lost	14-36	Daly T, Bailey T, Cromey T, Mayne T, Crowe C
25.2.1939	SCOTLAND	won	12-3	Moran T, Torrens T, Sayers GM, McKibbin P
25.1.1947	FRANCE	lost	8-12	McKay T, Mullan P,C
8.2.1947	ENGLAND	won	22-0	Mullan 2T,P,2C, O'Hanlon 2T. McKay T
6.12.1947	AUSTRALIA	lost	3-16	K Quinn P
28.2.1948	SCOTLAND	won	6-0	Mullan T, Kyle T
29.1.1949	FRANCE	lost	9-16	Norton 3P
12.2.1949	ENGLAND	won	14-5	Norton 2P,C, McKee T, O'Hanlon T
25.2.1950	SCOTLAND	won	21-0	Norton 2P,3C, Blayney T, Crowe T, Curtin T
27.1.1951	FRANCE	won	9-8	Clifford T, Nelson T, Henderson P
10.2.1951	ENGLAND	won	3-0	McKibbin P
8.12.1951	SOUTH AFRICA	lost	5-17	Browne T, Murphy C
23.2.1952	SCOTLAND	won	12-8	Henderson T,P, Lane T, Kyle T
8.3.1952	WALES	lost	3-14	Murphy P
14.2.1953	ENGLAND	drew	9-9	Mortell T, Henderson 2P
9.1.1954	NEW ZEALAND	lost	3-14	Henderson P
13.3.1954	WALES	lost	9-12	Henderson P, Gaston T, Kelly P
22.1.1955	FRANCE	lost	3-5	Henderson P
12.2.1955	ENGLAND	drew	6-6	Henderson P, Pedlow T
25.2.1956	SCOTLAND	won	14-10	Henderson T, Kyle T, O'Reilly T, O'Meara T, Pedlow C
10.3.1956	WALES	won	11-3	Cunningham T, Pedlow P,C
26.1.1957	FRANCE	won	11-6	Pedlow C,P, Brophy T, Kyle T
9.2.1957	ENGLAND	lost	0-6	
18.1.1958	AUSTRALIA	won	9-6	Henderson T, Dawson T, Pedlow P
1.3.1958	SCOTLAND	won	12-6	Pedlow 2T, Henderson P. Berkery P
15.3.1958	WALES	lost	6-9	O'Meara T, Henderson P
14.2.1959	ENGLAND	lost	0-3	
18.4.1959	FRANCE	won	9-5	Brophy T, D Hewitt P, English D
27.2.1960	SCOTLAND	lost	5-6	Wood T, D Hewitt C
12.3.1960	WALES	lost	9-10	Kelly 2P, N Murphy T
17.12.1960	SOUTH AFRICA	lost	3-8	Kiernan P
11.2.1961	ENGLAND	won	11-8	Moffett 2P,C, Kavanagh T
15.4.1961	FRANCE	lost	3-15	Kiernan P
24.2.1962	SCOTLAND	lost	6-20	Hunter P,T
17.11.1962	WALES	drew	3-3	English
26.1.1963	FRANCE	lost	5-24	O'Reilly T, Kiernan C
9.2.1963	ENGLAND	drew	0-0	
7.12.1963	NEW ZEALAND	lost	5-6	Fortune T, Kiernan C
22.2.1964	SCOTLAND	lost	3-6	Kiernan P
7.3.1964	WALES	lost	6-15	Keogh 2P
23.1.1965	FRANCE	drew	3-3	Doyle T
13.2.1965	ENGLAND	won	5-0	Lamont T, Kiernan C
10.4.1966	SOUTH AFRICA	won	9-6	McGrath T, Kiernan 2P
26.2.1966	SCOTLAND	lost	3-11	Kiernan P
12.3.1966	WALES	won	9-6	Bresnihan T, Gibson P,D
21.1.1967	AUSTRALIA	won	15-8	Gibson 2D,T, Duggan T, Kiernan P
11.2.1967	ENGLAND	lost	3-8	Kiernan P
15.4.1967	FRANCE	lost	6-11	Molloy T, Kiernan P
24.2.1968	SCOTLAND	won	14-6	Kiernan P,C, Duggan 2T, Bresnihan T
9.3.1968	WALES	won	9-6	Doyle T, Gibson D, Kinahan P
26.10.1968	AUSTRALIA	won	10-3	Bresnihan T, Goodall T, Kiernan C, Moroney C

DATE	OPP	RESULT	SCORE	SCORERS
25.1.1969	FRANCE	won	17-9	Moroney T,C,3P, McGann D
8.2.1969	ENGLAND	won	17-15	Kiernan 2P,C, Bresnihan T, Murphy T, McGann D
10.1.1970	SOUTH AFRICA	drew	8-8	Duggan T, Kiernan C,P
28.2.1970	SCOTLAND	won	16-11	Gibson T, Brown T, Molloy T, Goodall T, Kiernnan 2C
14.3.1970	WALES	won	14-0	Duggan T, Goodall T, Kiernan P,C, McGann D
30.1.1971	FRANCE	drew	9-9	Grant T, O'Driscoll 2P
13.2.1971	ENGLAND	lost	6-9	Grant T, Duggan T
29.4.1972	FRANCE	won	24-14	Kiernan 3C,2P, Duggan T, Flynn T, Moloney T
20.1.1973	NEW ZEALAND	drew	10-10	Grace T, McGann 2P
10.2.1972	ENGLAND	won	18-9	Grace T, Milliken T, McGann P,D,2C
14.4.1973	FRANCE	won	6-4	Gibson P, Ensor P
2.2.1974	WALES	drew	9-9	Ensor 3P
2.3.1974	SCOTLAND	won	9-6	Milliken T, McKinney P, Gibson C
7.9.1974	PRESIDENT'S XV	drew	18-18	McKinney T, Slattery T, Gibson 2P,2C
23.11.1974	NEW ZEALAND	lost	6-15	Ensor 2P
18.1.1975	ENGLAND	won	12-9	Gibson T, McCombe T,2C
1.3.1975	FRANCE	won	25-6	Ensor T, Grace T, McBride T, McCombe 2C, 2D, P
17.1.1976	AUSTRALIA	lost	10-20	Robbie 2P. McMaster T
21.2.1976	WALES	lost	9-34	McGann 3P
20.3.1976	SCOTLAND	lost	6-15	McGann 2P
5.2.1977	ENGLAND	lost	0-4	
19.3.1977	FRANCE	lost	6-15	Gibson P, Quinn P
21.1.1978	SCOTLAND	won	12-9	Ward 2P,C, McKinney T
4.3.1978	WALES	lost	16-20	Ward 3P,D, Moloney T
4.11.1978	NEW ZEALAND	lost	6-10	Ward 2P
20.1.1979	FRANCE	drew	9-9	Ward 3P
17.2.1979	ENGLAND	won	12-7	Ward P,D,C, McLennan T
2.2.1980	SCOTLAND	won	22-15	Campbell 3P,D,C, Kennedy T, Keane T
15.3.1980	WALES	won	21-7	Fitzgerald T, O'Driscoll T, Irwin T, Campbell 3P,C
7.2.1981	FRANCE	lost	13-19	Campbell 3P, McNeill T
7.3.1981	ENGLAND	lost	6-10	Campbell D, McNeill D
21.11.1981	AUSTRALIA	lost	12-16	Ward 4P
23.1.1982	WALES	won	20-12	Finn 2T, Ringland T, Campbell 2P,C
20.2.1982	SCOTLAND	won	21-12	Campbell 6P,D
19.2.1983	FRANCE	won	22-16	Campbell 4P,C, Finn 2T
19.3.1983	ENGLAND	won	25-15	Campbell 5P, T,C, Slattery T
4.2.1984	WALES	lost	9-18	Campbell 3P
3.3.1984	SCOTLAND	lost	9-32	Kiernan T, Murphy P,C
10.11.1984	AUSTRALIA	lost	9-16	Kiernan 3P
2.3.1985	FRANCE	drew	15-15	Kiernan 5P
30.3.1985	ENGLAND	won	13-10	Kiernan 2P,D, Mullin T
15.2.1986	WALES	lost	12-29	Kiernan 2P,C, Ringland T
15.3.1986	SCOTLAND	lost	9-10	Kiernan P,C, Ringland T
1.11.1986	ROMANIA	won	60-0	Crossan 3T, Dean 2T, Mullin 2T, Kiernan 7C, 2P, McNeill T, Bradley T, Anderson T
7.2.1987	ENGLAND	won	17-0	Crossan T, Matthews T, Kiernan T,P,C
21.3.1987	FRANCE	lost	13-19	Ringland T, Bradley T, Kiernan P,C
16.1.1988	SCOTLAND	won	22-18	Kiernan P,D,2C, Mullin T, Bradley T, McNeill T
5.3.1988	WALES	lost	9-12	Kiernan P,C, Kingston T
23.4.1988	ENGLAND	lost	10-21	S Smith T, McNeill T, Kiernan C
29.10.1988	WESTERN SAMOA	won	49-22	Crossan 2T, Francis T, McBride T, Matthews T, Mullin T, Kiernan T,2P,4C, Sexton T,D
31.12.1988	ITALY	won	31-15	Crossan 2T, Danaher 2P, Aherne T, Matthews 2T, Dean T, Cunningham C
21.1.1989	FRANCE	lost	21-26	Kiernan 5P,C, Mullin
18.2.1989	ENGLAND	lost	3-16	Kiernan P
18.11.1989	NEW ZEALAND	lost	6-23	B Smith 2P
3.2.1990	SCOTLAND	lost	10-13	J Fitzgerald T, Kiernan 2P
24.3.1990	WALES	won	14-8	B Smith T, Kingston T, McBride T, Kiernan C

DATE	OPP	RESULT	SCORE	SCORERS
27.10.1990	ARGENTINA	won	20-18	Kiernan T,4P, Hooks T
2.2.1991	FRANCE	lost	13-21	Kiernan 3P, S Smith T
2.3.1991	ENGLAND	lost	7-16	Geoghegan T, B Smith P
6.10.1991	ZIMBABWE (WC)	won	55-11	Robinson 4T, Popplewell 2T, Curtis T, Geoghegan T, Kiernan 5P,4C
9.10.1991	JAPAN (WC)	won	32-16	Mannion 2T, Staples T, O'Hara T, Keyes 4P,2C
19.10.1991	AUSTRALIA (WC)	lost	18-19	Keyes 3P,C,D, Hamilton T
18.1.1992	WALES	lost	15-16	R Wallace T, Keyes 3P,C
15.2.1992	SCOTLAND	lost	10-18	R Wallace T, Keyes 2P
31.10.1992	AUSTRALIA	lost	17-42	R Wallace T, Russell 4P
20.2.1993	FRANCE	lost	6-21	Malone 2P
20.3.1993	ENGLAND	won	17-3	Elwood 2P,2D, Galwey T
13.11.1993	ROMANIA	won	25-3	Elwood 6P,C, Geoghegan T
5.2.1994	WALES	lost	15-17	Elwood 5P
5.3.1994	SCOTLAND	drew	6-6	Elwood 2P
5.11.1994	USA	won	26-15	Geoghegan T, Bradley T, McGowan 3P,2C, O'Shea P
21.1.1995	ENGLAND	lost	8-20	Foley T, Burke P
4.3.1995	FRANCE	lost	7-25	Geoghegan T, Elwood C
18.11.1995	FIJI	won	44-8	Burke 4C,2P, Staples T, R Wallace T, Geoghegan T. P Wallace T, Francis T, Johns T
20.1.1996	SCOTLAND	lost	10-16	Clohessy T, Elwood P,C
2.3.1996	FRANCE	won	30-17	Mason 2P,2C, Geoghegan T, Wood T, Fulcher T. Corkery T
12.11.1996	WESTERN SAMOA	lost	25-40	Mason 6P,C, R Wallace T
23.11.1996	AUSTRALIA	lost	12-22	Burke 4P
4.1.1997	ITALY	lost	29-37	Burke 8P. Bell T
18.1.1997	FRANCE	lost	15-32	Elwood 5P
15.2.1997	ENGLAND	lost	6-46	Elwood 2P
15.11.1997	NEW ZEALAND	lost	15-63	Wood 2T, Elwood P,C
30.11.1997	CANADA	won	33-11	Nowlan 2T, Elwood 2P,C, McGuiness T, Maggs T, Costello T
7.2.1998	SCOTLAND	lost	16-17	Humphreys 2P,C,D, penalty try
21.3.1998	WALES	lost	21-30	Elwood 3P,C, Costello T, Ward T
14.11.1998	GEORGIA (WCQ)	won	70-0	Elwood 10C, Dempsey 2T, O'Shea T, Maggs T, Bell T, Duignan T, Johns T, P Wallace T, Costello T, Scally T
21.11.1998	ROMANIA (WCQ)	won	53-35	Bell 2T, Elwood 2P,3C, Humphreys 3C, O'Shea T, Scally T, Ward T, 2 penalty tries
28.11.1998	SOUTH AFRICA	lost	13-27	Elwood 2P,C, Wood T
6.2.1999	FRANCE	lost	9-10	Humphreys 3P
6.3.1999	ENGLAND	lost	15-27	Humphreys 4P, Dempsey P
10.4.1999	ITALY	won	39-30	Elwood 4P,C, O'Shea 2T, Bishop T, Dempsey T, Johns T
28.8.1999	ARGENTINA	won	32-24	Mostyn 3T, Wood T, Humphreys 4P
2.10.1999	USA (WC)	won	53-8	Ward 4T, Elwood 2T, Humphreys 5C,P, O'Driscoll T, Bishop T
10.10.1999	AUSTRALIA (WC)	lost	3-23	Humphreys P
15.10.1999	ROMANIA (WC)	won	44-14	Elwood 5C,2P, O'Driscoll D, O'Shea 2T, Ward T, Tierney T, O Cuinneagain T
19.2.2000	SCOTLAND	won	44-22	O'Driscoll T, Humphreys T,3C,P, O'Gara 2C,2P, Wood T, Horgan T, O'Kelly T
4.3.2000	ITALY	won	60-13	Horgan 2T, O'Gara 6C,6P, Wood T, Dawson T, Dempsey T, O'Driscoll T
1.4.2000	WALES	lost	19-23	Horgan T, O'Gara C,4P
11.11.2000	JAPAN	won	78-9	Hickie 3T, Howe 2T, O'Driscoll 2T, O'Gara 10C,P, Clohessy T, Henderson T, Murphy T, Stringer T
19.11.2000	SOUTH AFRICA	lost	18-28	Hickie T, Howe T, O'Gara 2P,C
17.2.2001	FRANCE	won	22-15	O'Driscoll T, O'Gara 5P,C
20.10.2001	ENGLAND	won	20-14	Wood T, Humphreys 3P. O'Gara 2P
11.11.2001	SAMOA	won	35-8	Howe T, Murphy T, Sheehan T, Staunton T. O'Gara 3P, 3C

DATE	OPP	RESULT	SCORE	SCORERS
17.11.2001	NEW ZEALAND	lost	29-40	Hickie T, Maggs T, Miller T, Humphreys 2P,2D,C
3.2.2002	WALES	won	54-10	Murphy 2T, O'Connell T, Hickie T, Gleeson T, O'Gara T,2C, Humphreys C,6P
2.3.2002	SCOTLAND	won	43-22	O'Driscoll 3T, Horgan T, Easterby T, O'Gara C Humphreys 2C,4P
23.3.2002	ITALY	won	32-17	Kelly 2T, Hickie T, Humphreys 4P. O'Gara P,C
28.9.2002	GEORGIA	won	63-14	O'Driscoll 2T, S Easterby T, G Easterby T, Hickie T Maggs T, O'Gara 5C,3P, Quinlan T, Humphreys 2C, Dempsey T
9.11.2002	AUSTRALIA	won	18-9	O'Gara 6P
17.11.2002	FIJI	won	64-17	Maggs 3T, Murphy 2T, O'Driscoll T, Bishop T, Dawson T, Foley T, Humphreys 5C,3P
23.11.2002	ARGENTINA	won	16-7	Dempsey T, O'Gara C,3P
8.3.2003	FRANCE	won	15-12	Humphreys 4P. Murphy D
30.3.2003	ENGLAND	lost	6-42	Humphreys 2P
16.8.2003	WALES	won	35-12	O'Connell 2T, O'Kelly T, Quinlan T, D Wallace T, Humphreys 4C, Murphy C
22.2.2004	WALES	won	36-15	Byrne 2T, O'Driscoll 2T, O'Gara T,3C, Foley T
20.3.2004	ITALY	won	19-3	O'Kelly T, O'Driscoll T, Horgan T, O'Gara 2C
27.3.2004	SCOTLAND	won	37-16	D'Arcy 2T, Murphy T, D Wallace T, Stringer T, O'Gara 3C,2P
13.11.2004	SOUTH AFRICA	won	17-12	O'Gara T,3P,D
20.11.2004	USA	won	55-6	Murphy 2T, Bowe T, Horan T, Miller T, Stringer T, Sheehan T, Humphreys 7C,2P
27.11.2004	ARGENTINA	won	21-19	O'Gara 5P,2D
27.2.2005	ENGLAND	won	19-13	O'Driscoll T, O'Gara C,2P,2D
12.3.2005	FRANCE	lost	19-26	O'Driscoll T, O'Gara C. 4P
12.11.2005	NEW ZEALAND	lost	7-45	Horan T, Humphreys C
19.11.2005	AUSTRALIA	lost	14-30	Horgan T, Humphreys P, O'Gara 2P
26.11.2005	ROMANIA	won	43-12	N Best T, Dempsey T, Murphy T, O'Connor T, Trimble 2T, Humphreys 5C,P
4.2.2006	ITALY	won	26-16	Flannery T, Bowe T, O'Gara 2C, 4P
26.2.2006	WALES	won	31-5	D Wallace T, Horgan T, Stringer T, O'Gara 2C,4P
11.3.2006	SCOTLAND	won	15-9	O'Gara 5P
11.11.2006	SOUTH AFRICA	won	32-15	Trimble T, D Wallace T, Horan T, Horgan T, O'Gara 3C,2P
19.11.2006	AUSTRALIA	won	21-6	Hickie T, Murphy T, O'Gara C,3P
26.11.2006	PACIFIC ISLANDS	won	61-17	S Easterby 2T, Hickie T, O'Kelly T, R Best T, Horgan T, O'Connell T, P Wallace 6C,3P,T

Neutral internationals in Lansdowne Road

27 Oct 1991	Australia	16	New Zealand	6	RWC semi-final
18 Nov 1998	Romania	27	Georgia	3	RWC qualifier
9 Oct 1999	Romania	27	USA	25	RWC group game
24 Oct 1999	France	47	Argentina	26	RWC quarter-final

Barbarians games in Lansdowne Road

26 Sept 1970	Wanderers	9	Barbarians	30
3 Dec 1994	Barbarians	23	South Africa	15
18 May 1996	Ireland	38	Barbarians	70
28 May 2000	Ireland	30	Barbarians	31

APPENDIX 2
SOCCER INTERNATIONALS AT LANSDOWNE ROAD 1900-2006

DATE	ATTENDANCE	COMP.	OPP	SCORE	SCORERS
17.3.00	8,000	HIC	ENGLAND	0-2	
27.4.27	20,000	f	ITALY 'B'	1-2	Fullam
10.5.71	25,000	EC	ITALY	1-2	Conway
18.10.72	25,000	WC	USSR	1-2	Conroy
10.5.75	50,000	EC	SWITZERLAND	2-1	Martin, Treacy
9.2.77	25,000	f	SPAIN	0-1	
30.3.77	48,000	WC	FRANCE	1-0	Brady
12.11.77	28,000	WC	BULGARIA	0-0	
5.4.78	10,000	f	TURKEY	4-2	Giles, McGee, Treacy
20.9.78	46,300	EC	NORTHERN IRE	0-0	
25.10.78	50,000	EC	ENGLAND	1-1	G Daly
2.3.79	35,000	EC	DENMARK	2-0	G Daly, Givens
22.5.79	23,000	f	W GERMANY	1-3	Ryan
17.10.79	18,000	EC	BULGARIA	3-0	Martin, Grealish, Stapleton
30.4.80	20,000	f	SWITZERLAND	2-0	Givens, G Daly
16.5.80	30,100	f	ARGENTINA	0-1	
10.9.80	30,000	WC	HOLLAND	2-1	G Daly, Lawrenson
15.6.80	40,000	WC	BELGIUM	1-1	Grealish
19.11.80	22,000	WC	CYPRUS	6-0	G Daly 2 (1p), Grealish, Robinson, Stapleton, Heighway
29.4.81	8,000	f	CZECHOSLOVAKIA	3-1	Moran 2, Stapleton
14.10.81	53,000	WC	FRANCE	3-2	OG, Stapleton, Robinson
13.10.82	21,000	EC	ICELAND	2-0	Stapleton, Grealish
17.11.82	35,000	EC	SPAIN	3-3	Givens, Stapleton 2
12.9.84	28,000	WC	USSR	1-0	Walsh
1.5.85	15,000	WC	NORWAY	0-0	
2.6.85	17,300	WC	SWITZERLAND	3-0	Stapleton, Grealish, Sheedy
13.11.85	15,154	WC	DENMARK	1-4	Stapleton
26.3.85	16,500	f	WALES	0-1	
23.4.86	14,000	f	URUGUAY	1-1	
15.10.86	29,203	EC	SCOTLAND	0-0	G Daly (p)
29.4.87	44,600	f	BELGIUM	0-0	
23.5.87	17,000	f	BRAZIL	1-0	Brady
9.9.87	18,000	EC	LUXEMBOURG	2-1	Stapleton, McGrath
14.10.87	26,000	EC	BULGARIA	2-0	McGrath, Moran
23.3.88	15,000	f	ROMANIA	2-0	Moran, D Kelly
27.4.88	12,000	f	YUGOSLAVIA	2-0	McCarthy, Moran
22.5.88	18,500	f	POLAND	3-1	Sheedy, Cascarino, Sheridan
19.10.88	12,000	f	TUNISIA	4-0	Cascarino 2, Aldridge, Sheedy
26.4.89	49,600	WC	SPAIN	1-0	OG
28.5.89	48,928	WC	MALTA	2-0	Houghton, Moran
4.6.89	49,600	WC	HUNGARY	2-0	McGrath, Cascarino
6.9.89	48,000	f	WEST GERMANY	1-1	Stapleton
11.10.89	46,800	WC	NORTHERN IRE	3-0	Whelan, Cascarino, Houghton
28.3.89	41,350	f	WALES	1-0	Slaven
25.4.90	43,990	f	USSR	1-0	Staunton
16.5.90	31,556	f	FINLAND	1-1	Sheedy
17.10.90	46,000	EC	TURKEY	5-0	Aldridge 3 (1p), O'Leary, Quinn
14.11.90	45,000	EC	ENGLAND	1-1	Cascarino
11.5.91	48,000	EC	POLAND	0-0	
22.5.91	32,230	f	CHILE	1-1	D Kelly
25.3.92	23,601	f	SWITZERLAND	2-1	Coyne, Aldridge (p)
29.4.92	27,000	f	USA	4-1	Townsend, Irwin, Quinn, Cascarino
26.5.92	29,727	WC	ALBANIA	2-0	Aldridge, McGrath
9.9.92	32,000	WC	LATVIA	4-0	Sheedy, Aldridge 3 (1p)

DATE	ATTENDANCE	COMP.	OPP	SCORE	SCORERS
31.3.93	33,000	WC	NORTHERN IRE	3-0	Townsend, Quinn, Staunton
28.4.93	33,000	WC	DENMARK	1-1	Quinn
8.9.93	33,000	WC	LITHUANIA	2-0	Aldridge, Kernaghan
13.10.93	50,000	WC	SPAIN	1-3	Sheridan
23.3.94	36,000	f	RUSSIA	0-0	
14.5.94	32,500	f	BOLIVIA	1-0	Sheridan
5.6.94	43,465	f	CZECH REPUBLIC	1-3	Townsend
12.10.94	32,980	EC	LIECHTENSTEIN	4-0	Coyne 2, Quinn 2
15.2.95	46,000	f	ENGLAND	1-0	Kelly
29.3.95	32,200	EC	NORTHERN IRE	1-1	Quinn
26.4.95	33,500	EC	PORTUGAL	1-0	OG
11.6.95	33,000	EC	AUSTRIA	1-3	Houghton
11.10.95	33,500	EC	LATVIA	2-1	Aldridge 2 (1p)
27.3.96	41,600	f	RUSSIA	0-2	
29.5.96	26,576	f	PORTUGAL	0-1	
2.6.96	29,100	f	CROATIA	2-2	O'Neill, Quinn
9.10.96	31,671	WC	MACEDONIA	3-0	McAteer, Cascarino 2
10.11.96	33,069	WC	ICELAND	0-0	
21.5.97	33,200	WC	LIECHTENSTEIN	5-0	Connolly 3, Cascarino 2
20.8.97	32,620	WC	LITHUANIA	0-0	
11.10.97	34,500	WC	ROMANIA	1-1	Cascarino
29.10.97	32,305	WCPO	BELGIUM	1-1	Irwin
22.4.98	38,500	f	ARGENTINA	0-2	
23.5.98	28,500	f	MEXICO	0-0	
5.9.98	34,000	EC	CROATIA	2-0	Irwin (p), Ry Keane
14.10.98	34,500	EC	MALTA	5-0	Keane 2, Ry Keane, Quinn, Breen
10.2.99	27,600	f	PARAGUAY	2-0	Irwin (p), Connolly
28.04.99	29,000	f	SWEDEN	2-0	Kavanagh, Kennedy
29.5.99	12,100	f	NORTHERN IRE	0-1	
9.6.99	28,108	EC	MACEDONIA	1-0	Quinn
1.9.99	31,400	EC	YUGOSLAVIA	2-1	Rb Keane, Kennedy
13.11.99	33,610	ECPO	TURKEY	1-1	Rb Keane
23.2.00	30,543	f	CZECH REPUBLIC	3-2	OG, Harte, Rb Keane
26.4.00	23,157	f	GREECE	0-1	
30.5.00	30,213	f	SCOTLAND	1-2	Kennedy
11.10.00	34,962	WC	ESTONIA	2-0	Kinsella, Breen
15.11.00	22,368	f	FINLAND	3-0	Finnan, Kilbane, Staunton
25.04.01	35,000	WC	ANDORRA	3-1	Kilbane, Kinsella, Breen
2.6.01	35,000	WC	PORTUGAL	1-1	Ry Keane
15.9.01	27,000	f	CROATIA	2-2	Duff, Morrison
1.9.01	35,400	WC	HOLLAND	1-0	McAteer
6.10.01	35,000	WC	CYPRUS	4-0	Harte, Quinn, Connolly, Ry Keane
10.11.01	35,000	WCPO	IRAN	2-0	Harte (p), Rb Keane
13.2.02	44,000	f	RUSSIA	2-0	S Reid, Rb Keane
27.3.02	42,000	f	DENMARK	3-0	Harte, Rb Keane, Morrison
17.4.02	39,000	f	USA	2-1	Kinsella, Doherty
16.5.02	42,652	f	NIGERIA	1-2	S Reid
16.10.02	40,000	EC	SWITZERLAND	1-2	OG
30.4.03	32,643	f	NORWAY	1-0	Duff
7.6.03	33,000	EC	ALBANIA	2-1	Rb Keane, OG
11.6.03	36,000	EC	GEORGIA	2-0	Doherty, Rb Keane
19.8.03	37,000	f	AUSTRALIA	2-1	O'Shea, Morrison
6.9.03	36,000	EC	RUSSIA	1-1	Duff
9.9.03	27,200	f	TURKEY	2-2	Connolly, Dunne
18.11.03	23,263	f	CANADA	3-0	Duff, Rb Keane 2
18.2.04	44,000	f	BRAZIL	0-0	
31.3.04	42,000	f	CZECH REPUBLIC	2-1	Harte, Rb Keane
27.5.04	42,356	f	ROMANIA	1-0	Holland
18.8.04	31,887	f	BULGARIA	1-1	A Reid

DATE	ATTENDANCE	COMP.	OPP	SCORE	SCORERS
4.9.04	35,900	WC	CYPRUS	3-0	Morrison, A Reid, Rb Keane (p)
13.10.04	36,000	WC	FAROE ISLANDS	2-0	Rb Keane 2 (1p)
16.11.04	33,200	f	CROATIA	1-0	Rb Keane
9.2.05	44,100	f	PORTUGAL	1-0	An O'Brien
29.3.05	35,000	f	CHINA	1-0	Morrison
4.6.05	36,000	WC	ISRAEL	2-2	Harte, Rb Keane
17.8.05	44,000	f	ITALY	1-2	
7.9.05	36,000	WC	FRANCE	0-1	
12.10.05	35,000	WC	SWITZERLAND	0-0	
1.3.06	48,000	f	SWEDEN	3-0	Duff, Rb Keane, Miller
24.5.06	41,200	f	CHILE	0-1	
16.8.06	42,400	f	HOLLAND	0-4	
11.10.06	35,500	EC	CZECH REPUBLIC	1-1	Kilbane
15.11.06	34,018	EC	SAN MARINO	5-0	A Reid, Doyle, Rb Keane 3 (1pen)

KEY

HIC: HOME INTERNATIONAL CHAMPIONSHIP
F: FRIENDLY
EC: EUROPEAN CHAMPIONSHIP
WC: WORLD CUP
ECPO: EUROPEAN CHAMPIONSHIP PLAY-OFF
WCPO: WORLD CUP PLAY-OFF

APPENDIX 3
LANSDOWNE ROAD INTERNATIONAL RECORDS: RUGBY

Most appearances

43 Malcolm O'Kelly (1997-2006)

37 Brian O'Driscoll (1999-2006)

35 Mike Gibson (1964-78), John Hayes (2000-06), Peter Stringer (2000-06)

34 Willie John McBride (1962-75)

33 Girvan Dempsey (1998-2006)

32 Anthony Foley (1995-2005)

31 Fergus Slattery (1970-83), David Humphreys (1996-2005), Kevin Maggs (1997-2005), Ronan O'Gara (2000-06)

30 Peter Clohessy (1993-2002), Paddy Johns (1990-2000)

Most appearances by non-Irish players

7 Jason Leonard (England, 1991-2003), Rory Underwood (England, 1985-95)

6 Rob Andrew (England, 1985-95), Will Carling (England, 1988-97), Scott Hastings (Scotland, 1986-96), Philippe Sella (France, 1983-95)

Most tries

17 Brian O'Driscoll (1999-2006)

11 Geordan Murphy (2000-06), Keith Wood (1997-2001)

10 Denis Hickie (2000-06), Shane Horgan (2000-06)

8 Keith Crossan (1986-88)

7 Girvan Dempsey (1998-2005), Alan Duggan (1967-72), Simon Geoghegan (1991-96), Kevin Maggs (1997-2002)

6 Brendan Mullin (1985-89), Conor O'Shea (1998-99), George Stephenson (1921-27)

5 Denis Cussen (1921-26)

Most tries by non-Irish players

4 David Campese (Australia, 1991-92), Christian Darrouy (France, 1963-65), Roy Laidlaw (Scotland, 1984-88), Arthur Smith (Scotland 1956-62), Georghe Solomie (Romania, 1998-99)

Most tries in one game:

4 Brian Robinson (Ireland) v Zimbabwe, 1991 (World Cup)

4 Keith Wood (Ireland) v United States, 1999 (World Cup)

3 Johnny Williams (Wales) v Ireland, 1910

3 Boetie McHardy (South Africa) v Ireland, 1912

3 Jan Stegmann (South Africa) v Ireland, 1912

3 Christian Darrouy (France) v Ireland, 1963

3 Keith Crossan (Ireland) v Romania, 1986

3 Denis Hickie (Ireland) v Japan, 2000

3 Kevin Maggs (Ireland) v Fiji, 2002

3 Matt Mostyn (Ireland) v Argentina, 1999

3 Brian O'Driscoll (Ireland) v Scotland, 2002

3 David Venditti (France) v Ireland, 1997

Most points

354 Ronan O'Gara (31 matches, 2000-06)

244 David Humphreys (31 matches, 1996-2005)

179 Eric Elwood (19 matches, 1993-99)

172 Michael Kiernan (23 matches, 1982-91)

108 Ollie Campbell (10 matches, 1976-84)

88 Brian O'Driscoll (37 matches, 1999-2006)

77 Tom Kiernan (29 matches, 1960-73)

70 Ralph Keyes (5 matches, 1991-92)

60 Geordan Murphy (22 matches, 2000-06)

Most points by non-Irish players

55 Petre Mitu (Romania, 5 matches, 1998-2005)

52 Neil Jenkins (Wales, 4 matches, 1992-2000)

49 Diego Dominguez (Italy, 4 matches, 1997-2002)

40 Andrew Mehrtens (New Zealand, 2 matches, 1997-2001)

Most points in one game

33 Andrew Mehrtens (New Zealand) try, 5 cons, 6 pens v Ireland, 1997

30 Ronan O'Gara (Ireland) 6 cons, 6 pens v Italy, 2000

26 Paddy Wallace (Ireland) 1 try, 6 cons, 3 pens v Pacific Islands, 2006

24 Paul Burke (Ireland) 8 pens v Italy, 1997

23 Ralph Keyes (Ireland) 4 cons, 5 pens v Zimbabwe, 1991

23 Ronan O'Gara (Ireland) 10 cons, 1 pen v Japan, 2000

Most penalty goals

58 Ronan O'Gara

36 David Humphreys

24 Ollie Campbell

23 Eric Elwood

20 Michael Kiernan

Most penalty goals by non-Irish players
10 Neil Jenkins (Wales)
8 Matt Burke (Australia)
7 Bob Hiller (England), Petre Mitu (Romania), Jonny Wilkinson (England)

Most penalty goals in one game
8 Paul Burke (Ireland) v Italy, 1997
6 Ollie Campbell (Ireland) v Scotland, 1982
6 Eric Elwood (Ireland) v Romania, 1993
6 Simon Mason (Ireland) v Samoa, 1996
6 Andrew Mehrtens (New Zealand) v Ireland, 1997
6 Ronan O'Gara (Ireland) v Italy, 2000
6 David Humpheys (Ireland) v Wales, 2002
6 Ronan O'Gara (Ireland) v Australia, 2002

Most dropped goals
4 Ronan O'Gara (Ireland)

Most dropped goals by non-Irish players
2 Guy Laporte (France), Doug Bruce (New Zealand), Guy Camberabero (France), Diego Dominguez (Italy), Mark Ella (Australia), Jonny Wilkinson (England)

Most conversions
51 Ronan O'Gara
40 David Humphreys
28 Eric Elwood
21 Michael Kiernan
13 Tom Kiernan

Most conversions by non-Irish players
10 Diego Dominguez (Italy), Andrew Mehrtens (New Zealand)
7 Petre Mitu (Romania),
6 Christophe Lamaison (France), Grahame Parker (England)

Most conversions in one game
6 Eric Elwood (Ireland) v Romania, 1993

6 Simon Mason (Ireland) v Samoa, 1996

6 Andrew Mehrtens (New Zealand) v Ireland, 1997

6 Ronan O'Gara (Ireland) v Italy, 2000

6 David Humphreys (Ireland) v Wales, 2002

Highest scores by Ireland

78-9	v Japan, 2000
70-0	v Georgia (RWCQ), 1998
64-17	v Fiji, 2002
63-14	v Georgia, 2002
61-17	v Pacific Islands, 2006
60-0	v Romania, 1986
60-13	v Italy, 2000
55-6	v USA, 2004
55-11	v Zimbabwe (RWC), 1991
54-10	v Wales, 2002
53-35	v Romania (RWCQ), 1998

Highest score by Ireland against other opposition

49	v Samoa, 1988
44	v Scotland, 2000
33	v Canada, 1997
32	v Argentina, 1999
32	v South Africa, 2006
30	v France, 1996
29	v New Zealand, 2001
25	v England, 1983
24	v Australia, 2006

Highest scores against Ireland

63-15	New Zealand, 1997
46-6	England, 1987
45-7	New Zealand, 2005
42-6	England, 2003
42-17	Australia, 1992
40-25	Western Samoa, 1996
40-29	New Zealand, 2001

Highest score against Ireland by other opposition

38	South Africa, 1912
37	Italy, 1997
35	Romania, 1998
34	Wales, 1976
32	Scotland, 1984
32	France, 1997
24	Argentina, 1999

Most tries in a match by Ireland:

11	v Japan, 2000
10	v Romania, 1986
10	v Georgia, 1998

COUNTRY	YEARS	GAMES	WON	DRAW	LOST	FOR	AGAINST	TRIES	CONS	PGS	DGS	GFM
IRELAND	1878-2006	244	118	17	109	3574	3026	444	240	395	43	3
ENGLAND	1878-2005	57	28	4	25	534	451	94	39	51	6	0
SCOTLAND	1894-2006	46	17	3	26	467	541	62	36	47	10	1
WALES	1882-2006	37	17	3	17	416	501	56	29	43	10	0
FRANCE	1909-2005	36	19	4	13	505	421	66	34	46	13	0
AUSTRALIA	1927-2006	16	11	0	5	257	180	30	18	28	5	0
NEW ZEALAND	1905-2005	13	11	1	1	270	112	35	22	23	3	0
SOUTH AFRICA	1912-2006	10	6	1	3	167	108	28	14	12	1	0
ROMANIA	1980-2005	8	2	1	5	131	286	14	7	16	0	0
ITALY	1988-2006	7	1	0	6	131	236	12	12	13	3	0
ARGENTINA	1973-2004	6	0	0	6	102	157	10	8	13	0	0
USA	1994-2004	4	0	0	4	54	161	6	3	6	0	0
SAMOA	1988-2001	3	1	0	2	70	109	10	6	4	0	0
FIJI	1985-2002	3	0	0	3	40	124	5	4	3	0	0
GEORGIA	1998-2002	3	0	0	3	37	160	4	4	3	0	0
JAPAN	1991-2000	2	0	0	2	25	110	3	2	3	0	0
PACIFIC ISLANDS	2006	1	0	0	1	17	61	3	1	0	0	0
CANADA	1997	1	0	0	1	11	33	1	0	2	0	0
ZIMBABWE	1991	1	0	0	1	11	55	2	0	1	0	0

LANSDOWNE ROAD INTERNATIONAL RECORDS: SOCCER

Most goals

22 Robbie Keane

12 John Aldridge, Tony Cascarino

11 Niall Quinn

10 Frank Stapleton

7 Gerry Daly

6 Kevin Moran, David Connolly

5 Tony Grealish, Kevin Sheedy, Ian Harte, Damien Duff, Clinton Morrison

4 Paul McGrath, Denis Irwin, Roy Keane, Andy Reid

3 Ray Treacy, Don Givens, David Kelly, Steve Staunton, Ray Houghton, John Sheridan, Andy Townsend, Tommy Coyne

Most penalties

4 John Aldridge

3 Robbie Keane

2 Gerry Daly, Denis Irwin

1 Ian Harte

Hat-tricks

3 (1 pen) John Aldridge v Turkey (EC) 1990

3 (1 pen) John Aldridge v Latvia (WC) 1992

3 David Connolly v Liechtenstein (WC) 1997

3 (1 pen) Robbie Keane v San Marino (EC) 2006

Biggest victories

6-0   v Cyprus (WC) 1980

5-0   v Turkey (EC) 1990

5-0   v Liechtenstein (WC) 1997

5-0   v Malta (EC) 1998

5-0   v San Marino (EC) 2006

Biggest defeats

0-4   v Holland (f) 2006

1-4   v Denmark (WC) 1985

Most consecutive wins: 10 (1987–89)

Most consecutive defeats: 4 (1900–72)

Most consecutive unbeaten games: 29 (1985–93), 17 (1993–95), 10 (1980–85)

		P	W	D	L	Ab		GF	GA
Ireland	(1900)	1	0	0	1			0	2
Rep of Ireland	(1927-2006)	126	69	33	23	1		205	93

IRELAND'S RECORD AGAINST ALL OPPOSITION

Switzerland	(1975-2005)	6	4	1	1			10	4
Northern Ireland	(1978-95)	5	2	2	1			7	2
England	(1900-95)	4	0	2	1	1		3	4
Spain	(1977-93)	4	1	1	2			5	7
Turkey	(1978-2003)	4	2	2	0			12	5
Denmark	(1979-2002)	4	2	1	1			7	5
Russia	(1994-2003)	4	1	2	1			3	3
Czech Republic	(1994-2006)	4	2	1	1			7	7
Portugal	(1995-2005)	4	2	1	1			3	2
Croatia	(1996-2004)	4	2	2	0			7	4
USSR	(1972-90)	3	2	0	1			3	2
France	(1977-2005)	3	2	0	1			4	3
Bulgaria	(1977-87)	3	2	1	0			5	0
Holland	(1980-2006)	3	2	0	1			3	5
Belgium	(1980-97)	3	0	3	0			2	2
Cyprus	(1980-2004)	3	3	0	0			13	0
Romania	(1988-2004)	3	2	0	1			4	1
Italy	(1971-2005)	2	0	0	2			2	4
West Germany	(1979-89)	2	0	1	1			2	4
Argentina	(1980-98)	2	0	0	2			0	3
Iceland	(1982-96)	2	1	1	0			2	0
Norway	(1985-2003)	2	1	1	0			1	0
Wales	(1985-89)	2	1	0	1			1	1
Brazil	(1987-2004)	2	1	1	0			1	0
Scotland	(1986-2000)	2	0	1	1			1	2
Yugoslavia	(1988-99)	2	2	0	0			4	1
Poland	(1988-91)	2	1	1	0			3	1
Malta	(1989-98)	2	2	0	0			7	0
Finland	(1990-2000)	2	1	1	0			4	1
Chile	(1991-2006)	2	0	1	1			1	2
USA	(1992-2002)	2	2	0	0			6	1
Albania	(1992-2003)	2	2	0	0			4	1
Latvia	(1992-95)	2	2	0	0			6	1
Lithuania	(1993-97)	2	1	1	0			2	0

Liechtenstein	(1994-97)	2	2	0	0	9	0
Macedonia	(1996-99)	2	2	0	0	4	0
Sweden	(1999-2006)	2	2	0	0	5	0
Italy B	(1927)	1	0	0	1	1	2
Czechoslovakia	(1981)	1	1	0	0	3	1
Uruguay	(1986)	1	0	1	0	1	1
Luxembourg	(1987)	1	1	0	0	2	1
Tunisia	(1988)	1	1	0	0	4	0
Hungary	(1989)	1	1	0	0	2	0
Bolivia	(1994)	1	1	0	0	1	0
Austria	(1995)	1	0	0	1	1	3
Mexico	(1998)	1	0	1	0	0	0
Paraguay	(1999)	1	1	0	0	2	0
Greece	(2000)	1	0	0	1	0	1
Estonia	(2000)	1	1	0	0	2	0
Andorra	(2001)	1	1	0	0	3	1
Iran	(2001)	1	1	0	0	2	0
Nigeria	(2002)	1	0	0	1	1	2
Georgia	(2003)	1	1	0	0	2	0
Australia	(2003)	1	1	0	0	2	1
Canada	(2003)	1	1	0	0	3	0
Faroe Islands	(2004)	1	1	0	0	2	0
China	(2005)	1	1	0	0	1	0
Israel	(2005)	1	0	1	0	2	2
San Marino	(2006)	1	1	0	0	5	0

INDEX

First published 2010 by The O'Brien Press Ltd,
12 Terenure Road East, Rathgar, Dublin 6, Ireland.
Tel: +353 1 4923333; Fax: +353 1 4922777
E-mail: books@obrien.ie
Website: www.obrien.ie

ISBN: 978-086278-910-7

British Library Cataloguing-in-publication Data
A catalogue record for this title is available from the British Library

1 2 3 4 5 6 7 8 9 10
10 11 12 13 14 15

Printed and bound in the UK by JF Print Ltd, Sparkford, Somerset.
The paper in this book is produced using pulp from managed forests.

Internal & cover photographs:
Introduction–Chapter 22: p 151 copyright © Brian Seed; p 154 & 157 courtesy of
Frank Greally; p 164,166, 168, 171 copyright © *The Irish Times*; p 234 courtesy of Jim
O'Brien; p 235 © copyright Patrick Anthony, used with permission; pp 236-239 ©
copyright *Sunday Tribune*.
Chapters 23-35: (except p 270 © *Sunday Tribune* and p 320) all photos copyright ©
INPHO.
Every effort has been made to trace holders of copyright material used in this book,
but if any infringement of copyright has inadvertently occurred, the publishers ask the
copyright holder to contact them immediately.